Cross-cultural Marketing

Cross-cultural marketing is an important element of the contemporary business environment. Many conventional accounts of the topic have conflated cross-cultural and cross-national marketing, but in this groundbreaking, new book, Burton argues that these generalizations have little meaning given the extent of multi-culturalism in many societies.

Given the importance of new emerging markets in the Far East, Middle East, Asia and Latin America, this book raises important questions about the applicability of existing marketing theory and practice, which was originally developed using the model of Western society. An extensive range of cross-cultural marketing issues is addressed, including:

- Cross-cultural consumer behaviour
- Cross-cultural management practice
- Promotional strategies
- Product development
- Distribution
- Marketing research methods

Cross-cultural Marketing offers a new, more complex and sophisticated approach to the important challenges for existing marketing theory and practice and their continued relevance for stakeholders. As such, it is an invaluable text for students of international and cross-cultural marketing, as well as for practitioners who wish to assess new developments in the field.

Dawn Burton has taught sociology and marketing at leading British universities. She has written widely on cross-cultural consumer culture and has held numerous research grants in this area. She is the founding editor of the journal *Marketing Theory*. Her work has been published in leading journals in the fields of sociology, marketing, geography and management.

Cross-cultural Marketing

Theory, practice and relevance

Dawn Burton

Routledge
Taylor & Francis Group

LONDON AND NEW YORK

First published 2009
by Routledge
2 Park Square, Milton Park, Abingdon, Oxon OX14 4RN

Simultaneously published in the USA and Canada
by Routledge
270 Madison Ave, New York, NY 10016

Routledge is an imprint of the Taylor & Francis Group, an informa business

© 2009 Dawn Burton

Typeset in Times New Roman by
Swales & Willis Ltd, Exeter, Devon
Printed and bound in Great Britain by
CPI Antony Rowe, Chippenham, Wiltshire

British Library Cataloguing in Publication Data
A catalogue record for this book is available from the British Library

Library of Congress Cataloguing in Publication Data
Burton, Dawn, 1961–
    Cross-cultural marketing: theory, practice and relevance/Dawn Burton.
        p. cm.
    Includes bibliographical references and index.
    1. Marketing.   2. Multiculturalism.   3. Minority consumers.   I. Title.
    HF5415.B7763 2008
    658.80089–dc22   2008017138

ISBN10: 0–415–44892–1 (hbk)
ISBN10: 0–415–44893–X (pbk)
ISBN10: 0–203–88934–7 (ebk)

ISBN13: 978–0–415–44892–5 (hbk)
ISBN13: 978–0–415–44893–2 (pbk)
ISBN13: 978–0–203–88934–3 (ebk)

For my son Wesley and my flat-coat Bryn

Contents

1 Dimensions of culture

The focus of this chapter is to explore some of the ways that culture can be analysed within a cross-cultural marketing context. The first task is to define what culture means taking into account historical patterns of thought and the contribution of different countries in arriving at the definitions that we use today. A second theme of this chapter is to explore the notion of national culture. Using the nation as a geographical unit of analysis and equating it with a distinctive culture is widely practised in marketing. Indeed within marketing cross-cultural and cross-national are often used interchangeably in books and research papers. The idea of a national culture is a concept that is of quite recent origin and some would argue is not sophisticated enough to deal with an increasingly culturally complex world. A third theme of this chapter is to assess what has become known as the globalization of culture. The globalization of culture was an idea that gained considerable currency in the 1980s, and refers to the way that global communications networks have resulted in a homogenized world of standardized products, advertising messages, and retail formats. The widespread use of the Internet is exacerbating these tendencies resulting in the globalization culture that supersedes local cultural differences. The fourth theme of the chapter is to consider what has become known as the glocalization of culture. This approach emerged largely as a critique of the globalization thesis which is arguably something of a blunt instrument. Supporters of glocalization maintain that it is still important to engage with differentiated local markets within the context of a globalizing world.

The fifth theme of this chapter is to recognize a trend around the world for countries to become more multicultural in their composition. In some respects the techniques used within the context of international marketing need to be used at home. Equating cross-cultural with cross-national marketing is missing the point, and in so doing is simplifying highly complex ethnoscapes comprising layers of cultural complexity. As ethnicity has become an important aspect of culture within different countries, the task of marketers has been to develop strategies that tap into this market. A sixth theme of this chapter is to engage with the issue of cosmopolitanism. The concept of cosmopolitanism was traditionally associated with well-travelled individuals from advanced nations that revelled in learning about other cultures. However, cosmopolitan consumer culture is also evident in definitions of culture. The final section explores the concept of whiteness and culture.

Definitions of culture

Culture is an incredibly complex concept that has attracted the attention of significant numbers of academics writing about the subject from very different standpoints (Jenks 1993). Some scholars within the field of anthropology have gone so far as to argue that the concept has become so problematic that it should be replaced with something that is more concrete and manageable (Geertz 1973). Raymond Williams has been one of the most prolific writers on the topic of culture documenting its historical roots and changing definitions according to societal conditions (Williams 1983, 1993). In his text *Keywords: A Vocabulary of Culture and Society*, Williams traces the historical roots of the word 'culture' in several European and Scandinavian countries. Initially, the word derived from *cultura* that had a range of meanings including 'inhabit, cultivate, and protect, honour with worship' (Williams 1983: 87). By the early fifteenth century the French word *culture* had passed into the English language and the primary meaning was then in husbandry, associated with the tending of natural growth in either crops or animals. From the early sixteenth century the concept of tending to natural growth was extended to human beings.

Culture as a noun was not common before the late eighteenth century. In eighteenth-century England, the term was often associated with *civility* that acquired social class associations connected to breeding and advantage. Williams cites Herder in his unfinished work entitled *Ideas on the Philosophy of the History of Mankind* (1784–1791) where he criticized the notion of a superior European culture in the world and referred to cultures in the plural: 'the specific and variable cultures of different nations and periods, but also the specific and variable cultures of social and economic groups within a nation' (Williams 1983: 89). Initially the term culture was used to differentiate between national and traditional cultures and subsequently the concept of folk culture. There is also a distinction between definitions of culture as a process of intellectual and spiritual development, and that which focuses on a material way of life of people, periods, groups or humanity in general. A third usage has emerged that refers to intellectual, especially artistic, activity – music, literature, painting and sculpture. Differences in the usages remain in various languages. In the German, Scandinavian and Slavonic language groups, the material production emphasis is apparent, whereas in Italian and French the process of human development dominates.

Cultural studies as an academic discipline is more highly developed in some countries than others, although its history as an academic discipline is highly contested (Werbner 2002; McGuigan 1999; Steele 1999; Carey 1997). It has a long history in Britain and the USA but is of more recent origin in South Africa (Nuttall 2006), India (Mukhopadhyay 2006), and Japan (Tumari 2006) where cultural studies can be traced to the 1980s. In Latin America there were studies of a distinctive Latin American culture in the opening decades of the twentieth century, but the discourse really emerged after the 1970s (Hart and Young 2003). There remain various differences in the usage of the term culture across academic disciplines. For example, in archaeology and cultural anthropology reference to culture, or a culture, is overwhelmingly connected to material production, whereas in history and cultural studies the primary focus relates to 'signifying or symbolic systems' (Williams 1983: 91). The cultural studies definition is aptly demonstrated by Tylor 'culture is that complex whole which includes knowledge, belief, art, morals, law, custom and any other capabilities and habits acquired by man as a member of society' (1964: 18). Best achievements in the spheres of art, literature and music became defining features of what constituted refinement, grace and civilization. In their review of twenty years of cross-cultural research, Sojka and Tansuhaj found that scholars rarely defined the term culture in order to clarify the concept. They provided their own definition 'a dynamic set of socially acquired behaviour patterns and meanings common to members of a particular society or human group, including the key elements of language, artefacts, beliefs and values' (Sojka and Tansuhaj 1995: 469). Geertz (1995: 42) describes cultures as 'many ways of "doing things", distinct and characteristic'. While Appadurai (1996: 13) stresses the dimensionality of culture when he notes 'culture is less a property of individuals and groups and more a heuristic device that we can use to talk about difference'. He concedes that not all differences are of a cultural nature, and suggests that differences that 'either express, or set the groundwork for the mobilization of group identities' should be included'.

The meaning and nature of culture is contested in marketing as it is in other disciplines (Arnould *et al.* 2004: 74) refer to a society's culture as 'dynamic blueprints for action and interpretations that enable a person to operate in a manner acceptable to other members of the culture'. However, it needs to be recognized that culture is indeterminant and therefore not fully predictable, it can also be subject to changes over time. They argue that blueprints of action are split into two parts: *cultural categories* and *cultural principles*. *Cultural categories* 'define and organize time, space, nature, the sacred and society' (75). For example, occupation, social class, caste, gender, ethnicity, and age are examples of cultural categories. Others include social categories such as families, temporal categories, for example the distinction between work and leisure, and natural and sacred categories that delineate between what is considered cleanliness and filth in different cultures. *Cultural principles* 'allow things to be grouped into cultural categories, ranked and interrelated . . . values, ideals, norms and beliefs' come into this category (77).

Much of the research in marketing centres on understanding *cultural values*. Values can be *instrumental values* that are shared beliefs about how people should behave. Or alternatively, they can be *terminal values*, for example desirable life goals (Arnould *et al.* 2004: 82). There have been several attempts by marketers to identify core values across societies, and those values that differ between and are a result of 'local' cultural differences. Particularly influential in marketing has been the work of Hofstede, although it has not been without controversy. Hofstede's work along with others that have attempted to identify cross-cultural value systems are critically evaluated in Chapter 9. Another value that marketers have been interested in is *ethnocentrism*, which is a belief that one's own culture is better/ superior than that of another cultural group. This concept has been used extensively to understand consumer attitudes to products from other countries/cultures.

While much of the work in marketing has focused on the importance of values, societies also possess *myths* and *symbols* that are an integral part of their culture. Myths are stories such as legends and fairy tales that are passed on from one generation to the next. Urban legends are stories that are supposed to be true but are fictitious, or at least there is some uncertainty about their authenticity. Myths and legends often have a symbolic and moral function, such as 'no good comes of nasty people'. Cultural symbols are objects that have a powerful significance within different cultures and they can have multiple meanings. For example, a national flag is something that binds people together. Marketers can use these symbols to promote products and services; for example, French wines and cheese are often stamped with a copy of the national flag. A final aspect of culture highlighted in marketing are rituals. Cultural rituals are behaviours that occur in a fixed order and tend to be repeated on a regular basis. Rook (1985) has distinguished between many types of ritual behaviour, including *grooming* (beauty products and services like spas), *disinvestment* (disposing of products, for example car boot sales), *exchange rituals* (gift giving at Christmas), and *possession rituals* where products are moved from the market to the home where they are consumed.

National culture

Considerable attention in marketing is given to the concept of *national* culture. The concept that nations have distinctive cultures is unproblematically accepted in cross-cultural research designs. Cross-national marketing looks at the responses of individuals in one country and compares them with another. The differences are usually attributed to national cultural differences. However, this approach to assigning to the nation a particular culture is not universally shared, and, more to the point, this way of thinking about culture is relatively recent in origin. A rather different perspective is that cultures are interconnected and exchange materials, thus no culture is due to the authorship of one group of people. Rather, 'cultures need to be studied in all their plurality and particular historicity, including their interconnectedness' (Wolf 1994: 5). The purpose of this section is to unpack the term of national culture and to consider how it evolved, the different ways that it has been used, and how plausible it is to continue this tradition.

Miroslave Hroch (1996: 61) describes the nation as a 'large social group integrated not by one but by a combination of several kinds of objective relations (economic, political, linguistic, cultural, religious, geographical, historical) and their subjective reflection on collective consciousness'. In order to successfully build a nation three central features are required:

- a 'memory' of some common past, treated as 'destiny' of the group – or at least of its core constituents;
- a density of linguistic or cultural ties enabling a higher degree of social communication within the group than beyond it;
- a conception of the equality of all members of the group organized as a civil society.

(Hroch 1996: 61)

Nationalism, the ideology that supports nation states, is historically contingent since it is linked to political intervention, the emergence of new ideologies and cultural change that manifests itself in new social identities. In some instances, nationalist movements directed at aligning the boundaries of the state and nation have employed or induced violence as in the case of Algeria, Basque Country (in Spain), Northern Ireland, Serbia, Somalia and Vietnam (Laitin 1999). In his text *Nation and Narration*, Bhabha (1990) argues that the notion of a static national culture that can be easily measured is flawed, since much of what constitutes the nation is at the level of discourse rather than practice. In his essay entitled 'What is a nation?' Ernest Renan (1990) argues that the concept of a nation is relatively new.

> Antiquity was unfamiliar with them; Egypt, China and ancient Chaldea were in no way nations. They were flocks led by a Son of the Sun or by a Son of Heaven. Neither in Egypt nor in China were there citizens as such. Classical antiquity had republics, municipal kingdoms, confederations of local republics and empires, yet it can hardly be said to have had nations in our understanding of the terms.
>
> (Renan 1990: 9)

A similar point is made by Laitin (1999) when he observes that states in the pre-capitalist period were multinational, and the boundaries were dictated by dynastic marriages, wars, and geographic convenience. The culture of the population within those somewhat arbitrary boundaries was of little interest to either leaders or the population at large. This situation changed with the advent of capitalism which fostered notions of individual citizenship and distinctions between different social classes. The ruling classes were pressed to legitimate their position of power and did so by inventing symbols that represented the common culture of the people in the form of a common language, ancestry, and territory. Hobsbawm (1990) suggests that as a consequence of this process nations are 'invented' or 'imagined' (Anderson 1983). Renan (1990) notes that the boundaries of nations are not dictated by language, geography, race, religion or anything else but are made by human will, it is a soul, a spiritual principle based on large-scale solidarity relating to what sacrifices one has made in the past and is prepared to make in the future.

Brennan (1990) has focused on what he refers to as the 'myths of the nation'. He argues that this concept is potentially confusing since it can offer multiple meanings and include 'myth as distortion or lie, myth as mythology, legend, or oral tradition; myth as literature per se; myth as shibboleth – all of these meanings are present at different times in the writing of modern political culture' (Brennan 1990: 44). Raymond Williams (1983) has explored the relationship between the use of the nation to make specific reference to the modern nation state, and the more general historical use of the term '*natio*' as denoting local community, family, domicile and a wide condition of belonging. He maintains that the two need to be distinguished.

> 'Nation' as a term is radically connected with 'native'. We are *born* into relationships which are typically settled in a place. This form of primary and

'placeable' bonding is of quite fundamental human and natural importance. Yet the from that to anything like the modern nation-state is entirely artificial'.

(Williams in Brennan 1990: 45)

The myths and popular symbols that are exported to economic and military dominions are powerful indicators of the culture of a country. An important vehicle in this respect was the novel that documented social life and presented the characteristics that imaged the community as nation. Johnson (1995) maintains that since the nineteenth century public monuments have been another way that national cultural and political identity at the popular level is constructed and maintained, in some instances by the fostering of imagined communities, for example associated with collective memories of war. He argues that the 'iconography of statues exposes how class, "race", and gender differences are negotiated in public spaces' (Johnson 1995: 62). National symbols and nation-building in post-apartheid South Africa have been built around the metaphor of the 'Rainbow Nation' promoting the racial, ethnic and cultural groups living in harmony. There is a new national flag, anthem, and a new constitution comprising a Bill of Rights that promotes 'democratic value of human dignity, the equality of all people, common citizenship and freedom'. However, not all ethnic groups value these attempts at nation-building with African Black groups being the most receptive (Bornman 2006: 385).

Featherstone (1995) maintains that nations can be considered imagined communities in the sense that they share a sense of belonging and attachment to those that share a symbolic space. An essential part of nation-building is the construction of a complex ethnic core and it is from this that a national community can be invented. A common repository of myths, heroes, events, landscapes and memories all contribute to developing a sense of nationhood. The generation of cultural media and artefacts reinforce this sense of collective identity over time and culminate in a shared sense of nostalgia. Consumers play out these myths such as those identified by Belk and Costa (1998) in the acting out of the 1825–40 fur trade rendezvous held in the Rocky Mountains in the American West, or in Wild West shows (Peñaloza 2001). Stern (1995) has focused on the myths that appear in consumer narratives, how they are related by particular characters, and what form they take in advertisements via her interpretive analysis of Thanksgiving food advertising.

There have been a significant number of studies in marketing that have focused on the concept of creating a national identity. Advertising is replete with what might be interpreted as national themes and influences. For example, some advertisements promulgate the national character of brands – the Irishness of Guinness, the Americaness of Levi's, and the Swedishness of IKEA (Frosh 2007). Advertising is also ingrained with national symbols and stereotypes of other nationalities (O'Barr 1994), while national conceptions of 'the self' shape the production of advertising strategies and campaigns. Nationalism is intimately related to consumerism. The concept of the 'citizen-consumer' has been advanced by Cohen (2004) when advertisers during the Second World War asked consumers to make daily sacrifices in the form of rationing and self-constraint to help the war effort, while simultaneously being 'purchaser consumers' that would support the free market system for which America was fighting. The success of Japan as a new democracy after the Second World War was driven by developing a mass consumer culture. Recent criticism has come as a result of the country failing to spend itself out of a protracted recession. The influence of advertising and other promotional techniques as shapers of national sentiment has been described by Michael Billig as 'banal nationalism'. He suggests that within established nations there is a constant circulation of discourses of nationhood that remind citizens of their national place in the world of nations. However, the process of reminding is so continual, and ever present that it is rarely consciously registered as a process of reminding.

The previous discussion suggests that nation and national are highly contested concepts. Acknowledging this debate has important implications for cross-cultural marketing since many marketing scholars have largely defined cross-cultural as cross-national, and that national differences are significant. Narayan (2000: 1083) has argued that this 'package picture' of culture where Western culture, non-Western culture, Indian women and Muslim women, and so forth, are depicted as homogenous groups is a gross simplification of reality. This issue is acknowledged by Featherstone (1995: 10) when he notes 'The very notion that we can undertake a comparative analysis based upon national cultures, consensual traditions or "organic" ethnic communities is being challenged and redefined'.

Alternative accounts of nation and the national, draw on another range of theoretical and conceptual ideas relating to globalization and multiculturalism and are serving to undermine the notion of cohesive, homogeneous, national cultures. The concept of culture has necessarily become more complex. The image of culture as something 'integrated, unified, settled and static; something relatively well-behaved which performed the task of oiling the wheels of social life in an ordered society' (Clifford 1988: 14), is inadequate in an era of globalization. Clifford emphasizes the shifting nature of culture, and its connectedness with a wider world:

> Cultural difference is no longer a stable, exotic otherness; self–other relations are a matter of power and rhetoric rather than of essence. Twentieth-century identities no longer presuppose continuous cultures or traditions. Everywhere individuals and groups improvise local performances from (re)collected pasts, drawing on foreign media, symbols and languages.
>
> (Clifford 1988: 14)

Scholars of international business suggest that while a range of dimensions used to define culture are used in research, the cultural grouping, or unit of analysis has usually been defined by national or geopolitical boundaries. Yet researchers have noted that culture is a construct and that cultures and nations are not equivalent. Cultural groups should not be inferred in this way nor should the unit of analysis be used in research designs as matter of convenience. From the outset, attention should be paid to identifying or, where appropriate, verifying different cultures, before examining cultural influences (Lenartowicz and Roth 1999, 2001).

Globalization of culture

During the 1960s, there was considerable debate about globalization, especially in connection with the social, economic and political effects of new communications technologies. Typical sentiments of the time referred to globalization as a world in which nation states are no longer significant actors or meaningful economic units; consumer tastes and cultures are homogenized and satisfied through the provision of standardized global products, created by global corporations with no allegiance to place or community (Dicken 2000: 315). The globalization thesis presents two images of culture. The first image relates to the *extension* of a particular culture outwards to its limit which is, in effect, the globe. Diverse cultures become incorporated into the dominant culture which eventually extends across the world. The second image of culture emphasizes the *compression* of culture. Values, norms, and, activities that were previously held apart, have been brought into contact as cultures connect with each other without any organizing principles. Following the globalization thesis to its logical conclusion, the world becomes a single space where everyone becomes assimilated into a common culture. The final outcome is that global culture becomes the culture of the nation state writ large (Featherstone 1995: 11).

Globalization of consumption and consumer behaviour are perceived as universal processes whereby global capitalism is responsible for the destruction of regional and local cultures. Some scholars equate globalization with Americanization, resulting from an intermeshing of the world's 'lead' (American) society and the world's 'lead ideology' (capitalism) (Bonnett 2006). The McDonald's burger stands for a way of life, it is a product from a superior global centre to which consumers on the periphery aspire. Time Warner has promoted itself under the slogan of 'The World is our Audience'. Along with Marlboro Man, Coca-Cola and rock music, they are icons of an American way of life, that constitute themes that are central to consumer culture – youth, fitness, beauty, luxury, romance and freedom (Featherstone 1995: 8). French critics of Euro Disneyland in Paris have referred to it as 'a terrifying step toward world homogenization' and 'a cultural Chernobyl'. The introduction of Coke and Pepsi in Mayan religious ceremonies instead of *poch*, the traditional alcoholic drink, and offering it up as a ritual offering, adds further fuel to the fire that these large companies are disrupting and shaping local cultures around the globe.

Technological developments, such as means of transport, facilitate the binding together of spaces and have been central to globalization. The same is also true of the mass media, including radio and television, along with new communications technologies – telephones, fax, computer networks, and the Internet. The first generation of communications technologies were designed for one-way communication while more recent versions comprise interactive devices. For Pieterse (2002), the present phase of globalization involves the relative weakening of the nation state, both economically and culturally. Globalization has been referred to as a process of 'McDonaldization' (Ritzer 1993) and 'Coca-colonization' (Hannerz 1992). The flow of cultural goods and images on a global scale raises difficulties with respect to reading culture and ascribing fixed meanings and relationships between a cultural sign or image, and the social attributes of the person that uses and consumes the item.

In his seminal paper 'The globalization of markets', Levitt (1983: 92) argued that standardization of product offerings was the order of the day and that 'companies must learn to operate as if the world were one large market – ignoring superficial regional and national differences'. Corporations were steered towards the standardization strategy based on the huge economies of scale that would follow with respect to production, distribution, marketing and management. Levitt adds:

> Gone are accustomed differences in national or regional preference. Gone are the days when a company could sell last year's model – or lesser versions of advanced products in the less-developed world. And gone are the days when prices, margins, and profits abroad were generally higher than at home.
>
> (Levitt 1983: 92)

His view was that standardization was not the only option, but one that should be pursued aggressively on cost grounds. He acknowledged that within the USA, companies do not standardize everything they make, sell, or do. There are neighbourhood, local, regional, ethnic, and institutional differences to work with and around. But the bottom line would be to search for sale opportunities in similar segments around the world, to achieve the economies of scale required to compete. Levitt makes the point that Japanese companies in the 1970s very often operated without the assistance of large marketing departments, yet 'cracked the code' of Western marketing through understanding what all markets have in common – dependable, world-standard goods and services at aggressively low prices.

Cultural transformations are a result of a two-way flow, and this corrects the view that non-Western and non-American cultures are merely passive recipients of cultural globalization. Berger (2002: 12) refers to the concept of 'alternative globalizations' to describe 'cultural movements with a global outreach originating outside the Western world' that can have a significant impact on Western cultures. For example, Indian religious movements have been very proficient at marketing themselves internationally. The Sai Baba movement has two thousand centres in 137 countries (Srinivas 2002). The Hare Krishna movement is an even more visible example. Some of the most important alternative global 'products' to emerge outside of Asia in the West are not religious, but what might be termed New Age culture that has affected the lives of many people in Europe and America at the level of beliefs (reincarnation, karma), behaviour (meditation, yoga, shiatsu, tai-chi, martial arts) and alternative medical traditions of India and China.

There are also a growing number of globalizing companies from emerging markets that are being fuelled by several features: rapid growth in domestic markets giving them cash to invest abroad; low production costs; the difficulties of working in emerging markets have made managers adaptable and resilient; finally liberalization of markets at home has opened up competition and the search for new markets. Tata's purchase of Land Rover and Jaguar from the Ford Motor Company added to Tata's acquisitions worldwide. Chery Automobile, China's largest car manufacturer and exporter, is planning to build plants in eastern Europe, the Middle East and Latin America. Johnson Electric based in Hong Kong has cornered half the world's market for tiny electric motors. Embraer of Brazil has made its mark as the third largest aircraft company, specializing in regional jets. Half of the sales of Sadia and Perdigão, two of Brazil's food companies, are exports (*The Economist* 2008).

Our capacity to understand the cultural effects of globalization in developing countries is limited because most marketing research is undertaken in developed countries, where advanced societies are also the focus of investigation. The challenge for marketing, as it has been in anthropology and other disciplines, is to transform its membership (academics and practitioners) into transnationals whose frame of reference is not limited or left unquestioned by virtue of their national identity (Ribeiro 2006; Cooke 2005; Paasi 2005). A study of 16 leading management journals (3,649 articles), demonstrated that all the journals were published in the first world, and were dominated by articles from the USA, and to a lesser extent Canada and the UK, while papers authored from the Third World were particularly marginalized (Wong-MingJi and Mir 1997; see also Zeleza 2002; Krotz 1997). Shultz (2001) has argued that consumer behaviour has centred on studying the world of the 'haves' – consumers who live in socioeconomic conditions above the poverty line, the 'have-nots' have largely been neglected. Yet the characteristics of developing and developed countries can be quite profound. Forty years ago, Lipson and Lamont (1969: 24) noted the following with respect to marketing in less-developed economies: 'Their middle class is small; the majority of people are poor. Markets are highly fragmented in terms of income, social class, language and tribal differences, and other socioeconomic characteristics'.

In recent years Latin America has received almost half of the total foreign direct investment going to emerging markets (Lenartowicz and Johnson 2002), yet it has received relatively little attention in the cross-cultural marketing literature. Furthermore, for companies like Proctor and Gamble developing markets are growing at double the rate of developed markets (Colvin 2007). It is estimated that 60 per cent of new business will come from emerging markets over the next decade for companies such as General Electric, Siemens, and Phillips (Steenkamp 2005). The reasons for the rapid growth is that 85 per cent of the world's population live in emerging markets and because these markets are at the earliest stages, growth could be rapid (Prahalad and Hammond 2002).

Social marketing in developing countries also promotes the globalization of culture. Fox and Kotler (1980) provide many examples of social marketing in developing countries such as family planning, encouraging people to boil their water, and build and use toilets. Development is big business and although few reliable figures exist, there are probably more expatriates employed by development agencies in Africa today than at any point in the colonial period (Stirrat 2000). Many consultants working for non-government organizations (NGOs) work across a range of specialisms and are employed to undertake reviews, formulate policy, planning, evaluation, and monitoring work. Government agencies involved with promoting international development also have an interest in new theoretical developments in cross-cultural marketing that could provide an additional frame of reference for their work (Eyben 2000). Debates about globalization and development that have been marginalized in marketing and often considered a niche area of macromarketing, should be brought into the mainstream (Kilbourne 2004).

Hunter and Yates (2002: 337) maintain that linguistic practices of a shared experience and perspective of American globalizers' is derived from debates within the 'social sciences, human rights, the market, and multiculturalism'. Whether for the purposes of public policy, consumer research, or program evaluation, all global elites employ the language and techniques of the social sciences to frame their agenda and to solve any administrative or programmatic problems. Under the circumstances it is unsurprising that among international non-governmental organizations (INGOs), professionally trained social scientists are employed in leadership positions and the same is true of multinational companies. Coca-Cola can boast of having fifty cultural anthropologists, sociologists, behavioural psychologists, and ethnographers working on matters relating to strategic marketing.

Some of these professionals work in contexts that are very different from mainstream cross-cultural marketers, that have potential to open up new areas of scholarship. A useful study in this context is that undertaken by Shultz *et al.* (2005) who make some interesting observations about war, marketing and societal welfare in the Balkans. They suggest that to date, marketing discourse has had little to contribute to the effects of war on marketing, yet there are huge implications for consumers. There have been more than 100 armed conflicts around the world in the last decade, which have claimed the lives of nearly 6 million people. They argue that food marketing systems in war-ravaged countries can be a force for good, indeed they can help mitigate and transcend ethnic boundaries. The deployment of marketing skills could be a real change for the good. Other areas that could be fruitfully studied include drugs and weapons trafficking, prostitution, people smuggling, money laundering, and non-legal and informal goods and services. Relatively little is known about these cross-cultural marketing activities, how they affect global markets, and the ways they sustain the economic health of nations (Nordstrom 2000; Kyle and Koslowski 2001; Cabezas 2004; Agustin 2006).

Glocalization of culture

As a result of some of the limitations levelled at the globalization thesis, there has been a different approach to understanding culture through the lens of 'glocalization'. Robertson (2002: 28–32) has provided a useful overview of the history of the term glocalization. The *Oxford Dictionary of New Words* (1991: 134) states that the term 'glocal' and the process noun 'glocalization' are formed by fusing *global* and *local* to make a blend. The term has its roots in Japan to denote the importance of adopting farming techniques to local conditions. The concept of *global localization* was used by Japanese business to suggest a global outlook that is adapted to take into account local conditions. By the 1980s, the terms glocal and glocalization were being widely used within the business community as a way of emphasizing the need to adapt the marketing of goods and services on a global, or near-global basis, to increasingly differentiated local markets. Hannerz (1990) suggests that one way of conceptualizing global culture is the increasing inter-connectedness of many local cultures both large and small. Robertson observes that in many accounts globalizing trends are in conflict with local views of identity and culture within the context of; 'the global *versus* the local, the global *versus* the "tribal", the international *versus* the national, and the universal *versus* the particular' (2002: 33). The outcome is the *hybridization* of national cultures.

At a most basic level, the global is associated with 'the space of sameness, and the local with a place of difference' (Ley 2004: 154). Featherstone maintains that it is becoming increasingly difficult for individuals living in advanced Western economies to view '"the other" through the long-distance lens implicit in terms such as "the savage", "the native" and "the oriental". These images are becoming challenged as fantasy projections and illusions, as "the other" seeks to speak back to us and to challenge our depiction of his or her world' (Featherstone 1995: 82). The result is that we have to deal with a greater degree of complexity when we assess the images of others. One important aspect of recognizing these changes is that of the fragmentation of the nation state. The concept of 'society' that has long been associated with the nation state or country, can no longer be regarded as homogeneous as far as its cultural composition is concerned. The cultures associated with separate countries are becoming more permeable due to global phenomena.

The ease with which images, goods, and practices can be transferred from one culture to another, and accepted by consumers in their daily lives, is a far cry from a few decades ago when the same goods may have been viewed as strange, exotic, and perhaps would even have been rejected because of their unfamiliarity. One perspective on globalization is that it has not led to homogeneity but quite the opposite, since it has created a greater diversity of local cultures as the global interacts with the local. The same goods and services circulating in the global economy may have different meanings to consumers living in different localities. The role of anthropology in understanding different cultures, and the increasing use of corporate anthropologists to interpret consumer behaviour and consumption in everyday life, are examples of these trends. The role of cross-cultural marketers in their capacity as transcultural professionals, is to use their global frame of reference to solve the practical problems associated with understanding consumers and markets in different places. Furthermore, they have to become skilled at 'packaging and re-representing the exotica of other cultures and "amazing places" and different traditions to audiences eager for experience' (Featherstone 1995: 99).

Local culture is something of a relational concept. How does one define local? Local is often understood as opposite from global and refers to the culture of a small bounded space in which people live, interact and have face-to-face contact. The stock of common values and shared practices that are relatively constant, enforce a common sense of place among those who inhabit these particular places. In the 1950s and 1960s, there was considerable emphasis on undertaking locality studies in disciplines such as sociology and geography in order to generate rich descriptions of people living in particular communities. These different cultures were reflected in films, novels, and soap operas. Often the subject was the lives of working-class people who were regarded as the 'other', by the upper middle classes. In practice, drawing boundaries around local cultures is extremely difficult because of the processes referred to earlier concerning the permeability of boundaries between different cultures in different places. This is not to suggest that maintaining local cultures is futile, since consumers can resist globalizing influences and thus strengthen local cultures. The process of resistance could serve to strengthen existing local traditions, rituals, and consumption practices or stimulate the invention of new ones. Ritzer neatly sums up the distinction between supporters of globalization and glocalization:

> There is a gulf between those who emphasize the increasing grobal [globally growing] influence of capitalistic, Americanized, and McDonaldized interests and those who see the world growing increasingly pluralistic and indeterminate. At the risk of being reductive, this divide amounts to a difference in vision between those who see a world that is becoming increasingly globalised – more capitalistic, Americanized, rationalized, codified, and restricted – and those who view it as growing increasingly globalised – more diverse, effervescent and free.
>
> (Ritzer 2004: 79–80)

Pieterse (2002: 45) argues that at any one time multiple views of globalization can be observed within different disciplines and critiques of the concept have emerged from a variety of sources raising different issues. The globalization thesis and the discourse of cultural imperialism attached to it, indicating that the world is being saturated by Western and essentially American culture, is increasingly being challenged. Robertson (2002) argues that cultural messages emanating from the USA are differently received and interpreted in different places. Furthermore, some of the largest producers of global culture including CNN and Hollywood, tailor their products to a differentiated global market. Hollywood films employ multinational casts of actors in a range of 'local' settings in order to capture diverse global audiences.

Cadbury, the British confectionary company, developed a strategy to enter the Chinese market in the 1970s, as soon as China's Open Door policy was announced. However, this was not a straightforward case of globalization whereby the company sold its existing products in new markets. The company was obliged to make changes to its recipes by reducing the content of sugar, and increasing the percentage of cocoa solids to accommodate local tastes. The names of the products and the packaging were changed, and the product was marketed as a prestige product for the better off, rather than a mass market product (Wood and Grosvenor 1997). Even a company like McDonald's, that is often used as an example to illustrate the globalization thesis, adapts its menus to account for local tastes. These examples and many others, indicate the existence and resilience of local consumption cultures which transnational companies need to accommodate if they are to be successful in different markets (Jackson 2004).

The degree to which the Third World is being swamped with Americanized culture 'seducing the world into sameness and creating the world of little Americas'

(Appadurai and Breckenridge 1995: 1), that is often framed in the context of development, is also questionable. There can be no doubt that transnational communications have resulted in a more globally interconnected world and the diffusion of cultural practices from advanced to developing countries has increased. What accounts of globalization often overlook, is resistance to global brands in different places. Most of the foreign goods available in China are sourced from Japan and the USA. Although foreign goods are equated with modernity, this sentiment is frequently moderated by China's long heritage of foreign domination that remains a source of humiliation. Beverley Hooper (2000: 452) demonstrates that in China nationalist sentiments have been used to evoke a very explicit voicing of consumer and competitor resistance. Placards at protests against some global brands indicated 'I'd rather die of thirst than drink Coca-Cola.' I'd rather starve to death than eat McDonald's'. Comparative advertising of global and local brands has also been used as a strategic tactic to generate consumer resistance. The US fast food outlet Kentucky Fried Chicken was involved in one such campaign, in which the Shanghai-based Ronghua Fried Chicken argued that it was more suited to local tastes, since it used a combination of twenty-one traditional Chinese herbs that also claimed to have health benefits in addition to other superior ingredients. It also needs to be acknowledged that the same products can have different meanings in different cultures. For example, in Asia branded goods might be bought more for 'face' reasons in regard for others, rather than because of an individual preference for the product (Schutte and Ciarlante 1998). In the Soviet Union jazz was banned as a product of capitalist decadence, and during another period it was promoted as the authentic 'voice' of an oppressed people. Both of these local interpretations were at odds with the meaning given to jazz elsewhere.

Multiculturalism

A further challenge to the concept of national culture is multiculturalism, referring to a greater ethnic mix within different countries. Appadurai (1990) suggests that the scope of existing and emergent 'ethnoscapes' are complex and shifting including tourists, immigrants, refugees, exiles, guest workers. The complexity of ethnoscapes makes the link between culture and nation difficult to justify in some instances, especially in connection with consumer culture. For example, in Kuwait over 80 per cent of the total workforce are expatriates predominantly working in the private sector (Ali and Al-Kazemi 2005); in Saudi Arabia the figure is also quite high at 33 per cent (Minority Groups International 2007). In the USA, ethnic groups comprise one third, and by 2050 will account for nearly half the population (Denton and Tolnay 2002). In Australia, New Zealand and Canada the ethnic market comprises approximately 40 per cent of the population (Wilkinson and Cheng 1999; Light 1997). In the UK, the ethnic market accounts for only 5–6 per cent of the population, yet the market is estimated to be worth 12 billion pounds a year (Golding 1998). At the other extreme, Japan's foreign population has always been small and, including naturalized Koreans and Chinese, it has traditionally been less than 1–2 per cent (Mouer 2004) although this figure has been regarded as an underestimate (Lie 2001).

Castles and Davidson (2000) highlight two novel features of current migration patterns that are intensifying levels of multiculturalism. The first feature is that multiculturalism is affecting all regions and most countries simultaneously. Millions of people hold multiple citizenships and live in more than one country, and millions of others do not live in their own country of citizenship. Globalization has increased the mobility of individuals across national borders, ensuring that populations become heterogeneous and culturally diverse. At the turn of the century, 150 million migrants celebrated the millennium outside their country of birth, and half were living in developed countries (International Organization for Migration 2000). Although employment-led migration is becoming more significant, family migration constitutes two-thirds of migration to the USA, and between a third and a quarter in Canada and Australia. The definition of the family is more restricted in the European Union and conforms to traditional marriage patterns. Only Scandinavia, the Netherlands, and the United Kingdom allow the in-migration of cohabiting couples or same sex couples providing they form a relationship akin to a family. Parents are permitted if they are dependent (Denmark, Spain, UK), for humanitarian reasons (Germany), or if in serious difficulties (Netherlands) (Kofman 2004).

The second novel feature of contemporary migration patterns relates to the diverse characteristics of immigrants who are arriving from ever more distant parts of the world, not just in relation to physical distance but in cultural terms. Early immigrants often originated from former colonies, or areas of presence of receiving countries. For example, Mexicans, Filipinos, Koreans and Vietnamese in the case of the USA; North and West Africans to France, and Caribbean, Indian, Pakistani and Bangladeshi people to Britain. Recent immigrants are being received from areas where economic and cultural linkages are more tenuous. For example, Arabs to the USA, South East Asians to Japan, and the Chinese to virtually all developed countries. Taiwan is emerging as one of the major exporter countries in the world, with migration increasing from 25,500 to 119,100 between 1990 and 1996 (Wang 2000). The majority of those leaving the country are business people, investors, and professionals.

A further feature of contemporary migration patterns is their complexity. Until recently, migrants moved from one country to another in order to settle permanently, or to return home at some later date. In the contemporary era of globalization 'there is a proliferation of patterns of recurring, circulatory and onward migration, leading to greater diversity of migratory experiences as well as more complex cultural interaction' (Castles 2007: 353). New transnational communities have emerged as a result of these more complex migratory patterns.

Furthermore, there are important implications for the localities in which migrants settle. Migrant populations are not static within particular localities, and thus require more effective measures of identifying population shifts from one place to another, and elucidating the implications for ethnic mix and segregation (Poulsen and Johnston 2006). Ehrkamp (2006) maintains that space features strongly in assimilation discourses since the spaces in which immigrants settle frequently become the basis for debates about difference, otherness and problematic unassimilability of migrants. Studying architecture through the theoretical lenses of globalization and postcolonialism provides insights about the material space – the built environment contemporary globurbs, technoburbs, ethnoburbs (King 2004). Mosques, grocers and other communal places are visible identifiers of migrant communities but they can also be the focus of negative discourse about features of this population (Ehrkamp 2006). As a response, some minorities are beginning to assert both their ethnic heritage and citizenship in socio-cultural political movements in their new home by becoming involved in ethnic celebrations within their communities. The relationship between citizenship, public space and public rituals in migrant communities is illustrated by Veronis (2006) who provides examples of the Canadian Hispanic Day Parade in Toronto, and Staeheli and Nagel's (2006) account of Arab–American community activists in three US cities.

Multiculturalism is not a new concept in marketing discourse. In the 1960s, Thorelli (1968) commented on the apartheid system in South Africa and its implications for ethnic marketing, and there was an established literature about blacks in the USA (Kassarjian 1969). However, it is probably true to say that multiculturalism has not received as much attention as it deserves as a global phenomenon in marketing and consumer research. There was a time lag in Western societies before their members realized that the so-called 'natives were no longer those exotic people living thousands of kilometers from their homes; they became neighbors' (Ribeiro 2006: 371), the rest were living in the West and many were unwilling to accept the cultural mythology of the nation (Hall 1992). The resulting 'ethnoscapes' (Appadurai 1990: 297) have generated more interest in targeting the ethnic market as a result of its increasing size, purchasing power and potential for future growth. Companies have attempted to reach ethnic consumers more effectively by using differentiated marketing strategies including new product lines, focused advertising and customized promotion programmes (Cui 2001). Kraft General Foods, Pepsi-Co, AT&T, Coca Cola, Nabisco and Sear are some of the organizations that have set up multicultural marketing departments to specifically target the ethnic market (Clegg 1996). More multicultural marketing texts have also appeared within the last decade (Halter 2000; Tharp 2001; Rugimbana and Nwankwo 2003).

It is important to acknowledge that multiculturalism is not a monolithic concept. Many forms of multiculturalism can, and do, exist (see Burton 2002; Hall 2000; Joppke and Lukes 1999; May 1999; McLaren 1994). Gunew (2004) has argued the case for *situated multiculturalism*, as a way of contextualizing local and global geopolitical and cultural dynamics of multicultural societies. Whereas Clifford (1997: 245) suggests that 'Words such as "minority", "immigrant", and "ethnic" will have a distinctly local flavor'. Said (1983) describes multiculturalism as a traveling theory disguising different struggles in different countries, cities and localities. Multiculturalism is always mediated by existing structures, policies and the conditions under which immigration takes place. It is therefore important that marketers understand the multicultural market *in context*, as opposed to merely using statistics of consumers within different ethnic groups taken out of their local context as a basis of their knowledge of the ethnic market.

Prior to the 1960s and 1970s, there was complacency within many receiving countries concerning the process of immigrant integration. There was an assumption, if not always stated explicitly, that immigrants would become fully integrated into the host culture. It was recognized that this process would not occur overnight, but would increase with each successive generation. By the 1990s, the so-called melting pot model of assimilation was questioned as a way of conceptualizing contemporary trends. Settler societies that assumed they had a single culture into which all their citizens should assimilate, found that the population included groups, whether long-established or new arrivals, whom it could not assimilate, or who would not assimilate. As a result, these societies faced unfamiliar challenges and the concept of multiculturalism, defined as the 'harmonious co-existence of differing groups in a pluralist society' (Cashmore 1996: 244) emerged as a response. Parekh (2000) quite rightly acknowledges, that settler societies embraced multiculturalism as a response to the demands of different ethnic groups, and many countries curbed their political and ideological assimilationist demands.

The concept of multiculturalism in Canada and Australia emphasizes ethno-culturally plural systems (cultural mosaics) in which immigrants are allowed to maintain the culture of their ethnic origin (Waldinger and Fitzgerald 2004). In the USA, the emphasis has been on the melting-pot phenomenon where the expectation is that individuals will eventually assimilate into the culture of the host country. A very different situation is evident in France where immigrants are expected to assimilate into French society. The founding ideal is of a French nation that is forged by 'coextensivity of citizenship and nationality and opposed to ethnic pluralism' (Simon-Barouh 2003: 16). The hard line reflects a policy of complete cultural submission by minorities so as not to disturb the image of French uniqueness, and is observable in the policy banning the wearing of Islamic headscarves in public schools (Thomas 2006). In Germany, ethnic homogeneity was the glue that kept the nation together, and while ethnic pluralism was part of the country's social fabric it was considered 'a threat by gatekeepers of national identity' (Harzig and Juteau 2003: 3).

A different ideology underpins racial and ethnic relations in Brazil. Gilberto Freyre (1959) developed the idea of an ethnic, racial democracy due to the blurring of group boundaries through miscegenation. Confronted with scientific racist beliefs of a superior white race and that mixed blood merely created inferior beings, Fryere maintained that cross-breeding produced hybrid vigour in humans. Portuguese colonizers made possible extensive racial mixing between three races: Africans, Europeans, and the Indigenous population. The Brazilian population is united in their Brazilianness and view society through an anti-racist lens as opposed to the racist lens of the USA. However, even within the Brazilian context marked by racial democracy, darker skinned members of the population occupy disadvantaged socioeconomic positions compared with those of lighter skin. In Brazil colour is lived as a continuum with the darker end of the spectrum associated with low status traits such as 'lack of education, crime, violence, sexual promiscuity, laziness, and a general lack of civility' (Bailey 2002: 411). By contrast, whiteness is the antithesis of these traits. An important issue in a multicultural world is the extent to which the melting-pot model is reproduced elsewhere; as yet our knowledge within this context is highly limited and somewhat untested (Gentry *et al.* 1995).

Diaspora

The term diaspora has a long history dating back to the third century BC but its contemporary usage is to challenge the once clearly demarcated parameters of nation with geography, national identity, and belonging. Diaspora is originally derived from the Greek word *diasperien, dia* meaning 'across' and *sperien* meaning 'to sow or scatter seeds' referring to the process where people move from their place of birth whether in the context of migration, immigration or exile (Braziel and Mannur 2003). This movement may be voluntary or enforced. For example, transnational notions of whiteness unite the old world racial nationalism (i.e. Europe and Scandinavia) with white diasporas of the New World (USA, Canada, South Africa, New Zealand, Australia and parts of South America) (Back 2002: 636). Transnationals have been defined as 'persons who live dual lives: speaking two languages, having homes in two countries, and making a living through continuous regular contact across national borders' (Portes *et al.* 1999: 217) However, there is no reason why transnationalism should be limited to the movement back and forth between just two places. Transnationalism associated with multiple ties and interactions that link people and organizations across borders of nation states, is not a new term. In her study of New York immigrants in the nineteenth and late twentieth century, Foner (1997) maintains that technological innovation has facilitated more frequent and closer transnational ties, that these are easier to maintain, and that dual nationality facilitates transnationality, as does a greater tolerance of ethnic pluralism.

Diasporic groups maintain a memory, vision, or myth about their homeland. They are committed to the maintenance or restoration of their homeland, and their consciousness and solidarity are defined by continuing relationship with home. For these reasons some governments in developing countries are targeting diaspora to invest back 'home' (Gillespie *et al.* 1999). Diaspora therefore relates to how individuals construct homes away from home, what experiences do they reject replace or marginalize. Consumer researchers are particularly interested in how migrants' use of products acts as a referent for these sentiments.

Cohen (1997) has argued that diaspora is often undertheorized, he provides a fivefold typology of victim, labour, trade, imperial, and cultural diasporas. The victim diaspora is illustrated by the transatlantic African slave trade that sent Africans to the Caribbean, Mexico and Brazil to work on tropical plantations. The indenture of millions of Indians under British colonialism who were used in British, Dutch and French tropical plantations comprised a labour, trade and imperial diaspora. Finally, he argues that Caribbean peoples constitute a new hybrid cultural diaspora since virtually everybody living there has come from some other place. In this respect diaspora poses problems for our understanding of the coherence of nations and the concept of a national culture. The value of the concept of diaspora is that it provides an alternative paradigm for understanding national identification.

According to Kalra *et al.* (2005: 10) the popular understanding of 'one nation – one people' is little more than a fantasy to underline a sense of nationalism that does not exist. They note that the 'formation of hyphenated identities, British-Cypriots, Greek-Australians, German-Turks, Italian-Americans can reinforce the sense of belonging to the nation states on both sides of the divide, but this can also result in the creation of new identities which have no affiliation to the nation-state form'.

Diasporic individuals tend to be identified with hybridity and heterogeneity in their cultural, linguistic, ethnic and national traits, reflecting a cultural mixing associated from moving from one place to another and one culture to another (Braziel and Mannur 2003). The concept of mixing is useful since it undermines the case for a 'pure' culture but it presupposes that culture was fixed and uncontaminated before it got 'mixed', which is clearly not the case. Some migrants also arrive from societies that do not have a strong national identity. Postcolonial societies are often in this category since they more closely resemble assembled collections of multiethnic populations, where regional or religious affiliations may override those of nation (Waldinger and Fitzgerald 2004).

Diaspora has been discussed from many different standpoints since there are many people all over the world who do not live in the country of their ethnic ancestry, but one single community can be maintained through the circulation of money, people, information and goods. Thapan (2005) has explored the issue of women and migration in Asia and its implications for identity. Breda Gray (2004) draws attention to women and the Irish diaspora in her investigation of national and cultural belonging among women who have left Ireland and those that have remained. Likewise, Donna Gabaccia (2000) provides an account of the Italian diaspora over several centuries, but she argues that it would be a mistake to categorize Italians abroad as part of a homogenized diasporic group. Diasporic Italians have their roots in many towns and villages with their own distinctive identities and comprise many different occupational categories. Furthermore, the Italian diapora is one of the most widely dispersed around the globe and their Italianness will be influenced by their country of residence. Similar observations are made by Caroline Brettell (2003) in her discussion of the Portuguese diaspora.

Tatla (1999) has charted the development of the Sikh diaspora that is concentrated in Britain, Canada and the USA and raises the issue of whether Sikhs comprise a religious community, an ethnic group or a nation. For sure, they make themselves noticeable with the men wrapping their uncut beards and hair in turbans. Outward physical displays such as this provide an indication that many Sikhs would not wish to go down the route of assimilation into the society in which they live, but rather that they work to maintain their cultural distinctiveness. Meanwhile, Khalid Koser (2003) focuses on the 'new' African diasporas that update a predominant focus on slavery within the African diaspora literature. In Paris it has been estimated that there are over two thousand African Associations. Ghanaians living in Toronto monitor the price of cement in Ghana so they can build houses at home as cheaply as possible. Somali communities in the USA and Europe send over $120 million back home, almost doubling household incomes in some parts of Somalia. Since

11 September 2001 migrant transnationalism defined as the ability to maintain ties and create new social spaces that are multilocal and span national borders is often being constrained by potential links to global terrorism. This particularly applies to Muslims and intensified Islamophobia in North America and Europe (Ehrkamp and Leitner 2006: 1591).

Cosmopolitanism

> The need for a constantly changing market chases the bourgeoisie over the whole surface of the globe. It must settle everywhere, establish connexions everywhere . . . the bourgeoisie has through its exploitation of the world market given a *cosmopolitan* character to the production and consumption in every country . . . The individual creations of individual nations becomes *common* property. National one-sidedness and narrow mindedness become more and more impossible.
>
> (Marx and Engels [1848] 1952: 46–47; cf Szerszynski and Urry 2002)

The above quotation reads as through it might have been written yesterday, however, it was written over a century and a half ago by Marx and Engels in their *Communist Manifesto*. Cosmopolitanism has been described as a sociocultural condition, a philosophy or world view, a political project concerning the development of transnational institutions, the multiple affiliations of citizens, an attitude or disposition, a practice or competence (Vertovec and Cohen 2002). At its core are two main features: first a political geography of global citizenship and a rejection of citizenship and loyalties based upon the nation (Binnie *et al.* 2006: 5). Frosh argues that consumerism is a key factor in the emergence and maintenance of cosmopolitan modern societies and 'a historical antidote to ethnic nationalism and its ultimate expression, violent conflict' (2007: 464). Second is a specific attitude and set of skills that facilitate an understanding of cultural diversity, an openness to otherness, difference, and a willingness to engage in divergent cultural experiences – a willingness to embrace *contrasts than uniformity* (Hannerz 1996). The skills are a crucial aspect of cosmopolitan consumer culture since they enable an authentic engagement with another culture. Research on inner-city cosmopolitan urban identities in Australia has noted that they tend to be constructed in opposition to an 'other', suburban, mainstream that is less culturally sophisticated and lacking in cultural capital (Rofe 2003; Bourdieu 1984).

Nava (2002) provides an interesting account of the cosmopolitan nature of the Selfridges department store in London in the first two decades of the twentieth century. Founded in 1909, it was one of the most frequently visited tourism venues in London. A reported one and a quarter million people visited the store in the first week that it opened. The owner, Gordon Selfridge, was a writer, a commercial visionary, he promoted equal opportunities for shop workers and was a supporter of the women's suffrage movement. Significantly, he also promoted cosmopolitan values in the organization's advertising campaigns that promoted a modern progressive worldview. For example, the store's publicity was advertised in twenty-six languages, it promoted the view that all races and nationalities were welcome, and this was reflected in the nature of products that were stocked. Nava concludes that 'cosmopolitanism at that time was a flirtation with difference, with the outside, the elsewhere, the other' (2002: 94). It was as a reaction to the perceived conservatism of the dominant culture. One of the 'cosmopolitan' posters published in 1914 to celebrate the fifth anniversary of the store had the caption 'Where East Meets West' (Nava 1997).

Contemporary accounts of cosmopolitanism have tended to focus on trans-national businessmen who have the opportunity to work on overseas assignments and thus experience being part of another culture as cosmopolitan professionals. For example, the cosmopolitan, middle-class expatriates described by Thompson and Tambyah (1999: 215) who relished traveling and experiencing a panoply of transcultural diversity. However, Ley (2004) maintains the extent to which transnational businessmen come into contact with local cultures may be overstated since postings may be for as little as two years. Furthermore, their lifestyles are often highly constrained and centred around 'work, bars, and sporting expatriate clubs' (Ley 2004: 157). Staff on non-Western assignments rarely interact with locals outside of work. Furthermore, he maintains that transnational workers who travel from city to city as part of their work tend to island hop from one expatriate enclave to another (Ley 2004: 157).

Cosmopolitanism has been discussed predominantly in the context of Westerners gazing upon the exotic others and predominantly in developing countries. Place-wars among cities to attract investors have intensified in areas such as South-east Asia. Urban regeneration, image making and branding have centred on the production and consumption of cosmopolitan culture, including the arts that are attractive to the transnational elite that these countries wish to attract. In practice this often means a heady mix of contemporary iconic buildings combined with touches of cultural authenticity (Yeoh 2005). However, marketers have become interested in cosmopolitan consumer culture in emergent economies due to the expansion of the middle-class in countries such as China, India and Latin America. What has become clear, is that there is no one form of cosmopolitan culture that can be predicted with a check list. Cosmopolitanism is location specific, different in content in diverse cultural worlds, thus the role for cross-cultural marketers is to understand how it is constructed and imagined by consumers (Szerszynski and Urry 2002).

It has been estimated that worldwide the number of high-net-worth individuals, those with over $1 million in financial assets, grew by 20 per cent between 2001 and 2006. Many come from emerging economies including China, India, and the Middle East, and are more likely to be self-made millionaires or billionaires rather than inheritors of wealth (*The Economist* 2006b). These high-net-worth individuals are emulating the consumption practices of the wealthy in advanced industrial societies. It does have to be recognized that 'middle class' is a subjective term and is culturally specific. In many developing countries there are significant material differences between the rich and the poor. China is an interesting example of this division. While there is a growing middle class in some of the largest cities, 800 million people, accounting for 60 per cent of the population live in the countryside on less than a dollar a day (*The Economist* 2005a). Likewise, South Africa has been described as 'two countries: a first-world one of comfort and plenty, and a far bigger third-world one of poverty and disease' (*The Economist* 2005b: 31).

At the same time as promoting cosmopolitanism as a more neo-liberal alternative to the dominance of national culture, others have pointed to its inherent politics. Cheah and Robbins (1998) have referred to cosmopolitics and its elitism, in their text *Cosmopolitics: Thinking and Feeling beyond the Nation*, where cosmopolitics comprises discourses and ways of doing politics that are concerned with their global reach and impact. Cosmopolitanism is frequently operationalized as consumption and aesthetics, and the importance of taste that constitutes a form of cultural capital (Bourdieu 1994). This has raised the issue of cosmopolitanism being referred to as elitist, exclusionary and devoid of political transformation or power. Who is included and excluded and on what basis? These are important questions for cross-cultural researchers yet to date they have not attracted significant attention. Some of the pertinent issues in relation to consumer behaviour are discussed in Chapter 2.

Whiteness

The previous discussion of culture has recognized the multiplicity of cultures that can arise in different countries and how different theoretical perspectives can lead to different conclusions. Conspicuous by its absence in these approaches has been the way *power* has been used to impose the culture of one group onto another. The Greeks and Romans built up huge empires and developed models in which there was a highly cultured and powerful centre or metropolis, a mother city, and beyond the core civilized areas were the lands of the barbarians 'clad in skins, rude in manner, gluttonous, unpredictable, and aggressive in disposition, unwilling to submit to law, rule, and religious guidance' (Wolf 1994: 2). This distinction between the civilized and the uncivilized and its link to race and culture was evident in many dominant rulers' worldview. Al-Azmeh (1991) makes a similar comparison in his discussion of barbarians in Arab eyes.

Of more recent origin are cultural anthropological studies exploring the colonial 'other' in Asia, Africa and Latin America that suffer from depicting other cultures as inferior to those of the predominantly white investigator: as simple, backward, unchanging and homogeneous (Kendall and Wickham 2001). In the case of Latin America, some indigenous scholars have begun to dissect the discourse of colonialism that existed from the Spanish invasion in 1492 up until the new imperialism of the USA after the Second World War, that persistently portrayed the Amerindian native as a 'monsterous, unlettered cannibal' (Hart and Young 2003: 2). Similar debates are ongoing in other former colonies such as India (Ganesh and Thakkar 2005). In the eighteenth and nineteenth centuries, evolutionary theories emerged which maintained that distinct races could be ranked according to their heredity, physical characteristics and intelligence. The architects of racial hierarchy positioned white Europeans at the top and other non-Europeans on intermediate rungs. Indians and African-Americans were in competition with each other as the lowest race of mankind (Gould 1996). Pseudoscience of this nature attempted to establish a theoretical framework that ordered and explained human variety, as well as to distinguish superior races from inferior ones.

Count Joseph Arthur de Gobineau has been described as the father of racist ideology (Biddiss 1970). In *The Inequality of Human Races* (1853: 208–210) he states:

> If the three great types had remained strictly separate, the supremacy would no doubt have always been in the hands of the finest of the white races, and the yellow and the black varieties would have crawled for ever at the feet of the lowest of the white . . . The white race originally possessed the monopoly of beauty, intelligence, and strength. By its union with other varieties, hybrids were created, which were beautiful without strength, strong without intelligence, or, if intelligent, both weak and ugly. Further, when the quantity of white blood was increased to an indefinite amount by successive infusions, and not by a single admixture, it no longer carried with it its natural advantages, and often increased the confusion already existing in the racial elements . . . Such is the lesson of history. It shows us that all civilizations derive from the white race, that none can exist without its help, and that society is great and brilliant only so far as it preserves the blood of the noble group that created it, provided that this group itself belongs to the most illustrious branch of our species.

The stratification of Europeans was noted by Benjamin Franklin in his classification of the world's population in 1751, when he made the distinction between the English that were considered white, and the Spaniards, Italians, French, Russians, Swedes and Germans who were considered non-white (Jacobson 1998). By the late nineteenth century the cultural and biological inferiority of Italians, Slavs, Jews and other Europeans was widely promulgated by scholarly experts (anthropologists, ethnologists, biologists) trade unions and racist popularizers. The belief that Europeans comprised a range of distinct and unequal relations found its way to a growing audience at the beginning of the twentieth century, via inexpensive and newsworthy illustrated monthly magazines and cheap daily newspapers. A whole range of metaphors have been developed over time, to indicate an individual's proximity to the desirable white standard including 'variegated' whiteness (Kolchin 2002), 'consanguine whites' and 'probationary whites' (Jacobson 1998), 'not-yet-white' (Roediger 1991), 'off white', 'not-bright-white', and 'not-quite white ethnics' (Arnesen 2001). Latterly, it is Europeans from the Mediterranean and Eastern European areas that have been perceived as less desirable racially, economically and culturally than North-western areas (Britain, Germany and Scandinavia) (Jacobson 1998). In Brazil, systems of race and colour are based on a clear racial hierarchy in which whiteness/Europeanness is prized and blackness/ Africanness is stigmatized (French 2000). In the USA, Noel Ignatiev's *How the Irish Became White*, Karen Brodkin's *How Jews Became White Folk*, and Matthew

Frye Jacobson's *Whiteness of a Different Color*, have tracked the shifting boundaries of the white population.

In most countries that experienced colonization, whiteness or proximity to whiteness remains a signifier of social class and/or wealth and status (Goudge 2003; Lopez 2005). In particular white skin or whiter skin has been important in defining someone as 'white'. In India, stratification according to skin colour is a historical legacy that predated colonialism. Indians from the north are lighter skinned, and therefore of higher status than those in the south. This was due to their Aryan influence through successive invasions from the Greeks (Shome 1999). Forster and Hitchcock (2000: 141) have observed that Kenya currently attracts a significant number of white Euro-American tourists who are referred to as *Mzungu* in Swahili, but the term has also come to mean a 'startling person, or an object of wonder'. In much of the Third World such as Africa and Latin America the most powerful and wealthy elites are also light skinned. On her travels in Latin America Goudge (2003) came across the term 'very white Nicaraguans', who were light skinned, upper class and described as 'imperialist'. Likewise, Lopez (2005: 4) refers to the persistence of colour-based socioeconomic caste structures in former colonies such as Jamaica and the Dominican Republic.

Foreign domestic staff are a persistent feature in world cities and developing countries, and a clear hierarchy is emerging with respect to the ethnicity of the staff. In Yemen, in the Middle East, domestic servants are predominantly women of Asian and African origin and they constitute a rank order within the elite. The hierarchy of foreign servants reflects different levels of prosperity of the employer. The most affluent families hire Filipinos and Sri Lankans, who are considered to be more efficient, cleaner, and more trustworthy than Indians, Egyptians, and East Africans (Vom Bruck 2005). Ethnicity also plays a significant part in the racialized sexual hierarchies of prostitution. In the American West at the end of the nineteenth century, white European and American women had elite status over impoverished women of colour including Asians, African-Americans, Native Americans and Latinas (Scully 2001).

Rosenthal's (2004) investigation of English portraiture demonstrates that post-1770s, feminine inner virtues were to be expressed through the *face alone*. The transparency of the skin showing blood vessels led to the blush being a key differentiating feature between whiteness and blackness. The blush became so common and obvious in portraiture that it was the subject of satire around 1800. The sales of cosmetic blusher flourished in the eighteenth century and were perhaps the first example of commodity racism. A contemporary manifestation of the power of whiteness is the huge growth in whiteness creams. From Manila in the Philippines, to Mumbai in India, to Japan, billboards extol the virtues of a lighter, whiter complexion akin to phenotypical white models. In India whiteness creams account for 60 per cent of all cosmetics sold, some of the sales of the high profile brands such as Lever's *Fair and Lovely* are sold in over 38 countries, and bring in a revenue of $140 million per year. Yet is has been known since the 1930s that there can be serious side effects of some of the ingredients like bleach (Leistikow 2008; Ashikai 2005; McFerson 2002; Harding 1976).

It is clearly important for cross-cultural marketers to be sensitized to how whiteness and white people have been used in history and how this has impacted upon the contemporary marketing environment in different countries. Treating whiteness and white people as a homogeneous entity and a marker against which all other ethnic and cultural groups are measured is far too simplistic.

Questions

- How have definitions of culture changed over time?
- What do you understand by the glocalization of culture?
- What are the implications of multiculturalism for cross-cultural marketing?
- How does the concept of cosmopolitanism assist cross-cultural marketers in developing their marketing strategies?
- Provide examples of how cultural understandings of whiteness have influenced product development and consumer behaviour in cross-cultural marketing.

Further reading

Clifford, J. (1997) *Routes: Travel and Translation in the Late Twentieth Century*, Cambridge, MA: Cambridge University Press.

Featherstone, M. (1992) *Consumer Culture and Postmodernism*, London: Sage.

Featherstone, M. (1995) *Undoing Culture: Globalization, Postmodernism and Identity*, London: Sage.

Halter, M. (2000) *Shopping for Identity: The Marketing of Ethnicity*, New York: Shocken Books.

Hannerz, U. (1992) *Cultural Complexity: Studies in the Social Organization of Meaning*, New York: Columbia University Press.

Hannerz, U. (1996) *Transnational Connections: Culture, People, Places*, London: Routledge.

Joppke, C. and Lukes, S. (1999) *Multicultural Questions*, Oxford: Oxford University Press.

Parekh, B. (2000) *Rethinking Multiculturalism: Cultural Diversity and Political Theory*, Basingstoke: Macmillan.

Willett, C. (1998) *Theorizing Multiculturalism: A Guide to the Current Debate*, Oxford: Blackwells.

Williams, R. (1983) *Keywords: A Vocabulary of Culture and Society*, London: Fontana Paperbacks.

Williams, R. (1993) *Culture and Society*, London: The Hogarth Press.

Wolf, E.R. (1994) 'Perilous ideas: Race, culture, and people', *Current Anthropology*, 35 (1): 1–12.

2 Consumer behaviour

The focus of this chapter is to assess the consumer behaviour implications of growing levels of cultural diversity, and how cross-cultural marketers might wish to respond to them. This is a huge area of research and it is not possible to cover all the relevant literature, so the emphasis in this chapter is on focusing on a few relevant themes. The first section of the chapter focuses on consumer behaviour and consumer society and the extent to which there has been a convergence across societies. The second theme focuses on the sub-cultural differences in the context of understanding the process of defining ethnic groups and boundaries within multicultural populations referred to in Chapter 1. An important debate is whether consumers will acculturate into the society in which they live or maintain their own culture. A third issue relates to understanding cosmopolitan consumer culture and how it is reflected in different national contexts and consumer groups. Materialism has been an important aspect of what has become known as consumer society. The symbolic role consumption has in consumer societies has important marketing implications and the situation becomes even more complex in cross-cultural contexts.

A fifth theme will assess the role of religion on consumer behaviour. Religion transcends national boundaries and has potential to produce different outcomes in different geographical contexts. Cultural perceptions of time have significant implications for consumer behaviour yet it is a somewhat marginalized aspect of consumer culture. The sixth section of the chapter will address a range of important dimensions of the cultural perception of time. The seventh section of the chapter will discuss discrimination on the basis of race and ethnicity in relation to consumption and consumer behaviour. The final section of the chapter addresses consumer movements and activism and how this aspect of consumer behaviour is reflected in different cultural contexts.

Consumer behaviour and consumer society

Levitt's analysis of the globalization of markets that was in discussed in Chapter 1, is a starting point for exploring cross-cultural aspects of consumer behaviour. According to Levitt, a convergence of markets would ultimately lead to a convergence in consumer culture and consumer behaviour. This is a very different proposition to that presented by Dichter (1962) in the 1960s, who was one of the first academics to advance the idea of the 'world consumer', and the need for marketers to understand the cultural differences that affected behaviour in advanced societies and developing economies such as South America, Africa and Asia. He noted that there were some striking similarities, yet at the same time a considerable degree of permanent difference between consumers and potential consumers all over the world. Nearly half a century later, the debate about 'local' and 'global' consumer culture is still raging. Although the convergence theories suggesting that as economic systems homogenize they lead to a homogenization in consumer behaviour is plausible, in reality it is not supported by anecdotal evidence. For example, a large-scale study of products purchased in Europe indicated that only in a very few categories was convergence occurring. Convergence was observable in connection with the purchase of television sets, telephone main lines, cars, sales of cleaning products and soft drinks. The two categories exhibiting the most convergence were cleaning products and soft drinks that have been dominated by US multinational firms (de Mooij and Hofstede 2002).

The USA is often presented as a model of modernity and development that other countries would inevitably emulate. The USA has a productive industrial base and is a leader in many areas of technological innovation. The country has a highly trained workforce, levels of material affluence that far exceed those in many other countries, it has educated and informed consumers, and established credit markets that have enabled the economy to pursue strategies of consumer-led growth. Because of these characteristics, America is held up as an exemplar of consumer society and there is a presumption that consumers are equipped with the social, psychological and behavioral attributes to enable them to become reflexive consumers. In this respect, American consumers are established as a marker by which other, less-developed, consumer cultures might be measured. Furthermore, trends in consumer behaviour are presented as a type of historical trajectory along which other cultures would travel, in much the same way as retailing institutions are thought to reflect the stage of economic development in each country.

The advanced nature of consumer behaviour in the USA, and its presentation as a homogeneous consumer culture has been questioned from a number of standpoints. Douglas (1976) argues that differences in behaviour patterns *within* a country are often marginalized in cross-national research, and differences between countries are often highlighted more than similarities. The outcomes are often 'national' consumer stereotypes that are unlikely to be particularly meaningful or useful (Douglas 1976: 12). There are many primitive aspects of consumption that are alive and well in contemporary American society that reflect kinship, ancestry, and ethnicity in consumption. The idea that consumer culture has been transformed along the line of 'out with the old and in with the new' is not an accurate representation of reality.

Hirschman (1985) explores the consumer behaviour and consumption of Blacks, Italians, White Anglo-Saxon Protestants (WASPs), and Jews in the USA, to indicate how their consumption traditions go back centuries. Contemporary WASPs are descended from English immigrants who founded the American colonies and established the social and political infrastructure of the USA. They have particular lifestyles that reflect their English ancestry:

> [They] dress in shabby-genteel clothing; enjoy needlepoint, yachting, golf, and squash in their leisure time; send their children to private boarding schools; eat mushy, bland, over-cooked foods; hang oil portraits of their ancestors on the walls; keep spaniels and setters as pets; prefer Heppelwhite, Chippendale, and Queen Anne style furniture in their houses; believe in cleanliness, promptness, and good sportsmanship; name sons after their fathers; and use the 'good silver' for everyday meals.
>
> (Hirschmann 1985: 147)

WASPs also have specific religious affiliations, Protestantism, which has its own doctrine on consumption. There is also an interest in ancestry tracing, establishing their lineage that reinforces their ethnic ancestry. By contrast, contemporary American Jews exhibit some contradictory tendencies. On the one hand, they adhere to some traditions that are ancient such as circumcising male babies, the *bar/bat mitzvah* ritual in which thirteen-year-old boys are declared as adults, and marriages performed under the *chuppa*, a canopy reminiscent of ancestral residences. Yet external consumption visible to non-Jews tends to reflect that of WASPs and can be summed up in the phrase 'dress British; think Yiddish' (Hirschmann 1985: 149).

The view that only affluent countries in the world, and those that embrace a Western philosophical tradition, can aspire to be consumer societies has been described as ethnocentric and based on inappropriate historical comparisons. Consumers in Third World countries often engage in aspects of conspicuous consumption before they have the basics to sustain life in the form of food, clothing and shelter. It is almost unbelievable to those of us living in advanced countries, that some 'premature' consumer cultures involve going without basic nutrition in order to sustain the consumption of 'luxury' Western items. A reason why this pattern evolves is due to more extensive information and communications networks which promote Western products and lifestyles around the globe. The recycling of Western products for use in Third World countries is also a factor.

Furthermore, it is not always consumers in higher income groups that lead the way. Belk (1988) indicates that low-income consumers in Ghana prefer to choose high-status, prestigious footwear for social and ceremonial uses, whereas the more affluent will buy shoes on the basis of durability. In shanty towns in India that are without basic facilities like water, people own television sets, pressure cookers, gas stoves and telephones (Prahalad and Hammond 2002). Communities in Africa and India used to assess wealth on the basis of livestock and other traditional goods. Under some circumstances, Western consumer goods are replacing these traditional signifiers of wealth. Within different developing countries there is often a 'local' consensus about the most desirable Western goods to acquire, yet there is little by way of a cross-cultural consensus which is indicative of globalization's 'local' effects. Dholakia *et al.* (1988) have also argued that the *average* Third World consumer is something of a mythological figure since the disparities between the rich and poor are so huge that to measure the population in terms of averages is misleading.

Arnould (1989) further questions the Western model of consumption and consumer behaviour in his study of the Niger Republic in Africa. The material poverty in the Province allows for a broader understanding of local forms of class and status dynamics, and local systems of meaning. How novel goods are used and made visible allows researchers to develop alternative paradigms of consumer behaviour that can be different from those in Western countries. Arnould's research with the Hausa generated three distinctive models that existed in parallel with each other: a *pre-market* model, a *Western market-mediated* model, and an *Islamic ethnonationalist* model. Pre-market societies are characterized by a range of factors including what is done with objects (their use value) rather than on their possession (their sign value). Objects are evaluated on the basis of their social history, their meaning and worth within a community, and not on their economic value. Substituting basic necessities for more desirable for goods is rare, and gift-giving rituals limit the accumulation of products for most members of the community. Innovation in consumption tends to be restricted to the elite and is always highly constrained. The introduction of European consumer goods into pre-market economies disrupts the existing order since the goods bring with them a distinctive cultural baggage. Furthermore, within Africa sophisticated economic systems of exchange exits that reflect consumption spheres segmented by age, gender and social status. These traditions are collapsing with the arrival of the cash economy. Crucially, the arrival of Western goods in pre-market societies needs to be assessed with reference to the meaning that consumers attribute to them. For example, it cannot be assumed that 'the Hausa in Zinder are becoming more Western just because they now eat salad or smoke Marlboros' (Arnould 1989: 258). Thus Third World societies should be regarded as a complex fusion of capitalist and pre-capitalist societies and consumer behaviour is fashioned by both.

The Western market model of consumption and consumer behaviour in Zinder was driven by the elite, who wanted to join the ranks for the supra-national elite, even if only temporarily. They adopted state policies, social policies and consumption practices from the French. The indigenous population made the link between Niger's national elite called *nasarai*, translated as white men, to denote that their consumption patterns were different from the mainstream. The taste for suits, cigarettes, radios, cassettes, motor scooters and LED watches among the urban elite was diffusing to the rest of the population. For the urban elite the emulation of Western consumption and consumer behaviour was one way in which they reinforced their legitimacy and status in the social hierarchy. It was a way that they signaled their new roles in a global division of labour in a global economy (Arnould 1989: 259–260).

A final sphere of influence in Zinder was popular Islam that denounced Western influences. The accumulation of wealth was looked down upon, antagonism was shown towards merchants, and the ransacking of marketplaces ensued. This movement increased the demand for Islamic goods: copies of the Koran, prayer shawls, rosaries, prayer mats. For the rich merchants involved and poor people within the community, popular Islam was conceived as a defensive form of conspicuous consumption, a way to maintain their status through the purchase of innovative Meccan goods rather than the imitation of Western offerings.

Ethnic groups and boundaries

One approach to understanding consumer behaviour is that individuals in different countries share the same values, and therefore understanding the importance of different values helps to understand cross-cultural aspects of consumer behaviour. However, as was noted in Chapter 1, even if certain values are associated with different national cultures (which is debatable) this still leaves the issue of accounting for difference between ethnic groups living within the same society. In multicultural societies using values frameworks to measure the indigenous culture is neglecting to consider significant sections of the population. In his classic work, *Ethnic Groups and Boundaries* (1969), Fredrick Barth argues that the notion of ethnicity resides in the boundary constructing processes which are used to demarcate group membership and non-membership. He argues that it is the differences between groups that create the essence of ethnicity, rather than the consistency of behavioral markers within groups. Much marketing research is premised upon Barth's model. Implicitly it places ethnic groups in opposition to the colonized standard of Americanism: White, Protestants of European, especially British, descent. Ethnicity is defined as the 'other', but whiteness is uncritically accepted as the marker of difference (see Chapter 1).

An important issue to address is how consumer researchers should measure ethnicity and its relationship to consumer behaviour. There is no one definitive answer to this question since consumer researchers are divided in their views: those that prefer objective and those that use subjective definitions. *Objective* definitions include country of birth, parents' nationality, religion, first or main language spoken at home, citizenship status, surname or ethnic/racial categories defined in large-scale surveys, including Census research. The vast majority of multicultural research favours the objective indicators, and there is an underlying assumption that group members have common characteristics that set them apart from the rest of the population. Racial stereotyping in marketing is necessary, since social reality is far too complex for every person to be represented accurately (Rossiter and Chan 1998). An alternative proposition is that categorization at a very general level of abstraction can reinforce in the idea of internal 'sameness', leading to stereotypical views of ethnic group homogeneity (Stansfield 1993). *Subjective* definition categories include various methods of self-identification including strength of *ethnic attachment* and *felt ethnicity* (Deshpande *et al.*1986). This approach recognizes that not all individuals within the same ethnic group share the same culture or will be equally committed to retaining their cultural identity. How they feel about their ethnic origins will differ and this will affect their consumption patterns. Those that have a strong ethnic attachment will purchase products that reinforce their cultural origins such as ethnic food, styles of dress, or choice of media. By contrast those that have a weak sense of ethnic attachment may actually resist conforming to cultural traditions in their behaviour patterns.

It should also be noted that many individuals change their ethnicity from one survey to the next. Since the 1980s, many more individuals in the USA have claimed Indian ancestry, in numbers that cannot be accounted for by factors other than large numbers of people changing their identity. Newer entrants tend to be from the higher socioeconomic groups. A similar pattern is replicated with individuals of Black and West Indian origin (Waters 2002). On the other hand, some ethnic groups defy national boundaries in the conventional sense. Gypsies have been referred to as a transnational minority rather than a national or international minority. Gypsies are a people in their own right and cannot be defined in contrast to the ethnic majorities of one or several states (Acton 1999; Holloway 2003). Another challenge to the concept of ethnic boundaries are mixed race consumers. Some scholars have preferred to use the term 'mixed descent' rather than mixed race, since it incorporates inheritance and ancestry that can often span race, ethnicity and nationality (Olumide 2002: 150; Blunt 2005). At the end of the millennium, mixed race children comprised 3.2 per cent of all annual births in the USA (Waters 2002), 2 per cent in Canada, and 0.6 per cent in Britain (Aspinall 2003). Each generation intermarries at a higher rate than the last, therefore magnifying the degree of "hybridity" within a society and creating 'new ethnicities' (Luke and Luke 1998).

Different countries have their own ways of defining ethnicity. In some instances individuals have considerable choice concerning their own ethnicity rather than it being ascribed. This is the case with respect to the Soviet Union and Russia which make things particularly complex, as Thelen and Honeycutt describe:

> the Soviet tradition of listing a person's ethnic identity in his or her domestic passport continues today in the former republics. At the age of 16, Russians receive their first internal passport and have the choice of taking either their mother's maiden name and ethnicity or their father's family name and ethnicity. Therefore, siblings may have different surnames and ethnicities listed in their internal passports.
>
> (Thelen and Honeycutt 2004: 62)

An important issue that marketers working in complex cultural environments need to consider is how ethnic minority populations differ from the indigenous population. If individuals from minority groups lose their ethnic identity by adopting the behavior of the indigenous population over time, a process of acculturation occurs. High levels of acculturation enable minorities to become assimilated whereby individuals become completely integrated into the host culture. If ethnic minorities adopt the assimilationist pattern of behaviour, marketers could safely assume that minority groups require no special targeting. In practice, the situation is rarely this straightforward as ethnic minorities often have different levels of acceptance of the host culture and are therefore at various stages of acculturation. There is also a question mark over the very linear process that the assimilationist model predicts.

Whether or not minorities adopt the culture of the host nation depends on a number of factors. The attitude of the host nation towards ethnic minority groups, and the attitudes of minority groups towards their socio-cultural settings are crucial. As was learnt in Chapter 1, host nations can respond to ethnic minorities in one of three ways: they can assimilate minorities on equal terms; subordinate them as second class citizens; or recognize cultural diversity in the private, communal sphere while maintaining a shared, public, political culture. Depending on how they are treated, ethnic minorities adapt their behaviour in various ways (Rex 1996). Berry (1990) argues that four models of acculturation are possible. These include *integration*, whereby an individual adopts some of the host culture while simultaneously maintaining their own culture; *separation*, where consumers refuse to integrate into the host culture; *assimilation*, where consumers adopt the host culture and forget their original culture over time; and finally *marginalization*, where consumers feel rejected by the host culture but do not want to maintain their original culture.

Although widely adopted in mainstream multicultural marketing research, the concepts of acculturation and assimilation have a number of limitations. Rex (1994) argues that there is no single ethnic identity shared by all members of an ethnic group. Ethnic groups have multiple identities and may differentiate themselves from non-members by a range of criteria including, 'primordial' characteristics and assigned roles in kinship groups and communities. Or they may unite with one another on the basis of a shared culture – moral, aesthetic behaviour, and religious beliefs. A second problem identified by Caws (1994) is the concept of a monolithic dominant culture into which minorities are acculturated. He questions whether a dominant culture has the unity and coherence that make it recognizably a single culture (see Chapter 1).

There have been many studies to assess the assimilation of ethnic minorities. One study of Latinos in the USA involved searching through their rubbish to establish what products they purchased (Wallendorf and Reilly 1983). The study found that Mexican-American's consumption patterns were not similar to either Anglos or Mexicans, which suggests that assimilation was not simply the result of a linear progression from one culture to another. In particular, the food categories of red meats, eggs, white breads, high-sugar dry cereal, caffeine products, sugary drinks and convenience foods were over-represented in the garbage. Wallendorf and Reilly argue that the Mexican-American consumption patterns were reminiscent of food patterns of Anglo Americans before consumer health education campaigns about cholesterol levels, calories, and tooth decay. They suggest that Mexican-Americans may have over-assimilated on their prior perceptions of Anglo cultural style, an internalized notion of American life.

Other scholars have noted the significance of place and how particular animals and practices take on a different meaning based on their spatial location (Philo and Wilbert 2000). Consumer research has investigated the relationship between Anglos and their animal companions in the USA, and the cultural meaning of the places of humans and animals depicted in stock shows and rodeos (Peñaloza 2001). Jerolmack (2007) has extended this discourse to reveal how animal practices among migrant populations affect ethnic identity. He notes: 'When humans migrate to new places they bring their cultural understandings – including those of animals – with them. Examining their animal practices and attitudes can thus be a window into how migrants either maintain or distance themselves from their ethnic identity and culture' (Jerolmack 2007: 892). He examines how keeping pigeons among Turkish migrants living in Berlin in Germany provides a tangible link with Turkey. Migrants referred to the fact that their ancestors kept pigeons, it was something they had been raised with and the bloodlines of the birds connected them with Turkey through its history and territory. They believed their hobby, which took up several hours a day, and cost considerable sums of money, connected them to an older and more traditional, superior form of Turkish culture. Lassiler and Wolch (2005) make similar observations about how the keeping of livestock in a city provides an important connection to the homeland and culture of Mexicans living in Los Angeles, and Filipinas in Los Angeles (Griffith et al. 2002).

Consumer researchers have argued that the view that migrants simply acculturate into the host culture is outdated, and the reality is far more complex. As a consequence new concepts have been used to emphasize the fluidity of ethnic boundaries. The concepts of bricolage (Bouchet 1995), hybridity, creolization (Sandikci 2001), self-colonialization (Hirschman 2001), black counter culture (Denzin 2001), culture swapping (Oswald 1999), and border crossing (Peñaloza 1994) to describe a process of cultural mixing and hybridization. Another concept that is often used in consumer research is *situational ethnicity* (Zmud 1992). This approach recognizes that individuals may be conscious of reinforcing their ethnic identity in some consumption contexts more than others. For example, at family gatherings such as Christmas and birthdays one might conform to cultural forms of dress, and food choice in order to meet cultural expectations in the wider extended family, but do not do so in business and work setting. In this sense consumption becomes performance, in which objects are the props, set and theatrical stage upon which we play out our lives. The use of language, blending different cultures in some instances and separating them out in others, the symbolic meaning of goods, all point to the idea of culture as commodity, that simultaneously transcends national cultures and collapses the boundaries between the nation state and its others (Oswald 1999). Ethnicity has become more about choosing a lifestyle and an image, rather than with reference to a particular social group (Bouchet 1995).

What has become known as post-assimilation discourse (Askegaard *et al.* 2005) has emphasized the fluidity of consumer identity and behaviour in different cultural contexts. But it needs to be acknowledged that there are limits to culture swapping in Anglo-Saxon cultures dominated by whiteness (see Chapter 1). Some ethnic minorities can transgress boundaries, the liminal spaces between categories for example, from minority to majority status, or from one minority status to a more acceptable minority status (Gubar 1997; Williams 1997). The phenotypical ambiguity of some individuals of Asian or Latino descent can facilitate passing back and forth from whiteness to escape their lower status ancestry and access a higher status one, but this is also true of any other ethnic groups (Oswald 1999). Some ethnic groups have a specific terminology for individuals with lighter skin that are phenotypically closer to whiteness. For example, Peñaloza (1994: 35) who is of Latino descent indicates 'In my family I am called *guera*, a Spanish term for women who can pass as white'. Passing for white has not always been perceived as a positive attribute and associated with self-hatred or disloyalty in both fact and fiction (Wald 2000; Pfeiffer 2003). Communications technologies make passing for white easier. In his discussion of virtual skin Bailey (2001: 338) notes: 'Online, the subject is more fully responsible for the persona into which she or he projects . . . It is a product of one's own words and acts.' At least for some groups, racial anonymity can be a liberating experience.

The mixed race market is substantial and growing yet some parents of mixed race children have problems in obtaining toys for their children that reflect their mixed racial heritage. Nakazawa notes:

> in our home we focus vigilantly on collecting *books* featuring multiracial children and families . . . With less success, we have also tried to find dolls that resemble our fair-complexioned, Asian-eyed daughter, Clare. Asian dolls are too dark in skin shade, and Caucasian dolls have eyes of an entirely different shape.
>
> (Nakazawa 2003: 32)

Nakashima (1996) provides a valuable overview of the mixed race movement in the USA, including its media. One example is the magazine *Interrace*, which has in excess of 25,000 subscribers and is full of advertising targeted at interracial consumers. Among the goods and services on offer are mixed race books, toys, dating and wedding services (Sandor and Larson 1994). The magazine also carries advertisements for counselors who specialize in services for interracial couples (see organizations such as http://www.mavinfoundation.org, http://www.hapaissues forum.org, http://www.ameasite.org (Association of MultiEthnic Americans), and http://www.mixedstudents.org (National Mixed Race Student Coalition).

A rather different issue is how individuals within the second generation acculturate and assimilate when they return to their parents' country of birth. Potter and Phillips (2006) have investigated this interesting aspect of acculturation in connection with second generation Barbadians in their 30s and 40s, who were born in Britain and who are colloquially known as Bajan-Brits. Local populations often regard returnees as something of interlopers who have had it easy abroad and they hold an ambiguous, although privileged, position in Barbadian society. Fanon's (1967) analogy 'black skin white mask' was relevant in this context since Bajan-Brits were viewed as symbolic whites through their English accents, their way of dress, food choices, work ethic, occupations, and general patterns of behaviour. In the UK, Bajan-Brits did not consider themselves either white or black. On returning to Barbados, the Bajan-Brits found that they occupied a third ambivalent space. A strong binary construction of race in Barbados on the basis of black and white served to locate Bajan-Brits in an inbetween hybrid category. In other words, the second generation did not blend into either society. The situation is far worse in South Africa, where xenophobia is a serious problem. There is considerable evidence of harassment and violence against immigrants, especially Black immigrants. It is ironic that Black African immigrants with whom South African Blacks had shared a common 'outsider' identity, are now severely discriminated against by their South African counterparts following the collapse of apartheid and their change of status to 'insiders' (Mensah 2003).

Striffler (2007) maintains that when Mexicans who have migrated to the USA visit home it enables them to escape from the mundane practices of everyday life but two themes usually structure their visits. First, they wish to go to places where they are 'normal' and fit, unmarked by race, language and occupation, but also where their travels gives them a higher social status. For a brief period of time they can afford to drink as much alcohol and eat the most expensive food that small town Mexico has to offer, and where young men become the most eligible batchelors in town. This is in contrast to their life in the USA where if they go out for a night they will tell women they are Italian because if they believe them to be European they would be more attractive. The men would not want to admit that they were Mexican, whereas in Mexico they could just be themselves. For two weeks they could live the life of princes, and revel in conspicuous consumption and ostentatious display. For older generations returning to a place where they are respected and because of their knowledge and experiences, means younger Mexicans turn to them for advice. For women a trip home means a return to traditional gender roles that are particularly foreign to younger women. They cannot drink, have more conservative modes of dress, are not allowed into town and have curfews imposed upon them.

Cosmopolitan consumer culture

It was noted in Chapter 1 that cosmopolitanism implies a particular view towards difference in the world, an openness to, and tolerance of diversity. Cosmopolitan consumer culture is intimately related to a globalized world, global awareness that transcends national loyalties. However, to draw the conclusion that there is one specific type of cosmopolitan consumer culture and consumer behaviour is an oversimplification of reality and has potentially misled marketers. There are several different types of cosmopolitan consumer culture that vary according to the context and consumer characteristics (Cannon and Yaprak 2002).

Thompson and Tambyah's (1999) account of cosmopolitans reflects most closely the view that they are individuals that like to travel, move beyond their familiar cultural surroundings, and experience new cultures. Self-development through the experience of cultural diversity is a prominent theme in their narratives, summed up by the phrases 'an eye-opening experience' and 'something we wouldn't miss for the world'. Their experiences often reflect what they perceive to be authentic, and are not superficial offerings available through conventional tourist sites. Some expatriates deliberately chose not to join expatriate organizations in the belief that they would have a much more rewarding experience by being included in the 'local'. Respondents provided evidence of cultural knowledge they had learnt about different 'communication styles, work patterns, interpersonal interactions, child-rearing methods, priorities in life, and locals' perceptions of expatriate professionals' (Thompson and Tambyah 1999: 226). The emphasis was on being adaptable and flexible and embracing all that the global economy had to offer, whether in the context of being invited to dinner by locals, or being told by locals about places to eat and shop that were off the beaten track.

The creation of global cultural cities plays a central role in place marketing strategies in the countries of South East Asia as they vie for the business of transnational elites (Yeoh 2005). In Singapore, the rhetoric of cosmopolitanism has required a shift from an early emphasis on the founding ideology of multiculturalism and nation-building, and the authenticity of the four founding races of Chinese, Indians, Malays and 'Others'. The current philosophy espoused by the government is for the population not to be parochial but to embrace influences from all over the world. The emphasis on re-engineering Singapore, is in order to make it a cosmopolitan city where professionals would want to work, complete with the benefits of having a cultural infrastructure of theatres and centres for the arts. However, in its quest for cosmopolitan status, Singapore is selective in whom it regards as cosmopolitan, and what status it gives to different sorts of foreigners. Yeoh (2004) notes that Singapore was not just built by the efforts of businessmen, academics and computing professionals, but unskilled labourers and semi-skilled workers in the construction industry and domestic service. Foreign workers in Singapore constitute 754,524 out of a population of 4 million (18.8 per cent) of which 80,000 are skilled and professionals.

In developing countries a cosmopolitan elite is emerging that often has more in common with cosmopolitans in advanced, Western societies than with citizens in their homeland. In Yemen in the Middle East, the *nouveaux riches* display cosmopolitan life-styles by visiting Europe and the USA for superior medical treatment, education, for business, and to purchase clothes, cosmetics and even china to demonstrate their cosmopolitan tastes to themselves and others. Businessmen are given lists of prospective purchases by their families, and on their return are laden down with toys, music tapes, videotapes, and even ordinary foodstuffs. One respondent bought cornflakes and croissants on visits to London because she could no longer afford them in San'a, the country's capital. Men invite each other out for meals and comment about the quality of local restaurants, and up-market restaurants in London and Paris, thus sharing and perpetuating cosmopolitan consumer knowledge (Von Bruck 2005)

In postcolonial societies cosmopolitanism has other important dimensions that reflect the history of colonization, and the relationship between the colonizer and the colonized. In her discussions of whiteness in Nicaragua, Paulette Goudge (2003) has undertaken interviews with Nicaraguans in which links are made between whiteness, cosmopolitanism, and imperialism. Several interviewees raised the issue of social class in connection to whiteness within the Nicaraguan hierarchy. The cosmopolitan elite, were lighter skinned and were from the upper social classes. She also notes that these attributes were also linked to imperialism and therefore colonialism. One respondent had this to say about Nicaraguan cosmopolitans, 'very white Nicaraguans. Very rich, upper class, pale skinned Nicaraguans – very Westernised in their outlook. They are quite separate from the rest of Nicaragua and could be seen to be imperialist' (Goudge 2003: 77). Professionals in Nicaragua who have lots of money go out dancing and drinking, behaviour which is not acceptable to the majority of Nicaraguans, and they are often a point of critical discussion.

In China, the concept of cosmopolitan culture has been commodified, and is targeted at foreigners who have a very different outlook from cosmopolitan consumers who revel in the new, authentic, and different. Soderstrom (2006) refers to a shop called *Cosmopolite, Boutique Living in China*, that was full of Western designer furniture, and a housing complex called Lido Courts that marketed itself as 'the oasis of cosmopolitan living'. The complex comprised 364 fully serviced apartments, an integrated shopping mall, sports facilities and play facilities for children. Its advertising website indicated the following:

> To make your life in Beijing as comfortable and rewarding as your life back home. Here you will experience a hassle-free transition into Beijing's life, a complete cosmopolitan lifestyle and the convenience of 'Turn-key' luxury. From fittings and furnishings of our serviced suites and parkland environment, Lido Courts give you a tranquil, safe, international oasis in Beijing.
>
> (Soderstrom 2006: 553)

A short distance away was another large housing complex under construction, *Phoenix City II*, that was marketed around the world on *expatriates.com*, the online community for expatriates. These places comprise cosmopolitan landscapes variously marketed as 'oases', 'havens', 'international' sites (albeit with an exotic flavour) for expatriates who are temporary dwellers in a foreign country (Soderstrom 2006: 555). This is in stark contrast to the original concerns of cosmopolitism in which cultural elites would revel in the opportunity to embrace another culture. Far from it, cosmopolitan spaces in the Chinese sense were safe places to limit the exposure to culture shock, rather than a means of engaging with the day-to-day realities of Beijing life.

A variation on global cosmopolitanism is *urban cosmopolitan culture,* in which localized versions of cosmopolitanism are constructed and practiced in urban centres around the world. A useful overview of this phenomenon in different countries can be found in *Cosmopolitan Urbanism* (Binnie *et al.* 2006). For example, in the 1970s and 1980s, Auckland in New Zealand, was considered something of a bland cultural setting. By the late 1990s, the inner-city had been transformed and a wide variety of upmarket restaurants comprising Mediterranean, Asian and South American cuisine had opened for business. Italian-style expresso bars and Manhattan-style drinking dens had emerged which sold a distinctive cosmopolitan lifestyle, but within an urban setting (Latham 2006).

Likewise the city of Manchester in the United Kingdom has extensively marketed the cosmopolitan style of loft living, helped by popular American television programmes. Estate agents selling city centre apartments promote the cosmopolitan lifestyle supported by bars, cafes, restaurants, arts, sports facilities, all in a central location. Interestingly, not all cultures were considered equal in the image of a cosmopolitan lifestyle that was being promoted. Cosmopolitanism was quite narrowly restricted to Western European cultures, especially the French lifestyle that was considered classy and trendy. The architecture of the flats, comprising minimalist style, spacious, open-plan, exposed brick work and wooden beams was indicative of a particular cosmopolitan lifestyle. Above all it was low maintenance living leaving plenty of time to play after work, rather than being bogged down with mundane household chores. Marketing is aimed at very specific groups that can live this cosmopolitan lifestyle 'predominantly young, professional, middle-class, able bodied, single or child-free couples, heterosexual and (despite some ethnic diversity) predominantly White' (Young *et al.* 2006: 1700).

The operation of 'local' or urban cosmopolitanism has also been discussed in the context of gentrification of neighbourhoods in Turkey (Ilkucan and Sandikci 2005). Some urban areas are attractive places to live because of the social diversity of the population. Particular segments of the population were attracted to areas suited to gentrification for example, students, academics and artists who moved to the area when house prices were affordable. Once restoration begins to occur, other social groups are attracted including creative types working in advertising and design, white-collar workers, and people who enjoy restoring historic buildings. This influx of money generates a revitalization of retailscapes, with increases in cafes, restaurants, gourmet food sellers, pet shops, hairdressers, and beauty salons. Local cosmopolitanism in this context is the appreciation of social diversity in a local setting rather than a looking to global trends to inform one's consumption and identity.

Materialism

Historians have noted that contemporary patterns of happiness-seeking via consumption emerged in the West in the fifteenth and sixteenth-century Europe, eighteenth-century England, nineteenth-century France, and nineteenth and twentieth-century America (Belk 1985). Perhaps the most prominent account of the role of consumption in social life is Thornstein Veblen's (1899) *Theory of the Leisure Class*. Veblen argued that in affluent societies, consumption is a social signifier through which individuals establish their social position. Conspicuous displays of wealth and leisure marked a person's worth to the outside world. Through their conspicuous consumption the rich advertised themselves to secure a place in the social hierarchy. Those located further down the social hierarchy aspired to the consumption patterns of the better off, giving patterns of consumption a trickle down effect. Bourdieu (1984) builds on work of Veblen in his *Distinction: A Social Critique of Taste*. Bourdieu's emphasis is on understanding social relationships of domination and submission being based not on people's possessions but their tastes that constitute symbolic or cultural capital. For Bourdieu (1984), practices of consumption are the sources of group-based social distinction generated through shared socio-economic constraints.

Lury (1996: 29–36) highlights a number of features that she believes characterize modern consumption and consumer behaviour; the availability of a larger and wide-range of goods for consumers to purchase; the commodification and marketization of a wider-range of goods and services, the expansion of shopping as a leisure pursuit, the emergence of different forms of shopping such as Internet shopping, political organization by and of consumers such as boycotts, a heightened visibility of sport and leisure practices, wider acceptance of credit and debt, an increase in the sites for consumption including shopping malls and theme parks; the growing importance of packaging, promotion, style design and appearance, the emergence of consumer crimes, illnesses associated with consumer society such as compulsive shopping, and an interest in collecting, such as art, antiques. Lash and Urry (1994) focus on the celebration of the creative and empowering possibilities of material consumption, consumers' pursuit of hedonism, and the heightened importance of style in the quest for personalized meaning and identity.

A consumption based orientation in societies where possessions occupy a central role in one's life, is commonly labeled materialism. Consumer researchers have become interested in materialism for four main reasons. First, to understand whether it is a positive or negative trait; second, whether marketing creates materialism or exacerbates it; third, to determine whether materialism is an egotistic trait as opposed to altruism and sharing; and fourth, to assess its impact on interpersonal relations, specifically whether the giving of material goods is a satisfactory sub-stitute for genuine love and affection.

While there is a debate as to whether lifestyles are reflected in, or are produced by advertising (cause or effect), what has been demonstrated is that ads have not necessarily visually portrayed the USA and Japan embracing more luxurious and comfortable lifestyle, but they have embraced themes that reflect this throughout most of the twentieth century (Belk and Pollay 1985).

Consumer researchers have sought to measure materialistic traits. For example, Belk (1985) has defined three aspects of materialism: *possessiveness*, relating to a desire for greater ownership of commodities rather than renting, borrowing, or leasing; *nongenerosity*, defined as an unwillingness to share one's possessions with others and a reluctance to donate or lend items to others; and *envy*, concerning an inability to be happy about the success, possessions or reputations of others. His results based on a sample of consumers in the USA indicated that, broadly speaking, 'more materialistic people tend to be less happy in life'. His study also addressed the issue of materialism across three generations, and found that the older generation was the least materialistic.

Richins and Dawson (1992: 304) came to similar conclusions when they measured materialism as a consumer value in the USA. They found that materialists highly value the means to acquire, and prefer to retain their resources for their own use. Materialists are less likely to share what they have, whether in terms of possessions or money, with individuals with whom they have close social ties. Finally, they concluded that materialists are more likely to be dissatisfied with their circumstances, than with themselves, in other words they did not perceive their materialism as a negative trait.

Ger and Belk (1999) have examined attitudes towards materialism in Romania, Turkey, the USA and Western Europe. They found that respondents reconciled the view that materialism is good/bad by using justifications that include passionate connoisseurship rather than vulgar materialism; instrumentalism and altruism, giving money to good causes. Excuses for their materialistic behaviour included compelling external forces, that it was the way of the modern world, and that they deserved their possessions. For example, the British respondents believed that the Japanese and Americans were more materialistic, and were cultures in which money mattered, whereas in Europe the emphasis was on education and recognition. The Turks considered ostentatious behavior crass due to a growing number of people engaging in conspicuous consumption that lacked subtlety and taste. Connoisseurship was about being intellectually curious, about aesthetics and culture for non-Americans, by contrast vulgar materialists are seen to spend money on bling. Materialism as a terminal value (an end in itself) was considered bad but as an instrumental value it was good. The Turkish and Romanian respondents especially appreciated the 'independence, power and security' that money can bring. Materialism was perceived as a something that was manufactured by society and the media. In the Romanian context, the respondents saw it as a condition that had been forced upon them after the 1989 revolution, for others it was just part and parcel of living in a consumer society.

A distinction has also been made between the public and private meanings of possessions. The public meanings of an object result from socialization and participation in shared activities within a particular culture. Whereas the private meaning is more personal and relates to how public meanings are shaped by private knowledge and experiences of the possessor, in connection to the particular object he or she owns. Objects to do with children (such as saving their first baby clothes/shoes), or relatives that have passed away (keeping objects of sentimental value such as watches and jewellery) often take this form (Richins 1994). The notion of public and private meanings are an important concept in cross-cultural marketing since cultural norms could play an instrumental role in shaping public and private meanings.

Griffin, Babin and Christensen (2004) conducted a study of materialism in Denmark, France and Russia, anticipating that there would be clear differences between the three countries since they would be regarded as having different value profiles. They maintain that one characteristic of Danish culture is that people tend to be modest, with little emphasis placed on personal accomplishments. The outward display of material goods is not a positive trait, and tends to be looked down upon. By contrast, the French culture places much more emphasis on success and achievement, and therefore it would seem more likely that the French place a higher emphasis on material goods as a measure of success than the Danes. Russian consumers have recently emerged from a situation of consumer goods scarcity which could work two ways, they could either place little emphasis on material goods since consumption is relatively low, or alternatively hold consumption as something central and meaningful in their lives given the difficulty of obtaining desirable goods. Overall, the study provided mixed results. Among the Danish sample, materialism was linked with success, happiness and centrality in one's life but the fit of the model was not sound when applied to the French and Russian sample. In the French sample, success was associated with happiness but centrality was not reproduced. The French sample did indicate that living well brings about success, but people are not defined by their possessions. In the Russian case, there was a much weaker association between success and the centrality of materialism in their lives.

Equally important are variations in identity between different generations of consumers in the same country. Thelen and Honeycutt (2004) suggest generational differences are particularly important to consider in transitional economies such as Russia. The former Soviet Union had a very clear ideology and citizens were told that they were leading the way to free workers from capitalist oppression. The Communist Party determined the blueprint for the good citizen, parent and patriot. Although the Soviet Union was multiethnic, the party created the new ethnicity of *homo sovieticus*. This is a very different worldview from contemporary Russia in which many individuals have embraced capitalism, and the opening up of the economy to international influences. A new sense of what it means to be Russian is emerging in a Russia with multiple political parties, different values, and lifestyles. As a consequence, different generations of consumers hold various views, values and opinions which have important implications for marketing strategy and promotional campaigns. For example, contemporary Russians are significantly more homogeneous than Soviet Russians. Soviet Russians are more ethnocentric, whereas contemporary Russians are more international in their outlook, and have much in common with consumers in the USA, Japan, Sweden and Mexico. Changes in gender roles have occurred. Women were the main consumers in Soviet times, in post-Soviet Russia the new Russian men have become more closely aligned with conspicuous consumption (Oushakine 2000).

Materialism has also found a very secure home among the population of China. Armani has plans to open 20–30 new stores in China by 2008. Prada has indicated that it will invest $40 million in order to double its number of shops to 15. By the end of 2004, Louis Vuitton had 13 shops on the mainland. Until fairly recently, 90 per cent of all luxury goods spending in China was by men, but this has started to change as more women come into the market. (*Economist* 2004f). There is also an emerging middle class in Indonesia comprising 18–20 million people that have an appetite for goods and services similar to young Western European and US professionals (Heuer *et al.* 1999). Srinivas (2002) maintains that significant amounts of poverty exist in India, but the poor are becoming engaged in global culture through imitating the behaviour of the middle classes. Maids in middle-class Bangalore homes used to wash their hair with indigenous soap-nut powder, but have now started using shampoos bought from local stores. They also have regular TV-watching schedules and save money to buy 'foreign' consumer items. Cultural globalization does in fact trickle down from the middle classes to the poor. (Srinivas 2002: 92)

Do Campo (2007: 22) maintains that 'people who call themselves middle-class in Latin America tend to be at the top of the scale: prosperous professionals with several servants, children at private schools and holidays in Europe or Miami'. The newly emergent middle class is more accurately described as a lower middle class that includes small business people, consultants to larger businesses, and those in new industries associated with computing and biotechnology. Between 2002 and 2006, 15 million households ceased to be poor in Latin America. In Brazil and Mexico, the incomes of the poorest half of the population are growing faster than those with average incomes. There are increasing numbers joining the middle class in Brazil and Mexico, with similar trends evident in Columbia, Peru and Argentina. Some aspects of consumption have been fuelled by new developments in consumer credit, as they have been in advanced societies (Burton 2008), although at a much lower rate. For example, in Brazil credit has risen to 32 per cent of GDP in 2007, up from 21 per cent in 2002. Typical patterns in credit utilization include consumer loans to fund car purchase and durable goods, followed by mortgages. In Mexico, the value of mortgages to fund house purchase has been expanding by about 35 per cent a year. Goods that have witnessed the greatest growth rates have included cars, computers, electronic goods, clothes, air travel and even household pets.

Sandikci and Ger (2002) have explored the concepts of materialism and modern identity and how the modern is interpreted in Turkey. They identified four different consumption orientations which they categorized as; *spectacularist, nationalist, faithful*, and *historical*. Spectacularist consumption was closely associated with highly fashion conscious urbanites. A range of beauty salons, fitness clubs, plastic surgery outlets and night clubs have been developed to cater for the needs of a more Western oriented lifestyle. Fashionable clothes and the 'in' garments to wear have a particularly high profile among this group that include singers, fashion models, DJs, high profile sportspeople, and television personalities. Consumers outside of this group either aspire to spectacularist consumption, and read celebrity magazines and watch television programmes about the rich and famous, or criticize these trends because of their 'artificiality, meaninglessness, indecency and wastefulness'.

Nationalistic consumption is more modest and less frequently advertised than other forms of consumption, and focuses on objects that symbolize nationalist ideologies or ethos. The most widespread manifestations of nationalistic consumption include objects, films, art, and books that are associated with the founder of the Turkish republic. Another aspect of consumption was a preference for domestically made brands and pride in the indigenous industry. Support and confidence in military acts as a form of collective pride, is reflected in tales of heroes in popular culture – films, folk stories, and cartoons about mythical characters abound. Nationalistic consumption revolves around the 'longing for a sense of worth, being proud of a national identity'. In part these sentiments are a reflection of a feeling of inferiority in relation to the West and a devaluation of the past that failed to develop a Westernized modern country.

Faithful consumption has a religious dependency upon Islam. Islamic media backed by Islamic capital has flourished following the state monopoly on television and broadcasting. There is currently a flourishing media including television, radio channels, pop music and romantic novels that compete with the secular media for audience ratings and advertising money. In 1996, a hotel for the religiously sensitive opened on the Aegean coast. Separate swimming pools, beaches, entertainment and leisure activities for men and women, offered a safe haven for the religious upper classes that want to enjoy the summer months but also maintain their allegiance to Islam. In the area of fashion, faithful consumption is particularly visible. The rise of political Islam created a demand for headscarves, turbans, overcoats and other religiously appropriate clothing items. However, the covering and dressing style is not only a signifier of being religious but also reflects the socio-cultural position of the wearer, both in terms of subgroups of Islamists as well as secularists. The newly emergent urban, middle-class covered women do not simply differentiate themselves from the Westernized, secular Turkish women; they equally distance themselves from the traditional Islamic women who wear a headscarf out of habit and from the gaudy and pretentious styles of the Islamic newly rich (Sandikci and Ger 2002: 468).

Finally, *historical* consumption emphasizes an interest in objects and customs that reflect a common, imagined past. These practices include a diverse range of activities from theatre to a revival of traditional wedding ceremonies. Traditional Turkish restaurants are emerging in major cities and cookbooks containing traditional Turkish recipes have been developed for consumers wanting to experiment at home. Turkish coffee has become more popular after it lost out for several years to Nescafé, and subsequently cappuccino, latte, espresso and filter coffee. Themed hotels have been constructed that reflect the country's Ottoman past. At Ciragan Kempinski Hotel in Istanbul guests, dine in a restaurant that serves old Ottoman cuisine, and its nightclub features classic Ottoman music and belly dancing. Sandikci and Ger conclude by suggesting that each of the groups differentiate their identities from each other and the mainstream middle class, by consuming specific objects and creating particular, pluralistic, 'modern' consumption styles.

Materialistic societies also have a dark side in the form of buying addiction. Research undertaken in the USA has demonstrated how respondents under-report their materialism values, compulsive buying, impulse buying and neuroticism, while over-reporting their self-esteem, thus producing socially desirable responses (Mick 1996: 116). In the early nineteenth century, the psychiatric literature provides evidence of lack of control in respect of buying behaviour. Yet it was not until the 1980s that research in the field began to increase momentum, and that contributions from other academic disciplines (sociology, psychology, social anthropology, medicine) appeared. Compulsive shopping, compulsive consumption (Faber *et al.* 1987), compulsive buying (O'Guinn and Faber 1989; Benson 2000), addictive shopping (Elliot 1994), compensatory consumption (Woodruffe 1996; Gould 1997; Rindfleisch *et al.* 1997), impulsive buying (Bellenger *et al.* 1978; Rook, 1987; Beatty and Ferrell 1998; Wood 1998) and excessive shopping (Dittmar and Drury 2000) have all been used to describe the dysfunctional processes whereby consumers are compelled to purchase regardless of the negative social consequences of doing so (Elliot *et al.* 1996; Baudrillard 1998). Additional subtypes of addictive shopping have also emerged, including collecting and compulsive gift-giving including the self gift (Benson 2000; Friese 2000). Compulsive consumption has been investigated over a number of domains in addition to shopping, to include drug abuse (Hirschman 1992), alcoholism (Blum and Noble 1994), and kleptomania (Marlatt *et al.* 1988).

The compulsive aspects of consumption have been reflected in the phrase 'I shop therefore I am' (Benson 2000) reflecting the need to shop to reinforce a sense of identity. Shopping provides people with a means to discover who they are, giving form to parts of the self that might otherwise have remained hidden. In this sense shopping can be viewed as a process through which individuals solve the problem of personal identity (Campbell 2004). Giddens (1991: 198) maintains 'The consumption of ever-novel goods becomes in some part a substitute for the genuine development of self; appearance replaces essence'. There is also some evidence that young adults raised in disrupted families are more likely to be more materialistic and exhibit higher levels of compulsive consumption than those reared in intact families. However, these results are partly mediated by the financial resources available and the degree of family stress (Rindfleisch *et al.* 1997).

Most research on compulsive consumption and overindebtedness focuses on advanced industrial societies including the USA (O'Guinn and Faber 1989), UK (Elliott 1994), Canada (Valence *et al.* 1988), Germany (Scherhorn *et al.* 1990), Finland (Lehtonen 1999), and Belgium (Dittmar and Drury 2000). However, Park and Burns (2005) maintain that compulsive buying among the fashion conscious is also being spurred on by credit card spending in the Far East. The numbers of consumers engaging in compulsive consumption or impulsive buying are not widely documented, so the scale of the problem is not fully understood. Estimates suggest that compulsive shopping affects 2–5 per cent of the population in developed Western economies (Dittmar and Drury 2000).

Religion

Religious differences are central to our understanding of consumer behaviour in different cultural contexts, yet the subject has not attracted significant amounts of attention from marketing and consumer researchers. Religion has been a persistent feature of consumer culture and considered a legitimate reason for discrimination in some quarters (Belk 1992). Mittelstaedt (2002) has proposed a framework for understanding the relationship between religions and markets which emphasizes three features. The first is how *religions and religious institutions affect the boundaries of market activity*. Most religions affect products that are available for consumers to purchase such as prohibiting, discouraging, encouraging or obligating the trade of certain goods. For example, Islam prohibits the payment of interest which has a major impact on the types of financial services that are permitted in Islamic countries. *Religion and religious institutions can influence the rules of trade and their subsequent enforcement.* For example, Jewish and Islamic jurisprudence developed independently of European legal thought, especially in connection to the status of contracts governing the conduct of market relationships. Within Western common law the equity of a contract is negotiated prior to an agreement and is not related to fairness of the outcome. Islamic jurisprudence, however, is concerned with the equity of the outcome of a contract such as one party acquiring unjust gains. Finally, *religious traditions affect the time and place when markets emerge*. For example, in the USA the so-called 'blue laws' prohibited shops opening on a Sunday in view of the Christian wish to keep the Sabbath sacred.

A second religious influence is the way that *religion holds authority over the activities of markets*, in the form of regulation of trade by religious sanctions. For example, in Saudi Arabia religious authorities, and not the government, control the courts and thus the activities of markets. Another way that religion holds authority over markets concerns institutional authority with respect to controlling some non-market aspects of life that feeds in to consumer behaviour in the marketplace, such as diet. One would be hard-pressed to find a cheeseburger in the Jewish or Muslim areas of Jerusalem, it is not necessarily illegal to sell them, there is just no demand. Social authority constitutes the right of religion to control the cultural beliefs about socially acceptable behaviour. For example, Hirschman (1983) has demonstrated that religion plays a significant part in the consumer behaviour of Jews, Catholics and Protestants through their sexual, political and economic doctrines. Finally, some religions compete directly in the market as in the case of religious hospitals and credit unions, and thus affect the market via their competitive authority.

The third aspect is *how markets affect religion*; when market offerings conflict with religious control of non-market social institutions believers are required to rethink their faith. For example, in 1968 the Catholic Church banned the use of contraception among Catholics which made some followers reassess the strength of their faith. In the USA, research demonstrated that in 1991, 58 per cent of women of childbearing age used artificial contraception compared with 60 per cent usage rate for the general population. In this instance it would seem that the market was influencing religious practices.

All major religions take a critical stance against consumption, especially in connection with the characteristics of greed, waste and self-indulgent hedonism (Ger 2005). In Buddhist philosophy, influential throughout south Asia and the Far East, the need to possess possessions is believed to be a major cause of psycho-pathology and suffering. Buddhist holy people beg for subsistence and a life devoted to contemplation is the ideal. The Buddhist middle way allows for the possession of products without the attachment to them, denoting that worldly goods are not a requirement of living a happy and fulfilled life. Worldly possessions are both meaningless and dangerous since they distract from one's spiritual goals. Buddhism influences consumers' attitudes and beliefs, general views towards materialism, and voluntary disposition behaviour. By contrast Christianity has been the dominant religion in Europe and some parts of the USA. Christianity is suspicious of worldly goods, the holiest life was one of poverty. Belk (1983) observes that material acquisition is tied to four of the seven deadly sins: greed, pride, gluttony, and envy. Monasteries and convents required that people did away with worldly possessions before they entered. In the bible it was stated that it was easier for a camel to pass through the eye of a needle than a rich man go to heaven.

Confucianism is the leading belief system of elites in China and other parts of East Asia. It is not a religion but the emphasis is on living a good life. The structure of society is deeply hierarchical and there is an acceptance that the upper classes would be wealthy and appropriately so. However, there are major religious objections to being obsessed with earning wealth, and conspicuous consumption is distained. For example, Confucianism insists on wearing appropriate clothing especially for ceremonial occasions, but money should not to be spent on frivolity (Stearns 2001). Yet interestingly, Gamble (2006) found that retail firms in China regularly used the phrase 'the customer is God' which they believed to be indicative of the situation in Western contexts. Yet as she observes, most Chinese are atheist and neither Buddhism or Confucian philosophy has a god which raises the issue of how Chinese people conceptualize the term god. Sometimes a local variation is used 'the consumer is the emperor', but as she points out the last Chinese emperor was overthrown in 1911.

Islam has a particularly distinctive approach that has implications for business operations, profits, business relationships, and consumer behaviour. There are in excess of one billion Muslims throughout the world and many live in developing markets. In twenty years time, it has been estimated that one third of the world's population will be Muslim and two thirds of those under 18 years of age will be Muslim. The most significant minority Muslim population is in China where Muslims comprise 2 per cent of the population and number nearly 20.5 million (Amine and Cavusgil 1990; Gladney 2007). Shari'ah law forbids the manufacture and sale of alcoholic drinks, pork and pork products, usury, gambling, deceitful transactions, hoarding and any other activities that can cause harm of any kind to other people. Any earnings or benefits derived from activities that do not follow the principles of Islamic teaching are illegal. Under Shari'ah law, Muslim individuals who accumulate wealth above a fixed level (*nisab*) are obliged to redistribute a certain amount among the poor and needy. This is done through a tax called *zakat*. Shari'ah law forbids the charging of interest on all types of credit, which makes Islamic banking operations fundamentally different from those in the Western world. Ethics play a pivotal role from their production of goods to their sale. Producers and retailers are required to familiarize customers with all the qualities of their products, both good and bad. Any extra costs resulting from difficulties in distribution should not be passed on to customers. Promotional activities should not appeal to emotions, include female personalities, sexual images, or exaggerated or false claims (Marinov 2007).

Jewish consumers are born into a religion and culture at the same time, and whether they adopt one or the other or both will have important implication for marketing. Hirschman's (1981) study of American Jewish ethnicity established that there were some important differences in the behaviour of Jews and non-Jews. She found that high levels of product innovativeness existed within the group which prompted shorter product lifecycles within the subculture. There was less brand and store loyalty, and the promotion effects of advertising wore out more rapidly in this group. Jews maintain aspects of their ethnic heritage in their language by using Yiddish expressions in their conversations. Kosher food is another example of maintaining ethnic traditions and although few households reportedly 'keep kosher', European foods that are aligned with their country of origin are eaten.

These include borscht, blintzes, latkes, cheesecake and smoked sturgeon, in addition to those that are more semitic in origin such as matzoh and bialys. During the Passover, foods associated with Jewish history are consumed in the home such as bitter herbs, lamb, and honey cake. However, in some aspects of consumption and consumer behavior, Jews adopt aspects of WASP culture including styles of dress and the architecture of their properties. Some Jewish women even undergo rhinoplasty in order to change their nose to one that looks more European (Hirschman 1985: 150).

Rastafari is a cultural and religious movement that began in Jamaica in the 1930s, and is ideologically informed by biblical scripture and Ethiopian history. It is a religion of an alienated subculture whose critique of history and ridicule of British cultural norms is a result of the experience of colonialism. Its followers are known as Rastafarians, Rastas or Dreads, and their religion and culture influence their fashion and lifestyle. Rastafarians follow an Ital diet that prohibits salt, sugar, white flour, tinned and processed foods and all flesh except for fish with scales that are less than twelve inches long. They have their own Iyaric language (dread talk), that is purged of negative associations and provides the power of secret communication. For example, sincerely translates to icerely or incerely, dedicate is livicate, and deadline becomes lifeline. The dreadlock hairstyle, sometimes covered in woven tams in red, green and gold, is another identifying feature. In some instances the style of Rastafarians has been co-opted but without the religious and revolutionary philosophy. During the 1980s, tourism attracted foreign women who wanted to experience being with a Rasta man on their holidays. In Negril, 'rentals', 'rent-a-dread', locally known as Rastatutes, traded sex for favours, using the cultural symbols of Rastafari but without the spirituality (Olsen 1995).

It is interesting that despite religious calls in opposition to consumption, many religious organizations have developed stores and websites to promote their religious artefacts, including religious souvenirs, home decoration, clothing, and music. Ger and Wilk (2005) have noted that the streets around Buddhist and Taoist temples in China are crowded with shops that sell religious objects for ancestor ceremonies, incense to burn at the temple, and figures of Buddha. Davis and Yip (2004) have discussed the growth of the New Christian Movement Churches in Australia that participate in a range of promotions from tele-evangelical services to websites offering online shopping. While Davis (2005) highlights the creolization of the Syrian Christian Roman Catholic marriage service in Kerala, that incorporates features of Indian traditions and Romanized practices. Glocalized practices have arisen in which the consumer chooses aspects of different religious elements to construct their own distinctive wedding ceremony.

Consumer perceptions of time

Time is a concept that is embedded in the language of many societies and is intimately related to consumption and consumer behaviour. Yet by the mid-1970s, relatively few marketing scholars had recognized and researched the use of time in consumer research (Jacoby *et al.* 1976). Edward Hall (1959) referred to the rules of social time as the 'silent language' so embedded in our culture that it is almost invisible. In his fascinating study entitled *A Geography of Time*, that examined the pace of life in 31 different countries around the world, Levine (1997: 9) noted the importance of five features 'People are prone to move faster in places with vital economies, a high degree of industrialization, larger populations, cooler climates, and a cultural orientation towards individualism'. Conversely, 'doing time' has become a colloquial expression for imprisonment in Western societies and research has been undertaken on how prisoners perceive time when taken out of the context of everyday life, where consumption and consumer behaviour are highly constrained (Brown 1998).

Anglo-Saxon perceptions of time allows for time to have a past, present and future that can be dissected into periods and have tasks allocated to them. If time is spent on a task and it is not finished, individuals have to make time to ensure that it is completed. Similarly, the concept of buying time is well understood in Anglo-Saxon cultures but elsewhere it is a baffling concept that would seem impossible. Understanding time as a consumer commodity introduces the idea that people can make choices about how to allocate their time, how much time to spend working, on leisure activities, time spent with the family, and so forth. The mental processes required to separate activities into discrete sets necessities an *allocation* scheme that maximizes *utility*.

In Anglo-Saxon cultures, time is a commodity just like any other consumer commodity. However, this viewpoint is not shared in all cultures. Graham (1981) provides three basic perceptual models to help us understand how consumers understand time – *linear-separable*, *circular-traditional*, and *procedural-traditional*.

The *linear-separable* model is comparable to the Anglo-Saxon one described above where a linear view of time predominates that separates out the past, present and future. The past is old in the sense that is has already been experienced, time spent in the past cannot be recovered. The future is new and comprises a different set of circumstances, and individuals can prepare for the future. A future orientation is very strong in the linear model since it is closely tied with the idea of progress, time spent in the past that does not contribute to the future is considered wasteful. Activities are not viewed as ends in themselves but are a means to an end, an end that lies some time in the future. Furthermore, dividing time into slices is equated with undertaking one task at a time. Graham argues that 'This discreteness allows time to be easily compared with other discrete items, such as money or consumer goods. One result is that time is often equated with money, and the notion of both time value of money and a money value of time arises' (1981: 336).

The *circular-traditional* model does not treat time as a continuous line stretching from the past into the future 'but rather as a circular system in which the same events are repeated according to some cyclical pattern' (Graham 1981: 336). This particular conception of time persists in traditional cultures where time is not regulated by clock time, but through the natural cycle of the moon and sun, seasons, agricultural tasks and hunting that depend on the predictability of these cycles. Individuals in these societies expect the past to repeat itself, and it is not to be anticipated with excitement or feared. Life is very much lived in the present and gives people a particular orientation to life. It is typical of that found in the mañana attitude of Latin America, where people will perform tasks that have to be done today with the benefit of immediate rewards and leave the rest. In these cultures time is not really planned or segmented and as a consequence there is little relationship between time and money. This way of viewing time can also exist within advanced Western societies among the poor and less educated. Graham cites the case of poor people using food stamps to purchase the highest quality merchandise and thus living in the present, since buying small things that they really want compensates for the drudgery of everyday life. A wealthier person may have less to spend at the supermarket because they are paying off a mortgage on a house which is an investment for the future. These different perceptions of time result in different types of consumer behaviour and consumption practices.

The *procedural-traditional* model treats the time spent on a particular activity as irrelevant, since activities are procedural rather than time driven. The most important feature of any activity in these cultures is to do the job properly, as opposed to being disciplined according to time. This approach to time is prevalent mainly in cultures that are based on oral history, and whose cultural traditions are passed through rituals. Events are performed when the time is right, and the right time may have little to do with the task in hand. Within this model there is little by way of a relationship between time and money, and time would not be perceived as a consumer commodity. A strong ethic towards haste is perceived as a negative factor, heightening the importance of material advance at the expense of social obligations. But even within these societies a division can arise between traditionalists and progressives with respect to conceptualizing time with younger generations becoming more educated and exposed to outside experiences, such as being in the army. Those that favour modernization and/or Westernization mark themselves out by their appearances, 'usually wear trousers rather than the traditional sarong; they also affect dark glasses and wrist-watches. In some instances, the wrist-watches may not work, but they continue to function as a symbol for the acceptance and importance of a more precise treatment of time (Raybeck 1992: 333).

Perceptions and use of time can be modified by rulers and economic domination of different cultures resulting in the existence of parallel traditions of time. In Amis villages in Taiwan, traditional ways of keeping time are based on differentiating between day and night, changes in the moon, the tides, and times of the year. Japanese government rule resulted in the imposition of a formal education system and the introduction of the clock and clock time. Time of the Taiwanese and mainlanders refers to rituals and political events relating to the Chinese. Time of the whites is linked to the introduction of Christianity and going to church on a Sunday and other events on the Christian calendar, such as Christmas and Easter (Huang 2004).

Cultural aspects of time are also evident in multicultural societies as minority groups make a point of distinguishing their own shared temporal norms from those of the majority. Perkins (1998) draws attention to 'dreamtime' and 'walkabout' that are distinctive of aboriginal culture which has been criticized by mainstream, white Australian society. North American Sioux Indians have no single word in their language for 'time', 'late', or 'waiting'. Many Mediterranean Arab cultures use only three conceptualizations of time: no time at all, now (which is of varying duration), and forever (too long). American Indians like to speak of 'living on Indian time'. Mexican-Americans differentiate between *hora inglesa*, which refers to the actual time on the clock, and *hora mexicana*, which treats the time on the clock considerably more casually. African-Americans often distinguish their own culture's sense of time, what they sometimes refer to by the no longer fashionable term 'colored people's time' (CPT), from the majority standard of 'white people's time' (Levine 1997: 10).

Timestyles have been defined in the context of customary ways that people perceive and use time. A social orientation to time includes 'me time' or 'time with others'. A temporal orientation is the significance that individuals attach to the past, present or future, and has been tied to personality differences. A planning orientation is how people approach time management. Analytic people extensively plan and account for every minute, whereas spontaneous people do not plan ahead and think of time in macro units – things to do this week – and rely on their memory. Time orientations can be used as a basis for consumer segmentation including time allocated to the mass media (Hornik and Schlinger 1981), television viewing (Jackson-Beeck and Robinson 1981), travel time savings (Cherlow 1981), allocating discretionary time (Holbrook and Lehmann 1981), how consumers understand the concept of time scarcity (Kaufman-Scarborough and Lindquist 2003), and the effects of polychronic (multitasking) versus monochromic (one thing at a time) time (Cotte *et al.* 2004). Time is a source of product innovation: the use of time-saving appliances such as microwaves and their approval in different cultures (Guirat 2007), the marketing of fast and convenience food (Brewis and Jack 2005), attitudes to waiting times on satisfaction and service evaluation (Usunier and Valette-Florence 1994). Props that enable us to measure and allocate time include wrist watches which appeared in the 1850s (Freake 1995) and contemporary self-help books on time management which are a relatively new spin on an old idea (Larsson and Sanne 2005).

Holidays are considered a special time to spend with the family that are more deeply embedded in the 'holiday time surplus' nations of Europe, as opposed to the holiday time deficit societies of the USA and Japan (Richards 1998). Westwood (2002) writes of 'diamond time', which refers to periods of romantic imagery and the role of diamonds as signifiers of love. The familiar phrase 'Diamonds are forever', transcends clock time and stretches out to eternity in Western societies in the context of heterosexual love. Cross (1998) maintains that toy gifts from parents to children are intimately related to time in the form of markers of seasonal and annual celebrations, and rites of passage during various stages of the lifecycle. In early twentieth-century America, the white middle-classes began to view children as 'priceless', not just economic assets to be sent to work to provide parents with income. Children became emotional capital for parents, valuable because they were protected from the labour market and thus were allowed to enter a world of imaginative play. As a consequence, toy making moved from a small-scale craft to a mass-production industry.

Globalization through the widespread use of the Internet requires a convergence in our understanding of time. Castells has focused on 'timeless time', Negroponte emphasis 'absolute time for everybody' and 'virtual time' and 'universal time' (c.f. Lee and Liebenau 2000: 43). One of the practicalities of doing business in a global age, is the need to engage with colleagues or business partners or consumers in a synchronized fashion. The existence of different time zones and the need to translate times can cause difficulties. In October 1998 Swatch, the Swiss matchmaker, declared that they had invented a new way of thinking about time that was appropriate for the digital age. They maintained that 'Internet time' which has no time zones will alleviate the problematic consequences of time in the Internet age. Internet time is based on a new format called the 'beat'. A day comprises 1,000 beats, and one beat is the equivalent of 1minute 26.4 seconds; 12 noon in GMT is the equivalent of @500 beats in Swatch's new system. So individuals could arrange to meet to have a conversation on the Internet @500 or meet to have a coffee at some allocated place @500. The creation of a new meridian Biel Mean Time (BMT) (Biel is the location of Swatch in Switzerland) was designated as the universal reference for Internet time. A day begins at midnight BMT (Central European Wintertime). At the opening ceremony the company announced 'Internet time is absolute time for everybody. Now is now and the same time for all people and places. Later is the same subsequent period for everybody. The numbers are the same for all' (Lee and Liebenau 2000: 44).

Discrimination in the marketplace

Discrimination has not yet received a great deal of attention within consumer research, although discrimination is part and parcel of consumer culture. Discrimination can be based on a range of group criteria, rather than individual differences such as age and gender. In theory, marketplace discrimination should not exist since it is in the interests of marketers to treat all consumers equally to enhance business opportunities. Discrimination is a culturally specific phenomenon since some groups are discriminated against more than others in different places. For example, the study by Gilly *et al.* (1998) of American expatriates living in Spain showed that they felt as though they were discriminated against because of an anti-American sentiment associated with the Afganistan war. Sometimes the women were mistaken for being British, but they did not correct the error because they thought they might be treated better.

One of the most thorough analyses of discrimination in the marketplace has been provided by Crockett, Grier and Williams (2003), in their examination of the experiences of African-American men. Their findings demonstrated that respondents regularly perceived that they were faced with marketplace discrimination and in fact had become resigned to the fact that it was an inevitable part of life. When asked about the reasons why they had suffered discrimination, most felt that this was a consequence of negative stereotypes of African-American men that were prevalent in US society. These negative sentiments were reflected in the personal interactions of store personnel. In particular, the high status men in the sample recalled incidents where they felt their status was being questioned. One main issue in consumer-service provider interaction was discrimination on the grounds of consumer inferiority, specifically 'not having enough money to buy', being regarded as 'shoplifter' or 'threat' as opposed to confrontational, overt hostility. They were followed around stores under suspicion as a consequence of widely held views about African-American men being associated with crime and poverty, views propagated in the media.

African-American men in the sample used status oriented consumption to combat stereotypes about their perceived low status. The ability to pay for expensive goods, such as expensive perfume that sales personnel initially thought out of their financial reach, was a way that they enjoyed resisting and undermining prevalent stereotypes. Despite the inferior treatment meted out to this group of men, they were rarely confrontational about it in consumption contexts. Rather, they tended to protect themselves emotionally from any potentially negative outcomes. For example, having multiple ways of paying for goods just in case one was refused, and deliberately thinking about self-presentation when they went shopping by choosing clothes that would project a high status image. African-American men generated communal knowledge of their experiences to make others aware of their unhappy encounters, a case of forewarned being forearmed. Some men did make formal complaints, but they were in the minority and the emotional upset of being angry and making a fuss was balanced against the likelihood of behavioural or procedural change occurring as a result. The issue of relatively infrequent complaining behaviour is significant since the true scale of the problem may be hidden.

The somewhat passive acceptance of marketplace discrimination in the case of American-American men is radically different from the next example of market-place discrimination in Peru. A very different cultural context and norms of social interaction between retailers and consumers produce an overt discriminatory outcome. Traditional markets, bazaars, or suqs are common in rural and urban areas of developing countries. They closely resemble the open-air events of the European Middle Ages as Bakhtin explains:

> The marketplace of the Middle Ages and the Renaissance was a world in itself, a world which was one; all 'performances' in this area, from loud cursing to the organized show, had something in common and were imbued with the same atmosphere of freedom, frankness and familiarity. Such elements of familiar speech as profanities, oaths, and curses were fully legalized in the marketplace and were easily adopted by all the festive genres, even by church drama. The marketplace was the center of all that is unofficial; it enjoyed a certain extraterritoriality in a world of official order and official ideology, it always remained 'with the people'.
>
> (1984: 153–154)

Linda Seligmann (1993) provides additional insights into consumer racism in her analysis of daily market transactions between Peruvian market women (*cholas*), and their clients, comprising peasants from the countryside (*campesinos*), and urban residents (*mestizos*). *Cholas* are proud and feisty people that have rural origins in a society that is known for its *machismo*. They are identifiable by their dress comprising many cotton or velveteen skirts, tall hats that have white crowns and wide black or coloured bands, and large earings. Their world is distinct from that of both *campesinos* and *mestizos*. Seligmann argues that language exchanges within the marketplace can be understood as a politics of culture and ethnicity that reflect wider concerns of nationalism and 'nationness'. When asked in interviews, market traders indicated that all Peruvians were either *cholas* or *mestizas* and that they came from the same ethnic heritage. However, this underestimates the cultural poles of Indian and European that provide a historical backdrop, with *mestizas* having European associations and *cholas* Indian. But when market women distinguished themselves from others it was within the context of education, ownership of property, clothing, and where they lived in the countryside or the city (Seligmann 1993: 189). However, the following extract is an exchange between Elena Vega a *mestiza* client who has visited the meat market with her servant and Susanna Mora the butcher which graphically indicates that in everyday life a hierarchical distinction is made between the two:

Elena: Señora, how much is your kilo of beef?

Susanna: Very cheap, mother. Buy some. The meat is fresh.

Elena: Then why is it so dirty? It's covered with dirt.

Susanna: But, little mother, all you have to do is wash it.

Elena: But, Senora, don't you understand that the meat is already contaminated? Why do you [plural] sell in these conditions? The municipal agents should control this. How can you sell in this manner?

Susanna: But you, who do you think you are to reject the meat I'm selling in this way? If you are such a clean lady, then go buy somewhere else. You shouldn't buy in the market.

Elena: But who do you think you are, refined *chola*, that you can tell me where I should buy? I can buy wherever I want.

Susanna: And you, who are you? Who do you think you are, stinking dame? You don't remember where you are from, who your grandparents are? Maybe they were worse *cholas* than I. And you, now you come calling us *cholas* without knowing who you are. Now you dress in pretty clothes, elegant clothes, you use makeup. With that, you think you are superior to us.

Elena: But you, what an insolent Indian you are. You don't even know how to treat your clients properly. I'm sure you never set foot in a school. You aren't educated or cultured.

Susanna: So, maybe you've gone to school or maybe you haven't. Maybe you're refined. Go away, lady of high heels. You're making me furious. Be careful or I'll throw this piece of meat at you.

Elena: Go ahead and throw it, greedy Indian queen bee [metaphor referring to those who opportunistically accumulate wealth for themselves]. You don't know what I'll do to you.

Susanna: [speaking loudly so her fellow vendors will hear] Lady, you are rich. Perhaps you're a millionaire who made your money as a prostitute. Go to your house. Don't fuck me over here.

Elena: [turns to her domestic servant] What did she say?

Servant: [smiling] I don't know. What could she have said?

Elena: [speaking again to her servant] But you know Quechua. What did this woman say to me? I won't leave things this way. I'll denounce her to the authorities.

Susanna: Right. Go ahead, bring your husbands and your lovers [referring metaphorically to authorities]. What are they going to do to me? Go ahead and bring them. If you like, I'll go with you. You're a lady like a pig with lice eggs between her thighs.

Elena: You'll see, you foul-mouthed *chola*. Perhaps you don't realize the kind of power I have to do something about this. I'll come back tomorrow.

Susanna: Go ahead, stinking dame. I'm not scared of you. Bring whomever you like. How ridiculous! Surely you wanted me to give away the meat to you. You say you have money and you still look for the best, you should buy imported meat and not come here to try my patience.

(Seligmann 1993: 192–193)

These types of interactions occur on a regular basis in the marketplace. Despite the dominant class and ethnic categories to which *mestizas* subscribe, social relations in everyday life open up the spaces for a reassessing relational categories of difference and for market women to reject them or deliberately call attention to them (Seligmann 1993: 191). In her interpretation of the text, Seligmann notes that it is unusual for wealthy urban residents to visit the market with their servants. She maintains that Elena probably visited the market in person in order to assert her authority to get a better deal. The exchange begins in Spanish using formal, polite terms of address; 'Señora' on Elena's part and 'Mother' by Susanna. The conversation then degenerates into ethnic slurs, with Elena referring to Susanna as a 'foul-mouthed *chola*' and Indian, and Susanna calling Elena a 'stinking dame' and 'prostitute'. Susanna confronts the stereotypical views about non-*mestizos* being 'uncivilized' and uneducated, by speaking in Quechua rather than Spanish, to get one up on Elena who does not understand the language. The world to which *cholas* belong is distinct from Quechua peasants or *mestizos* but they interact freely with each insulting whom they please in an aggressive fashion. Furthermore, market women do control *mestizos*' access to urban goods thus making the latter vulnerable. Indians acting in urban ways are perceived particularly threatening by *mestizos* because they do fit ethnic and class stereotypes.

Consumer resistance and boycotts

The concept of the ethical consumer is one that has generated considerable attention within recent years (see Harrison*et al.* 2006). A range of issues have been addressed including what constitutes ethical consumption (Barnett *et al.* 2006), historical approaches to consumer activism (Lang and Gabriel 2006), pressure groups and the campaigns they develop to influence the behaviour of companies (Harrison 2006; Kozinets and Handelman 2004), ethical consumer behaviour (Worcester and Dawkins 2006; Shaw 2006), and the development of corporate strategy in response to consumer concerns (Adams and Zutshi 2006). Others have focused on whether consumers can escape the power and lure of the market in everyday life (Firat and Venkatesh 1995), and commitment to boycotting action (Miller 2001). Kozinets (2002) provides an example of the Burning Man festival in the USA, a week-long, anti-market event that promotes itself as a temporary antidote to consumer culture. Participants engage in debates about corporate greed, passive consumption, employ alternative exchange modes beyond money, and share experiences about alternative ways of life.

A useful summary of academic research pertaining to consumer motivations for boycott participation has been provided by Klein, Smith and John (2004). They found that during the 1990s, businesses were reporting that boycotts were occurring more frequently and were often successful. Furthermore, boycotts were more likely to be focused on corporate practices of specific companies than a broader remit, such as improving civil rights. Recent examples have included the multi-country boycott of Nike, as a response to the sweatshop conditions operated by their Asian suppliers. Because of the significant investment corporations expend in brand building, developing their reputations and a wider public interest in corporate social responsibility, they become more vulnerable to the actions of boycotts. Klein *et al.*'s research demonstrated that four factors influenced consumer boycott participation in the USA: the desire to make a difference; scope for self-enhancement; an awareness of counterarguments that prevent boycotting; and finally, the costs to the boycotter in terms of constraining their consumption.

Consumer boycotts have not received a great deal of attention in the cross-cultural marketing literature and much of what exists tends to be informed by the perspectives of consumers and boycotters in advanced industrial societies to the exclusion of 'local' boycotts in less developed countries. When boycotts in developing countries have been acknowledged, it is often in the context of protests occurring in Western countries in support of consumers and workers in emerging economies, as the example of Nike cited above demonstrates. Clearly, this situation is not particularly satisfactory since it provides only one perspective. Furthermore, practitioners need to be aware of the various cultural contexts in which boycotts can take place. In many countries, boycotts have a long history, thus contemporary boycotts may belong to a trajectory that is not new.

There are few historical accounts of cross-cultural consumer boycotts within marketing and consumer research. One of the few is Terrence Witkowski's (1989) paper entitled 'Colonial Consumer in Revolt: Buyer Values and Behavior During the Nonimportation Movement, 1764-1776' which blends the concept of colonialism, consumption and identity through a historical reading of accounts of the relationship between the colonizer (Britain) and the colonized (USA). In the 1760s, most of the purchases made by Americans were locally produced, but 27.5 per cent of expenditure was on items produced in other British colonies, especially the Caribbean or England. Most manufactured goods were almost always made in or shipped through England. The elites set themselves apart from the ordinary colonist by adopting some of the purchasing behaviour of the upper classes in Europe, resulting in goods advertising one's social position. Once established such consumption patterns would be emulated by others resulting in further imports, especially from England. One consequences of increasing importation was that America went into deeper debt to the 'mother' country.

The nonimportation movement began in 1764 and continued until 1776. The main focus of the movement was to reverse imperial policies on taxation which would stop the flood of imports from the mother country. The purpose was to inflict economic hardship on English merchants and manufacturers who would then lobby Parliament for changes in legislation. The nonimportation movement became America's first organized consumer revolt. English goods were disparaged in the media but local artisans advertised their English, particularly London connections. The appeals of the movement were not unequivocally shared among the population. Moral rhetorical appeals of patriotism had more influence among the more disadvantaged members of society than the upper classes, and women showed more enthusiasm than men. Nonimportation was a desire for cultural independence, a rejection of tea drinking was a rejection of the cultural meaning that was embedded in that quintessentially English pastime. How successful the nonimportation movement was in the longer term is a point of conjecture. Witowski maintains that luxury goods from England were replaced with those from other European countries (France, Spain, and Holland) during the nonimportation ban, and when the importation movement disbanded English imports were once again imported with vigour.

In India *swadeshi* campaigns, translated as 'buy Indian products and boycott foreign goods', began after 1905 with the import of British-made cloth into India which destroyed many areas of handicraft production. Bayly notes:

> In the hands first of Bengali leaders and later of Mahatma Gandhi and his supporters, the need to support *swadeshi* (home) industries and boycott foreign goods was woven through with notions of neighborliness, patriotism, purity, and sacrifice, all of which provided unifying ideologies more powerful than any single call for political representation or independence.
>
> (1999: 285)

The import of foreign cloth became an important material symbol for nationalists compared to literary or legendary motifs in other countries. This was due to the qualities and symbolic role various types of cloth played in Indian. The *swadeshi* led to the boycott of English goods and was similar to other nativistic upsurges in Asia and Africa that rejected European products, or refused to grow European crops as symbols of local and/or national oppression. Periodically it re-emerges especially among the poor, unemployed and disgruntled labouring classes that blame foreigners for their woes (Vicziany 2004). Some older Indian consumers still refrain from purchasing British goods as a consequence of the legacy of colonialism

(Murray 2002). More recent consumer protest has focused on hi-tech, international food chains that threaten the livelihood of farmers and agricultural workers. Examples include Kentucky Fried Chicken outlets in Bangalore that have been attacked by Karnataka farmers (Shirin 2004). Hindustan Lever discontinued two of its ads for whiteness cream after a year-long campaign by protestors. It was accused of using social stigma to sell products and being discriminatory on the basis of skin colour. Its ad showed depressed women becoming happier and more successful after they had used the cream and obtained whiter/lighter skin (Leistikow 2008).

The boycott of American brands in the Middle East is a fairly persistent occurrence and tends to be particularly pronounced in circumstances of political conflict that has religious foundations. Britain's Muslim grocery stores stock a bewildering variety of Islamic alternatives to Pepsi and Coca-Cola. The most popular is Mecca Cola whose founder maintains that it is targeted at individuals who resent 'Coca-Colonization', but identify with the image that Coke coveys of the free and easy lifestyle. Mecca Coke allows consumers to drink an American-style drink while at the same time being subversive. Qibla Cola (referring to the direction of Mecca) is another alternative that is brewed in Derby in the UK. In its publicity it plays down its Islamic roots and focuses upon charitable donations and injustice and exploitation, including the 'unjust colonialist war in Iraq'. Zamzam Cola is an Iranian drink that is named after a holy spring in Mecca, and is more closely aligned to market principles focusing on market share and production capacity. 'Political food' is not just confined to Coke. Another recent example has been Zaytoun olive oil harvested from groves on the West Bank. Demand was so strong from consumers concerned about the plight of Palestinian farmers, that the first two shipments of the product had been pre-sold to distributors and shops (*Economist* 2004c).

Another religious boycott was targeted at Arla Foods of Denmark in its Middle Eastern markets, by Muslim consumers. The source of the boycott were cartoons depicting the prophet Muhammed in ways that were considered inappropriate. Arla had been making dairy foods in Saudi Arabia for 20 years, and had regional sales of $465 million. Arla already sold the Middle East's best-selling butter and saw potential to double sales by 2010. The company had been based in the country for so long it thought consumers viewed it as a local dairy. The company was so confident of increasing sales, that it relocated the production of processed cheeses from its home country to Saudi Arabia. However, the good times were not to last and at the start of 2006 it was hit by a boycott of Danish products throughout the Muslim world, resulting in losses of $1.8 million each day (*Economist* 2006a). Another protest in the Muslim world against Western products occurred when Endemol launched the 'Big Brother' reality show. There were protests by con-servative religious leaders that resulted in the withdrawal of the programme, however, in this case it was against a background of audience interest (Husted and Allen 2006).

Coke is a company that has attracted considerable boycott attention through its activities in the Third World. In the Spring of 2006, the membership of the Board of the Society for Cultural Anthropology began a deliberation on a resolution and subsequently endorsed a boycott actions against the Coca-Cola Company. What they termed the 'Coke Complex' was concern about the company's use of unjust practices which had environmentally detrimental effects (Fortun and Fortun 2007). The company has been criticized for its activities in Mexico for using water which is in short supply for commercial purposes. As a result water has become contaminated, forcing locals to buy bottled water that they can ill afford (Nash 2007). Even more concern has been aired about the company's activities in India. The soft drinks and bottled water market in India is worth $2 billion year and will eclipse soft drinks consumption in the USA over the next few years. Coca-Cola and Pepsi between them control 80 per cent of the soft drinks market, and 40 per cent of the bottled water market. The bottled water market is expanding at an average of 25 per cent per year making India the tenth largest consumer of bottled water in the world. The reason for the significant increase is due to the expansion of the Indian middle class. In India bottled water is primarily underground water that is treated and purified and costs next to nothing to produce, thus generating huge profits. The company's activities have caused water shortages, it has dumped sludge waste, and high levels of pesticide have been found in Coke resulting in it being banned in some outlets (Aiyer 2007). In Fiji, Coca-Cola has been accused of distorting the national economy since bottled water is now a significant sector in the country's export economy and there is a growing dependency on the company (Kaplan 2007).

While there is a growing literature that focuses on cross-cultural consumer boycotts of specific companies, the strategic responses of competitor organizations in the market has received far less attention. One example that backfired was when the Citrus Marketing Board of Israel that sold its fruits under the Jaffa brand name, tried to cash in on the boycott of South African oranges. The company engaged Saatchi and Saatchi to design an advertising campaign. Unfortunately, Saatchi and Saatchi fell foul of cultural codes of conduct. Its advertising caption 'Jaffa: the chosen fruit' was banned by television watchdogs on the grounds that it was anti-Semitic (Fendley 1995).

Questions

- What implications does Levitt's analysis of the globalization of markets have for consumer behaviour?
- How does the concept of culture swapping undermine conventional cross-cultural marketing theory that takes national culture as its main frame of reference?
- Why is the concept of materialism important in our understanding of cross-cultural consumer behaviour?
- How does Rastafari influence consumer behaviour of its followers?
- Provide examples of consumer boycotts in Third World countries?

Further reading

Arnould, E. (1989) 'Towards a broadened theory of preference formation and the diffusion of innovations: Cases from Zinder Province, Niger Republic', *Journal of Consumer Research*, 16 (September): 239–266.

Askegaard, S., Arnould, E.J. and Kjeldgaard, D. (2005) 'Postassimilationist ethnic consumer research: Qualifications and extensions', *Journal of Consumer Research*, 32 (June): 160–170.

Hirschman, E.C. (1985) 'Primitive aspects of consumption in modern American society', *Journal of Consumer Research*, 12 (September): 142–155.

Klein, J.G., Smith, N.C. and John, A. (2004) 'Why we boycott: Consumer motivations for boycott participation', *Journal of Marketing*, 68 (July): 92–109.

Peñazola, L. (1994) 'Atravesando froneras/border crossings: A critical ethnographic exploration of the consumer acculturation of Mexican immigrants', *Journal of Consumer Research*, 21 (June): 32–42.

Potter, R.B. and Phillips, J. (2006) 'Both black and symbolically white: The Bajan-Brit return migrant as post-colonial hybrid', *Ethnic and Racial Studies*, 29 (5): 901–927.

Witkowski, T.H. (1989) 'Colonial consumers in revolt: Buyer values and behavior during the Nonimportation Movement, 1764–1776', *Journal of Consumer Research*, 16 (September): 216–226.

3   Products

Introduction

The globalization of brands has been an important theme in cross-cultural marketing for many years. The first part of the chapter reviews some of the main issues in the debate about the globalization of products. In reality, even the huge global companies adapt their product offerings to different cultures. The second theme of the chapter is to assess how some companies adapt their products for different markets, and what effects the Westernization of aspects of consumer culture has on the built environment. A little commented upon aspect of product innovation is the evolution of transnational products, yet as more consumers do not live in their own country of origin they are an expanding area of product innovation. The concept of transnational products will be illustrated in the context of money transmission services and how various cultural groups deal with sending money back 'home' will be the theme of part three. The fourth part of the chapter will deal with the concept of crossover products. Crossover products are designed for ethnic minority consumers and then become part of main-stream culture. Products that have been specifically designed for diasporic groups (see Chapter 2), are an important growth area, and will be discussed separately in section five.

Product authenticity has attracted considerable attention since fakes can cost companies dear. Within a cross-cultural marketing context, marketers need to understand how consumers within different cultures conceive authenticity and fakes. These issues will be discussed in section six. Section seven deals with consumer ethnocentrism which relates to the beliefs consumers have about the appropriateness or morality of purchasing foreign made products. Ethnocentric consumers regard purchasing imported products as wrong, since this could damage the economy, cause unemployment, and is unpatriotic. An important issue for cross-cultural marketers is to understand consumers' objections so that they can be overcome. Consumer animosity is a variation on consumer ethnocentrism and concerns remnants of antipathy related to previous or ongoing military, political, or economic events. In some circumstances consumer animosity can effect consumer decisions to purchase products from various countries. Consumer animosity will be discussed in section eight. Consumer racism refers to antipathy toward an ethnic group's products or services as a symbolic way of discriminating against that group in the domestic marketplace. Consumer racism is a relatively new cross-cultural marketing concept, some of the tentative findings to date will be reviewed in the final section.

Globalization of brands

Local distinctions are disappearing as products are sold all over the world. Brand names and images signal the same or similar meanings all over the world. International marketing companies are well aware that market segments do transcend national boundaries and form global communities of consumers or brand specific 'image tribes' (Firat and Dholakia 1998). Branding has it roots in Western economies, although that is not to indicate that developing economies did not, or do not, develop their own brands. Coke is bound up with the culture of the USA, living the American Dream, living in a consumer democracy and tied to American ideology and economic values. In 1990, the World of Coca Cola museum opened in the company's headquarters in Atlanta Georgia. Coke as a global product that reaches even the most remote, exotic, and less affluent parts of the world is a recurrent theme. Foreign advertisements reflect the company's global reach showing 'Coke aboard camels in Egypt, bicycles in Indonesia and long-tailed *hang yao* boats in Thailand' (Ger and Belk 1996: 271). Yet despite being found in these far flung contexts, Coke advertises in English despite the fact that English is spoken by a minority of the population. The intention is to promote the product as a high status symbol of Western consumer culture. However, with global brands comes the possibility of making huge marketing blunders. Changing the formula for Coke in the mid-1980s, cost the company $4 million in development costs and the result was 8,000 calls a day, and 40,000 letters from customers across cultural groups that complained. The company finally relented to customer pressure and changed the formula; the episode has been referred to as the biggest marketing blunder of the century (Prendergast 2000).

Whether global, icon brands will be generated in the future is a debate, Kapferer thinks not.

> The empires built by Marlboro or Coca-Cola will not be replicated as they benefited from particular historical and time factors. The international expansion of Coca-Cola was fostered in great part by two world wars and the presence of GIs in Europe and Asia.
>
> In reality, there are very standardized global brands. An early example was Ford's model T car that was totally standardized. Although the US was by far the largest market, the car sold in excess of 20 million cars worldwide. In 1981, the launch of the Ford Escort in the US ad Europe was heralded as a sign of globalization. However, the two models of cars manufactured for the two markets had only one part in common, the radiator cap.
>
> (Kapferer 2008: 455)

Globalization announces itself in the form of McDonald's, Sony, IBM, Marlboro and many other global corporations that are now commonplace in countries that have recently moved to marketized economies including Russia, Tanzania, Malaysia and China. Every day 400–700 new brands are added to the 2.1 million brands that are tracked by media intelligence companies. Many old brands have also made reappearances through the retro-marketing of commodities such as the Volkswagen Beetle (Brown *et al.* 2003). It is an easy task to develop a brand for the market, but much harder to guarantee that it will be noticed. Brands have no objective existence, they are a collection of perceptions in the mind of the consumers but they do add structure and meaning in a person's life, akin to a relationship, and those relationships can cultivate consumers' perceptions of the self (Fournier 1998). For example, Harley Davidson riders learn about the brand from their interaction with each other, but this goes further to present a way of life – a subculture (Schouten and McAlexander 1995). A more recent development is for US parents to name their children after global brands such as Armani, L'Oreal, Chevrolet, Del Monte, and Courvoisier after the cognac (BBC 2003). An even more intimate association was made by Den Fujita, the president of McDonald's in Japan who took the globalization theme a bit too far when he indicated 'The reason Japanese people are so short and have yellow skin is because they have eaten nothing but fish and rice for two thousand years . . . If we eat McDonald's hamburgers and potatoes for a thousand years we will become taller, our skin white and our hair blonde' (Love 1987: 426).

Brand name standardization is particularly problematic in a cross-cultural context. Religion can cause difficulties in some environments. For example, in Islamic countries it is forbidden to sell beer and even selling food under the Budweiser brand is unacceptable. Nike's reference to the ancient Greek goddess of victory is also unacceptable since the reference to a god other than Mohammed is frowned upon in Saudi Arabia, and consumer boycotts have ensued. There have also been pronunciation difficulties; brand names that are difficult to pronounce are hard to remember; consumers are less likely to ask for the product by name; less likely to discuss the brand with others, all of which can result in fewer purchases. In Chile, consumers had difficulty pronouncing Schweppes ginger ale, and the company had to launch an ad campaign to teach people how to say it. Phonetic sounds can also cause problems in translation. Goodyear's Seivitekar tire store pronounced in Japanese means 'rusty car'. Unilever's Le Sancy soup sounds like 'death to you' in certain Asian, local dialects (Alashban *et al.* 2002).

Global brands bring with them Western values, but whether they will come to dominate local patterns of meaning is another issue. Research suggests there are local interpretations of meaning, resistance, and acceptance. In their survey of 1,800 respondents in 12 countries, Holt *et al.* (2003) questioned individuals about their perception of globalness and how it was reflected in their brand preferences. The results indicated that the most important factor was that brands act as an indicator of quality; followed by increased status that comes with being associated with globalness; the third factor was image and special characteristics such as country of origin; the fourth factor was increased responsibility in business practices that comes from being a high profile brand; and finally, brands reflected an American image and way of life. Individual's product and brand decisions are also influenced by family and peer based reference groups. Family involvement in the socialization of offspring has been referred to as intergenerational influence. Childers and Roa (1992) sought to unravel the relationship between comparable samples of consumers in Thailand and the USA to assess what effect culture had on the consumption of public and privately consumed luxuries and necessities. There is an important difference between nuclear families that are the norm in the USA, compared to the extended family in Thailand. They found that within nuclear families there is a higher degree of influence from peers, for public more than for private products and brands (necessities). This observation was not true of Thailand where the existence of a wider network of family members serves to reduce the influence of peers. The distinction between necessities and luxuries is not as pronounced in Thailand as it was in the USA. Even when purchasing conspicuous brands, purchasing brands that are used by one's parents is more pronounced in Thailand. They conclude that the social consequences of owning the 'wrong' brand in the USA is likely to be very negative. However, owning the same brand as one's parents in Thailand is less likely to be viewed as socially inappropriate.

Typically global brands are designed for the domestic market and then exported worldwide to provide a uniform marketing image. However, it is possible that consumers can interpret brands in ways not intended by marketers. It is important that brands are viewed through the lens of cultural values in different markets. In some developing countries values are in a constant state of flux. Eckhardt and Houston (2002) address this issue in the context of the brand meaning attributed to McDonald's in Shanghai in China. But the wider role of brands within different cultures is also significant. In China the social use of branding can be traced back to the Ming and Qing dynasties (1368–1911) and evolved due to uncertainties about a person's social status due to class divisions and the rise and fall in family wealth.

In the old Soviet Union some commentators have suggested that brands did not need to exist because there was no competition in the market. Virtually everything was supplied by state-owned companies and the state also set prices. There was little or no incentive for suppliers to produce innovative goods or improve quality (Ahmad 2005). There are two rebuttals to this argument. First, it is quite true that some categories of foods such as everyday basics (bread, cheese, butter, milk) were not branded. However, that is not to suggest that consumers did not discriminate between products. When all products were supposed to be the same, consumers learnt how to read barcodes by way of a substitute for brands to identify goods that came from reliable factories (*Economist* 2005d). Second, some 'common luxuries' and novelties did proliferate, and these were given brand names. For example, Kazbek, Kosmos, and Stiuardessa were brands of cigarettes; there were also brands of chocolates, cognac, wine and vodka.

Manning and Uplisashvili (2007) divide products in the former Soviet Union according to staples fulfilling basic human needs which were brandless; and *luxury goods* (Soviet or Western) that fulfilled specific human desires that were branded. Branded goods formed the core of the Soviet concept of 'culturedness', and the basis of the second economy of informal *blat* (valuable gifts) (Ledeneva 1998). In addition to the socialist branded goods that imitated Western brands, there were also 'firm' goods, brands from Western or East European socialist countries that presented almost mythical images of the 'imaginary West'. The transition from socialism to postsocialism and the influx of Western brands destabilized the existing complex brand infrastructure, as opposed to introducing Western brands into a country that had managed without.

In many developing countries Western brands are perceived as high status products. However, marketers also need to be aware of high status branded products in local markets with which they have to compete. An intriguing example in this respect is provided by Ritson's (2008) discussion of Panda luxury brand cigarettes in China. The Shanghai Tobacco Corporation manufactures the Panda brand which it established in 1956. It soon became the cigarette of choice of Deng Xiaoping the leader of the Chinese Communist Party, and subsequently generals and politicians, and became synonymous with power and social standing. Keeping production levels small created a mystique about the brand, and even today, the Panda brand signifies that the smoker is a person of influence in China. Until 2004, the distribution system was something of a mystery, and it was impossible to purchase the product in traditional retail settings. Over the past four years the availability of the brand has increased, but it has still maintained its exclusivity by only allowing the cigarettes to be purchased in exclusive hotels and restaurants. Its design also adds to the sense of uniqueness. One third of the cigarette comprises a filter that moderates the strong taste of the high nicotine content. The premium priced product costs 85 Yuan for a pack of 20, equivalent to around £6. Panda's cost fifty times as much as a regular packet of Chinese cigarettes, and five times as much as foreign prestige brands like Marlboro. The popularity and scarcity of the brand has resulted in a black market and copycat versions. As a result, each Panda packet contains six anti-counterfeiting measures. Some of the people that buy the cigarettes are not smokers themselves, but buy them to give to officials. The brand has also developed a strategy of celebrity endorsements when it asked China's most famous athlete who won a gold medal at the Athens Olympics to become a spokesman for the brand.

Glocalization

Globalization of brands is apparent in some contexts as noted above, but large international companies have been forced to cater to diverse cultural segments and consumer behaviour. In his article published in the *Journal of Marketing* in 1961, entitled 'Selling the Tropical African Market', Marcus made some interesting observations about product modifications required to tractors for sale in Africa, 'Picks and shovels must be adapted to the African's physical attributes, and even the tractor seats must be altered, for the African's posterior is generally smaller than the American's or European's' (Marcus 1961: 5). Unilever is a large multinational company competing in detergents, foods, chemicals edible fats and dairy, and personal products. The company continues to design different products and brands, with various brand names, using different formulations and packaging for different cultures. For example, habits of washing clothes, the temperature of the water in which clothes are washed, and the types of machine used all vary greatly, which impacts on the type of washing detergent used. The full harmonization of brand image, formulation, and packaging remained elusive even when a strong international brand proposition existed. A case in point was Lux soap, that was produced in eight different weights in Europe in the 1970s. When Mentadent toothpaste was developed, it had numerous local variations from the outset. It was promoted everywhere as a gum health product, but it had a different taste in different countries. The product was also promoted in different colours to reinforce the brand; in Austria and Italy it was a green gel, in Sweden it was white. The packaging was also varied to appeal to various national segments.

Food products are particularly susceptible to local differences. For example, Nescafé has hundreds of blends of coffee to suit the local palette (Jones 2005). The importance of food choice in reaffirming the culture of white Anglo-Saxons (Wallendorf and Arnould 1991), other ethnic groups (Oswald 1999; Crockett and Wallendorf 2004) and the population of countries such as China (Veeck *et al.* 2005) has been widely documented in consumer research. For example, In the USA chile and mangos are imported from Mexico to meet the needs of Latino and Asian migrants in Los Angeles, since chile is a staple part of the diet for these populations. The rapid growth in these ethnic markets populations in addition to the demand from other ethnic groups that seek culinary diversity, have led to new techniques in global fruit and vegetable processing (Alvarez 2005).

An example of the glocalization of food, drink and housing design is presented in the next section.

Pizza Hut and Domino's in India

America's global pizza purveyors: Pizza Hut and Domino's are battling it out for premier position in India. At stake is the significant Indian middle-class currently numbered at 50 million but projected to grow to 583 million by 2025. This huge increase will be fuelled by significant numbers of younger people that are likely to be more Westernized than their parents and have the disposable income to spend on eating out. Pizza Hut has 13,000 outlets worldwide, and 134 locations across India. The statistics for Domino's are 8,500 and 149 respectively. Both organizations are increasing their number of stores in India by around 50 each year, quadruple the number in other markets, with Pizza Hut aiming for 300 stores by 2012 and Domino's 500 by 2010. There is also considerable geographic concentration of stores in particular places where new technologies and industry are generating lots of jobs. Bangalore is a prime example of a hi-tech hub. Domino's has 20 outlets there and planned another five by the end of 2007. There is also plenty of room for expansion since India has 35 cities with more than a million people, compared with just nine in the USA. The two pizza chains have had a presence in India for over a decade, but the competition became much fiercer when Pizza Hut began a push to double the number of its outlets, and Domino's started to add in-house seating. Prior to this they both had their own spheres of business; Domino's primarily take out and Pizza Hut eat in.

The reason why the pizza is popular in India is because of its similarity to the nation's traditional diet. Indians eat leavened bread (*naan*) and a popular traditional way of serving it is to spread it with butter and garlic. The end result is not unlike garlic bread which is often ordered as a side dish in Domino's and Pizza Hut in India. The ingredients associated with pizza are found throughout India. Cheese (*paneer*) is used extensively in northern Indian cuisine. Tomatoes and sauces are found everywhere and the combination of all of these ingredients into a pizza that you can eat with your hands, as is the norm in Indian dining etiquette, means the pizza has found popularity among the locals. It is estimated that around 80 per cent of Indians are vegetarian and the pizza is able to accommodate these 'local' cultural differences. Both Pizza Hut and Domino's are meticulous in keeping vegetables and non-vegetables separate in their kitchens to a point where they invite customers to inspect them. A further concession to the host culture is adapting meals to meet the needs of the country's 5.2 million Jains, whose religion forbids them from eating onions and garlic. Finally, stores that are located in areas where there is a large Muslim population do not use pepperoni. To provide for a distinctive servicescape and make the atmosphere more relaxed, Pizza Hut engages in what it calls 'customer mania' when the crew do a dance during peak hours every day. At $6.25 for a four course meal for two, it is more expensive than local restaurants but a meal at Pizza Hut or Domino's has become an aspirational event in an increasingly affluent India.

On the delivery side of the business, things are a little more problematic. Problems with traffic congestion, the monsoon rains, and new neighbourhoods that are emerging on a continuous basis, make delivering to tight timescales difficult. Nevertheless, the competition in the marketplace has meant that Domino's has enlisted a strategy that it abandoned in the USA in 1993; the 30-minute-or-free delivery guarantee. In unfortunate circumstances that inevitably arise, outlets have to give away as many as 70 pizzas in a weekend, comprising 2 per cent of the total orders. Pizza Hut has retaliated by offering a 50 per cent reduction on orders that take over 30 minutes (Prasso 2007). There is also local competition in the Indian pizza market. As local entrepreneurs saw the success of Domino's and Pizza Hut they entered the market and positioned themselves as local brands, making local appeals, stressing local values and cultural capital. However, in the minds of consumers the local pizza offerings were not perceived as local but global and foreign. The reasons for consumer responses were as much related to the context in which pizzas were consumed as much as the product. Pizza restaurants contravened local norms in which food was traditionally eaten at home with family members. Pizza restaurants offered a public setting where family and friends could eat together, in mixed sex groups, and stay on and chat (Eckhardt 2005).

The differences in the synergy between the pizza and the indigenous food culture is more problematic in relation to burgers. McDonald's has had more difficulty in penetrating the Indian market and has just 105 outlets in India, despite studying Indian consumers' tastes for six years before entering the market. McDonald's introduced a radically different menu due to protests that it was introducing a foreign fast-food culture in India. All beef products were eliminated and vegetarian foods and a mutton burger were introduced. The rejection of beef products by consumers is due to their incompatibility with India's predominantly Hindu culture that worships the cow. Furthermore, there is a large section of the population that is vegetarian, and even Hindus who eat non-beef meat products have days of the week when they do not consume meat. In this environment McDonald's had to drastically change its global model. Some vegetarian options have been adapted to include more spices to meet the need for tastier food. In these respects the Indian consumer can be viewed as 'Indianizing' McDonald's as apposed to the chain 'Americanizing' India. Indeed the McVeggie burger developed for the Indian market is now available in many other markets including the USA, Canada, and the United Kingdom (Eckhardt and Mahi 2004).

Starbucks

Thompson and Arsel (2004) take a closer look at the glocalization debate by assessing how Starbucks' marketing is perceived by different groups of consumers. They argue that although the globalization thesis may be flawed, nevertheless, it can function as a folk theory that consumers can use to interpret the meaning of global brands in the context of local alternatives. They argue that to be dismissive of globalization's culture effects, could marginalize the effects that global brands can have on local markets and consumer preferences. To theorize these aspects in the context of glocalization they develop the concept of the hegemonic (culture-shaping) brandscape. Brandscape commonly refers to the way that consumers engage with the symbolic meaning of brands. Thompson and Arsel reconfigure consumercentric views of brands to assess the extent that global brands impact on local competitor brands and the meanings that consumers derive from these glocal servicescapes. As they indicate:

> A hegemonic brandscape is a cultural system of servicescapes that are linked together and structured by discursive, symbolic, and competitive relationships to a dominant (market-driving) experiential brand. The hegemonic brandscape not only structures an experience economy market . . . but also shapes consumer lifestyles and identities by functioning as a cultural model that consumers act, think, and feel through.
>
> (Thompson and Arsel 2004: 632)

In the coffee shop market, small-scale independent coffee shops occupy competitive positions that can be mapped in relation to global brands like Starbucks that have attained iconic cultural status. In 1990 there were around 200 free standing coffee shops in the USA, fifteen years later there were in excess of 14,000. Starbucks own 30 per cent of the total, and have exported the format globally including Canada, China, Japan, Taiwan, Britain, and Europe. Anti-Starbucks slogans and critiques of the company's strategy have ensued on the back of undesirable business practices, negative effects on local competitors, the environment and Third World coffee growers. It is argued that anti-Starbucks discourse has become part of coffee culture which is reflected in consumers' patronage of local coffee shops and gives political meaning to their consumption patterns.

Housing design

It has been a common trend for anthropologists and archaeologists to examine material aspects of culture, including buildings and other objects, to help uncover the norms that govern the behaviour within society. Analysing the physical setting of domestic space, such as its furnishings and treasured possessions, are often used as a basis for describing and discussing the activities of the occupant. Housing design reflects the socio-economic status of the owner and the values of the community at large and those of the owner (Howell 2003). One of the most important implications of the integration of cities into the world economy is the shifting terrain of land values that have important implications for property values. The relationship between global economic restructuring, shifting land values and social equity with respect to accessing suitable housing has not just been an important issue for cities of developed countries, but also developing countries. In Southeast Asia, the pace of internationally linked property development has radically altered the spatial development of metropolitan areas and caused huge transitions from urban to rural housing. Urbanizing trends are particularly apparent in the large cities of Bangkok, Jakarta and Manila, but similar processes are also apparent in secondary or tertiary cities. Sajor's (2003) account of urban property development in a secondary city (Metro Cebu) in the Philippines, maintains that property development was initially driven by a surge in foreign investment in manufacturing that generated high-end residential housing. This development led to the pricing out of low income households and the urban poor, reducing land allocated for mass housing while simultaneously providing significant profits for developers and speculators.

The increase in land values is a different issue to the globalization of residential architecture as a consequence of transnational migration; however the two are linked. In some developing countries emigrant remittances have enabled families to build the home of their dreams. In some instances the styles of property chosen have been contrary to indigenous cultural traditions of appropriate design, and reflect American ideals of good taste. In some contexts this has presented professional dilemmas for local architects over 'good' design. Housing design is an important product in its own right but it also has implications for the consumption of household durables. Ozaki and Lewis (2006) explore the boundaries and meanings of social space in Japanese households compared with housing in Western societies. An important distinction in Japanese households is the boundary between inside and outside space that is closely related to cultural notions of cleanliness. A consistent feature of Japanese households over the years has been a place to remove and store shoes before entering the main part of the house to ensure that it is kept clean. Another design feature is a separate toilet and bathroom which is a similar symbolic difference to inside–outside boundaries, with the toilet as dirty, and the bathroom as a place of cleanliness. For the same reasons properties that have the washing machine in the kitchen do not sell well, since dirty clothes contaminate clean kitchens where food is prepared. A great deal of emphasis is not placed on dining rooms since it is considered more intimate to eat in a lounge. A more Western influence is evident in relation to bedroom space and the use of substantially constructed walls, rather than paper screens. Japanese housing design has adopted some Western influences but maintained integrity to cultural traditions.

The design of Japanese houses also has implications for consumer goods. Small Japanese homes do not have a great deal of storage space, thus larger boxes of diapers that are perfectly acceptable in many Western homes, prove problematic in Japan. This factor was compounded by the fact that Japanese families change their children's diapers far more frequently than Americans. As a result Proctor and Gamble began producing thinner diapers sold in smaller boxes and the product Ultra Pampers took off. Refrigerator manufacturers from Western Europe also had problems selling their goods in the Japanese market. Further investigation revealed that the refrigerator motors were just too noisy for Japanese homes with their paper thin walls. Once refrigerators were adapted to local conditions the products sold well (Ricks 1993).

Similar moves to westernize housing design are evident within the cosmopolitan elite in Yemen. The country has a very strong Islamic tradition which curtailed many aspects of consumption considered Western, such as listening to music and viewing advertisements incorporating uncovered women. There is a move among the elites to move to new areas in the suburbs and out of the older cities. A new style of housing that is bungalow-style has emerged, and these houses have fewer multi-purpose rooms than traditional houses. The new accommodation reflects the trend towards living in nuclear families, whereas older houses were designed to accommodate several generations of the same family. These new houses have bedrooms incorporated into the design reflecting a Western influence towards intimacy and individualism. A longstanding tradition in Yemeni households was for couples to share a bedroom until the birth of children, at which time the husband would move into his own room while the children slept with their mother. Household members often slept on mattresses on the floor. In the new homes children are allocated their own bedrooms, leaving their parents to enjoy their own space. One indicator of the importance of bedrooms as domestic spaces is the importation of bedroom furniture (Vom Bruck 2005).

Transnational products

Transnational products are a group of products that have been designed with migrants in mind. Developments in information and communications technology, cheaper air travel, and modern capitalist production relations have given rise to people, goods, money, and ideas that connect disparate parts of the globe. One product of central importance to migrants is the remittance service, or money transmission service, since many migrants send home a sizeable proportion of their income (Ozden and Schiff 2006). A study by the World Bank indicates that migrant remittances sent back 'home' reached $268 billion in 2006, a little over twice the amount recorded in 2000. Workers from developing countries account for most of the total, with Mexicans, Indians, Chinese and Philippino workers sending by far the largest amounts of money home (*Economist* 2006e).

Remittance transfer systems are presented as a positive way of helping people manage their livelihoods and connecting them to a wider financial services system. Furthermore, the best way to secure transmission is to shift more of them to the regulated and commercialized money transfer sector. Pieke, Van Hear and Lindley (2007) question the view that commercialized services are the most appropriate method for many consumers, and that alternative methods are often cheaper, more reliable, accessible, and convenient. It has been estimated that informal remittances comprise 1.5 times the value of formal remittances. Transfers are made through a range of systems. In value transfer systems, money is transferred without it being physically being moved. The *hawala* system used in the Horn of Africa, the Middle East, Pakistan and Afghanistan, and the *hundi* system in South Asia involve the customer giving money to an agent in the host country who communicates instructions to pay the same amount to a nominated individual. The agent charges a fee for the service.

Another method is the hand carrying of cash by migrants on a return visit. In this method the costs are integrated in the travel costs, and the costs of exchanging the money into local currency. There are some limitations to this method, for example customs restrictions, customs corruption, or crime in home countries may mean that this is a risky option. Furthermore, some groups of migrants are unlikely to return home, refugees are in this category. Taxis are also used to move money across borders in southern Africa, for their service taxi drivers are known to charge about 20 per cent of the transfer value. Some cash intensive businesses, import/ export and shipping companies, grocery businesses, brokers, gold and jewellery shops, also offer remittance transfer systems. The agents involved make a profit on the exchange rate spread, and from fees charged to the customer. Other means are dedicated money transmitters, small-scale versions of big mainstream companies including Western Union and MoneyGram. These companies often specialize in customers from one country. Some organizations also offer in-kind services; for example, the company WatuWetu offers vouchers that can be redeemed in stores in Kenya, while Leppe delivers goods, pays bills and organizes religious ceremonies that link migrants in the USA and France with Senegal. These companies tend to advertise on websites, in telephone directories, and in local ethnic media. Finally, the growth of microfinance institutions in many developing countries has allowed these institutions to offer money transmission services.

A number of factors have been found relevant in consumer decisions to use the different methods available. Accessibility is an important consideration since not all migrants from a specific country have equal access to remittance services. In countries like Senegal, there is a low cap on foreign-exchange transactions, and in other countries there is lack of access to distribution points (banks, agencies and post offices) especially in rural and remote areas. Cost and speed are often an issue and Pieke *et al.* (2007) found that alternative methods are cheaper and faster than regulated methods. Trust is a final factor and it is nearly always mentioned as an advantage of informal systems and linked with ethnic solidarity and reciprocity. The poor performance of banks, especially those based in Africa, encourages the use of non-bank methods due to high levels of corruption and lack of security.

The method chosen largely depends on the legal and regulatory environment in the countries concerned. Inadequate or absent regulation is a factor, especially in African countries which are some of the poorest in the world with large informal economies. Governments often have little capacity or expertise to design or enforce regulations. Legality is another consideration since in some countries particular remittance systems are illegal. The h*awala*/*hundi* system is illegal in India, yet in Afghanistan it is used by the government and major NGOs. Furthermore, the regulatory environment in some developing countries is often in a state of flux, resulting in some systems that were legal being made subsequently illegal.

The consumption patterns of migrants shape local economies and their home communities. Walton-Roberts (2004) provides an interesting account of the impact of remittances in two villages in the Doaba region of the Punjab in India. The remittances play a valuable role in assisting India to develop within the global economy but maintain economic and political control. At the turn of the millennium India was the single largest remittance receiving country at around US$ 10 billion annually. While the precise amount of money being devoted to various good causes in the villages varies, it is not insignificant. Educational facilities tend to be highly funded, including the building of institutions of higher education. Community halls are another popular way of donating funds to the community, alongside the temples. At the local bank in one of the villages the bank manager estimated that 20–30 per cent of the money processed by his branch came from non-resident Indians and was being used to purchase land, build houses, and finance weddings.

Another aspect of transnational remittances is to fund funeral payments. Mazzucato, Kabki and Smith (2006) argue that the lack of attention is due to a Western bias in the literature that perceives funerals as more of a cultural rather than economic phenomenon. Funerals involve large sums of money and after business, housing and education they can often be one of the main sources of non-subsistent remittances. In their study of the participation of Ghanaian migrants living in the Netherlands who were financing, planning, and carrying out a funeral in Ghana many migrants criticized the lavishness of the funerals which they were required to fund but under the circumstances they felt it difficult to renege on their social responsibilities, since the lavishness of a funeral was a source of prestige in the village. In the Ashanti region it remains common practice to keep a record of peoples' donations to funerals. Some migrants become responsible for the dependents of the deceased and in so doing incur large debts. The debt of the funeral was therefore only one aspect for which migrants became accountable. Participation in funerals also has other spin-offs including acting as wedding markets, and retaining links with their homeland. Despite residing in different areas of the world many migrants want to be buried in their homeland, and some participants in the study were already having homes built in preparation for them to return home in the future.

Crossover products

The concept of crossover products is important in the context of cross-cultural marketing, since it concerns the ways that a product targeted for one segment of the market has the potential to appeal to other cultural groups. Crossover has traditionally been used to describe the process whereby products move from the margins to the mainstream. For example, how ethnic-oriented products originally targeted at a particular ethnic minority group are adopted by consumers in the mainstream rather than the reverse. Indian cultural artefacts are consumed on a global basis. Srinivas (2002: 90) notes that 'silk sari bedding is advertised at Bloomingdale's, Indian jewelry and dress, henna tattoos, Darjeeling tea, and toe rings are all bought every day by Europeans and Americans'. The marketing may be Euro-American to adapt to the market but the product's cultural origins are unquestionable. The more consumers adopt ethnic-oriented products, the higher sales are likely to be, however, marketers have to be vigilant to retain a degree of authenticity and not to sell out to watered down mass produced versions. The situation becomes more complicated when crossover products are viewed in their wider international context and in relation to multicultural societies. For example, indigenous Indian products could be adopted by the wider Indian diaspora and while these groups may share some aspects of the same ethnic culture they may be different in other respects which require the adaptation of product features. Another aspect of product crossover is ethnic minority to ethnic minority crossover. In some instances overseas companies may provide products for the dispora, but do not wish to actively target mainstream consumers. A preferred option is to target other ethnic groups that may have some synergy with the diasporic market.

To illustrate the crossover process in the USA, Grier, Brumbaugh and Thornton (2006) note that 60 per cent of hip-hop (traditional black music) is purchased by white consumers, salsa sales have exceeded those of ketchup, and over 1,000 grocery stores have sushi counters. Despite marketers' attempts to diffuse their products to a wider audience, some ethnic-niche products do not crossover. The most highly rated television programmes in the USA show a high degree of segregation between blacks and whites – blacks watch television programmes designed for black audiences and whites watch television programmes designed for whites and mainstream audiences. The question that marketers need to address is why some products cross over more easily than others.

Several factors are relevant. The first relates to the *product characteristics* and the extent to which they are congruent with the one ethnic group for which they have been designed. For example, hair care products and make-up designed for consumers of African origin would not easily transfer to other ethnic groups. Many ethnic products are not constrained in this way and thus *product cues* become important. The ethnicity of the spokesperson in an advertisement or ethnic characters and symbols on a product's packaging provide ethnic product cues. If marketing features such as packaging and promotion present a consistent ethnic image, they can be said to be strongly ethnically embedded and thus likely to be viewed favourably by the target group, but not necessarily by other ethnic groups. Advertisements that feature mixed ethnicity characters and incorporate aspects of mainstream culture, including language and background, could be construed as indicative of low ethnically embedded products. Another example is the difference between mass produced goods distributed by large US companies, and handmade products from family-run organizations, packaged with ethnic language labels. The mass-produced versions are less ethnically embedded than the more authentic versions.

Another aspect of the mix includes *consumer characteristics*, and specifically how consumers relate to ethnic goods and brands. Of particular importance is whether consumers have an interest in a particular culture, or different cultures in general. The context in which the product is consumed is also significant. Social beliefs and norms influence consumption and this is especially the case where ethnic products are consumed in public rather than in private. For example, an African-American aerobics class may appeal to a non-black fitness enthusiast but attitudes towards the class might be more favourable if they went with a friend from the African-American group. Finally, *product familiarity* may enhance product crossover. For example, eating out in an Asian restaurant could have the effect of mainstream consumers purchasing Asian readymade meals from the supermarket, or Asian ingredients so that consumers can experiment cooking Asian food at home.

In order to test some of these issues Grier *et al.* (2006) undertook an experimental study to assess the crossover of ethnic films in the USA. Participants were provided with descriptions of films that varied in ethnic congruence and levels of ethnic embeddedness, and responses were assessed according to the participants' diversity-seeking behaviour. The study found that black consumers preferred black movies over white ones. A diversity-seeking orientation improved attitudes towards white movies among black participants. Familiarity with dominant cultural themes in movies made participants more favourably disposed towards other ethnic mainstream movies. The results for the white participants found that higher levels of diversity seeking were associated with higher levels of positive attitudes towards black movies, and among respondents who were more likely to go and see the movie alone. Authenticity was important; a highly ethnically embedded plot and low promotional budget were indicative of authenticity.

An additional example of product crossover is illustrated in the context of the different strategies two food companies developed to target the transnational Jamaican community living abroad. Grace, Kennedy and Co, and Walkerswood are both food companies based in Jamaica, and both target the market in the United Kingdom. In the mid-1990s, Caribbean food was expected to be the next big crossover food of the mainstream market following in the footsteps of Indian, Chinese, and Tex Mex food. Caribbean food sales had doubled from £10.1 million in 1993 to 20.4 million in 1995. The UK food market was worth in excess of £600 million and its growth trajectory was set to continue. Cook and Harrison (2003) have provided a valuable case study of the two companies' strategies: one that maintained a niche market strategy, and another that managed to cross over into the mainstream.

Grace, Kennedy and Co. was founded in 1922 and imported products to Jamaica where the company processed and branded them. The company established itself as the largest grocery supplier in Jamaica. However, the small Jamaican market comprising a population of 2.5 million who were not particularly affluent, prompted the company to target the larger and wealthier community of 9.5 million Jamaican people living abroad. In the mid-1990s, it extended its international network through wholly owned subsidiaries and modernized its production facilities in the Caribbean. The company also modernized its brand logo 'Grace' and bilingual labelling that promoted the brand as being of 'Genuine Caribbean taste, enjoyed worldwide'. By the end of 1998, the company was launched in 15 countries outside Jamaica, and offered 180 commodities from canned kidney beans to specialist foods like jerk barbecue sauce. According to the company, the thrust of the campaign was to exploit the 'emotional bond between Caribbean persons overseas and their yearning for the tastes and smells of home food and the Grace brand' (Cook and Harrison 2003: 300). The company's strategy emphasized the view that Grace was a modern Caribbean company manufacturing 'authentic Caribbean foods'.

The company directed its efforts towards the ethnic market abroad especially in connection with exporting to America and the UK. Despite its heavy reliance on these markets the company did not envisage crossing over into the mainstream market. The General Manager of the Export Division maintained that the mainstream was a fringe market for the company. Interestingly, they did not rely on the Caribbean commodity fetish such as blue skies, beaches and sunshine. The reasons for not over-emphasizing images of the Caribbean in their promotional strategies were twofold. First, they did not view the Jamaican or indeed the Caribbean market, as a discrete cultural and economic market in its own right. The reason for this was the ambiguous position of second and subsequent generations of migrants that provided a different context from first generation migrants that had first-hand experience of Grace products in Jamaica and wanted to continue to purchase them in their 'new home'. By the time Grace had re-branded itself there had not been significant waves of in-migration to the UK for many decades. Many of the first generation of migrants had either died or had returned to the Caribbean to retire. Their children were very different consumers in terms of their ethnic identity and lifestyles and the company needed to recognize that fact if it wished to increase sales. Many of these potential consumers could scarcely remember their relatives making meals with Grace products and did not have time to make meals from scratch using basic ingredients given their busy lifestyles.

A second reason for not promoting images of the Caribbean was that the company hoped to attract consumers from other Third World countries since culinary traditions of many Latin American, African, and Asian countries are similar. For example, coconut milk is used by all these groups and in that sense the promotion of the product was better served by being culturally neutral. These two distinct markets used mainstream supermarkets for general provisions but the company's market research indicated that specialist ethnic retailers were used to purchase ethnic goods. The company saw little real merit in attempting to move into mainstream supermarkets and all the extra costs associated with increased production capacity and quality controls to meet the strict conditions of British supermarkets.

A rather different strategy was adopted by Walkerswood, a brand name for five companies comprising a co-operative based in the Walkerswood area of Jamaica.

The company was of relatively recent origin having been established in 1978. The company was made possible by the donation of land by a white former plantation owner, and is famous in Jamaica for being an example of a successful company run by black Jamaicans, for the benefit of Jamaican people, in a rural area that would otherwise have been overcome by poverty. The company was originally called Cottage Industries that manufactured jerk, a traditional mixture that was used to flavour pork and other meats. The product was sold in one supermarket in the Ocho Rios area of Jamaica. This area was populated by foreign tourists staying in nearby hotels and day trippers visiting the island from cruise ships that stopped over on their way around the Caribbean. Tourists purchased the bottled jerk and took it home and as a consequence the company built up a demand for its products in a range of countries on the back of tourist purchases.

The strategy that the company adopted was to export a narrow range (15 products in 2000) of Jamaican sauces, seasonings, and ingredients. All the products were overwhelmingly sourced in Jamaica, the exceptions being nutmeg, black pepper and packaging – bottles, labels, caps and cartons. The company had a small workforce of around 60 people and used ingredients grown by around 100 local farmers. Products were exported to the USA, Canada, the Netherlands, Germany, Belgium, France, South Africa and Japan. Mainstream supermarkets in the UK had listed the company's products for several years. Walkerswood products are an example of an ethnic food that had managed to become a crossover food. Unlike Grace, Kennedy and Co., Walkerswood fully exploited images of Jamaica – 'colourful, native paintings featuring scenes from Jamaican life' (Cook and Harrison 2003: 305) – on its packaging and labelling. The emphasis was on focusing on authenticity, local ingredients, local people that appealed to the mainstream market.

Diasporic products

Diasporic products are those that have been specifically developed for the diasporic community (see Chapter 1). To some extent, the examples of Jamaican food marketing in the United Kingdom described above can be understood as diasporic products, since the original concept was to appeal to the Jamaican diaspora. A further example in connection to food marketing, is provided by Elisha Renne (2007) in her account of mass producing food traditions for West Africans living abroad. During the 1980s and 1990s, manufactured West African food, with African brand names began to be distributed through African grocery stores and advertised in US-produced African newspapers. This development 'has allowed West African men and women living abroad to maintain their memories of food and African childhood as well as global connections with their families, hometowns, religious and ethnic groups, and national associations' (624).

Appadurai (1996: 35) has suggested that *mediascapes* (especially television and film) are an important source of 'images, narratives, and *ethnoscapes* to viewers throughout the world, in which the world of commodities and the world of news and politics are profoundly mixed'. Within the context of mediascapes, the marketing of films has started to become significant. Craig, Greene and Douglas (2005) have examined foreign box office receipts in eight countries for the top 50 US films, over a period of six years. They examined the effects of two main variables: film character and country character (cultural distance from the USA, the degree of Americanization, and language). They found that films released in countries culturally closer to the USA were likely to perform better at the box office. The performance of the films within the market was linked to cultural distance, specifically, the extent to which the country embraced elements of American culture. Interestingly, they measured the extent of Americanization by calculating the number of McDonald's outlets per head of the population. The more MacDonalds, the better the films were received and this was especially the case in countries where English was widely spoken.

Indian films screened overseas are examples of diasporic products since research has demonstrated that South Asian cinema, television and Bollywood, help to shape and reshape cultural practices and social attitudes in India and the wider South Asian diaporic communities around the globe. Viewers in India and the Indian diaspora have a shared knowledge of images and narratives that are now in global circulation, and they also have the ability to interpret central messages in films that might be hidden to other audiences. Filmmakers position their films to appeal to different types of Indian and diasporic audiences through their use of characters and places in which the diaspora are located. This geographical spread allows for a wider range of issues to be dealt with in a variety of ways within different films. For example, Rajan (2006) assesses how masculinities are differently constructed in three South Asian films to demonstrate the interaction of class, sexuality, gender and nation. The Middle East and Africa have traditionally been the location of the Indian diaspora and therefore the main destinations for Indian films. In the 1990s, some Indian directors in Bollywood took the decision to specifically make films for the diaspora since it was perceived as a more secure market than India. The targeting of the new markets required filmmakers to invent methods of relocalization at the shooting and post-production stages, especially in connection with dubbing in foreign languages (Grimaud 2005).

The downloading of Bollywood movies from the Internet is thriving. Rajshri Productions, one of India's oldest movie distribution houses, has created India's largest Bollywood portal (rajshri.com) comprising 6,000 hours of movies and Hindi songs. Older movies cost $4.99 to download or are free in streaming video, with new releases available in download format only for $9.99. When the site was launched in 2006, it was immediately successful logging 10,000 downloads and five million video streams from the site in the space of eight months. Consumers were attracted from as far a field as Togo and Estonia. The success has prompted other online competitors to establish a similar online presence including BigFlicks.com and Yashrafilms.com. It has been estimated that India's box-office revenue will rise from $5.9 billion in 2005, to $7.4million by 2010. Over the same period downloaded content is estimated to increase from $17 million to $1.4 billion. The activity is not without its problems. High-speed bandwidth required to download the movies is not widely available, illegal downloading is a problem, and consumers can only download using a US dollar credit card (Tippu 2007a).

Deterritorialization refers to ways in which cultural forms and identities migrate from their original environment and reconstitute themselves in new contexts as diasporic forms. This process has an impact on both the original and migrant cultures transforming products and in so doing creates 'new' local identifications. Schelling (1998) provides the example of how some Latin American musicians whose music was originally located in specific regions, have become 'world music' superstars since they represent 'Latiny-within-Globalization. South Americans 'at home' and within the diaspora are offered an image that they appropriate in a multitude of ways dependent on their particular context creating a multitude of 'Latinites'. This new 'Latiny' may bear only a passing, if any, resemblance to the lives and customs of those that originally produced the music (Franco 1996).

Product authenticity

Brand and product pirating and the loss of intellectual property rights, were estimated to have cost American industries $200 billion at the turn of the millennium. Furthermore, losses from product pirating have quadrupled over each decade over the last twenty years. An estimated 5 per cent of all products sold worldwide are counterfeit. Some commentators have even argued that piracy can be as lucrative as pushing heroin. The returns are so high that international counterfeiting is almost irresistible to some people. Very often piracy begins at the point of production. For example, Mexico's piracy rate is thought to exceed 50 per cent for videos, audio and business and entertainment software. Indian pharmaceutical companies are one of the world's largest suppliers of drugs that have been based on pirating the products of other companies. Approximately 10 per cent of Brazil's pharmaceutical production is either falsified or stolen. Western medicine is entering the private market in many developing countries and is often dispensed without prescription or information. Increasing amounts of these drugs are fakes resulting in many unnecessary deaths in developing countries (Larkin 1998). The company Electronic Arts is one of the world's largest entertainment software companies and it has estimated that 95 per cent of the sales in Thailand using its name are pirated. Fortune 500 companies spend around $2–$4 million per year to combat counterfeiting, and for some companies the figure is much higher at $10 million. Counterfeit goods seized by US Customs are overwhelmingly from China (38%), three times as many as Taiwan which is the next biggest country, and ten times as many from the whole of Western Europe.

An important aspect of cross-cultural marketing is the concept of product authenticity denoting that products for sale are the real thing. In a world of mass-produced goods international property rights (IPR), laws such as copyright, patents and trademarks are used to denote a clear distinction between the authentic and the fake. Historically, intellectual property rights have been based on legal decisions in Europe and the USA that linked authorship to ownership, privileged originals over copies, and interpreted ideas as property (Rose 1993). IPR laws are used to determine which products are authorized, legitimate and authentic by contrast to the unauthorized, illegitimate and the inauthentic. Despite these laws being enforced internationally, consumers in different countries may perceive the relationship between ideas, goods, authors, creators and property rights and ownership very differently. For example, in China there has been no sustained tradition of recognizing intellectual property, and the failure of European and US governments to recognize this fact has caused years of economic and political conflict (Alford 1985).

China is widely believed to be the international capital of counterfeiting. Estimates suggest that at least $16 billion worth of goods that are sold in the country each year are counterfeit. Proctor and Gamble maintains that 10–15 per cent of its revenues in China each year are lost to counterfeit goods. An astonishing 90 per cent of musical recordings sold in China are believed to be pirated. China is also becoming a leading exporter of counterfeit goods. This trade relies on sophisticated distribution networks that are increasingly run by organized crime syndicates that use many of the routes established for narcotics. However, it would be wrong to believe that counterfeiting is limited to poor countries. For example, a recent survey in the US, found that Milan is the leading producer of counterfeit luxury goods. Reconnaissance International, an anti-counterfeiting research group, suggests a range of reasons for the boom in counterfeiting that is being witnessed. First, technological advances have allowed companies to move their operations to countries with low labour costs. However, many businesses paid insufficient attention to intellectual property rights in these locations and are now paying the price. Second, the relocations abroad coincided with a huge growth in the importance of brands, especially designer brands. Much of the product's value is now closely integrated with its intellectual property and its brand, rather than its material constituents. It has become easy for counterfeiters to exploit consumers' expectations of quality without having to realize them (*Economist* 2003b).

What is of particular interest in relation to our focus on cross-cultural marketing is how consumers in different countries perceive counterfeit goods. Vann's (2006) analysis concerning perceptions of authenticity in Vietnamese consumer markets revealed significant differences in consumers' understandings compared with what might be viewed as the norm in advanced Western societies. Vietnam is an interesting case study since many Vietnamese believe they are witnessing an epidemic of false goods and consumer deception. Some estimates suggest that 90 per cent of goods that are promoted as authentic are in fact fakes. It is significant that the reestablishment of diplomatic and trade relations with the US after years of war, embargos and mutual distrust, relied on Vietnam's willingness to recognize and protect US property rights. Vann maintains that customer's perceptions of brand authenticity do not neatly align with IPR laws but take the form of a four-fold categorization. Consumers make the distinction between *mimic* goods that IPR laws would recognize as counterfeits, and *model* goods which are the famous brands that mimic goods imitate. Shoppers also make the distinction between *real* goods and *fake* goods, in effect whether the product as opposed to the brand is legitimate. For example, whether the product inside the box delivers what is illustrated on the label.

Vann maintains that Euro-American definitions of authentic collapses two sets of distinctions between authentic and inauthentic, and real and fake, whereas in

Vietnam these two sets of terms are clearly distinguished by shoppers. The market for consumer products in Vietnam is one where counterfeits or 'mimic' goods predominate and authentic or 'model' goods are in the minority. The existence of large numbers of mimic goods is perceived as a consequence of capitalism where manufacturers will attempt to emulate prestigious goods that are unaffordable for the vast majority of the population. This is particularly the case for the emergent middle classes in developing countries that aspire to follow trends generated by middle-class consumers in advanced societies. Furthermore, mimic goods are not perceived to damage the reputation of authentic goods since the fact that they are being copied enhances their status as desirable commodities. The dangers that Vietnamese shoppers associate with mimic goods are through their *sale* not their *manufacture*. The practice of shopkeepers misrepresenting goods that they are selling for high prices as the authentic brands is something that consumers need to safeguard against.

A rather different issue concerning product authenticity are products that occupy the boundary between the formal and informal economy. Willis (2003) provides an interesting example of this phenomenon in the context of a new generation alcoholic beverages that began to appear in Kenyan bars in the 1990s. The distinction between illicit and legal alcoholic beverages has been a feature of the Kenyan marketplace for many years. Expensive branded beers that were out of the reach for many individuals on the one hand, and home made brews associated with a series of health scares and poisoning on the other. Illegal beers were drunk out of old tin cans or recycled bottles without their labels. They were not sold or consumed in bars or hotels, nor were they on display in shops or other formal places of sale.

During the 1990s, a new generation of drinks emerged; labelled 'traditional', they were produced by small firms and thus avoided expensive taxes. The new generation drinks adopted many of the practices associated with legal drinks. The advertising focused on the fact that it was a respectable drink for development minded people. People could afford to buy a drink and not squander household budgets in the process. Moreover, the beers were promoted as safe and were sold in labelled bottles that included a list of ingredients and sell by dates. By 1997, there were around 40 'breweries' producing these 'new generation' drinks and they became an integrated part of public consumption in a way that informal sector liquors never had. Although there were public bans of new generation drinks, largely orchestrated by legitimate brewers in order to protect their market share, the results were patchy since the new generation of beers had gained legitimacy in the eyes of the consuming public.

The country of origin, in addition to having a brand name, is relevant in lesser developed countries with respect to product authenticity, especially in connection with food. Careless handling of food and drink are commonplace in developing countries. Even reputable companies such as Coke have had incidences where problems with hygiene have made people ill. Branded goods from the USA and Western Europe give a guarantee to consumers that the goods will not damage their health. The language of labelling can affect people's perceptions of the product. For example, in Africa some companies have created labels in the consumers' local language rather than English or French in order to adapt to the local culture; however sales declined because the perception of the product was deemed inferior to those with a Western label (Lipson and Lamont 1969).

In the Cameroon, American beauty products occupy a special place and they cannot be replaced by those from Europe and Asia. American cosmetics companies have lines of products that been specifically designed for African-American women that transfer easily to the Cameroon. A degree of trust in the quality of authentic American brands is unlike some African counterfeits from Nigeria, that have flooded the market and have undesirable side-effects due to their inferior quality. The way that entrepreneurs gain access to imported products is varied and includes informal social networks. In some instances informal imports are generated by extended families. These products form the basis of businesses in the informal sector of the economy that provide services for women that are unable to access similar products in the mainstream sector because they are too expensive. Some beauticians even provide credit facilities due to the economic situation of their clients (Monga 2000).

Closely related to product authenticity is product liability and, with it, legal constructions of the consumer in different cultural contexts (Everson 2006). A recent article in *Fortune* entitled 'China's newest export: Lawsuits' reflects a significant number of product scares and recalls (Parloff 2007). The incidents involve potentially deadly, defective or contaminated products imported from China and have included pet food, toys, tires, toothpaste, cough syrup and shrimp. An important issue is where the liability lies in instances where the product is made in China but sold in another country. In the US law suits against retailers selling the products have proliferated since US importers are deemed responsible for ensuring that foreign made merchandise conforms to US standards. Some companies involved in product recall are verging on bankruptcy. For example, Foreign Tire Sales (FTS) is a small family owned business employing 16 people, that was sued in Philadelphia after its tires were believed to be responsible for an accident in which two people were killed and another suffered brain damage. The company have initiated a recall of 450,000 of Chinese-made tires at a projected cost of $90 million. FTS has sued the manufacturer, Hangzhou Zhongee Rubber Co. Ltd, in the US courts as has the family but the manufacturer did not respond to either action. Furthermore, Hangzhou Zhogee have denied liability for the defects. Even if the US plaintiffs win default judgements it is unclear whether they will be able to enforce them anywhere.

Another case has involved Menu Foods, a pet food manufacturer based in Ontario, Canada whose melamine-laced gluten poisoned dozens of brands of American pet foods and resulted in over 100 law suits. In this case big name brands that it supplies – Proctor and Gamble, Wal-Mart and Safeway – are also appearing as defendants and could be called upon to provide funds for compensation when Menu Foods' insurance runs out. None of the organizations in the spate of problems with Chinese products have contemplated suing Chinese companies in Chinese courts. In the past, tiny damages and hostile judges often made litigation a pointless exercise. These incidences and others like them, raise issues about stronger regulation and legal accountability on the part of Chinese companies.

Consumer ethnocentrism

Ethnocentrism is a sociological concept that was developed over a century ago. The concept was used to distinguish between in-groups, referring to groups of people with whom an individual identifies, and outgroups, defined as groups that are oppositional to the in-group. Ethnocentrism refers to the view that people see their own group as the centre of the universe and interpret the world from their perspective, while simultaneously rejecting people who are culturally dissimilar, and blindly accepting those that are culturally similar. The symbols and values of one's own ethnic or national group become a source of pride and attachment, whereas the symbols of other groups are objects of contempt. William Graham Sumner in his book entitled *Folkways* first published in 1906 defines ethnocentrism as the following:

> Ethnocentrism is the technical name for this view of things in which one's own group is the center of everything, and all others are scaled and rated with reference to it. Each group nourishes its own pride and vanity, boasts itself superior, exalts its own divinities, and looks with contempt on outsiders.
>
> (Sumner 1906: 13)

Shimp and Sharma (1987) have extended the concept of ethnocentrism to 'consumer ethnocentrism' to draw attention to beliefs consumers have about the appropriateness or morality of purchasing foreign made products. Ethnocentric consumers regard purchasing imported products as wrong, since this could damage the economy, cause unemployment, and is perceived as unpatriotic. Non-ethnocentric consumers evaluate foreign products on their own merit without giving a great deal of attention to where they were manufactured. In a practical sense, consumer ethnocentrism provides consumers with a sense of identity, a feeling of belongingness and an understanding of what purchasing behaviour is acceptable or unacceptable within their ingroup. In order to measure the existence and extent of consumer ethnocentrism they developed the CETSCALE. The scale was a measure of *tendency* rather than *attitude*. Tendency captures a more general notion of a disposition to act, as opposed to an attitude which is more closely tied to consumer feeling towards a specific object such as particular models of products.

Their original study focused on consumer ethnocentrism in America and comprised a seventeen item scale on which consumer s had to rank responses on a seven point Likert-type scale, where 7 = strongly agree and 1 = strongly disagree.

The results of their study concerning motor vehicle purchase among U.S. customers indicate that general attitudes towards foreign-made products are strongly negatively correlated with ethnocentric tendencies. Furthermore, the stronger one's consumer ethnocentrism, the more likely they were to purchase an American car, or intend to purchase a domestically made car. They also found that individuals within lower socio-economic groups were more likely to be threatened by foreign competition and were more ethnocentric in their consumption patterns. This pattern of behaviour was intensified when ages of respondents were added to the equation. Older consumers in lower socio-economic groups were the most ethnocentric of all. The study also revealed that consumers in some geographic regions were more ethnocentric than others. They found that areas that were most threatened by the decline in the American manufacturers' share of the domestic car market were the areas where consumers were most ethnocentric. They argue that the concept of consumer ethnocentrism can improve marketers' understanding of how consumers and corporate buyers assess domestic and foreign made products and how their product judgments may be subject to bias and error. How consumers are socialized into these particular views during their lifetime is an important area of research. From a practitioner's viewpoint, ethnocentrism could be made into an important promotional tool via 'made in America', 'buy American' messages, at least for some consumer segments. The geographical aspects could also be fruitfully used in localized marketing campaigns.

There have been other studies that have used the CETSCALE in other cultural contexts. For example, Sharma, Shimp and Shin (1995) have examined the antecedents and moderators of consumer ethnocentrism in Korea. They wanted to assess whether product necessity had an effect on consumer ethnocentrism. They used ten products that differed in perceived necessity for everyday living, those that were deemed necessary included medicine, beef, personal computers and kitchenware. Products considered relatively unnecessary were golf clubs, liquor, bananas, insurance, large refrigerators and jewellery. They concluded that CETSCALE was shown to be positively related to the collectivist culture in Korea and patriotic/ conservative attitudes, and negatively correlated with cultural openness, education and income. Korean consumers were more ethnocentric than Americans and the more a product was viewed as unnecessary, the higher the overall level of consumer ethnocentrism.

The focus of a study by Balabanis and Diamantopoulos (2004) was to explore whether domestic country bias of ethnocentric individuals is uniformly dispersed across different product categories and different countries. They asked participants in the UK to rank eight products (cars, food, televisions, toiletries, fashion wear, toys, do-it-yourself tools and equipment and furniture) from six developed countries (Britain, USA, France, Germany, Japan, and Italy). All of the goods had the same properties and all had the same price. Their results revealed that only 13.3 per cent of respondents had Britain as a first choice for all eight products and 7.7 per cent did not have Britain as a first choice category for any of the products. The second most common first choices after Britain were Japan and Germany. The view that consumers prefer domestic products over imports was not sustained. An analysis of product category and country of origin revealed that Britain was overwhelmingly the first choice for food products, toys, do-it-yourself tools, but not so for televisions, cars, and fashion wear.

These findings suggest that domestic manufacturers cannot count on domestic consumers to purchase their products over imports. Furthermore, Balabanis and Diamantopoulos note 'wholesale generalizations that a company's products will *necessarily* suffer in a foreign market based on evidence of similar incidents in *other* product categories have to be discounted' (2004: 91). Across all the product categories consumer ethnocentrism was found to account for only a small amount of the variance in consumer preferences. It was also the case that economic competitiveness and cultural distance did not affect the links between consumer ethnocentrism and preferences for foreign products. They suggest that a wider range of concepts need to be explored that may account for consumer preferences including economic nationalism, stereotyping, and categorical thinking.

Research on consumer ethnocentrism suggests that the demand for domestically produced products is often weaker in underdeveloped or developing economies. For example, Jaffe and Martinez (1995) demonstrate that Mexicans have a poor perception of domestic goods, and rate Japanese and American electronic household products above Mexican products. In China, manufacturers endeavour to pass off local products as Western ones because they are thought of more highly. So endemic is the process, that it has a name 'maoyang' (Gilley 1996). This practice has also been reported in other countries like Nigeria (Okechuku and Onyemah 1999). Consumers in former socialist countries prefer Western to domestic products. Ettenson (1993) found that price was also relatively less important than country of origin in Russian, Polish and Hungarian consumer purchase intentions for television sets. Okechuku and Onyemah (1999) highlight a similar pattern in Nigeria where consumers place a higher profile on country of manufacture than price; superior reliability and technological advancement of foreign products are other important factors in consumer product choices.

Consumer animosity

While consumer ethnocentrism has attracted considerable attention from marketers, animosity has been somewhat neglected. Animosity within the marketing literature has been defined as 'the remnants of antipathy related to previous or ongoing military, political, or economic events' (Klein *et al*. 1998: 90). This definition has been extended by Ang *et al*. (2004) who propose four types of animosity: *stable* versus *situational* and *personal* versus *national*. *Stable* animosity refers to historical realities that are passed on from one generation to the next. *Situational* animosity refers to contemporary difficulties which are a cause for concern among consumers. *Personal* animosity relates negative personal experiences that have happened to individuals. Finally *national* animosity is directed towards countries. Some recent examples of the marketing consequences of consumer animosity were reflected in attitudes to the American war on Iraq. In Argentina, demonstrations occurred outside McDonald's with placards stating 'Here they sell happy meals to finance the war'. In retaliation some US consumers were so angry that a few restaurants in New York removed all French wines and champagne from the menu as a protest against France's opposition to US-led coalition against Iraq (Amine *et al*. 2005). Negative associations with a country's products in this way can cause problems for marketers since they have little option but to reveal the country of manufacture and brand name. Negative associations associated with a product's origin can affect consumers' decisions, independent of product judgement, and consumers can find actions difficult to forgive. Minority Groups International (2007) has indicated that there are minority–majority conflicts occurring all over the world: Europe, Africa, the Americas, Asia and the Pacific and the Middle East (MGI 2007). Furthermore, over the last decade there have been more than one hundred armed conflicts around the globe which suggests animosity could have a considerable impact on consumer behaviour (Shultz *et al.* 2005).

There is an important difference between consumer ethnocentrism and animosity. Consumers who score low on the CETSCALE and therefore believe it is perfectly acceptable to purchase goods from other countries, may nevertheless not purchase goods from countries where there is a history of animosity. For example, Jewish consumers in the USA refraining from purchasing German-made products (Hirschman 1981). Another example is the boycott of French products by Australians and New Zealanders because of nuclear tests being carried out by the French in the South Pacific. From a marketer's viewpoint, knowing consumers score high/low on the CETSCALE model is of little value, and possibly even misleading since consumers can demonstrate considerable animosity towards a product but without denigrating the quality. An understanding of this process has led some marketers to use the term 'nation equity' to refer to the fact that countries like brands have equity associated with them, and that equity extends beyond product perceptions and includes an emotional component (Maheswaran and Chen 2006).

Klein *et al.* (1998) tested the level of animosity towards Japan and Japanese-made products among consumers in China. They specifically controlled for *war-based animosity* and *economic-based animosity*. In the late 1990s, Japan was China's number one trading partner and largest source of direct investment. However, several foreign investors, including Japan, were accused of 'buying and burying' Chinese brands in order to champion their own products. As a consequence, Japanese products and brands proliferated at the expense of China's domestic brands and industries. These factors could be the basis of economic animosity. War-based animosity has a long history between the two countries. Over the years Japan has been an enemy of China many times, most recently in the Second World War. Japan invaded China in 1931 and although the country was never fully conquered, China suffered a brutal Japanese occupation. The results of Klein's consumer survey demonstrated that animosity towards Japan and consumer ethnocentrism were distinctly different constructs. Chinese consumers' animosity toward Japan was reflected in their negative views about Japanese products and their subsequent unwillingness to purchase them. These attitudes persisted independent of Chinese consumers' views about the quality of Japanese products. Those consumers that scored high on animosity stipulated country reasons for not buying, rather than poor product perceptions. Historical, war-related factors were associated more closely with animosity, rather than contemporary economic concerns.

A further study assessed the consumer animosity of predominantly female, US consumers in the context of purchasing a motor vehicle from Japan and South Korea. Both Japan and South Korea are highly advanced Asian manufacturers of technological goods. There is no history of animosity between South Korea and the USA, whereas there is between the USA and Japan, especially in connection with the Second World War and the Nanjing Massacre in which many US lives were lost. In the economic sphere there has been a considerable backlash in the

USA against the import of Japanese cars, the negative effect on the indigenous auto industry, and what is perceived to be unfair Japanese competition. The results of Kelin's (2002) study indicate that consumer ethnocentrism was negatively related to preferences for Japanese over US products, and animosity was negatively related to preferences for Japanese over South Korean products. Animosity was indicated by war and economic animosity as in the previous example. Older consumers were more likely to have higher levels of war animosity than younger ones, and men held more economic animosity than women. This final point raises the issue about the extent to which animosity could be related to other segmentation variables, and used within the marketing mix to target specific goods (Klein 2002).

In another study Dale Russell (2007) demonstrates that consumer animosity can be manipulated. He explicitly designed a scenario to openly activate animosity in the belief that the threat of cultural incursions would make consumers more defensive and therefore resistant to foreign products. Consumer movie choices were assessed specifically in the context of the threat of world domination by Hollywood and cultural homogenization by the USA through movies and television. The research participants were French, and animosity was manipulated by asking them to read a press article about trade relations between the USA and France, before participating in a movie survey sponsored by the American or French Film Institute. The participants were then required to choose an American or French movie to watch. As might have been predicted, the preference for domestic movies increased when consumers' animosity was fostered and they were reminded of the US presence in their movie industry. In a further experiment, participants were told that the US dominance of the movie industry was invasive and detrimental to the local culture. This stimulus also had the effect of creating animosity to US movies in favour of supporting the local movie industry. Russell (2007: 149) notes that these experiments demonstrate that animosity can be manipulated. Making visible a culturally threatening nation can generate consumer resistance and foster allegiance to one's own country and products.

The animosity model was first developed to explain inter-country animosity, but Shoham *et al.* (2006) have used it to study intra-country animosity between two ethnic groups which adds a further dimension to the debate. Specifically, they explore the impact of the second Intifada on the buyer behaviour of Jewish Israelis and Arab Israelis. Thousands of Israelis and Palestinians have been killed since the second Intifada started in 2000, under normal (pre-Intifada) circumstances each group purchased products from the other group. Anecdotal evidence suggests that behavioural changes among these two groups of consumers emerged during the hostilities. Shoham *et al.* assess the impact of animosity on product quality judgements and examine the effects of dogmatism (the extent to which a person asserts his/her opinion in an unyielding manner), nationalism (one's country is superior and should be dominant) and internationalism (acceptance of other nations and cultures) as antecedents of animosity.

Their study examines the change in purchasing behaviour of Jewish Israelis in six product categories produced or marketed by Israeli Arabs. They also include six product categories for which Arab Israeli and Jewish Israeli goods or services were widely available (bread and pastry, olives and olive oil, car service and repairs, restaurants, tourism, and fruits and vegetables). They found that Jewish Israelis' dogmatism was related positively to their animosity toward Arab Israelis, nationalism predicted animosity towards Arab Israelis, whereas internationalism is inversely related to animosity. Animosity did negatively affect Jewish Israeli's quality judgments of Arab Israeli products and services and their willingness to purchase them. There was a possibility that changes in purchase behaviour were a result of Jewish Israelis not wishing to venture into Arab Israeli areas to do their shopping, rather than specifically avoiding purchasing their products. However, Shoham *et al.* discount this possibility during the course of their analysis. They maintain that animosity can be regarded as a form of hatred and is potentially subject to swings in intensity, dependent on outside events.

The role of animosity in purchase behaviour could also be pertinent in other societies that harbour hostile relationships between ethnic groups. For example, the Serbs and Croats harbour ill-feelings and animosity due to the Balkan wars after the break up of the former Yugoslavia. Other similar contexts include Muslims and Christians in Lebanon and the Hindu–Sikh conflict in India. Animosity between different groups living in the same country is evident on a worldwide basis. Market research can be used to determine which segments score high on animosity, and marketing activities can be designed accordingly. For example, one strategy may be to emphasize or deemphasize the origin of a product. Managers could also separate the image of the product from its cultural underpinnings and emphasize attributes that are unrelated to the people who produce the product.

Consumer racism

In the previous section it was suggested that consumer ethnocentrism, patriotism and animosity can have an effect on consumer decisions to purchase goods and services from countries other than their own. This literature is valuable in aiding our understanding of how consumers in one country view the products of another country. However, this emphasis neglects to address variations within the country given that many countries are now multicultural in their composition. The focus of this section is to consider the concept of consumer racism and its effects on domestic cross-ethnic product purchase, in order to understand how consumers living in the same country view patronising stores and purchasing goods from ethnic 'others'.

The concept of applying consumer racism to purchase patterns is a relatively new concept in marketing although we know from scholars working in other areas of the social sciences that racism is a part of everyday life for some sections of the population. Racism has been defined by W. J. Wilson (1973: 32) as 'an ideology of racial domination or exploitation that (1) incorporates beliefs in a particular race's cultural and/or inherent biological inferiority, and (2) uses such beliefs to justify and prescribe inferior or unequal treatment for that group'. According to this interpretation, racism has shifted from being associated with biological inferiority to incorporate a much broader range of real or imaginary features including languages, cultures, customs and lifestyles. Arguably, overt racism has declined in recent years in many Western societies although it is alive and well in some developing countries (see Chapter 2). The decline of overt racism in Western societies has not meant that racism has disappeared but that it has reappeared in a more subtle form.

Ouellet (2007) suggests that the racism that has been detected in service contexts also exists in the context of product choice. He defines *consumer racism* as 'the antipathy toward a given ethnic group's products or services as a symbolic way of discriminating against that group' and notes that this 'affects consumer behaviour in the domestic marketplace' (Ouellet 2007: 115). He makes the distinction between *ethnocentrism, animosity* and *consumer racism* as three distinct levels of analysis. The distinction between *ethnocentrism* and *ethnic ethnocentrism* is one dimension. Ethnocentrism refers to the beliefs consumers have about purchasing foreign made products in place of locally made goods. Ethnic ethnocentrism refers to the negative evaluations of products and services at the sub-national, cross-ethnic level which is an alternative explanation of consumer racism.

A second dimension involves a shift from *national animosity* to *ethnic-based animosity*. National animosity refers to the possibility of consumers displaying a hostile attitude to specific countries and this attitude being reflected in their purchasing decisions, as opposed to consumer ethnocentrism which refers to consumer's judgement or evaluation of those products. The basis of hostile attitudes could be historical, for example associated with colonialism, or contemporary economic and political relations associated with war or religious differences. This emphasis may also be applicable at sub-national level. For example, in the USA Latinos may show animosity to Anglo Americans because of their perceived exclusion to well-paying jobs. Algerian immigrants to France may feel ill will towards the indigenous French population due to the poor treatment of civilians during the French–Algerian war. In the United Kingdom there is often resentment between the English, Scottish and Welsh based on historical experiences and contemporary allocations of economic resources between these different countries. This example highlights the importance of white ethnicity that is often a neglected aspect of ethnic research. Ethnic-based animosity can affect consumers' purchase decisions in the domestic marketplace. The dynamics are important in ethnic-based animosity since it reflects the animosity of the currently dominated group to the dominator, or previously dominator group.

Ouellet (2007) argues that consumer racism and ethnic-based animosity are different constructs. While ethnic-based animosity refers to the dominated ethnic group's attitude towards the dominator (or previous dominator), consumer racism works the other way around. Consumer racism is located in the dominant group's inability to impose the dominant culture on minorities, which resist assimilation. The lack of conformity to the dominant culture results in negative beliefs about products that emanate from those ethnic groups which can result in refusal to purchase goods. For example, in the UK and USA this may result in a dominant white view that goods purchased from stores owned by individuals of Pakistani and Bangladeshi origin are less desirable because of perceived differences in standards of cleanliness.

In order to test the distinctions between ethnic-based ethnocentrism, ethnic-based animosity, and consumer racism more directly, Ouellet conducted a study of attitudes among consumers in Grenoble, France, Montreal, Canada, and Boston in the USA. A range of products and services were included since racist consumers might be more inclined to purchase products from ethnic minorities, if the products have little importance to them, thus are low involvement products. By contrast, majority consumers might be less inclined to purchase services in which they are in close physical proximity to the service provider, and thus are examples of high involvement products/services. The mix of products and services reflected the spectrum of high and low involvement products and included wireless speakers, ethnic packaged goods, ethnic goods, convenience stores, ethnic restaurants, and auto repair shops.

The results indicate that consumer racism is not related to socio-demographic status or national ethnocentrism. However, ethnic ethnocentrism is significant with respect to product judgment in the USA, in connection with product ethnicity of origin. Consumer racism is related to the product's ethnic origin, thus influencing a consumer's willingness to purchase products that originate from dominant ethnic minorities in each country. Furthermore, consumer racism also influences judgements about products that originate from dominant ethnic minorities in every country. Yet interestingly, the results indicate that consumer racism has no significant effects on judgements or willingness to purchase products that originate with the second largest ethnic group. Only consumers scoring highly on the consumer racism model differentiate between purchasing high and low involvement products. This group of consumers, and this was observable in all countries, evaluate high contact products/ services that include direct contact with ethnic minority groups particularly poorly.

Oullet's study of consumer racism is a very valuable addition to the marketing literature since it draws attention to racism which has been studied extensively in other areas of the social sciences. From a policy viewpoint, measures that give support to ethnic minority businesses could be justified since they suffer prejudice by majority consumers in each of the countries studied. The findings also raise issues for marketing managers operating in different countries with large multicultural populations. Strategies should be adjusted to accommodate ethnic perceptions and could include deemphasizing a product's ethnic origin, for example by branding strategies. Another way of looking at this problem is whether ethnic entrepreneurs should attempt to hide their ethnic origin to placate racist majority consumers at the expense of alienating ethnocentric consumers in their own ethnic group.

Questions

- Why are standardized cross-cultural branding strategies problematic?
- Explain how Pizza Hut and Domino's have used a glocalization strategy in India.
- What do you understand by the term crossover products?

- Explain the term transnational products using examples.
- Why do marketers need to consider consumer ethnocentrism, consumer animosity, and consumer racism when designing cross-cultural product marketing strategies?

Further reading

Ang, S.H., Jung, K., Kau, A.K., Leong, S.M., Pompitakpan, C. and Tan, S.J. (2004) 'Animosity towards economic giants: What the little guys think', *Journal of Consumer Marketing*, 21 (3): 190–207.

Balabanis, G. and Diamantopoulos, A. (2004) 'Domestic country bias, country-of-origin effects, and consumer ethnocentrism: A multidimensional unfolding approach', *Journal of the Academy of Marketing Science*, 32 (1): 80–95.

Cook, I. and Harrison, M. (2003) 'Cross over food: re-materializing postcolonial geographies', *Transactions of the Institute of British Geographers*, New Series, 28: 296–317.

Eckhardt, G.M. (2005) 'Local branding in a foreign product category in an emerging market', *Journal of International Marketing*, 13 (4): 57–79.

Grier, S.A., Brumbaugh, A.M., and Thornton, C.G. (2006) 'Crossover dreams: Consumer responses to ethnic-oriented products', *Journal of Marketing*, 70 (2): 35–51.

Klein, J.G. (2002) 'US versus them, or us versus everyone? Delineating consumer aversion to foreign goods', *Journal of International Business Studies*, 33 (2): 345–363.

Klein, J.G., Ettenson, R., and Morris, M.D. (1998) 'The animosity model of foreign product purchase: An empirical test in the People's Republic of China', *Journal of Marketing*, 62 (January): 89–100.

Oswald, L.R. (1999) 'Culture Swapping: Consumption and the ethnogenesis of middle-class Haitian immigrants', *Journal of Consumer Research*, 21 (June): 32–54.

Ouellet, J. (2007) 'Consumer racism and its effects on domestic cross-ethnic product purchase: An empirical test in the United States, Canada, and France', *Journal of Marketing*, 71 (1): 113–128.

Pieke, F.N., Van Hear, N. and Lindley, A. (2007) 'Beyond control? The mechanics and dynamics of "informal" remittances between Europe and Africa', *Global Networks*, 7 (3): 348–366.

Shimp, T.A. and Sharma, S. (1987) 'Consumer ethnocentrism: Construction and validation of the CETSCALE', *Journal of Marketing Research*, XXIV, August, 280-289.

Vann, E.F. (2006) 'The limits of authenticity in Vietnamese consumer markets', *American Anthropologist*, 108 (2): 286–296.

Wallendorf, M. and Arnould, E.J. (1991) 'We Gather Together': Consumption rituals of Thanksgiving Day, *Journal of Consumer Research*, 18 (June): 13–32.

4 Promotional strategies

Introduction

The need for appropriate cross-cultural communications strategies in different markets around the world is an accepted part of marketing practice. It is therefore interesting to note that academics in the early 1960s found little support for this new area of work among their colleagues (Dunn 1994). At the time companies were split as to whether cultural differences between consumers should be taken into account when designing advertising campaigns (Donelly 1970). A recent analysis of international advertising articles published in major advertising, marketing, and international business journals between 1990 and 2002 revealed 122 articles (Zou 2005). Articles concerned with cultural values came in fifth position with 14 articles behind those concerned with standardization (34), consumer response (26), advertising content (18) and social issues (17). Interestingly, some of the articles with the highest citations were those that focused on cultural differences (Zinkhan 1994).

The first part of this chapter discusses the role of advertisers as cultural brokers. Understanding how consumers are configured in the minds of marketers and reflected in promotional strategies in different cultural contexts is an important and interesting issue. The second theme of the chapter is to assess historical depictions of the 'other' in advertising images as a way of understanding the role of colonialism and postcolonialism in marketing discourse. It is important to understand cross-cultural advertising as a historical process, to understand that some cultures have been depicted more favourably than others, and that important continuities exist with previous eras in contemporary advertising. A third theme is a recurrent one and focuses on the globalization of advertising. The glocalization of advertising is the fourth issue to be addressed in the chapter and emphasizes strategies that marketers have adopted, and crucially what consumers think of them. Multicultural advertising is an expanding area of marketing research although much of the existing literature relates to the experiences in the USA which is one specific cultural context.

Language and literacy have not attracted significant amounts of attention in the advertising and promotional literature. Part of the reason for this neglect can be attributed to the fact that most attention has been paid to marketing in developed countries in which literacy rates are high. Marketing to ethnic minorities whose first language may not be the same as the indigenous population, and marketing in developing countries where there are low levels of literacy, requires that language and literacy be placed higher up the agenda. Understanding how language and literacy can impact on advertising and promotion is discussed in the fifth part of the chapter. An interesting yet marginalized area of discussion, concerns cross-cultural perceptions of colours that are discussed in part six. The relatively new methods of promotion of celebrity endorsements and product placement in movies and soap operas are the focus of discussion in parts seven and eight respectively. The final two aspects of advertising and promotion that are discussed include social responsibility in advertising, and adverting regulation.

Advertisers as cultural brokers

A central concept in promotional strategies is the issue of *representation*. Academics, marketers, and consumers engage in the process of representation. Academics make choices about what types of consumer behaviour they want to represent, and how, and the outcome is a subjective view of the consumer. Consumers represent themselves when engaging in consumer research, or when using products and services to construct their identities. Finally, marketers also spend a great deal of their time imagining and constructing consumers. Representations appear in the images of consumers on television and in printed advertisements. Managerial practices and processes involved in depicting consumers have been neglected in marketing research, yet for many years anthropologists have assessed marketing practice as a form of discourse for framing consumers. Consumer researchers have placed more emphasis on evaluating representations and their impact on consumer behaviour, and representations as objects of interest in their own right, but not on the social, economic and political context in which representations are constructed and why some characteristics are highlighted and not others. Understanding how consumers are configured in the minds of marketers and are incorporated into marketing practice helps us understand the boundaries and links between representational paradigms of marketers, consumer researchers, and consumers (Cayla and Peñaloza 2006).

There has recently been much more awareness of the relationship between advertising and anthropology and how ethnography has become an important tool in consumer/market research (de Waal Malefyt and Moeran 2003). Kemper (2003: 37) argues that 'If anthropology is understood as "writing" culture, what advertising "writes" ends up producing culture'. When ethnographers create an image of remote places and peoples as exotic and native people view the advertisements, they begin to inhabit the cultural forms in those pictures, and that is both direct and powerful. The idea that both anthropologists and advertisers are doing the same thing, namely discovering an underlying and existing cultural order, avoids engaging with 'multiple mediations' – advertising and marketing among them – that serve to re-work and reproduce what we think of as culture and cultural difference (Mazzarella 2003: 62).

One outcome of advertising representations of the 'other' are stereotypical versions of reality. This issue has been raised by Kjeldgaard and Askegaard (2006) in their discussion of global youth culture in Denmark and Greenland. They maintain that marketers in stressing the homogeneity of youth culture have generated a myth of a global youth segment that is at odds with reality. The view of homogeneity is a result of the 'marketers' own ideologically framed cultural constructions via advertisements, practitioner-oriented literature, and various other forms of cultural production' (Kjeldgaard and Askegaard 2006: 246). Julien Cayla (2006) argues that over the last two decades Indian advertisers have presented Indians as global consumers in two distinctively different ways. The first favours images of India as a self-sufficient socialist nation, and created the patriotic consumer who rejected British and other foreign goods in favour of locally produce products. More recently this image has been surpassed by representing India as a new postcolonial nation embracing globalization that reflects the hybridity of East and West.

In depicting images of the new India, some scholars have arguesd that advertisers have neglected to take into account the complexity of the subcontinent. For example, advertisers often borrow from Hindu religious imagery and heritage to appeal to upper middle-class Indians who wish to join the global elite. But these images fail to consider in excess of one hundred and forty million Muslims in Indian, who are largely neglected by advertisers apart from a few billboards, films and a television series representing Muslim families. In reality, while middle-class consumers are quite happy to engage in consumption practices akin to global consumers, significant resistance is apparent among the lower social classes that identify more with consumption, television programmes and products from the Middle East.

Sandikci and Ger (2006) have examined representations of Islamic women in fashion advertising in Turkey and how these representations have changed over time. Conventional images of Islamic women have focused on oppression, non-modern and non-fashionable representations. Their analysis of media, advertising and company catalogues indicated that covered women were depicted as attractive, well groomed, with shapely bodies and thus had much in common with uncovered women. The global ideals of beauty of the face and body are clearly observable in these images and constitute a global look that is religiously acceptable in a Muslim country. These representations thus question the assumption that covering is a practice of faith and secularization, and that the view of a covered women as ugly is outmoded. The shift from what they term 'religious attire' to 'fashionable outfit' is indicative of a shift in identity from the 'pious woman' to a 'modern consumer' (Sandikci and Ger 2006: 460).

The important parallel between anthropologists and advertisers is not that they seek to understand 'culture' but that they are engaged in public cultural practices. A pertinent question is what they have to teach each other. Anthropologists' work is in narrow circulation and they have often gone to pains to explore their responsibilities vis-à-vis representation. By contrast, advertising professionals have to operate according to industry standards and self-regulation but also have their own interests at heart. Within a cross-cultural marketing context, there is often a difference between how advertisers within multinational organizations want their company's products presented in a foreign market, and views of appropriate representations of the population in indigenous ad agencies with whom they are dealing. By arguing for the distinctiveness of local markets for the production of local advertising campaigns, indigenous ad agencies have leverage power at the expense of head offices to establish a vibrant and viable local ad industry. Moeran (2003) suggests that for this reason the advertising industry in Japan has been able to fend off the huge mega agencies such as JWT, Saatchi and Saatchi, and so forth. This is not just true of big countries like Japan but also true of small ones like Trinidad (Miller 2003). Moeran (2003: 105) also argues that advertisers suffer from time and space constraints that enable them to do little more than generate 'mouthfuls of exotica to be consumed by rapidly masticating media bites'. In reality, this could be a single printed page, or a television commercial of relatively short duration. In Japan, commercials normally last no more than 15 seconds and there is little time to become involved in 'complicated or complicating issues' and thus the existing systems and norms are reproduced.

The conflict between ad agencies and companies constituting the politics of representation has also been noted in India. A study of company–ad agency relations in Bombay in India found that many advertisers berated their foreign clients for their 'value arrogance' and for failing to understand that Indian consumers needed to be addressed in ways that respected their essential cultural specificity. Equally, these same executives had nothing but scorn for the apparently condescending way in which any transnationals had tried to 'Indianize' their advertising or their products, by arguing that Indians deserved the same quality as everyone else. Either way, the transnationals were trashed for their neo-imperialistic assumptions. Of course the advertising agencies knew full well on which side their bread was buttered, and they managed to salvage for themselves a highly strategic role. Positioning themselves as expert brokers between the ambitions of their clients and the cultural inscrutability of Indian consumers, they turned what had initially been a profound crisis of value into a virtuoso display of legitimation. Rhetorically, they presented themselves as a new kind of popular hero: defending Indian cultural integrity against transnational imperialism (Mazzarella 2003: 65–66).

The localized nature of advertising agencies is also a feature of contemporary China. The business risks of entering China are significant compared to other countries but most multinationals believe it is more important to have a presence than not. As a consequence, there has been significant interfirm competition for advertising contracts. Local firms are the leading advertisers in China, only two foreign brands made the Top 10 in 2002, Proctor and Gamble's Safeguard (5th place) and Crest (6th place). The pressure to advertise has also encompassed local, state-owned organizations whose advertising spend increased by 41 percent in 2003. Foreign ownership of media is tightly controlled and is only allowed to take the form of a joint venture. This policy has resulted in huge local media companies attracting most of the business. For example, in 2001, CCTV the only national television station attracted 75 per cent of television advertising spend through its 13 channels (Hung *et al.* 2005).

Depictions of the 'other' in advertising images

How images communicate, how people decode them, and how they circulate in consumer societies have all become important issues in image intensive societies. Visual communication can take a number of forms, such as art, photography, websites, comics and so forth (Schroeder 2002; Beck 2006).The previous section introduced the notion of the social, economic and political drivers in the cultural representation of images of 'others'. It is also important to recognize the role of history in the construction of representations of other cultures. Technological innovation has played an important role in the development and dissemination of cultural images. Photography and postcards bore images of indigenous people that would not otherwise have been available to Western publics (Landau 2002; Waitt and Head 2002).

Landau and Kaspin (2002) in their text *Images and Empires: Visuality in Colonial and Postcolonial Africa* draw together a collection of folk art, photography, film and dance, cartoons and other topics. They note that images change depending on who is looking at them, and how images have underwritten and undermined hierarchies that governed colonial Africa. The accounts are instructive and they have contemporary relevance since they relate to the wider issue of how people use amorphous images and social meanings from their *own* society, and how they use these resources to recognize people from *other* societies.

The practice of playing with images and distance is taken up by Kim (2002) in her analysis of how the exotic 'other' was depicted on European trade/business cards, shop signs, and product labels in the eighteenth century. These artefacts provided an important cultural function since they were sources of visual information about non-European peoples. In some depictions Africans were 'whimsical, carefree cherubs', in others 'ennobled savage princes', and slaves hard at work producing goods for shipment. Western clothed and lighter skinned models were more acceptable. Trade cards depicting Chinese workers in the tea industry were of a different order and reflected their higher status in the racial hierarchy. These focused on happy trading alliances between 'civilized' mercantile societies striking bourgeois poses, sometimes drinking tea, 'as consumers of high quality teas, coupled with their western drawing-room postures, in fact position them on a par with cultivated Europeans' (Kim2002: 161).

Burke's (2002) analysis of advertising in Zimbabwe in the early twentieth century indicates that there was a strong sense within the advertising community and the wider public concerning appropriate content for African consumption especially, with respect to depicting white women as objects of desire and refraining from promoting a social world that was too far removed from colonial society. From 1950 to 1970, print advertising throughout southern Africa predominantly portrayed Africans achieving an elevated social and economic standing through their use of a particular commodity. Burke notes:

> One campaign for Castle Lager, for example, showed Africans fly-fishing in the mountains and picnicking next to their car, transposing black men and women directly into images that had initially featured white subjects.

Campaigns for Ambi, a skin lightener, featured a wealthy African couple relaxing at Victoria Falls and a light-skinned African doctor reviewing charts, contrasted with his dark-skinned janitor. Other campaigns were careful to show African achievements as more suited to the standards of colonial society: a regular series of print ads for Lifebuoy soap showed African men in a variety of 'appropriate' work settings, including mining, bricklaying, clerking, and teaching.

(Burke 2002: 49)

Interestingly, Burke suggests that some advertisements that were shown in the USA and UK would not be shown in the same form in colonial Africa. One constant theme was the ability of a good soap to turn blacks into whites. One ad promoting Gossage's Soap which centred on a caricatured African whose face was half black and half white, was run in the USA. The caption read 'Soap Makes Black White'. The ad would not have appeared in this form in Africa since the promise to make Africans white through their use of soap would not be acceptable. An assumption that toiletries can make Africans lighter was fine, but not white. However, the use of Africans as a symbol of the cleaning properties of soap to consumers in Western countries was acceptable.

The practice of cross-cultural marketing that emerged in the 1950s also had an impact on the practices of advertising professionals in Southern Africa. An important issue in this respect was the emphasis on using visual images since they were more accessible, easier for different cultural groups to translate and they helped to avoid linguistic blunders. However, one of the most controversial ads of the time focused on the misunderstanding of pictures rather than words. An ad for Raleigh, the bicycle manufacturer, showed an African boy riding his bike to escape from a lion, in an attempt to demonstrate the bicycle's superior performance. A rapid drop in sales followed, and when the matter was investigated it emerged that the ad was interpreted as lions would chase anyone that rode a bicycle. Another concerned the wrapper of Stork margarine depicting a baby on the wrapper; this was misunderstood as the product being manufactured from rendered baby fat.

One might wonder what contemporary relevance these examples of colonialist advertising practices have in the current postcolonial era. There are a number of scholars who maintain that the legacy of colonialism remains with us in the way we depict 'the other' in marketing communications. For example, O'Barr's (1994: 79) account of otherness in the world of advertising in print media in America in the late 1980s and early 1990s demonstrates that representations of ethnic and racial groups appeared in three main categories: in *travel advertisements*, in *product endorsements*, and advertisements dealing with *international business*. By far the most common representation was as foreigners in advertisements by airlines, hotel chains, travel companies, and governments. These advertisements were asymmetrical with respect to the characteristics of the tourist and the indigenous population. Natives smile, work and dance for the tourists who do touristy things like go to the beach, swim, relax and sightsee. The natives work while the tourists enjoy their leisure. The tourist was always depicted as an American often with blonde hair, blue eyes and fair skin, in contrast to the native who was routinely darker.

Product endorsements operated in two ways. The first context was in connection with a product from the model's own country. The Columbian farmer dressed in national clothes holding a bag of coffee is illustrative of this practice at its most basic level. Often the products being endorsed have little or no connection with their country or nationality but rest upon the imagery that is associated with different foreigners. A glamorous African woman advertising European lingerie makes associations with Africa, its primitive nature, and the supposed raw sexuality of black women. In this respect the advertisement reflects ideas about Africa that circulate in Western culture. The advertisements for international business tend to focus on convenience and efficiency of trips abroad and having a home from home. A significant amount of information about flights and hotels falls into this category. The power relationships in these contexts can be more complex since the subordination of a foreigner to an American in a business setting is not always a reality

Some contemporary versions of the 'other' in advertising focus on the products of other countries rather than the people. A specific example is the role of products in improving the situation of impoverished indigenous people. Carol Hendrickson (1996), in her analysis of selling Guatemala through a reading of Maya export products in US mail order catalogues, highlights the use of certain phrases such as 'primitive'. Primitive objects are described as being produced in small communities without the tools and technologies normally found in the West. Products are often referred to as being sourced in 'villages'. Yet the reality is very often different from the advertising text. In some catalogues towns with 62,000 inhabitants are described as 'a tiny village in Guatemala' (Hendrickson 1996: 106). Another strategy is to make liberal use of the words 'rainforest' and 'jungle'. For example, silver necklaces and earrings were reportedly 'handmade in a tiny town high above the Guatemala rainforests', when the town actually had 42,500 inhabitants. Furthermore, most of the places where the goods were made were nowhere near the rainforests.

Similar patterns of the 'other' being perceived as inferior to white, Western populations is replicated in the context of ethnic marketing in advanced societies. Early studies of ethnic minority marketing date from around the 1960s and tended to focus on African-Americans. For example, Kassarjian's (1969) study of blacks in American advertising from 1946–1965 was highly critical of the stereotypical and inferior depiction of 'Negroes'. Pollay *et al.* (1992) examined racial segmentation in cigarette advertising in the USA from 1950–1965 and found that ethnic segregation existed with black models in black media and white models in white media. The black models were invariably athletes. However, the two markets were not treated equally since there was a two to three year time lag in advertising safer, filtered cigarettes to black consumers.

By the 1970s, research on minorities tended to focus on descriptive differences between black and white consumers but the unequal treatment and negative stereotyping persisted. Stern (1999: 3) concludes that 'Blacks featured centrally were cast predominantly in negative roles such as menial worker, poor recipient of charity, and social problem. The few exceptions were one-in-a-million figures such as athletes, musicians, and entertainers'. Moreover, they tended to be token blacks, faces in a crowd and frequently children. By the 1980s, multicultural research began to re-examine the issues of ethnicity from a multidimensional perspective. Since the 1990s, ethnicity has received far more attention from advertising researchers and has enjoyed a much broader base than solely directed towards African-Americans and has included Hispanics and Asians (Taylor and Stern 1997; Davila 2001). As already noted in Chapter 1, more attention has been paid to ethnic marketing in different countries. Novel theoretical and conceptual approaches emerged including new ethnicities, heterogeneity, hybridity, multiplicity, creolization, consumer resistance, counter-culture of the Black diaspora (Denzin 2001; Sandikci 2001), culture swapping (Oswald 1999) and border crossing (Peñaloza 1994). These new approaches raised questions about appropriate methods of targeting advertising at ethnic groups and the impact of advertising messages on target and non-target audiences (Aaker *et al.* 1998; Grier and Brumbaugh 1999; Holland and Gentry 1999). Furthermore, the contribution of socialization variables (Bush *et al.* 1999), intra-ethnic group variables (Green 1999), the impact of cultural and sub-cultural knowledge (Brumbaugh 2002), and ethnic self awareness (Dimofte *et al.* 2004) were indicative of a more complex approach to ethnic portrayal in advertising images.

From a strategic viewpoint, advertisers need to respond to the needs of the ethnic market due to its size, purchasing power and potential for future growth in many advanced societies. Previous research has demonstrated that the racial composition of advertisements affects identification, evaluation and purchase intentions among white and non-white groups, across mass and racially targeted media (Green 1999). Overall, efforts to attract ethnic minorities have been found to fare better when advertisements mirror the consumer's own ethnic group (Whittler 1989; Aaker *et al.* 1998). This feature is especially apparent for white and black consumers; although not necessarily the case for those of multiethnic origin, Asians, and Indians when multiple ethnic groups have been used in research designs (Braumbaugh and Grier 2006). From a societal point of view, there are also issues around the realistic representation of minorities rather than negatively focused stereotypical images that are distanced from reality (Taylor and Stern 1997; Bush *et al.* 1999; Stevenson and Swayne 1999).

There is still much work to be undertaken in some cultural contexts vis-à-vis multicultural advertising. We know most about the situation in the USA but relatively little about other contexts. How Chinese children's commercials differ from those in the USA was a theme addressed by Ji and McNeal (2001) who found some of the Chinese commercials included ethnic (non-Han races) but few (6.1%) contained Western models. By contrast American commercials included blacks (30.4%), Asians (7%) and Hispanics (5.4%). Elias and Greenspan (2007) have provided an interesting case study of the advertising challenges of appealing to Russian immigrants living in Israel. They found that products were largely invisible to immigrants unless they were specifically targeted at them. The Russian diaspora is estimated to number around 10 million of which 1 million live in Israel. Furthermore, they are highly educated and employed in professional, scientific and white-collar occupations. Yet interestingly, manufacturers thought that immigrants were already aware of their company's offerings because they were large successful companies with a high profile brand profile among the indigenous population. The reasons why advertising was unsuccessful in attracting immigrant groups varied according to the product. For example, a honey producer failed to attract immigrants because these consumers were unable or unwilling to read labels that were written in Hebrew. Only advertisements that used cultural symbols that were familiar to immigrant communities overcame the language barrier, even people who could not read the label could identify the company's products. A bear, that is a popular character in Russian folktales, was shown eating the honey to get the message across. A further problem related to the spelling of the manufacturer's name which in Russian meant 'poison'. This issue was resolved by changing the spelling to avoid confusion and subsequently the market share amongst this group was increased.

Another company that targeted the Russian immigrants was a manufacturer of meat products. This was a more challenging case than the one connected with honey, since honey was already an integral part of the Russian diet whereas Kosher meat was not. The company adapted an existing advertisement designed for Hebrew-speaking audiences. Follow-up research demonstrated that 26 per cent of respondents reported purchasing the company's products as opposed to 6 per cent purchasing those of the competitor. In 2003, the company decided to invest in an advertisement specifically designed to reflect Russian immigrant's authentic experience and cultural symbols. The main characters in the ad were an immigrant father preparing his daughter's lunch while she practised on a violin. The use of a violin and classical music reflected cultural signifiers of the intelligentsia with which many Russian immigrants identified. The company therefore made the connection with immigrants of high socioeconomic groups and its own products. The advertisement was a success and increased both sales and awareness without resorting to below the line advertising such as points of sale advertising and tasting. This outcome was a real achievement since it was based upon consumers' willingness to change their culinary patterns and purchase kosher meat products.

Globalization of advertising

One of the most recurring themes within cross-cultural marketing is the standardization of advertising which reflects Theodre Levitt's view of the globalization of markets (see Chapter 1). International advertisers generally have three choices: *standardization*, *adaptation*, and a *contingency approach*. The *standardization* philosophy maintains that although there are variations between different countries they are more a matter of degree as opposed to direction. It is therefore of benefit to focus on the similarities of consumers in different countries resulting from the cost savings associated with planning, brand building, and maintaining a good corporate image. The *contingency* approach, as the term suggests, emphasizes evaluating each case on its own merits. It takes the middle ground recognizing the cost savings of standardization but also the pitfalls of getting things wrong balanced against the more expensive option of adapting to different cultures.

The *adaptation* approach emphasizes the differences rather than the similarities of consumers in various countries. Countries could differ along a number of variations including culture, economic stage of development, the availability of suitable media and legal regulations. A number of international advertising mistakes have resulted from not taking into account some of the important but also subtle differences between cultures. A couple of examples demonstrate how a lack of cultural understanding can waste valuable advertising expenditure. The toothpaste Pepsodent's promise of white teeth was inappropriate in many regions of Southeast Asia where betel nut chewing was an elite habit and where black teeth are a symbol of prestige. The slogan 'Wonder where the yellow went?' was equally baffling. Another example is a Canadian advert for canned fish run in Quebec, which showed a woman playing golf with her husband. The caption stressed that she could enjoy a day playing golf with her husband and still cook the dinner. Anthropologists argued against the advertisement since it broke numerous cultural norms: wives were not likely to be golfing with their husbands, women would not been seen wearing shorts on a high class golf course, and French-Canadians did not serve that particular type of fish for the evening meal (Ricks *et al.* 1974: 48).

In his analysis of 40 years of the standardization/adaptation debate, Agrawal (1995) identifies major shifts within the discourse. In the *1950s*, practitioners placed considerable emphasis on adapting to local markets and avoiding costly mistakes. The shrinking of distance aided better communications and made the adaptation a more realistic possibility. The two main difficulties that were raised when designing advertisements for foreign markets were language problems and difficulties in obtaining copy. Avoiding figures of speech, slang, and puns in advertising copy and trying to translate humour into other languages was highly problematic. While there was some consensus in the 1950s around the issue of adaptation, in the *1960s* there was a greater degree of variability, and overall, there was a trend for practitioners to increase levels of standardization in order to cut costs. For example, BMW, the car marker, had to launch advertising campaigns in 27 countries as diverse as Latin America, Africa, the Arab States, and Europe establishing a similar reputation in all of them. It decided to focus on high quality in all markets, and then, depending on the market, to adapt different features – 100 mile per hour cruising speed, safety features with respect to construction economy, unique suspension system and so forth. All products prominently displayed the BMW symbol.

In the *1970s* there appears to have been a trend back to adapting ads as opposed to the standardization approach that was witnessed in the previous decade. There was a recognition among some advertising agencies located in different parts of the world that they could not just buy local media and have US ads translated into the local language. The 'people are alike' theory had become in danger of becoming grossly simplified, and there was a move among practitioners to incorporate local knowledge of cultural differences in ads. During the *1980s*, there seems to have been a move back to standardization among companies although ad agencies were somewhat split over the standardization/adaptation issue. A survey of executives working in advertising agencies in the late 1980s indicated that 43 per cent of the sample had positive attitudes towards standardization, whereas 57 reported reservations. The standardization approach was particularly strong among the giant Cola companies (Pepsi-Cola and Coca-Cola) that wished to cultivate a single identity throughout the world. As Coca-Cola president Roberto Goizueta stated 'People around the world are today connected to each other by brand-name consumer products as much as by anything else' (Prendergast 2000: 448). In a global survey of teenagers only 40 per cent could correctly identify the United Nations logo, but 82 per cent identified Coke's symbol. Agrawal's review of the standardization versus adaptation debate is useful because it provides an overview of changes over time and demonstrates that there have been trends when standardization has been in vogue and others when the reverse was true. It does need to be acknowledged, however, that the globalization thesis became more powerful in some advertising circles than others.

Saatchi and Saatchi, one of the largest advertising agencies in the 1980s, exposed the globalization view in its annual reports. Cultural and language barriers would progressively decline in importance due to media such as satellite television. So enamored were they of Levitt's work on global marketing, that in 1986 he sat on the boards of the operating and consulting divisions of Saatchi and Saatchi (Kleinman 1987). One of their first ads for British Airways was symptomatic of their view of globalization and they presented it as the most globally co-ordinated branded ad ever. The television ads were show in the USA, Canada, Australia, and Britain on the same day. Twenty five other countries including the Gulf States, Egypt, Hong Kong, South Africa, India and Thailand saw it shortly afterwards (Fallon 1988).

Within advertising scholarship there has been a great deal of emphasis on whether or not organizations should standardize, and little by way of investigating how they go about it (Harris 1994). For example, the way decisions are made about common objectives and budgets (Banerjee 1994), and creative media decisions about the whole corporation (Wills and Ryan 1977). Okazaki *et al.* (2006) suggest that the relationship between standardization and global measures of financial and strategic performance has also been marginalized. While there have been pronouncements for many years about the financial benefits of standardization, the evidence to prove the point has been largely absent. Okazaki *et al.* (2006) conducted a study of US and Japanese subsidiaries of multinational companies in the UK, France, Germany, Italy, and the Netherlands. They found that despite the hype surrounding the entity of a single European market, practitioners perceived important differences in the infrastructure of European markets.

Often the standardization debate is couched as a binary either yes or no, and McDonald's is a company that is cited as typical of the standardization of advertising. Yet, this is not how the company views its cross-cultural marketing strategy. McDonald's vice president for corporate communications uses the term 'multilocal' to describe his approach to cross-cultural advertising;

> We're over 80 percent owned and operated by franchisees or joint venture partners. We have people from the community who work in our restaurants and manage them. They are involved in our local marketing approach, our

advertising approach, and in adapting our core menu to local tastes and local culture. We're not creating advertising in some big agency here in America or London or Hong Kong and then shipping out with a 119 voice-overs. We absolutely believe that the brand needs to be portrayed as a Moldavian company in Moldavia, as a British company in the UK, as a Japanese company in Japan.

(Hunter and Yates 2002: 343)

Duncan and Ramaprasad (1995) have taken this issue further by assessing which aspects of multinational advertising are standardized more than others. Their study made the distinction between the standardization of *strategy*, *executions*, and *language*. The countries included in the survey were from Europe, the Americas, Asia including the Pacific Rim, and Australia. They found that 68 per cent of multinationally advertised brands used a standardized strategy in *all* the countries, 24 per cent indicated *some* countries, and only 7 per cent indicated not at all. The standardization of executions was similar, with 54 per cent of brands using it in all countries, 36 per cent in some countries and 8 per cent not at all. They found that the standardization of language was not common. Only 11 per cent of brands standardized language in all countries, 41 per cent used it in some countries, and 43 per cent did not standardize language at all. Overall, they discovered that Western region advertising agencies standardized more than non-Western region agencies. However, there was a difference in the standardization of different elements. Western region agencies standardize strategy and execution more and language less, than non-Western region agencies. A factor that was important in decisions to standardize was the expertise in 'local' countries. The view of the companies was that in many small countries ad agencies did not have the clients or agency expertise to produce great advertising.

Despite the years of debate on the standardization issue few studies have actually addressed what factors lead companies to standardize their advertising. One study undertaken by Laroche *et al.* (2001) sought to determine the level of advertising standardization of 230 multinational corporations (MNCS) across North America, Asia (mostly Japan), France, Germany, Spain, Italy, UK, Netherlands, Scandinavia and South America. It was found that the more 'the market positions or country environmental conditions are similar between MNC's and subsidiary's countries, or the more the MNC's manager is familiar with the context of the foreign country, the higher the MNC's degree of control of the subsidiary' (Laroche *et al.* 2001: 261). The converse was also true, the less decisional power awarded to the subsidiary the higher the MNC's degree of control. Consumer similarity across markets has also been an important feature in decisions to adopt standardized strategies. In order to assess whether this is feasible organizations have to identify the presence of intermarket segments in target countries, in other words establish that consumer segments transcend national boundaries and share common dimensions. Of particular relevance are segmentation characteristics in the area of lifestyle, tastes and habits.

Another study by Samiee *et al.* (2003) assessed MNC's country of origin upon the standardization of advertising programmes at the subsidiary level in four culturally similar nations. The study compared the responses of US, European and Japanese multinational subsidiaries in China, Hong Kong, Singapore and Taiwan. Their research indicated that despite the cultural similarities across the four markets, the extent and drivers of standardization were largely different. An important finding was that Japanese multinational companies that were culturally closer to the Asian markets used in the study, were the least likely to standardize their advertising programmes. This was consistent with previous research that indicated that is was easier to standardize advertising programmes for European markets because of their closer proximity and similar levels of economic development than Asian countries which are more diverse in these respects. On the other hand, three of the countries chosen had relatively high standards of living and so were relatively homogeneous. Interestingly, the level of advertising standardization within US and European multinational companies was more prevalent in these markets. Thus the level of standardization would appear related to the multinational company's country of origin. It was also evident from the findings that there was more standardization within the larger subsidiaries which was consistent with earlier research which noted head office takes a keener interest in larger business units.

Glocalization of advertising

There are many issues that prevent standardized advertising messages being promoted cross-culturally. A significant number of blunders have occurred due to organizations not understanding 'local' cultural differences in advertising. Ricks *et al*. (1974: 48) maintain that advertising blunders overseas result from 'tremendous optimism about a particular product or product line, vast confidence in business know-how and past success formulas, and failure to fully understand and appreciate the foreign environment'. Unicultural management that takes all the decisions regarding advertising in different cultures is a high risk strategy.

Public display of affection between members of the opposite sex is acceptable in many Western societies but in many countries it is regarded as offensive and unacceptable. Thailand is one such country where an ad for mouthwash that showed a young couple holding hands was unsuccessful. The company changed the ad to include two women which was deemed acceptable. Another taboo relates to parts of the body that are acceptable to be shown in public. For example, an American shoe manufacturer promoted its product through showing photos of bare feet. This would be acceptable in many areas of the world but not in Southeast Asia where exposing the feet is considered an insult. Other companies have encountered similar problems with ads that depict an executive at a desk on the telephone with their feet propped up against it. In the Middle and Far East, showing the sole of the foot or shoe is considered a terrible insult (Ricks 1993).

It would be a mistake to think that cultural errors only occur across different countries. In the USA where there is a big ethnic population similar problems have occurred with respect to the Latino market. Ricks (1993) provides some interesting examples in this respect. A telephone company tried to incorporate a Latino flavour in its commercial by employing Puerto Rican actors. In the ad, the wife said to her husband, 'Run downstairs and phone Mary, tell her we'll be a little late'. This commercial contained two major cultural errors: in a traditional household, Latino wives would seldom dare order their husbands around, and almost no spouse would feel it necessary to phone to warn of tardiness (Ricks 1993: 64). McDonald's has used various 'Hispanic ads' in several Spanish-speaking markets within the USA. However, these same ads proved unsuccessful when introduced in Puerto Rico. Apparently Puerto Rican consumers deemed them to be 'too Mexican' so separate ads had to be developed (65).

In Southeast Asia, Vietnam and Thailand are geographically adjacent and culturally quite similar and this may prompt organizations to use similar advertising strategies in these countries. In her content analysis of advertising in newspapers and magazines between 1994 and 2004, Sar (2007) found that there were considerable differences in the ads that appeared in the two countries. Vietnam came out as the more traditional of the two countries with ads that focused on themes associated with respect, modesty and collectiveness. Furthermore, these trends intensified rather than reduced over the period. Whereas an emphasis on convenience, sexiness and humour increased over the period in Thai ads and not for the Vietnamese ads, which reinforces Vietnam as more Eastern and less Western of the two countries. Significantly, more emotional appeals (happy, surprised, pleasant, interesting) were used in Thai ads and this trend intensified over the period. The results therefore indicate that Vietnamese print-ad audiences will respond more positively to traditional Asian appeals – sexual conservatism, collectivity, an emphasis on product information. Thai audiences will respond more positively to ads that have a more Western appeal. For the future, Vietnam may grow more Western as it moves further away from its communist roots. Whereas the Thai ads appear to reflect a culture that has accepted a significant degree of Western influence and is more akin to a cosmopolitan mix of East and West.

Although the standardization debate has received considerable attention Zhou and Belk (2004: 63) maintain that existing scholarship tends to focus on 'advertising content analysis or on how advertisers say they create advertising in foreign markets'. They argue that an implicit assumption within these studies

> is what an ad says or what its creator intends it to convey is also what it means to consumers; thus, the presence of global images and foreign appeals or advertiser preferences for such images and appeals are taken to mean that local culture is becoming more globalized and that consumer values are changing accordingly.
>
> (Zhou and Belk 2004: 63)

It is both interesting and puzzling that few studies have actually investigated consumer acceptance or rejection of local and global appeals in advertising and that they have tended to use small student samples.

If a central focus of marketing is about the fulfilling of consumer needs and wants then it is crucial that feedback on consumer preferences is obtained. This argument about the importance of consumer meaning is also addressed by Domzal and Kernan

(1993: 1) who argue that 'Global advertising succeeds when it is perceived in semiotically equivalent ways by multicultural consumer segments'. They argue that what makes a campaign global is the 'culturally transcendent meanings of the advertised product or service'. Yet there are many examples of advertisements that send out contradictory cross-cultural messages to consumers. In his visit to Tokyo, Boyle (2003) describes an advertisement for Virginia Slims cigarettes incorporating the words 'Be you'. At first sight this may not seem out of place since there has been a movement towards depicting self-determination in advertising. The confusion arose because not only was the slogan presented in English, rather than Japanese, but the two girls in the picture were obviously American. How should the locals read that kind of complex demand? Be you, but also be us? (Boyle 2003: 288).

The distinctiveness of Japanese television advertising is a theme discussed by Johansson (1994) particularly in connection with the meaning consumers attribute to soft-sell approach compared with Western standards. He notes, 'the lack of emphatic selling demonstrations, the limited exposure of unique features, the seemingly irrelevant usage situations, the preference for cartoon characters, and the popularity of persistently upbeat musical soundtracks all add up to a fantasy-filled, mood-creating, "unserious" audience experience in Japanese TV advertising' (Johansson 1994: 17). One reason for the soft-sell argument is the relationship between the buyer and the seller, where the buyer has a very high status and the quality of products and services is guaranteed. Japanese consumers are very suspicious of any company that needs to push the virtues of a product and this results in a degree of distrust. The soft-sell approach is designed to invite consumers to take a closer look at the product. This philosophy is reflected in the approach to television advertising that is considered an imposition on the consumer's time, leaving advertisers to justify why they have interrupted their viewing schedule. The hard -sell is not conducive to a softly, softly apologetic approach. Furthermore, considerable importance is attached to protecting members of the household from outside influence and keeping a good atmosphere within the home.

Miller (2002) has explored the local meaning of global products and the implications for advertising strategies in his discussions of Coke in Trinidad. From the perspective of consumers, the key conceptual categories are not the flavours and colas that marketers hold in high regard, but what are referred to locally as the 'black' sweet drink and the 'red' sweet drink. The red sweet drink is a traditional Trinidadian beverage that has the highest sugar content of the two drinks. The Indian population in Trinidad is particularly fond of sugar and sweet products and is supposedly linked to their arrival in the country as indentured labourers to work in the sugar cane fields. The centrality of the black sweet drink is associated with the alcoholic drink of choice on the island, rum and coke. In Trinidadian culture rum is never drunk alone but is always accompanied with a mixer. However, the centrality of Coke as the black drink is not widely adhered to since any black drink will do. This is especially true of the cheaper end of the market where locally produced black drinks are substituted. The vernacular expression in the bar is 'gimme a black' or 'gimme a red', and within this cultural context Coke is an example of a high status black drink.

There is also an ethnic dimension to the status of Coke as a black drink. Indians spoke of Coke as a 'white' and 'white oriented people' drink. Miller interprets the term 'white oriented' as 'a synonym for Black African Trinidadians' since many Indians assume that Africans are more inclined to emulate white tastes and customs and become 'Afro-Saxons'. Africans would dispute this interpretation by arguing that Indians are more deferential to white people. Leading on from this Miller argues that black culture has replaced colonial culture as the mainstream, and Indians have become the 'other'. This observation was acknowledged by a marketing official responsible for organising advertising spots on the radio, when he remarked 'we want an Indian programme, since marketing soft drinks has become very ethnic' (Miller 2002: 255). The ethnic segmentation of the soft drinks market was also reflected in the marketing of Canada Dry that was not marketed as ginger ale, but a 'tough soft drink'. As Miller notes:

> The advert was produced in two versions. One had a black cowboy shooting several bottles, as on a range, and finding that Canada Dry deflected his bullets. The other had an American Indian having his tomahawk blunted by this brand, having smashed the others. As the company told me, the idea was to cover the diversity of communities and (as it were) 'red' Indian was adopted only after marketing tests had shown that there would be empathy and not offence from the South Asian Indian community of Trinidad.
>
> (Miller 2002: 255)

It is interesting that market research had demonstrated that associating red with Indian and black with African does not reflect the reality of consumption. A higher proportion of Indians would appear to consume more Colas while Kola champagne, as red drink is commonly known, is more frequently drunk by Africans. While Coca-Cola is often highlighted as an image of superficial globality, in Trinidad quite the opposite is true. Coca-Cola as a generic black sweet drink and a brand developed as much through local contradictions of popular culture, and part of a wider debate of how people should be.

Variations on the 'standardize versus localize' theme have been around for a long time. Some scholars have argued that since materialism seems to be permeating most societies, albeit at different rates, the specialization versus globalization duality has become something of a blunt instrument. Perhaps it would be more useful for practitioners if the dichotomy was replaced with a continuum on which different cultural groups could be mapped (Lin 2001).

Language and promotion

Understanding the relationship between language and promotion in cross-cultural marketing is particularly complex. The sheer numbers of languages used in some cultural contexts is mind boggling. Furthermore, language use can be a highly political issue that should be considered when designing a promotional strategy. Ryan (1990) has documented the existence of 127 ethnic groups in the Soviet Union but the proportion that considered the language of their ethnic group as their mother tongue, was highly variable between different ethnic groups. Latin America has largely been described as a 'Spanish-speaking', and culturally Hispanic part of the world. An imaginary homogeneous communicative scenario and longstanding history of a common cultural and linguistic heritage conceal the region's great linguistic and cultural diversity and complexity. More than 450 different languages are spoken in the region. Nowhere is this linguistic and cultural complexity more true than in the Andean sub-region, from Venezuela to Chile, which has more than 200 Amerindian linguistic groups. Furthermore, more of the indigenous languages are being accepted and used as languages of education, having officially recognized alphabets and writing systems (Lopez 2001).

Language systems in India are equally complex. Children who complete 10 years of schooling will have learned to read and write in three languages – the mother tongue/regional language, Hindi (the national language) and English (the international language). In the 1961 Census of India, 1,652 mother tongues were listed. More recent Censuses have recognized 105 languages spoken by more than 10,000 people. Of the 105 languages, 96 can be classified as Indian languages. However, of the 96 recognized languages, only 50 are considered written languages, the remainder are 'technically or actually "unwritten"'. Most Indians speak more than one language or dialect and even those who speak only one language will understand other languages and dialects (Daswani 2001). India has around 300 large newspapers with a combined circulation of 157 million. Only a few dozen papers with a circulation of over 35 million are in English but these papers attract nearly half of all advertising funding. English is the language of aspiration, a remnant of colonialism and the medium of aspiration is the newspaper. These findings suggest that newspapers could increase in importance in the near future (*Economist* 2007a).

Probably more research has been undertaken on language use and ethnic minorities in the USA than any other country. La Ferle and Lee (2005) have addressed the issue of whether English language media can connect with ethnic audiences. Their survey of Anglos, African-Americans and Latinos demonstrates that advertising agencies are spending far less on researching Latino and African-American consumers, than their spending power merits. With respect to media use, all of the groups spent more time with broadcast media than print media. The African-American group spent more time watching the television than listening to the radio than the other two groups. Around 60 per cent of all groups indicated that they spent less than one hour during a weekday reading English language newspapers and magazines. Around 27 per cent of Latinos did not read English language newspapers and magazines and thus broadcast media was the most reliable method of targeting all the groups. In terms of representation in the media, the Latino group was most likely to report that they were under-represented in the media, followed by the African-Americans. There was widespread disagreement with the statement 'the portrayal of my ethnic group in ads is offensive to me'. African-Americans and Latinos were more predisposed to support companies that supported their ethnic groups via sponsorship of ethnic festivals and sporting events and so forth.

Spanish-language advertising in the USA has increased Latinos' perception of advertisers' sensitivity to Latino culture and people, and made them more predisposed towards advertisements. When advertisements were exclusively presented in the Spanish-language, this decreased the affect towards the advertisements. They suggest that Latinos have language-related inferiority complexes that affect the way they view advertising directed at their sub-culture (Koslow *et al.* 1994). Marin and Marin (1991) provide an explanation of this finding when they argue that there is a common misconception in the portrayal of Latinos as monolingual in the USA, and of being of a singular Hispanic identity. The reality is that many Latinos view themselves as Latino and American at the same time and marketers and others need to recognize this fact. To provide advertisements in only Spanish or English ignores the importance of multiple identities.

The issue of language use in advertising is also evident in Europe. Dutch consumers are increasingly being presented with television commercials using three variants of English: British English, American English and Dutch English. In nearly three quarters of commercials where English was spoken, the English used was Dutch English with an American accent. One quarter used pure American English, and only 2 per cent British English. English was even used in advertisements that promoted Dutch products. For example, one advertisement for Dutch cheese was accompanied by an English song. The reason for the extensive use of English is financial. Companies choose not to translate because it is too expensive. The view of advertising agencies is that everyone understands English and its use is also good for the product's image: young, dynamic, international. However, consumer attitudes towards the use of English were not positive, this was even the case among young people who are more accustomed to it than older consumers. Negative images could result in consumers not buying the product, thus savings made through not translating were lost as a result of negative attitudes towards the use of English. A question mark also remains about how much English consumers actually understood. Although 80 per cent said that they understood the English used in commercials, only 36 per cent were able to explain the narrative. Understanding was enhanced when text of the spoken word was shown on screen.

In some instances it is not the language of the advertisement that is problematic but the order in which advertisements are presented to consumers. For example, Proctor and Gamble launched a laundry detergent in Saudi Arabia in the mid-1990s. The series of advertisements depicted dirty clothes being placed in a washer, the detergent being added, and the clothes coming out nice and clean. The series of pictures were arranged in a horizontal manner to be read from left to right as is the practice in Western cultures. Unfortunately, for Proctor and Gamble, in Arab cultures consumers read from right to left and as a consequence the ad made little sense in the context in which it should have been understood and was a total failure (Saporito 1994). Language blunders in promotional translations can also be problematic. Translation errors occurred when an American airline advertised plush 'rendezvous lounges' on its jets in Brazil, to find out that rendezvous in Portuguese meant a room hired for love making. Colgate-Palmolive introduced its Cue toothpaste in French-speaking countries to find that 'cue' was a pornographic word in French. Faulty laundry soap advertising can wipe out sales. One American company advertised in French-speaking Quebec that its product was particularly good for the dirty part of the wash – 'les partes de sale'. Only to find out that the phrase was indicative of the American idiom for 'private parts'.

Literacy and promotion

The concept of literacy has not loomed large in analyses of consumer behaviour or marketing thus reflecting the discipline's Anglo-Saxon roots and middle-class bias (Hirschman 1993). Within the wider social sciences there has been far more emphasis on understanding cross-cultural approaches to literacy, and conceptualizing literacy in an age of multiculturalism and pluralism (Lankshear and McLaren 1993; Street 1993; Durgunoglu and Verhoeven 1998; Olson and Torrance 2001; Schmidt and Mosenthal 2001). Cross-cultural aspects of literacy are important for advertisers to understand for a number of reasons. First, reading and writing have different meanings in different cultures, and cultures require different levels of literacy to be an active participant (Wallendorf 2001). Ultimately, levels of literacy will affect how products are promoted in different cultural settings. Literacy is often cited as a characteristic of modern societies and a precursor to economic efficiency, although this linear progression has been extensively criticized. In some countries a high proportion of the population may have literacy difficulties, especially in some developing countries without a well-established educational system and a high dependence on an oral tradition. In 1991, the national literacy level in India was 52.21 per cent (Daswani 2001) it has since increased to 60 per cent (*Economist* 2007a). In many societies gender and literacy are intimately related. In India the male literacy rate in 1991 was 64.13 per cent, compared with only 39.29 per cent for females. Around 70 per cent of children who do not attend school are girls. (See also Rockhill (1993) on Hispanic women in the USA.)

Second, there is a discourse surrounding ethnic literacy, for example black literacy and Jewish literacy are specific domains (Wallendorf 2001). In multicultural societies many consumers may use a first language that may not be the dominant language spoken in country in which they are residing. For example, we know that large numbers of adults for whom English is not their first language comprise a significant proportion of the functionally illiterate in the USA and many other societies (Adkins and Ozanne 2005).

Third, the dominance of the English language in global communications may disadvantage some consumers more than others. Furthermore, English has developed as a glocal language with a range of different variants. In the not too distant future the number of native speakers will be outnumbered by non-native speakers and therefore the centre of dominance will change. Furthermore, whiteness theorists maintain that language is one mechanism by which ideologies of whiteness are reproduced and in this respect language becomes synonymous with power (Wetherell and Potter 1992; Steyn 2005; Taylor 2005). Whiteness is intimately related to the English language and Westernization but its reading will be different according to the standpoint of the participant. The use of English is unlikely to be perceived in the same way in India, which underwent colonization by the British for 200 years, and Denmark, an affluent, white, advanced society that has historical links with British English (Yano 2001). Furthermore, there are differences of opinion between Indian academics, some of whom consider the imposition of English during colonialism as a form of violence (Shome 1999) and others who view it as an agent of decolonization that effectively connects those that have historically been linguistically disenfranchised to a global system (Valsh 2005).

Literacy is crucial to our understanding of consumer behaviour since there are significant numbers of consumers even within advanced Western societies that are functionally illiterate, whose reading levels are poor, who have difficulty interpreting and comprehending prose and documents, and performing simple mathematical calculations. Even larger numbers of consumers are marginally illiterate referring to the ability to locate basic information in texts and to make simple inferences (Adkins and Ozanne 2005). Marketers should be interested in illiteracy since research has shown that low levels of literacy can be related to a range of negative market outcomes. These have included choosing incorrect products and the inability to understand pricing information (Adkins and Ozanne 1998); effort versus accuracy trade-offs involved in making purchasing decisions (Viswanathan *et al.* 2003); making sub-standard product choices because of being overly dependent on visible cues such as product advertising and packaging (Jae and DelVecchio 2004); and the vulnerability that consumers face during the purchase process and the high levels of stress that this can induce (Adkins and Ozanne 2005).

Further complications occur in differences between ideographic writing systems, such as in the languages of the Asia-Pacific region (e.g. Chinese), that are very different from the alphabetic systems used in Western languages. The structural differences between languages may impact on consumer information processing. Consumer memory is affected in Chinese and English by 'presentation mode', the way brands are learned, and in 'memory mode', the way they are remembered. Chinese consumers are more likely to recall information when the visual memory, rather than the phonological memory, is accessed. Whereas the reverse in true for native English speakers. Marketers should therefore structure their communication strategies to reflect this by using visual representations to Chinese speakers to enhance their natural tendency to rely on visual memory. For native English speakers, exploiting the sound quality of the brand by use of jingles and onomatopoeic name creations may be more successful (Schmitt *et al.* 1994).

Cross-cultural perceptions of colours

Colour is an integral part of the communications mix and has been found to influence moods, emotions, consumer perceptions and behaviour in both consumer and industrial marketing (Clare and Honeycutt 2000). There has also been an undercurrent of racist ideology concerning perceptions of colours. In the past, advertisers commissioned research that allegedly found evidence that Africans perceived a narrower range of colours than whites. Later the biological determinism was replaced with cultural determinism but the taboos about colour remained and were reproduced by advertisers. Burke (2002) spoke to advertisers that maintained Africans were frightened of bright colours.

Colour choice and usage differs among cultures at various levels of economic development, and in different geographical locations. In areas where the light is extremely bright, colours and contrasts tend to decline in intensity thereby making it more difficult to distinguish between colours. Economic development and technological advancement also influence colour use since companies in industrialized nations have a wider range of colours from which to choose than those in less developed countries, and there are also cost considerations to factor into the equation. The use of more colours usually means more expense which companies in less developed countries may not be able to afford. Colour has become a competitive tool in its ability to differentiate one organization's profit offerings from another. Most of the research that has been undertaken on colour in marketing focuses on Anglo-Saxon cultures. Insufficient attention has been paid to culture differences in perceptions of colour and how they can result in communication failures. For these reasons, some marketers have suggested consulting local agencies on the use of colours rather than international advertising agencies (Ricks 1983). It would seem that a systematic colour theory that takes account of cultural differences would be a valuable addition to the cross-cultural marketers' armoury (Aslam 2006).

One of the most authoritative accounts of the relationship between culture and colour is Gage's (1993) text *Colour and Culture*. Cultural beliefs about colour have existed since antiquity. In the fifth century BC, the Greeks referred to the distinctions between black and white, or darkness and light and introduced a scheme of primary colours; white, black and red, and a range of mixes from yellow to green. Medieval and Renaissance colour use reflected religious symbolism. The four elements of nature were related to four colours, scarlet (later red) with fire, white (later black) with earth, blue with air, and purple (later white) with water. Colours were also given mystical interpretations: blue denoted heaven, scarlet charity, purple martyrdom, and white was devoted to chastity and purity. Some colours were associated with precious metals: gold, scarlet and purple extracted from precious pigments became symbols of power, authority and opulence. In the fifteenth century colour was recognized as a function of light and Newton was the first to establish a colour wheel comprising seven colours lined in a circular arrangement.

Aslam (2006) identifies two schools of thought with respect to human behaviour and colour: that colour perception is innate, or that it is learned. The innate perspective maintains that colour signals to the brain trigger an affective response when confronted with a colour stimulus. Whereas the learned perspective argues that over time, colour preferences are learned and are the subject of shared meanings and associations with language, literature and myths. Colours have different meanings and aesthetic appeals in different cultures, but our understanding is largely confined to English speaking and Asian countries.

A study in the United Kingdom demonstrated that colour signals product attributes such as quality and price. The colour white was referred to as 'crap' and below average, beige/neutral equated to being dull and boring but considered expensive for a particular segment (including older people), pink was viewed as looking young, red garish and tacky. A similar study in the USA indicated that dark colours were associated with richness and value, and dark grey with expensive, high tech products. Perceptions of food are also associated with colour. The flavour of cakes and ice creams are often anticipated from their colour. Colour has also been linked to product associations in the USA: blue with toys, health foods, dairy foods, deserts, and financial services, red with toys and pizzas, silver with dairy foods, green with health foods, vegetables, toys and financial services, yellow with toys, dairy, health and deserts, and pink with cosmetics and Barbie dolls.

Different cultures have different colour preferences that are akin to country of origin effects. The colour red is most favoured by Americans, green by the Lebanese, blue-green by Iranians and Kuwaitis. Some countries are also associated with certain colours more than others. China is often associated with red, purple with France, green with France and Italy, blue with the USA, and red with Asia. These associations could be used for the packaging of country of origin products in foreign countries. It has also been noted that in some countries colours are paired with others that have a similar meaning. Colour has also been used to reflect consumer values in advertising. For example, Volkswagen showed a black sheep in a flock in Italy as symbolic of the characteristics of a VW owner, meaning being independent and self-assured. A black sheep in Italy has positive associations with independence, whereas in other cultures a black sheep is symptomatic of being an outcast.

Celebrity endorsements

Celebrity endorsements are a widely used method of promotion. In the mid-1990s, it was estimated that in the order of 20 per cent of all television advertising in the USA featured a famous person, a celebrity, as an endorser (Agrawal and Kamaura 1995). Many successful personalities in countries around the world are obtaining the status of celebrities. Celebrities are drawn from fields as diverse as entertainment, sport, cuisine, politics, and business. The media are saturated with celebrity and magazines have been developed to feed the insatiable appetite to know the intimate details of celebrity lifestyle. In his book *Celebrity Sells*, Pringle has this to say about the prevalence of celebrity:

> Celebrities are giving us ideas on how to dress, what to say, what to do, what to eat, what to buy, how to have sex and with whom, where to live, what to drive, and where to go on holiday. Increasingly they are telling us how to modify our appearance, not just by means of cosmetics, clothing and other accessories, but by use of medical treatments and cosmetic surgery.
>
> (Pringle 2004: 46)

From a marketing viewpoint, the ability of celebrity to overcome advertising clutter and generate high recall rates, differentiate product images, and generate sales and profits makes celebrity endorsements a lucrative strategy. Various approaches have been advanced to explain how celebrity endorsements work. The first, the *source credibility model*, relating to effectiveness of the message, depends on the level of expertise and trustworthiness of the source. Expertness in this context refers to the *ability* of the source to be informed enough to make assertions, and trustworthiness is the perceived *willingness* of the source to make valid assertion. For example, in the context of high-technology oriented products, expert endorsers, rather than celebrity endorsers, have more impact on consumers' risk perceptions (Biswas *et al.* 2006). The *source attractiveness model* also has its roots in social psychology. According to this approach, the effectiveness of the message depends on the familiarity, likeability and similarity of the source. However, some celebrities who are athletic and attractive also antagonize people, and they too have been successful endorsers. John McEnroe the tennis player, was famous for upsetting viewers when he questioned the umpire's call with the phrase 'YOU CANNOT BE SERIOUS', yet he successfully endorsed disposable razors in the mid-1980s (Kahle and Homer 1985).

Cultural significance of celebrity is that it adds value over and above what could be achieved by an anonymous model. Celebrities deliver meanings that add 'extra subtlety, depth, and power': for example, they offer a range of personality and lifestyle meaning that enhance the product that an anonymous model could not provide. Models and actors are merely playing a role or reading a script, whereas celebrities are a feature of real life, and celebrities 'own' their own meanings because they created them in the public arena (McCracken 1989: 315). The value of celebrity endorsements for marketers is how closely the meanings the celebrity brings can be aligned to and enhance the marketing plan. This synergy will allow the consumer to first identify and then transfer meaning. Some people are more sensitive to celebrity endorsements than others, people moving on from one age category to another, people going through role changes or status mobility, and those who are newly arrived from a culture use the meaning of celebrity endorsements to help navigate meanings in consumer society (see McCracken 1989: 315).

Some celebrities attain the status of global celebrity. It was for this reason that Michael Jackson was signed up by Pepsi following the global success of his *Bad* album that demonstrated his hold on young people. Michael J. Fox was signed up for precisely the same reasons – global brands and global celebrities are a good combination. In order to attain worldwide status celebrities have to transcend national borders and overcome cultural differences in global marketing communications. Yet in order to be successful celebrities have to encompass the cultural values and aspirations of different societies, since advertisers have demonstrated that successful advertisements are those that are congruent to the norms and values in which the ad is disseminated.

Choi *et al.* (2005) maintain that despite the importance of celebrity in marketing promotional strategies, there have been few studies of the different incidences of celebrity endorsements across countries and they tend to be limited to assessing the frequency of appearance, rather than the ways in which the strategy is implemented cross-culturally. This is an important omission since the percentage of advertisements worldwide that feature a celebrity have doubled in a little over a decade to number 17 per cent (Money *et al.* 2006). Most research on celebrity endorsements has focused on the positive aspects of this promotional strategy. Little attention has been given to the negative aspects of celebrity endorsements such as what damage occurs to a brand when the celebrity tarnishes his or her public image. Yet it is clear that negative information about celebrities can have a negative effect on the brand and sales of the products they endorse. Madonna has moved beyond national markets and established a reputation around the world as a global icon. She agreed to shoot a Pepsi ad in 1989 to her new song 'Like a Prayer'. The campaign cost $5 million and debuted in the USA and in 40 other countries. She had not told Pepsi she had filmed a sacrilegious video for MTV in which she 'cavorted in front of burning crosses, displayed Christ's stigma on her hands, and made love with a black saint on a church pew'. Amid huge public outcry of the video, Pepsi decided to pull its own ads (Prendergast 2000: 377). The British model Kate Moss had her contracts terminated by *Chanel* and *Burberry* because of reports of her association with cocaine. Research has indicated that negative information about celebrities attracts far more attention than positive attributes and is more easily recalled by consumers.

Money *et al.* (2006) have explored the effect of a negative celebrity endorser in the two different cultural contexts of Japan and the USA, which both make extensive use of celebrity. The national culture of the two countries is different and this feeds into promotional strategies. For example, the differences in advertising have already been noted: Japanese ads tend to be symbolic compared to the information-based approach that is common in the USA. The advertising message in Japan is more subtle and is related to Japan's 'high context' culture compared with the 'low context' culture of the USA that favours more explicit communications. Furthermore, celebrity endorsements are incredibly popular in Japan, as many as 70 per cent of advertisements feature a celebrity and 90 per cent of the most popular ads include a celebrity. An important reason why celebrity ads are so popular in Japan concerns the issue of trust. Japanese consumers are particularly swayed by advertising messages that incorporate trust as a central issue. Given the strongly collectivist culture in Japan it might be expected that negative celebrity endorsement information may be perceived as more important than in the more individualist nature of US culture.

Results of the experimental study found that negative information about a celebrity who endorsed a brand did not lead to negative perceptions of the brand, and the same pattern of results were similar for US and Japanese respondents. When the negative information was given by the celebrity rather than from some other source it had a more positive effect on purchase intentions in both groups. Money *et al.* (2006) maintain that self-oriented, negative information can evoke sympathy and empathy among consumers that in effect augment the product. The practical outcome for many endorsers when a celebrity misbehaves is to drop the celebrity as a damage limitation exercise. Money *et al.* indicate that this course of action may not be necessary or justified, and rather than being a liability the celebrity may become more of an asset.

Product placements

Product placement involves incorporating brands in movies, soap operas, video and computer games, books and other forms of media in return for money, some promotional transaction or other forms of recompense. This type of placement has been viewed as something of a hybrid between advertising and publicity, and has proven itself a valuable addition to the promotional mix. The majority of the product placement literature has focused on product placement efficiency as a method of promotion and its ethical acceptability. Some scholars have reported that prominent product placements, as opposed to lesser props, are better than television advertising in generating brand recognition, recall, and attitude, but little of this work focuses on purchasing behaviour. As far as ethical issues are concerned, consumers tend to differentiate between ethically charged products such as cigarettes, alcohol and guns as being more unethical than soft drinks, automobiles and cameras (Gupta and Lord 1998). Relatively little attention has assessed the performance of product placement in a global context (Gould *et al.* 2000). This neglect is interesting to note when one considers that many of the carriers of product placements are media intended for global audiences.

The issues of standardization versus adaptation are as relevant to product placement as they are to other areas of global marketing communications, and an important concern is how they are perceived by consumers in different cross-national and cross-cultural groups. While cultural products such as movies are marketed around the world it is impractical to have different international versions based on different versions of product placements. It is rather a case of having standardized product placements or nothing. Nevertheless, it would be helpful to have an understanding of how a global marketed product would be perceived in different cultures.

The history of product placements in movies dates back to the Lumière films of the 1890s (Newell *et al.* 2006). In her book *Product Placement in Hollywood Films: A History*, Kerry Segrave (2004) indicates that product placements only became an integrated part of Hollywood movies in the mid-1930s. At this time there was a noticeable trend to show branded products in entertainment feature films but also to mention them by name. Product placement grew sharply from 1978 to 1981, partly due to the emergence of product placement agencies that acted as brokers between manufacturers and movie makers but the most significant milestone was the movie *E.T.* that was released in 1982. The film's success in establishing sales for the confectionary product Reese's Pieces was the start of a spectacular period of growth for product placement. Sales of the candy jumped 70 per cent within a month of the film being released. Two months later, 800 cinemas that had not previously sold the item, stocked the candy at concession stands.

Following the success of *E.T.*, major Hollywood producers publicly opened themselves up for placement business and some even published price lists. At the end of 1983, 20th Century-Fox became the first major Hollywood filmmaker to offer manufacturers a display of their branded products in return for cash. Another high point in the history of product placement was in the summer of 1993, when *Jurassic Park* was released, including in excess of 100 corporate tie-ins. Lining up manufacturers to have products placed in movies was nearly as important as the hiring of a big-name star and director. Segrave suggests that at the turn of the millennium, there was a shift from 'Hollywood the Dream Factory to being Hollywood the Ad' (2004: 212). Product placement had certainly become a significant source of funding.

The reason for the success of product placements in the movies tends to centre around the fact that movies have consumers' full divided attention. A hero or heroine can endorse the product in the film, placing products in a 'naturalistic' setting rather than an artificial ad, and a verbal mention rather than just the visual was found to aid brand recall. Various studies have demonstrated that US consumers do not mind product placements, providing it is not overdone. Consumers do not view product placement as a form of intrusion. Successful lifestyle product placement is not just about getting the product on screen, but to have it associated with the right stars, movie and image. Some companies have also become more sensitive to the way their products are used in movies, or indeed whether they are included at all. Having beer brands used in a violent film about a drunken wife abuser would do little to enhance the brands concerned, and in fact could be highly detrimental. Coca-Cola has long been recognized as a convenient symbol of Western civilization, and not always a healthy one. In *The Gods Must be Crazy* and *The Coca-Cola Kid*, the drink is indicative of a sinister force and a harbinger of unhealthy values (Prenderast 2000: 448).

While Hollywood was first to introduce product placements, the practice has caught on around the globe. Nelson *et al.* (2005) have undertaken a content analysis of brand placement in Bollywood movies at four points in time (1991, 1996, 2001, 2002) since the liberalization of markets in India. The results demonstrate that over the period, international brands were more likely to be woven into the plot than domestic brands. A survey of middle-class respondents reported both positive and negative effects towards product placements. Among the cosmopolitan section of the sample, the Westernization of product placement was welcomed since they look for cues in films to inform their product purchase decisions. However, ethnocentrism among some consumers had negative effects on perceptions of Western products. The opening up of the national television network, allowed private sponsors to become involved in programme production and the film industry quickly became the source of supply for television since there were many film producers that wished to work in a new medium. In recent years the television viewing population in India has dramatically increased from 60 million in 1985 to around 250 million. Large national and international corporations such as Tata, Godrej, Proctor and Gamble and Colgate quickly got involved as they saw it as an opportunity to directly or indirectly promote their products (Pendakur 2003).

Gould *et al.* (2000) are amongst of the few academics to research cross-cultural product placement in movies in their study of consumer attitudes in Austria, France and the USA. Their results indicate that country, product and individual differences exist. And although country variations exist, they are not huge. The Americans came out as the most accepting of product placements, and more likely to purchase products they saw at the movies. It may be the case that product placements may need further advertising support in some countries. With respect to products, ethically charged products (cigarettes, alcohol, guns) were less acceptable across all countries. As far as individual differences were concerned, women had a more negative attitude towards product placements than men especially where ethically charged products were concerned. The limitation of the study is that it focused on Western countries and samples need to be more wide ranging. For example, in Japan consumers prefer the soft sell rather than the hard sell associated with USA. Therefore, overt or explicit product placement may be received unfavourably, whereas a more subtle approach may work better. Also differences within countries that might perhaps be based on ethnic origin need to be given consideration. Another range of issues relevant to cross-cultural research are country-of-origin effects, associated with ethnocentrism and animosity in relation to the movie and products placed in it.

Most of the research on product placements has focused on movies. However, of greater significance in the cultural realm are soap operas that are exported around the world and are often the media of choice among the population. Most of the literature has tended to focus on television soap operas, but radio soap operas were a popular medium for product placements in the USA from the 1930s, especially in their connection with promoting labour-saving devices, and disseminating product-related expertise (Lavin 1995). The continuity over long time scales makes them an important promotional vehicle for marketers. Soap operas are a global phenomenon and their audiences can be huge and extremely loyal. It seems that each country has its favourite soaps that reflect the important social, economic and political issues of the day (Allen 1995). They were first developed by Proctor and Gamble the multinational detergents organization (hence *soap* opera) who targeted them at female audiences scheduled for afternoon viewing. Indeed Proctor and Gamble owns several day-time soap operas which it sells around the world as a vehicle for advertising its own products (Das 1995). When scholars have analysed the product placement strategies in the soaps of different countries some interesting differences emerge. A comparison of product placement strategies in New Zealand and American soap operas found that American programmes displayed more consumption imagery relating to leisure and appearance-related items. By contrast, the New Zealand soaps tended to focus on products that were related to transport and food. Overall, almost half (46%) of the episodes contained actual brand references but the figure was much higher in New Zealand (70%) than the USA (26%) (Pervan and Martin 2006).

In Brazil product placements are the main funding source for soap operas along with some government funding. They are also limited to 180 to 200 episodes, unlike the format in other parts of the world where soap operas can go on indefinitely. The inclusion of government funding has had an important impact on the themes that soap operas address. There is more of an emphasis on social merchandising strategies that include social and educational messages as well as commercial concerns. Plots tend to focus on class conflict and social mobility and include activities relevant to political, cultural and economic issues. The reading of product placements are not necessarily viewed in promotional or advertising terms, but rather as part and parcel of the lifestyles of upper-class urbanities (Pastina 2006). Brazilian soap operas have been exported to 112 countries and have been particularly well received in Asia and China where some joint productions have spun off (Schelling 1998). Soap operas were introduced into India in the 1970 from Mexico. The early Mexican soaps were fashioned as education programmes, akin to social marketing to spread the doctrines of family planning, literacy and to promote social harmony (Das 1995).

One of the newer product placement strategies is to place them in computer game advertising (referred to as in-game advertising) to attract the millions of people worldwide who play consumer games rather than watch television (Nelson *et al.*, 2006). Sales of computer and video games in the USA grew to $7.3 billion in 2004, comprising the sale of 248 million products. Around 50 per cent of the population play, 35 per cent under the age of 18, and 43 per cent between the ages of 18 and 50. Although brand names in games can be traced back to the 1980s, there has been an increase in this advertising expenditure from $79 million in 2003 to $250 by 2008. For the video and computer games industry product placement can bring in additional revenue in addition to adding to the realism of the game. But as yet there is little by way of significant evidence of the payback in terms of brand recognition or increases in sales. These factors are especially significant in computer game advertising since games require the player to respond to the game using the controller rather than to just watch the film passively as is the case with movies. The interactive characteristics could interfere with the ability of the player to recall the placed brands (Yang *et al.* 2006). This final issue has been addressed more recently by Lee and Faber (2007) that the location of the brand message in the game (referred to as proximity), game involvement and prior game experience all interact to influence brand memory. They conclude:

> Although experienced players in the moderate-involvement condition recognize focal brands better than peripheral brands, the recognition superiority of the focal brands over the peripheral brands disappears when experienced players' involvement is high. The interaction between proximity and game involvement does not emerge for inexperienced players, however.
>
> (Lee and Faber 2007: 75)

Far less emphasis has been given to the product placements in books. Examining popular language usage in bestselling novels after the Second World War Friedman (1985) identifies a huge increase in brand names and generic names in texts. Product categories given a high profile included cars, magazines, sweets, beer and toiletries, while Coke was the leading brand name. Friedman developed the phrase 'word-of-author advertising' and suggested it had important implications for marketers, consumers and consumer researchers. The product placement literature is rapidly evolving with new areas including gender responses to different types of product placement in television sitcoms in the USA (Stern and Russell 2004), characteristics, types of programmings of product placements on the television in the USA (La Ferle and Edwards 2006), and their use in game shows (Gould and Gupta 2006).

Social responsibility in advertising

The theme of social responsibility is one that permeates virtually every aspect of cross-cultural marketing, and advertising and communication is no exception. Indeed 'Responsibility in Advertising' was the theme of a special issue of the *Journal of Advertising* in the summer of 2007 (see Polonsky and Hyman 2007) but disappointingly only two papers were written from a cross-national perspective (Dolnicar and Jordaan 2007; Hassan *et al.* 2007). Responsibility in advertising can be operationalized in a range of ways including understanding the role of persuasion in consumers' behaviour patterns (Hassan *et al.* 2007), the effects of deception in advertising (Shabbir and Thwaites 2007; Shanahan and Hopkins 2007), and privacy concerns (Dolnicar and Jordaan 2007).

Advocacy advertisements are a controversial aspect of corporate advertising since they intend to influence audiences about the issues that are outside of the usual domain of products and services. Advocacy ads are most commonly used by organizations that sell products that carry some element of risk attached to them. For example, these may include oil and gas, alcohol, tobacco, and pharmaceuticals. Sinclair and Irani (2005) maintain that in the USA, Shell Oil's ads on driver safety, or Budweiser's effort to promote responsibility in the context of drinking and driving, differ from public service initiatives since the advocacy ads fulfill the function of protecting the company's market. The goal is to generate an awareness of an organization and enhance its image in a positive light. They argue that marketplace advocacy ads 'can be defined as messages that emphasize building acceptance for a particular product or service by addressing consumer concerns' (Sinclair and Irani 2005: 59). Three types of advocacy ads have been identified as focusing on the marketplace, political concerns and values. Marketplace advocacy ads are designed to provide a platform for acceptance about the company's products or services, or the business practices that create them. As a consequence there is an increasingly blurred line between what passes as public service announcements, paid advocacy ads, and editorial content.

One of the first companies to use this strategy was Benetton, a well-known clothing retailer that has outlets in 120 countries and is recognized for targeting controversial advertising appeals to many cultures, races, religions, lifestyles and challenging consumers' values. In its advertising promotions in 1991–1992, the company used photograph-posters and prints of catastrophes that were indistinguishable from what Falk (1994: 180) describes as 'catastrophe aesthetics' of the network news. Some of these images included a ship packed full of Albanian refugees, some of them failing overboard, pictures of a burning car, another of a dead man lying in a pool of blood, the image of an AIDS victim and his family shortly after his death. The Benetton ads were novel because they transgressed the traditional boundaries of advertising that overwhelmingly depicts the good things in life. When Benetton was questioned about how the ads came to be developed, the owner maintained that it was a waste of resources to focus on the clothes, rather that the idea was to make them feel the reality of living in an unjust world in order to pave the way for a brighter tomorrow. Noble intentions that are laudable, but Benetton nevertheless were successful in mobilizing an undercurrent of popular opinion and commodifying it in a way to sell clothes. Global issues that travel well can be valuable promotional tools. More recently, research has been conducted to assess the match between consumers' values, values consumers associate with Benetton and its advertising, and liking the company and its advertising. Polegato and Bjerke (2006) conducted a study of consumers in Germany, Italy and Norway to study this aspect of Benetton's advertising, and found advertising to be effective when directed at consumers' value systems and the potential for that to be transferred to the brand and buying intentions.

Lash and Lury's (2007: 155) study of the operation of global culture industries noted that in Latin America, and emerging economies worldwide, the culture industry is vastly different from Anglo-Saxon and even Continental media regimes. The reason why it differed was because culture industries were much more closely tied to the state and politics. The important role of the state in transforming the advertising context in India is supported by Oza (2001). She maintains that the visible changes in India are remarkable where retail outlets have replaced the old brand names with multinational goods and billboards advertise Citibank and Levis jeans. However, the most dramatic change of all was the privatization of television. In 1987, there were three state-owned channels available in the major metropolitan areas and by 1996 the number of channels had increased to around 40 international and domestic satellite and cable channels. This rapid expansion has given rise to a television software industry to fill airtime and provide an alternative to English-language programmes such as soap operas and game shows. Several satellite channels were beamed from outside India thus outside the jurisdiction of the state. This has caused cultural conflict and law suits centering on the representation of women, offensive advertising, and films. One high profile example was the mobilization of opposition against the Miss World beauty pageant.

One major problem for marketers in an age of global communications is the heterogeneous local conditions that may prevent organizations standardizing international advertising. Governments around the world confront many similar challenges concerning the protection of consumers and the promotion of fair market conditions, and this commonality may form a common round in the resulting advertising despite profound social, economic and political differences. Advertising regulation can take a number of forms that correspond to different degrees of control of the host country and include anything from laissez-faire to varying degrees of government regulation and self-regulation in between. International trade organizations have also been proactive in providing models on which national marketing self-regulation should be based.

The form that regulation takes varies from one country to another and is based on ideological positions concerning the nature of capitalism and protection of the consumer interest. Classical economic theory maintains that foreign ownership of the mass media should be unhindered along with foreign equity positions, the number of foreign personnel that work in ad agencies and the scope and nature of advertising strategies. The situation is rather different in some of the poorer countries of the world and there has been some concern about allowing the dominance of foreign owned advertising operations and the regulatory implications have been more stringent. For example, Tansey and Hyman (1994) maintain that dependency theory as a major paradigm of development economics has been a significant force in Latin America where perceptions of advertising regulation are concerned.

According to dependency theory, governments in weaker economies should act to rectify the social inequities resulting from free markets. The percentage of foreign ownership in promotional media should be restricted, foreigners should hold only minority equity positions in ad agencies and that the extent and reach of advertising should be limited. Dependency theory would support investment in local infrastructure, facilitating technology transfer and providing white collar local jobs rather than less developed countries being part of an outpost of foreign multinationals. The role of advertising in generating an environment of conspicuous consumption among the wealthy and the poor is another concern, since it may promote unhealthy lifestyles and distort the indigenous culture. The trend of the wealthy to emulate consumption and lifestyles of affluent Western consumers increases the demand for imports. Advertising promotes luxury and non-essential goods among the poor, for example cigarettes. Furthermore, dependency theorists maintain that the dominance of multinational companies and the advertising messages they promulgate amount to cultural imperialism that assists the substitution of different values and beliefs.

A different perspective of the relationship between advertising and regulation is evident in the Soviet Union. Wells (1994) questions the wholesale adoption of Western concepts and maintains that Western advertisers and academics held misperceptions about advertising in the Soviet Union. He argues that there were three misperceptions '(1) the Soviets had not created, produced, or used advertising to promote goods and services; (2) prior to 1988 there were no advertising agencies in the Soviet Union; and (3) the only "correct" advertising system is one based on a free-market Western model' (Wells 1994: 83). The central concerns of Western advertisers have been circulation, reach and frequency in the production and placement of advertising. However, in the Soviet advertising context these factors were not perceived as critical for a number of reasons. First, television and radio advertising was highly constrained due to the difficulties of scheduling broadcasts across the eight time zones across the country. Magazine and newspaper production and circulation were dependent on paper and ink and the ability to deliver copy to news stands and people's homes. Furthermore, the Soviet population was perceived to be a captive audience since which ever mass channel was chosen it was state-owned and was distributed throughout the Soviet Union.

Foreign companies that approached the indigenous advertising agencies were keen to be the first in a new marketplace and were eager to understand the complexities of a new terrain. A problem was that Western advertisers wanted to stick with methods that they knew worked back home. So if they advertised in a particular way they believed they were more likely to control consumer response. While Western advertisers sought to establish brand names customers were not familiar with Western-style advertising methods, the products that were being offered, the high retail prices or the fact that the products were more difficult to source in retail outlets than domestic products. In the rush to be the first they made mistakes, as Wells notes.

Proctor and Gamble and Colgate-Palmolive had imported personal hygiene products in selected markets in the Soviet Union. The advertising objective was to establish brand names. However, Soviet consumers were unaccustomed to Western-style advertising, much less products that were higher priced and less readily available through retail outlets than domestic products . . . In the Soviet Union such advertising was perceived as an invasion of homes and personal lives. It touted goods that were relatively unaffordable, unavailable, and simply inconsequential in the prevailing lifestyle.

(Wells 1994: 89)

This approach came across as ignorant of the cultural differences and thus prompted speculation that these companies did not have any long-term commitment to the marketplace.

Wells maintains that organizations in Russia understood that they needed to selectively adopt Western marketing practices to avoid losing out on important marketing opportunities. Russian culture and traditions in the context of language, art, music and literature contribute to debates about what advertising means. He notes that 'domestic firms were reluctant to eliminate symbols of the Russian culture in structuring advertising messages or traditional media use, whereas foreign firms resisted using cultural symbols for their products. Indigenous advertising agencies attempted to revitalize advertising with 'Russians' enchantment with animals, fables, and word plays' (Wells 1994: 90). However, agencies counseled against using these symbols in the international marketplace. Wells maintains that as each former Soviet republic attempts to develop its own identity through re-visiting its own history, Western advertiser should be concerned with viewing advertising as cultural communication that is embedded in social and economic contexts and not just a way of accessing a new marketplace.

The cultural diversity in Malay society is particularly significant in the context of understanding the regulatory environment. Malays live side by side with Chinese and Indians, and there is significant religious heterogeneity (Islam, Buddhism, Taoism, Christianity, Hinduism). The variety of spoken languages – including the official language, Malay, plus English and Chinese dialects such as Hakka, Mandarin, Cantonese and Hokkien – create a challenging environment for those involved in promotion and advertising (Marinov 2007). Waller and Fam's examination of advertising regulation in Malaysia is focused on protecting the indigenous Islamic culture from the influence of foreign values. The Malaysian *Advertising Code for Television and Radio* (1990) prohibits

[the] adoption or projection of foreign culture which is not acceptable to a cross section of the major communities of the Malaysian society either in the form of words, slogans, clothing, activity or behavior ways of life that are against or totally different from the ways of life followed by Malaysians.

(Waller and Fam 2000: 11)

Also disallowed are images and products that offend religious, racial, political, or sentimental susceptibilities of any section of the community. It is interesting to note that if English is used in advertisements that are broadcast or published, 'Malaysian English' must be used.

Questions

*   In what ways do advertisers operate as cultural brokers?
*   What are some of the criticisms that have been levelled at multicultural marketing strategies within different cross-cultural contexts?
*   How do language and literacy impact on cross-cultural advertising strategies?
*   Describe how celebrity endorsements work in diverse cross-cultural settings.
*   Why have product placements become an important cross-cultural marketing method?

Further reading

Agrawal, M. (1995) 'Review of a 40-year debate in international advertising: Practitioner and academician perspectives to the standardization/adaptation issue', *International Marketing Review*, 12 (1): 26–48.

Burke, T. (1996) *Lifebuoy Men, Lux Women: Commodification, Consumption, and Cleanliness in Modern Zimbabwe*, London: Leicester University Press.

Duncan, T. and Ramaprasad, J. (1995) 'Standardized multinational advertising: The influencing factors', *Journal of Advertising*, XXIV (3): 55–68.

Gould, S.J., Gupta, P.B. and Grabner-Krauter, S. (2000) 'Product placements in movies: A cross-cultural analysis of Austrian, French and American consumers' attitudes toward this emerging, international promotional medium', *Journal of Advertising*, XXIX (4): 39–49.

Kjeldgaard, D. and Askegaard, S. (2006) 'The glocalization of youth culture: The global youth segment as structures of common difference', *Journal of Consumer Research*, 33 (2): 231–247.

Landau, P.S. and Kaspin, D.D. (2002) *Images and Empires: Visuality in Colonial and Postcolonial Africa*, Berkley: University of California Press.

Money, B., Shimp, T.A. and Sakano, Y. (2006) 'Celebrity endorsements in Japan and the United States: Is negative information all that harmful', *Journal of Advertising Research*, March: 113–123.

Nelson, M.R., Deshpande, S., Devanathan, N., Lakshmi, C.R. (2005) 'If the table for McWorld has been set by Hollywood, What is served by Bollywood', *Advances in Consumer Research*, 3 (1): 473.

Sinclair, J. and Irani, T. (2005) 'Advocacy advertising for biotechnology: The effect of public accountability and corporate trust and attitude toward the ad', *Journal of Advertising*, 34 (3): 59–74.

Stern, B.B. (1999) 'Gender and multicultural issues in advertising: Stages on the multicultural research highway', *Journal of Advertising* 28 (4): 31–46.

Wallendorf, M. (2001) 'Literally literacy', *Journal of Consumer Research*, 27 (4): 505–512.

Wells, L.G. (1994) 'Western concepts, Russian perspectives: Meanings of advertising in the former Soviet Union', *Journal of Advertising*, XXIII (1): 83–93.

5 Distribution

Introduction

The spatial concentration of ethnic populations is a feature of most societies and it is therefore an important aspect of cross-cultural retailing. A more recent development has been the emergence of gated communities. The first section of the chapter focuses on these two developments. The second section of the chapter traces the development of the department stores as a cross-cultural phenomenon, followed by the internationalization of the supermarket format. Supermarkets are an established retailing format in advanced societies but this is not the case in developing economies where small shops better suite the needs of consumers' consumption patterns. Shopping malls have achieved almost iconic status as temples of consumption in consumer societies of the Western world. It is important to note the importance of culture in the context of the design, the service delivery, and the profile of the consumers that frequent the stores.

An interesting feature in many countries is the persistence of traditional methods of retailing. An interesting example are traditional markets that date back centuries and are a good fit with consumers' consumption patterns and religious norms. Alternative variations on markets are more informal methods of retailing such as car boot sales and secondhand markets which will be discussed in section three. The fourth section of the chapter spotlights direct selling as a cross-cultural retailing strategy. First developed in the USA it has rapidly spread around the world. The big players in the market include Avon, Amway, and Tupperware who have successfully adapted their sales techniques to new markets. The penultimate theme discussed in the chapter is outshopping. Outshopping refers to the process of travelling beyond the local urban market to shop. International outshopping requires moving beyond one's national boundaries to shop and it is becoming an important part of life for some consumers. The final section of the chapter takes up the theme of racism and discrimination through a discussion of redlining in retailing.

Spatial concentration of ethnic populations

In many societies ethnic groups are concentrated in geographic enclaves. World cities including Los Angeles, London, and Paris are central nodes in a global system of trade, communication and migration (Sassen 1991). These cities have been joined by urban areas that are experiencing ethnic diversity that is of more recent origin giving rise to the concept of 'EthniCities' (Roseman *et al.* 1996). The spatial concentration of minority groups in specific localities is a feature of many advanced societies (Marin and Marin 1991). In the USA, metropolitan areas including New York, Los Angeles, San Francisco and Washington, DC have ethnic populations (African American, Asia American and Hispanic American) that easily comprise more than 50 per cent of the population (Frey 1998). In Canada many ethnic minorities have settled in Canada's three largest cities, Toronto, Montreal and Vancouver, alongside a few immigrant gateway cities. Ethnic minority populations comprise 40 per cent of the population of Toronto and Vancouver and about 14 per cent in Montreal. Furthermore, the concentration in three cities has intensified in recent years (Hou 2006). In Britain, 30 per cent of the current population of London has either been born abroad or are the children of parents born abroad (Penn 2000). In New Zealand, 53 per cent of the ethnic minorities live in Auckland (Light 1997). At the turn of the millennium, 42 per cent of the non-Western ethnic population in the Netherlands lived in the four largest Dutch cities (Tesser *et al.* 1999). Recently, ethnic segregation has also been found in the former state socialist countries of east central Europe and the former Soviet Union, within major metropolitan areas and medium sized industrial cities (Gentile and Tammaru 2006). Ethnic residential segregation has intensified for most groups in Sweden over recent years, and this is especially true for new immigrants (Brama 2006; Harsman 2006).

Massey suggests that social scientists in the USA have been reluctant to acknowledge or address the consequences of the 'new' immigration or its spatial implications. This neglect results from a 'fear of cultural change and a deep seated worry that European Americans will be displaced from their dominant position in American life'. However, a failure to engage with geography will result in broadly based generalizations in assuming that individuals with similar cultural, demographic and lifestyle characteristics will have similar consumer behaviour patterns regardless of where they reside. There is also an assumption that the same marketing strategies will work equally well in different places.

The residential segmentation of cities along the lines of social class and ethnicity has been a feature of the urban landscape for many years. Some of the most extreme cases are in the large cities of developing countries. For example, Mumbai (formerly Bombay) is India's financial and industrial capital and the fifth most populated city. Home to a global elite, property prices in the centre are extremely high. Among the obvious affluence, there is significant poverty with over half the city's population living in slums. This situation has earned the city the name of 'Slumbay'. Housing conditions are very poor with 80 per cent of houses smaller than 100 square feet (9 square metres) (Mukhija 2003). This pattern is repeated in other parts of India including Madras (de Wit 1996), in Bangladesh (Pryer 2003), and Manila in the Philippines where 40 per cent of the city's population live in informal settlements (Shatkin 2004). This scenario is repeated in many other areas of the Third World where the globalization of major cities is occurring. However, Firat and Dholakia (1998) maintain that enclaves of the poor and rich are appearing in both the economically developed and underdeveloped world to such an extent that it is becoming difficult to apply the labels of economically developed or underdeveloped at the level of the country.

Gated communities have emerged in many countries around the world and they provide a form of total exclusion across the lines of social class and ethnicity (Atkinson and Flint 2003). Mycoo maintains that:

> the ancient self-contained walled cities were places of grandeur where all members of the community had access to shared facilities such as baths, recreation space, churches, and community meeting places, and walls served as a mechanism for defence against invaders. The modern gated community is a residential area with restricted access, where normally public spaces have been privatised, and public goods are privately provided or maintained.
>
> (Mycoo 2006: 131)

The design of gated communities have much in common with the ancient walled cities with respect to keeping undesirable characters out, reinforcing notions of inclusion and exclusion through the use of security guards, armed guards, and entry-phones. Contemporary gated-communities appeared in the USA in the 1970s and in the developing world in the mid-1990s. Sassen (1991) argues that gated communities developed in global cities as a consequence of global restructuring. International competition has led to a highly stratified workforce of a transnational elite and significant numbers of working class engaged in low paid insecure work and the unemployed. In everyday life this polarization leads to a dual-city structure where the guarded elites live in enclaves and organize their own consumption, education, leisure and housing.

The emergence of gated communities in the developing world has occurred in the last two decades. Within Latin America and the Caribbean gated communities emerged in the 1990s, with many individuals in the middle and upper classes choosing to live in gated communities in cities such as Caracas, São Paulo, Buenos Aires, Mexico City, Kingston, Puerto Rico, Port-au-Prince and Port of Spain. Mycoo (2006) maintains that a number of features are responsible for the upsurge in gated communities in Latin America including some of the highest rates of homicides and other violent crimes, drastic cuts in public spending, unemployment, poverty, social and cultural heterogeneity and diverging lifestyles under the influence of globalization. Strong economic growth meant that the richer became richer and wished to move away from crowded busy centres to the suburbs. The gated communities were marketed as a new way of life that was copied from the US model.

> They are characterised by 'artificial worlds' of shopping centres, housing, and leisure ghettos that represent spaces for the realisation of their consumption needs and image, as well as the new spaces of social contact. These artificial worlds also exist in the cities of the Caribbean where elites share space in glitzy shopping malls, citadels of luxury housing, and members-only clubs.
>
> (Mycoo 2006: 133)

Gated communities are representative of residential segregation as opposed to racial segregation and the overriding factor for their emergence in Latin America are security needs of locals and expatriates. In Cape Town, South Africa, gated communities have arisen for the same reasons (Lemanski 2006). In Saudi Arabia gated communities have a different function from those in advanced Western societies, Latin America, South Africa, and the Caribbean. Gated communities in Saudi Arabia are designed to contain expatriate culture, for the benefit of those inside and outside the gates (Glasze and Alkhayyal 2002).

Retail formats

Department stores

In this section of the chapter, three retail formats are discussed; department stores, supermarkets and shopping malls. In 1840 department stores did not exist, the retail wisdom of the early nineteenth century stressed specialization as opposed to the wide assortment of merchandise that became the defining characteristic of the department store. Over the next 50 years the department store would flourish and the retail format would be exported to far flung parts of the world. Susan Benson (1988: 12) suggests that department stores are often defined as downtown stores that sell an extensive range of household goods, furnishings as well as dry goods and clothing. However, she argues that this definition is somewhat narrow since it fails to appreciate the lead role managers took in developing management strategy and a public presence for the store. From the late nineteenth century the department store was symbolic of consumer culture and became established in every major city of the Western world. The stores became acceptable spaces for respectable and unaccompanied women, along with other public spaces including 'great exhibitions, galleries, libraries, restaurants, tearooms, hotels and department stores' (Nava 1997: 61). Luxurious architecture was used as an important way of attracting attention. Department stores in Paris, London, New York and Berlin often took up whole blocks of the street and their architecture often surpassed the most important public buildings. Department store owners drew on religious imagery, calling stores 'cathedrals', and their goods as 'objects of devotion'. Women were referred to as 'worshippers', consumption a moral act, and shopping was often depicted as the religious duty of women (Domosh 1996).

Department stores signalled a new era of retailing by providing diversified offerings, adopting a one price system, a commitment not to misrepresent merchandise, promising refunds/exchanges for unsatisfactory goods, and allowing free access without having to buy. A woman shopper could spend the whole day in just one store, browsing the merchandise and socializing with friends. A one price strategy was a necessity, with over one hundred people being employed in some department stores. Not all employees could possibly be trusted to negotiate prices with customers. The free entry strategy was to exploit impulse buys and thus move stock more quickly throughout the store. Giant sales were a feature at the end of the season to make way for new stock that could be adaptable to taste and demand. This practice was in contrast to traditional stores that kept goods in stock at the same price until they were sold. Department stores were also innovative in the ways they promoted themselves. They advertised widely across a range of media, and made sure their huge windows were dressed with enticing 'prestige' products for customers to buy. Department stores also worked hard to present a convincing case to women to buy their merchandise on the basis of fashion, quality or price (Benson 1988).

Integral to the department store ethos was the quality of the service that was on offer. Benson provides some insights into the attention to detail:

> Doormen bowed customers into the store while uniformed chauffeurs whisked their cars off to the garage and attendants received their wraps and packages. When shopping became too wearing, they could relax in a restaurant to the music of live musicians, refresh themselves with a hot bath, or distract themselves by attending a lecture, viewing an art exhibition, or planning a vacation at the travel bureau.
>
> (Benson 1988: 85)

The quality of service accorded to consumers was not always as high as women expected, however. In marketing surveys women customers often complained that sale assistants lacked warmth and a natural friendliness, and that stores were bureaucratic. While (male) managers perceived women customers as too demanding and articulated their desire for more male customers.

In Russia department stores were located in major cities by the 1850s. The stores were built on elite consumerism compared with urban markets and necessities for poorer sections in society. Foreigners dominated the stores in Moscow, especially the French, and the stores were called *magazin*, the French word for shops. Instead of shopkeepers, new stores were staffed with polite, well-dressed clerks. Another feature was the standardization of prices which did away with the bargaining process. By contrast with the new department stores, the existing older types of stores looked unmodern and non-Western as a consequence of Russian contact with Asia (Stearns 2001).

In Egypt, Abaza (2001) notes that shopping centres were first introduced in the late nineteenth century, coinciding with their introduction in Europe. By 1910, an eighth of Cairo's seven million inhabitants were foreigners and at the time the rich indigenous population reflected the tastes and lifestyles of rich Parisians. Even now, for many older people in Cairo department stores evoke 'nostalgia for refined taste and images of fashionable, upper-class women being attended to by skilled sales women and men. The staff became known for their good manners. The experience of shopping in such stores was in itself a form of elevation' (Abaza 2001: 103).

From the 1870s onwards, the Bon Marché in Paris organized concerts attended by thousands of people. The Dufayel department store in Paris had a theatre for 3,000 guests and a Cinematograph Hall for 1,500; both acted as a form of advertising. In 1902, a new Marshall Field and Co. store opened in Chicago and was decorated with cut flowers on every counter, shelf, showcase, and desk as well as banners and string orchestras playing over several floors. Interestingly, Marshall Field refused to allow shoppers to purchase goods on its first day, focusing all the attention on the lavish show. The department stores encouraged leisurely window shopping. Unlike the *flaneur* of the Parisian arcades, the modern shopper was not regarded as a suspicious character, but was encouraged to linger and make use of the lavish surrounding without having to make a purchase. Until the early nineteenth century, entry into a shop came with the obligation to make a purchase. When the Bon Marché store was opened in 1852, all the prices of goods were fixed and clearly marked, doing away with lengthy negotiation of the value of a product. The focus on a more rational shopper, and a design that focused on more modernist principles of simplicity and the generous use of space as an indicator of taste and luxury, emerged in the early decades of the twentieth century (Grunenberg and Hollein 2002).

Not everyone was in favour of the elegant and flamboyant department stores. Not least the small shop and mail order businesses that thought they were losing ground. Indeed there was hostility to department stores in many countries at the end of the nineteenth and twentieth century in Germany, France, Canada and the USA (Coles 1999). Department stores went through some difficult times towards the end of the last millennium. Their huge premises, expensive high street sites, the out-of-town malls, and the return of the designer boutique all took their toll on the department store which came to look as though it was a relic of retailing of a bygone age. In the 1990s, Lowe and Wrigley (1996) suggest that the department store began to enjoy a revival in the United Kingdom. They are no longer just associated with major retail groups, but have been reinventing themselves in some locations as 'flagship stores', incorporating their own label as their only product identity. The 'Dr Marten's Department Store' in Convent Garden, London is one example and there are many others in upmarket shopping areas around Bond Street. As Lowe and Wrigley note:

> Like their nineteenth-century equivalents the contemporary department stores combine within their 'spaces', designer interiors, rituals of display and leisure, sexuality and food. At Donna Karen in Bond Street, for example, DKNY mineral water, New York bagels and New England cheesecake allow the contemporary consumer to lose themselves in the ultimate 'own label' experience.. . .Dolce and Gabbana 'flagship' in Sloane Street has been designed on a palazzo style and combines both classical and modern elements. Furniture includes gilt picture frames and baroque divans.
>
> (Lowe and Wrigley 1996: 25)

Supermarkets

When people go food shopping, over 95 per cent of them do their main shopping at a supermarket. This was the startling finding of the state of food shopping in Britain provided by William Young (2004) in his book *Sold Out: The True Costs of Supermarket Shopping*. Even more astonishing is that the four largest supermarkets sell around three quarters of the country's groceries. Supermarkets are such an integral part of the culture of Western societies that it might be taken for granted that it was always like this, and similar developments will occur around the globe.

It is important to recognize that food shopping has not always taken place in supermarkets. In the middle of the nineteenth century, going food shopping for the middle classes in Britain would have involved visiting a local store, called a Grocer's, that specialized in selling traditional food and sugar, spices, tea, coffee and so forth, and buying fresh eggs, butter and cheese in open-air markets, or from specialist cheese mongers. Ironmongers would sell a whole range of goods associated with keeping the home in good order, such as paints, brushes, coal, firewood, various sorts of tools and oils. In this era, the grocers were a skilled group of people who were very knowledgeable about their products. They would provide a personalized service to their regular customers and were often considered upstanding members of the community. Businesses were often handed down from one generation to the other, and business success was dependent on the quality of goods on offer and the owner's honesty. By contrast, the working classes would purchase goods from open markets, or market halls that were being built in the cities. However, there were some undesirable downsides of this quaint retailing era. The opportunities for cheating on measures was present because much of what was sold was prepared by the grocers, very few commodities came pre-packed. Also, prices were seldom fixed and as a consequence customers had to be prepared to bargain.

The term supermarket did not come into common usage until 1956, although supermarkets as recognizable entities were established in California in the late 1920s, and a few years later in some of the eastern states of America. The term supermarket evolved from the term *super* meaning 'that which surpasses' and *market* referring to 'place' (Charavat 1961: 6). The design of the stores aimed to bring different areas of food retailing, including credit facilities (in some cases), and delivery under one roof. This was a more convenient way of shopping for the consumer and economies of scale that arose from high volume sales could be passed on to customers in the form of cheaper prices. In many instances the old style grocers and corner shops have been unable to compete due to smaller mark-up in a competitive area, and the inability to buy in bulk which mitigates getting a good price from wholesalers and manufacturers. Many small stores have competed by selling very high quality specialized goods, or by opening longer hours. As the power of the new supermarkets grew, they developed into large chains, resembling what exists today. Systemized and huge buying power enabled retail chains to make new demands on retailers and manufacturers and in some cases dispensed with wholesalers completely and invest in manufacturing plants (Strasser 2006).

In advanced Western societies there has been considerable concern about the power and dominance of supermarkets and their ability to influence consumer culture. In the USA, there has been considerable concern over Wal-Mart's domestic and global operations. The company is regarded as the largest profit-making business in the world, and does more business than Target, Home Depot, Sears, Kmart, Safeway, and Kroger combined. It has in excess of 5,000 huge stores around the world of which 80 per cent are located in the USA. It employs 1.5 million people around the globe and is the largest private employer in the USA, Mexico and Canada. It imports more goods from China than either the United Kingdom or Russia. The company operates a low wage, low-benefit personnel policy and seeks to employ young people, retirees, and those that are willing to work part-time. In the United Kingdom, the dominance of supermarkets has led to a major decline in specialist independent stores such as butchers, bakers and greengrocers, and the availability of local and regional produce. There are also concerns about the way supermarkets bully suppliers and farmers who are often at the mercy of a small number of supermarkets to purchase their produce (Young 2004). Concerns have also been expressed about their location policies; invariably they choose the most affluent areas to establish stores, leading to food deserts in poorer areas.

Of the world's top 250 retailers, 104 have no international operations at all. The retailer that has the most international outlets is France's Carrefour, which has stores in just 29 countries. Carrefour is the leading supermarket in China having in excess of 300 stores in this lucrative market. Low levels of internationalization in retailing contrasts sharply with multinationals in other industries that might operate in 100 or more countries (*Economist* 2006d). The internationalization of retailing literature is replete with examples of retailers entering new markets and having to withdraw shortly afterwards (Bianchi and Ostale 2006). There is often an assumption that formats that work well at home, can be transferred unproblematically elsewhere. Variations in consumer culture, shopping habits, and the existing retailing infrastructure that is embedded in local cultures have caused problems for Western retailers seeking to expand abroad. The wider the cultural differences between the retailers and the indigenous culture, the more pronounced the difficulties seem. There appear to be particular difficulties in developing countries, yet theoretically they hold the greatest potential due to extensive population growth, and the emergence of a significant middle class.

In 1974, Stanley Hollander, a famous and well-respected marketing historian, noted the foreign inspiration of many retailing developments in the USA in his paper 'Cosmopolitanism and chauvinism in American retail trade', published in the *Journal of Retailing*. He also reported 'an unfortunate indifference to foreign *retailing* developments' (Hollander 1974: 3) among academics and practitioners due to the long period of American leadership in self-service, accounting and mechanization and the view that foreigners have little to offer. He noted that comparisons are often made between country X and country Y being like America ten or twenty years ago. The emphasis was on the new and exciting and little else is brought to the agenda. It is too simplistic to suggest that all supermarkets borrowed the format from the success of the USA. For example, Goldman (1974) provides evidence of the emergence of supermarkets that grew from small family stores in Latin America and Israel, by increasing their product lines and then moving to produce, and then fresh meat; developments that were independent of applying the of US model. In Israel, consumers persist with traditional forms of shopping even when well-developed, supermarket infrastructure exist (Goldman 1982). There is even some confusion about the term supermarket when viewed in its cross-cultural context. What qualifies as a supermarket in one country may not qualify in America. Furthermore, a whole variety of different terms and formats fall under the 'supermarket' label: discount supermarkets, regular supermarkets, superettes, superstores, and food emporiums are just some of these different terms. Assessing the development or antecedent forms of the supermarket in the USA may widen the possibilities of formats to use in the developing world (Goldman 1975/6).

India has the highest density of retail outlets in the world, approximately 15 million compared with 900,000 in America where in value terms the market is 13 times bigger. In India retailing is the largest provider of jobs outside of agriculture accounting for 6–7 per cent of employment and about 10 per cent of GDP. Organized retailing only accounts for 2–3 per cent of the total and 96 per cent of that is concentrated in the ten biggest cities and 86 per cent in the biggest six. However, despite its low base, organized retailing is growing at 18–20 per cent per year (*Economist* 2006f). India has 12 million small traders, street sellers and mom-and-pop shops called *kiranas* that provide small amounts of credit and cater to people making purchases on their way home. Consumers use these shops for purchasing small quantities 'two or three sweets to children, a single cigarette to another customer, and tiny tobacco sachets every few minutes' (Elliott 2007: 14). Further down the retailing hierarchy are traders in city marketplaces and roadside shopping areas selling a range of produce including vegetables, herbs, fruit and flowers, betel leaves, banana or dry lotus leaves that are used as plates, and snacks. Many vendors operating in 'unofficial' street markets pay no rent but bribes paid to police takes its place (Lessinger 2001).

Retailing in Latin America follows a similar pattern to that in India with large numbers of small retailers supplying a significant proportion of goods, especially to lower income consumers. D'Andrea *et al.* (2006b) indicate that lower income consumers in Latin American countries comprise 50–60 per cent of the population and 30–40 per cent of the purchasing power. In real terms these percentages equate to 250 million consumers who spend $120,000 million a year on fast moving consumer goods. This group of consumers are not destitute but live in houses with running water, electricity and basic domestic appliances. Around 90–100 per cent of all consumers in the socio-economic categories C and D have a television, radio and refrigerator.

During the 1990s, a number of foreign retailers established a presence in the region in an attempt to attract the purchasing power of this segment of the market, although with mixed success. Wal-Mart has achieved considerable success in Mexico which it entered in 1991 by acquiring Cifa the leading chain of self-service stores. In 2004, it had 696 stores generating sales equivalent to $12 billion. With 101,000 employees it is the country's largest private employer and some have argued that it is a threat to sovereignty. However, Tilly (2006) argues that three factors will limit the company's growth in the future: imitations, inequalities in incomes that make Wal-Mart prohibitively expensive for some parts of the population, and economic crises and stagnation that result in consumers reverting to more traditional methods of shopping. Large supermarkets account for 45 per cent of sales in Brazil, 45 per cent in Mexico, 51 per cent in Argentina, 38 per cent in Colombia, 53 per cent in Chile and 55 per cent in Costa Rica. Traditional stores account for 13 per cent of sales in Brazil, 47 per cent in Mexico, 18 per cent in Argentina, 46 per cent in Colombia, 27 per cent in Chile and 38 per cent in Costa Rica. However, the more astonishing figures are the numbers of traditional stores in each country compared with large and small supermarkets. There are 285,000 traditional stores in Brazil, 432,550 in Mexico, 98,600 in Argentina, 159,000 in Colombia, 60,600 in Chile and 10,000 in Costa Rica (D'Andrea *et al.* 2006c).

D'Andrea *et al.* (2006b) maintain that traditional stores tend to be relatively small affairs and provide an over-the-counter service, small self-service stores are a subset of small supermarkets but are low tech and usually operate without cash registers by the owners, and open air street fairs are characterized by a semi-permanent or mobile infrastructure. The persistence of small retailers is a consequence of a number of features. First is their location since many lower income consumers make daily purchases and need a retail outlet near where they live and work. The convenience of having a shop available lowers their total purchases costs since they do not have to pay travel costs. The stores are often cluttered and less tidy in appearance but consumers tend not to mind, hygiene is the most important factor and owners ensure that their premises and goods are hygienic. Many low income consumers perceive large modern supermarkets as a cost since ultimately it is the consumer that has to pay in the form of higher prices. Sales in these shops can be as little as 10 per cent of what a large supermarket would achieve per square meter but they compensate for this in other ways.

Second, the small retailers offer an appropriate range of products to meet their consumers' needs, and these include goods from the 'informal sector', in other words stolen goods. The traditional stores focus on selling 'fresh food, drinks, and basic dry goods, along with a limited selection of cleaning products, personal care items, and luxury food items (canned fish, cookies)' (D'Andrea *et al.* 2006b: 665). Most of the goods stocked are well-known brands. The store owners also stock small sizes of products that are more affordable to those on low incomes. For example, the smallest packet of washing powder for sale at a large supermarket is 500 gram; whereas small retailers stock 150g and 250g packets and some store owners will divide these into smaller quantities. Open air markets sell fresh produce and consumers can purchase as much or as little as they want. Consumers indicated that they would feel ashamed asking for such small quantities in a large supermarket. Knowing what their consumers want to buy is the key to the success of traditional retailing, since inventory turnover is twice as high in this sector as it is in large supermarkets. This enables inventory to be effectively converted into cash.

Third, the smaller quantities come at a price with exact substitutes costing 5–20 per cent more in traditional stores than in the large supermarkets. However, from a supply side perspective this is understandable since the traditional stores did not sell anywhere near the volumes of their larger competitors and are at a procurement disadvantage because of purchasing relatively small volumes. The higher costs do not put customers off shopping in traditional stores, what they are more concerned about is the total value of the purchase. Street markets do provide price advantages in the context of fresh produce. Furthermore, large supermarkets sell only good quality produce whereas street sellers provide a range of quality which makes them flexible on price.

Finally, small-scale retailers benefit from being locally owned and part of the community, and as a consequence they can provide a personal touch. Being friendly and offering appropriate advice develops a rapport with the consumers and helps enhance customer loyalty. Some shops accept credit cards and others provide their own informal credit facilities. Informal credit can take the form of writing the amount in a notebook to be paid at some time in the future. Another method is the 'virtual wallet' allowing customers who are short of change at the checkout to pay the next time they visit the shop. In this way credit operates as an informal loyalty programme, debtors within the community tend to be stigmatized thus loans are usually repaid. It is for all of these reasons that the dominance of large supermarkets and hypermarkets will not capture extensive market share within the lower income segments any time soon.

The trends that have been noted above with respect to India and Latin America are also observable in parts of the Far East. In Vietnam there have been some significant changes in the retail environment: traditional wet markets and bazaars have been superseded by stores shopping malls and supermarkets. Interestingly, Mai *et al.* (2003) suggest that this new shopping environment has generated a situation in which impulse buying is flourishing. Impulse purchases tend to be small and relatively inexpensive due to the low standard of living in Vietnam. Clothing, items used within the home, music items and gifts predominate among impulse purchases, and products for personal use are more susceptible than those for collective use.

In Malaysia in 2002 it was estimated that there were 29,656 retail outlets, of which more than 95 per cent were grocery stores which account for two thirds of consumer expenditure. Big brand names dominate the large department stores and hypermarkets in which the more affluent urban consumers shop. International retailers including Carrefour and Tesco own about half of the hypermarkets in Malaysia. Nestlé and Kraft dominate the dairy sector; Kellogg leads on breakfast cereals, McDonalds, KFC, and Pizza Hut have between them cornered the fast food market, and Cadbury–Schweppes, Mars and Van Houten between them dominate the chocolate, sweets and snack market. Brand recognition for these goods is high, however, there is also a thriving domestic food production sector that comprises small local companies that cater to individual tastes. It has been estimated that in excess of 3,000 small, family-owned companies cater for traditional local tastes producing favourites such as noodles and cakes. The products from these outlets are reputedly preferred by most rural and about half urban consumers. Most consumers shop daily and favour small quantities of high quality at low prices. The relationship the store owners have with their consumers is an important aspect of retaining business (Marinov 2007).

Shopping malls

Shopping centres were first developed in California in the USA in the 1920s. Supermarkets would serve as an anchor in the area and attract other smaller stores. In 1922, the Country Club Plaza was built in the suburbs of Kansas City and was the first shopping centre to be built that was only accessible by car. In 1931, the Highland Park Shopping Village in Dallas was the first group of stores that had its own stores and located with their front away from an access road. The first proper enclosed mall was developed in a suburb of Minneapolis in 1956. The venue was marketed as a place to escape the harsh weather, life, crime, dirt, and trouble. These aspects of mall shopping are major advantages, the controlled environment that eliminates a suggestion of unpleasant realities is reassuring to mall shoppers. Malls were developed as a response to what shopping in the city could not provide – clean, safe environments where people could walk and see each other. By 1960, there were 4,500 malls in the USA accounting for 14 per cent of retail sales, and these figures had increased to 16,400 centres accounting for 33 per cent of retail sales by 1975. In 1987 there were 30,000 malls accounting for over 50 per cent of retail sales. Some malls are so large that they are retail, social, and community centres (Feinberg and Meoli 1991). In the USA they have been heralded as the new town square where diverse groups of people come together. By contrast, the centres of many cities that were the shopping hub have been abandoned to the homeless and drug dealers after office hours (Staeheli and Mitchell 2006).

The vast mast majority of shopping in the USA is undertaken in malls. Most department stores are in malls, so are national chains of shops, restaurants and professional services such as legal and medical services. Malls are of considerable financial significance but they have also become a way of life – a consumer paradise to some. One survey indicated that Americans were spending more time in malls than anywhere else apart from, home, work and school. They certainly provide for a one-stop shop but much more besides. Malls are spaces where consumers can play out their fantasies in an enclosed space away from the outside world, where retailers provide the staging, props, lighting, and mannequins. People-watching is an activity in which people engage when they are not necessarily looking for something to buy. The 1970s witnessed the segmentation of malls, especially those catering to the tastes of the nouveau riche. White Flint in Washington is an example of a 'speciality mall'; it specializes in providing goods and services for rich people, high-end fashion shops, a greater variety of eating places and is anchored by a very fashionable department store. These high-end malls also function as cultural centres, for staging art exhibitions and Shakespearian festivals (Kowinski 1985).

Mall mania is not confined to the USA; it is a retail format that has been widely replicated in many countries all over the world. The West Edmonton Mall in Canada was until recently the largest mall in the world, containing 800 stores, ice skating and 24 movie screens (Feinberg and Meoli 1991). Malls exist all over Western Europe, South America, the Far East and Russia. In Japan there is an underground mall in Tokyo that has 46 movie theatres, more than 1,500 restaurants, 15 discos, and 699 Mah-Jongg parlours (Kowinski 1985: 23). Just five years ago there were shopping arcades but no malls in India, today there are around 100 big shopping malls. The country's largest mall is being built in Bangalore at an estimated cost of US$250 million, not in the sprawling suburbs but in the city centre a kilometre away from the central station in order to attract passing traffic (Tippu 2007b). Despite their popularity, malls are not always great places to work or shop. The work is tedious, employees have to work long hours, and they are underpaid. The working conditions are poor, shop assistants cannot see what is going on in the outside world, there is a lack of clean air and the light is bad. For their part, consumers complain about inattentive and inexperienced staff, or are alienated by false chirpy staff putting on a show, or the banality of the décor.

The focus of existing research has centred on advanced industrial societies which raises the issue of the extent to which similar developments exist in developing countries and whether they perform the same retailing functions. In some countries like Taiwan and Thailand malls have become part of the urban landscape over the last decade, that have attracted many foreign entrants (Feeny *et al.* 1996; Trappey and Lai 1996). In other countries they are more firmly established. In Egypt contemporary shopping malls are highly differentiated according to the customers that use them. The World Trade Centre caters for middle-classes and in its welcome to shoppers it describes itself as combining 'the old touch of Egyptian Islamic bazaars with ultra-modern European galleries' (Abaza 2001: 112). The mall includes 75 shops selling a range of high quality goods including clothes, accessories, furniture, art galleries, coffee shops, etc. Leisure facilities are also included such as cinemas, fitness centres and discotheques. Hotels and housing apartments are also part of the package. The Bustan Centre would hardly qualify as a mall in the eyes of many Europeans and caters for lower middle class youths that frequent cheap coffee houses and bowling and billiard centres. It is largely an extension of a huge car park. The Yamamah Centre is Saudi owned and provides for specific tastes including 'high-heeled shoes, glittering clothes and children's games, attracting mainly Saudis' (Abaza 2001: 109–110). The most exclusive is the recently opened First Mall in the District of Guizeh, and it is one of the most lavish buildings in Cairo. Its exclusivity is preserved by high levels of security and expensive restaurants and coffee shops that exclude the poor. Women shop assistants remove Islamic scarves when taking up their positions and put them on again when they go home.

In Turkey shopping malls and new shopping districts appeared in the main cities in the post-1960s period and shopping visits and window shopping became part of the middle-class women's lifestyle. Durakbasa and Cindoglu (2002) maintain that a rapid proliferation of shopping malls has occurred in the 1980s but that stratification among shopping habits of women within different social classes exists. Before the malls were built department stores did exist but the number of overseas stores that have relocated suggests that their development will expand considerably in the future. The emergence of the mall has transformed gender relations in the shopping experience and the physical architecture. The *charshi* was an integral element in the planning of Ottoman town centres and comprised small shops under the control of guild associations. Traditionally a sex-segregated shopping culture existed in which buyers and sellers were men. Women had limited access to the *charshi* and their visits would be accompanied by men, children and servants. The sex-segregated nature of shopping persists in many provincial towns.

In China, foreign companies have been allowed to participate in the retail sector since 1992 and in that year the government gave its permission for a joint venture with the Japanese company *Yaohan* to build a 120,000 shopping centre in Shanghai. By 1997, there were 500–600 retail joint ventures in China. China is currently home to the world's largest mall, the South China Mall in Dongguan. Developers travelled abroad for two years in search for the right model. By 2010, China is expected to be home to at least seven of the world's ten largest malls. Chinese malls generally have a different architecture from those in the USA. They usually have many levels that rise up rather than out in the two-level style found in the USA. Chinese consumers arrive by bus and train and increasing numbers are driving there. On a busy day, one mall in the southern city of Guangzhou attracts around 600,000 shoppers. A wide range of consumer goods are for sale: mobile phones, DVD players, jeans, sofas and self-assemble furniture. There is food from many areas of China and franchises of large international companies such as McDonalds and KFC, along with IMAX theatres. Stores without Western roots sell Gucci and Louis Vuitton goods (Barboza 2005). However, not all malls are successful and there are many huge malls that are almost empty. Attracting the right mix of tenant is key to attracting shoppers (Tippu 2007b).

Before the reforms consumer choice was severely constrained, since purchases had to be made from state-owned shops. These offered a limited range of products, at the same price. There was little incentive for consumers to make price comparisons, and the quality of the service was usually poor. Prior to the reforms, customers were not allowed to touch products and thus foreign retailers have adapted their storescapes for this reason by making displays more elaborate. The Chinese are also very brand conscious, and this has meant organizing displays by brand rather than function in some stores. The stores of foreign retailers in China employ more employees than, say, a UK store of a similar size. This partly reflects the differences in labour costs but is also due to higher expectations of customer service on the part of Chinese consumers of foreign companies. Indeed some consumers aggressively assert their rights as consumers. The whole concept of self-service was novel to Chinese consumers and as a consequence they were compelled to shop in a different way. Foreign shops were more trustworthy in a country where fakes are abundant (Gamble 2006).

Far less attention is paid to the socially divisive nature of malls, in reflecting the inequalities between the rich and the poor, the haves and the have-nots. An extreme example that reflects these differences is the police helicopter that patrols over Plaza Las Americas in San Juan, Puerto Rico to demonstrate that the area was safe during the busy Christmas shopping period (Kowinski 1985). The shopping mall has even become part of the retailing landscape in Cuba that has long demonized mercantilism and consumerism. Carlos Tercero in Central Havana is a self-contained mall that was opened in 1998. Shoppers must possess dollars or convertible pesos to make purchases in Carlos Tercero. It is a space full of new, Western products with few reminders of the scarcity and dilapidation of the Havana outside its walls. The mall provides Cubans with a window on the global economy, both in relation to the goods on sale and the shopping experience itself. However, the vast majority of Cubans are not active participants in consumer society and shopping at Carlos Tercero and other similar outlets is beyond their means. Gordy makes the point that consumer culture is not the same as popular culture in Cuba. Shopping malls like Carlos Tercero provide opportunities for conspicuous consumption that few Cubans can participate in, but perhaps more importantly, they represent a culture that is at odds with Cuban socialism that promotes unity, equality and nationalism:

> The mall offers everything: home appliances, cosmetics and perfume, clothing, pet supplies, shoes, a food court, and more. There is a Benetton store where T-shirts for children cost $25. The grocery store sells sugar cereals, peanut butter, imported apples that cost up to a dollar each, olive oil, and other tinned products that most Cubans could never afford. There is even an 'everything for a dollar' store in the US tradition, where one can buy plastic toys and flowers, buckets, and pencils, much of it made in China. Everything is 'only a dollar' even when a dollar's worth of Cuban pesos can buy you sixty bus rides . . . ten cinema tickets, ten pounds of oranges, on five packs of unfiltered cigarettes. However, a dollar in the world of dollars in Cuba gets you very little. In the grocery store like the one in Carlos Tercero, a can of *Tropicola*, the Cuban-brand cola, costs forty-five cents and a beer costs sixty cents. A stick of butter can cost up to a dollar, more than what it costs in the USA. Toilet paper costs $1.40 for four rolls. Eggs cost from ten to fifteen cents each. When the highest salary in Cuba is $40 a month [2000 prices], these prices are very high indeed.
>
> (Gordy 2006: 404)

Freitas (1996) has compared various shopping centres in Brazil with the Parisian Forum des Halles. Freitas maintains that the shopping centre symbolizes the ideal city, protected from pollution and nature. Paralleling the increase in violence in Brazil, shopping centres increased from one in 1980, to 19 in 1995, as a way of providing a safe shopping experience. The Barrashopping is the largest shopping centre in Latin America and its selling point reflects its role as 'humanizing' space against violence (cf. Abaza 2001). The issue of safety in the shopping experience is also noted by Frosh (2007) in connection with ongoing conflicts in Israel. He notes,

> One would expect people to never quite get used to being checked for explosives on their way into shops or cafés or even actively to resent it. But as I have said, the security check and the security guard have become routine, unstoryable components of everyday life. More telling still, there is no evidence of great discomfort and opposition to them. Extra security charges are frequently added to restaurant and café bills to cover the wages of guards, and these rarely meet opposition from customers. Security checks and guards appear to be perceived by consumers and advertised by cafés and restaurants as necessary and welcome features of the landscape of consumption.
>
> (Frosh 2007: 471)

Somewhat similar issues have been addressed in connection with gunmen terrorizing shoppers in Washington DC in the USA. Consumers changed their shopping behaviour as a response and preferred to shop at central, well-known stores as opposed to those off the beaten track, switching to on-line shopping, and being more aware of the location of the parking in the context of the store (D'Rozario 2004). While George Ritzer (1999) has referred to shopping malls as cathedrals of consumption, in some cultural contexts they are also fortresses of consumption, denying the noise of the outside and shutting out its terrors (Frosh 2007).

The examples discussed above demonstrate some of the continuities and differences in the history, development, segmentation and use of malls in various countries. Far less emphasis has been devoted to research on ethnic consumers in shopping malls in different countries yet there is considerable research on shopping centres facilitating ethnic identity maintenance (Miller *et al.* 1998). Shopping malls all over the world are beginning to cater to the needs of consumers with different ethnic backgrounds, cultures, lifestyles and values. Understanding in more depth ethnic and cultural variations will enable mall operators to adjust their offerings including layout, promotional activities and store choice more effectively. Large mall companies in the USA have begun to accommodate the ethnic characteristics of their customers. At Christmas, the majority of malls have all the tree lights and other trappings of the season, but for those that cater for predominantly Jewish and Muslim consumers Santa Claus only makes a cameo appearance. Greenbriar Mall in Atlanta is almost exclusively targeting African-Americans. Yaohan Plazza in Chicago's Arlington Heights, attracts Asian consumers from as far away as Michigan, Ohio, and Kentucky. In Canada, Asian owned shopping malls in Richmond, British Columbia attempt to attract non-Asian clients by developing promotions with ethnic themes (Michon and Chebat 2004). Kowinski (1985) has noted how malls in the suburbs that have been deserted by mainstream white shoppers have reinvented themselves to target the Africa-American market. Landover Mall in Washington DC is a case in point; when it opened in 1972, 35 per cent of shoppers were black, by the mid-1980s the figure had increased to 80 per cent.

Michon and Chebat (2004) have looked at the use of malls by English and French speaking Canadians in Montreal (17% and 83% respectively). Their study found some differences between the two groups. The French were less likely than the English shoppers to use the mall for activities other than purchasing goods and services, although the French shoppers did score more highly on the hedonistic dimension. There were no significant differences in the consumption of various services between the two groups, apart from the fact that the English shoppers were more likely to use the banking services.

Direct selling

Direct selling is a very old form of retailing. For thousands of years, peddlers have carried goods on their backs and pushed carts full of goods to sell to consumers from door-to-door. Peddlers were mostly men, who were nomadic, and worked independently of each other. In the past hundred years this way of doing business has changed. Direct selling has become a highly feminized area of retailing, direct sellers rarely leave their own communities, and the industry is highly organized. Nicole Biggart (1988) has suggested that within America, direct selling has gone through three important stages of development. First were the independent peddlers that hawked their goods throughout the colonial economy. They brought goods, services and information to rural populations without access to small shops in towns and cities. However, when mass merchandising developed in the mid-1800s peddling declined. Not all manufacturers were pleased with the new retail outlets and some organized direct sellers into sales forces to sell their wares. A wide variety of goods were sold in this way including religious books, textiles, shoes, hosiery and personal care items. Automobiles were also sold through direct selling distributors until the First World War.

After the Second World War direct selling began a new era comprising network direct selling organizations and the party plan, a form of selling that exploits social networks. During the Depression direct selling schemes boomed in the USA due to mass unemployment, the offer of casual employment, and no necessity for capital outlay and formal skills. It grew again in the 1970s when people were looking for work at a time of economic stress. This method of retailing also worked well in the USA because it was a good fit for the social and political conditions – the individualist and entrepreneurial culture and the open character of social ties. Feminized areas of retailing grew, where in exchange for a gift the party host would provide a room in her home and some refreshments. Hostesses were encouraged to become commission-based agents themselves. The home party sales system was also a response to legislative changes in the USA that protected house holders from aggressive door-to-door sales people. Since its foundation, the home party system has been used by many companies and exported around the world (Biggart 1998).

Consumers' experiences of home parties have not attracted significant amounts of attention from marketing scholars. What little research has been undertaken suggests that the social relationship between the host and her guests is essential to the success of the parties (Burton 2002). Gainer and Fischer (1991) identified two distinct types of buyers in the USA: 'enthusiasts' purchased at least one major item quickly, were knowledgeable about the products and had obviously attended before, often with the same group of people. The second type of buyer made small token purchases.

Laura Klepacki (2005) provides one of the most detailed accounts of Avon. Avon, the global cosmetics retailer, is the largest direct selling company in the world and operates in 143 markets in 50 countries. Founded in 1886, there are currently 4.9 million Avon representatives across the world, of which 650,000 are in the USA. Avon sells direct over the Internet (http://www.avon.com) but the vast majority of its sales still come from its 'ladies'. Brazil has more Avon ladies (900,000) than it has men and women in its army and navy. The global revenues for 2005 were $7.7 billion. In 2004 Avon sold 2.3 billion products to more than one billion customers. The firm produces 600 million brochures in more than 100 versions in nearly as many languages. The content of the brochures can vary between 10–20 per cent. This variation is due to gift categories outside of beauty since each culture has different gift giving occasions. More beauty products carry the Avon name than any other name in the world. Some 80 per cent of Avon's products are distributed globally and the remaining 20 per cent are regional specialities. By 1990, international sales exceeded those generated in the USA for the first time. Mexico and Brazil were the second and third largest markets respectively. Furthermore, it has proven itself to be a recession proof business; while families may cut back on big purchases women find enough loose change to buy a new lipstick or eye shadow.

In developing countries such as Mexico the sales model resembles the original sales model where people go from door to door to search for new customers, whereas in developed countries Avon is rolling out its Sales Leadership model that provides more of a managerial structure and opportunities for training among agents. The exception is in China where the company hires and trains local staff to run the business to ensure compatibility with the local culture rather than using expatriates. Some of the stories of Avon ladies providing goods for their customers are a million miles away from the glamorous looking assistants behind the make-up counters in department stores. In Iceland Avon ladies have to cross huge swathes of ice with products on their backs, and after the Turkish earthquake in 1991, one entrepreneurial lady rebuilt her family's fortunes by paying for her first package of Avon products on credit and then built up a thriving business by selling lipstick from tent to tent. Yet another example was of an Avon lady in Brazil who paddled canoes through the piranha-infested waters of the Amazon to seek out customers who could only make it into town twice a year.

Avon has also paid attention to the ethnic composition of some of its markets. For example, in response to the growing Latino population in the USA in 1988 it was already investigating targeting Latino consumers including developing the company's first Spanish language television commercial. In 2002 it introduced *Eres Tu* a brochure specifically aimed at Latin women, not just in Spanish, but with products selected to appeal to their unique beauty and lifestyle needs. Latina women use more perfumes than the general population so the focus has been on developing more perfumes to meet the demand from this segment. Avon's selling model has worked well within the social Hispanic culture where there is admiration for the extended family.

Avon has tapped into the global beauty business. A widely reported study by David Buss that logged the mating preferences of 10,000 people across 37 cultures found that women's physical attractiveness came top or very close on every man's list. Beauty in women is often characterized by a number of features; long shiny hair has been a sign of good health, mascara makes eyes look bigger and younger, and blusher and red lipstick supposedly mimic signs of sexual arousal. In most cultures relatively light flawless skin is a testament to youth and health. The beauty business is a global business comprising of skin care worth $24 billion, make-up $18 billion, $38 billion of hair-care products, and $15 billion of perfumes. And it is growing at a rate of around 7 per cent each year. This exponential growth is being driven by wealthier, ageing baby-boomers with higher levels of discretionary income in advanced societies. In developing societies the growing ranks of the middle class have become important consumers in countries like China, Russia and

South Korea. In India anti-age creams are enjoying huge popularity and sales are increasing by 40 per cent a year (*Economist* 2003c).

Tupperware manufactured its first plastic tumbler in 1940. It offered essential household items that no self-respecting middle-class family would be without. Earl Tupper's goal was the 'tupperization' of America. By 1954 the company had a network of 20,000 dealers, distributors and managers, predominantly women between the ages of 24 and 40. The internationalization of the Tupperware sales system began in 1952 when dealers in Puerto Rico wanted their own management teams. Between 1952 and 1956 sales teams developed markets in Africa, Canada, France, Germany, Hawaii, India, the Bahamas, Guatemala and Mexico. In 1957 local sales teams were established in South Africa and Iran. By the 1970s, Tupperware products were being sold in the Americas, 15 European countries, Asia Pacific, the Middle East and South Africa. Initially, there was concern that cultural differences in food preparation, storage and associated domestic rituals would negate widespread adoption. This did not occur as products were appropriated in different culturally embedded ways. For example, Econo-Canisters were defined as Kimono-Keepers for the Japanese market, ideal for keeping ceremonial clothes free from insects and humidity. There were tales from Africa of Tupperware canisters being entirely appropriate for the tropical climate where they were used for storing 'magic' witchcraft powder and replacing traditional ceremonial vessels in connection with palm milking and ox bleeding. It seemed that one thing that Tupperware highlights is the 'cross-culturally recognizable position of women as an economically disenfranchised group, performing labour ostensibly undervalued in a capitalist system' (Klepacki 2005: 190)

Up until the 1970s the industrialized north was targeted but subsequently viewed lesser developed countries as a way of increasing sales. Amway has web site pages that promote 'Amway's Global Village', 60 headquarters in 50 countries and territories. Tupperware and Avon have a global network of around 100 countries. For US direct sales companies substantial earnings come from the 'Third World' and the former Soviet Union where direct sales can bring modern products to far-flung regions without a well-developed retailing infrastructure. Approximately one-third of Avon's sales and one half of its total profits were being generated by new markets in Latin America and the former Soviet Union, Asia and the Pacific. Together, the markets in these regions were growing at many times the rate of those in the mature markets of industrialized countries. Similar trends are also evident at Amway, with one third of Amway's sales occurring in Japan, Australia, Taiwan and Thailand (Wilson 1999). Biggart (1988) suggests that there are cultural reasons why direct selling works well in Asia. First, because they are structured societies where everyday social interactions, including family, are built on a notion of status hierarchy which is not too dissimilar to direct selling. Entrepreneurial spirit is strong within the Confucian ethic which serves as an ideological support as the Protestant ethic did in the USA. Finally, the existence of extended family networks make recruiting and selling easier. These conditions have increased direct selling organizations in Asia but they are not the same as those that have driven expansion in the USA.

Tupperware entered Thailand in 1969, Avon Cosmetics began its operations there in 1978 and Mary Kay in the late 1990s. By 1993, 13 direct sales organizations collaborated to form the Thai Direct Selling Association and sales increased dramatically; US $240 million in 1993, US$400 million, and by 1997 US$ 800 million. The backgrounds of direct sales workers is highly varied as Wilson (1999) explains.

> Direct selling has recruited many women (including *tom*), some men and some third gender *Kathoey*. In Thailand, sellers come from many classes and social worlds: office workers, sex workers, and NGO workers sell from catalogues, as well as farmers, bureaucrats, professionals and wealthy Sino-Thais . . . The diversity of sellers in Thailand offers a revealing index of social flux: wealthy, middle-class and poor people see the need for extra income, and identify direct sales as one self-determining tactic with which to obtain it.
>
> (Wilson 1999: 412)

However, not all of the sales force align their sales practices with those of the company. This is especially true of existing shopkeepers who are merely looking for another line to sell in their store and the office worker that stocks up on favourite products and sells them off at work.

China is emerging as one of the biggest markets for direct sales despite banning 'pyramid schemes' in 1998. The ban came in response to thousands of complaints against pyramid groups. Ten foreign direct selling organizations were allowed to continue operating providing they converted their businesses into 'retail business models'. Single-level, direct selling was allowed in the context of directly contracted sales representatives. Chain-selling or *chuanxiao*, interpreted as multi-level marketing, continued to be banned. Sales representatives were not allowed to buy and resell company products or obtain rewards outside of the commission from products that they had personally sold. The reorganization restricted sales representatives to specific districts, and companies were required to assume liability for their sales representatives. Amway has annual sales of around $2 billion in China, comprising 20 per cent of its global sales, making China its largest market. The company has 130,000 sales reps, selling 180 products and, unlike any other location in the world, it has 130 retail stores in order to comply with the 1998 rules. Mary Kay cosmetics has swapped its trademark pink Cadillac for a pink Volkswagen in China. It has a market worth $120 million and an all women sales force of 120,000. Avon was the first direct seller to enter China and unlike Amway and Mary Kay, it has a retail directed sales model encouraged by the Chinese government. It has 6,300 beauty boutiques and 1,700 beauty counters owned and operated by local Chinese in 74 cities. Stores are less profitable than direct sales because of staff and overhead costs. However, while sales in the USA are falling, revenues from China are increasing by 30 per cent each year comprising $220 million (*Economist* 2005c).

Direct selling is also an option being trialled in rural India by Hindustan Lever, a subsidiary of the giant Unilever consumer goods giant that manufactures detergents and personal goods such as shampoo. Having lost market share to rivals it established self-help groups called *Shakti* to extend its marketing. Tiny loans are offered under the auspice of microcredit to support a direct-to-home distribution network. The company hoped to enlist 25,000 *Shakti* entrepreneurs to cover 100,000 villages and 100 million rural consumers (*Economist* 2004d).

Outshopping

Outshopping refers to the process where consumers travel beyond their local urban market to purchase goods. Outshopping can take a variety of forms, including visiting an out-of-town store, or urban dwellers shopping at country stores. In this particular section of the chapter two specific aspects of outshopping are considered: international outshopping relating to customers shopping in a neighbouring country to take advantage of lower prices and a greater variety of products; and ethnic outshopping in which consumers visit multicultural areas within their own country to shop for the variety of goods on offer.

International outshopping

Piron (2002) observes that each month 900,000 Singaporeans cross the causeway to the Malaysian border town of Johar Baru in order to shop. In extreme cases some Singaporeans buy daily necessities in this way instead of purchasing them in their country of residence. Foreign retailers in Malaysia benefit from lower operating costs and can offer more competitive prices compared to retailers in Singapore where a scarcity of land and shortages of labour drive up overheads. In a sample of 180 Singaporeans who had engaged in outshopping in Johar Baru two thirds of them engaged in the activity at least once a month and a little over half travelled by car. The most popular purchases were food and beverages (27.4 per cent), groceries (24 per cent), and fashion products (17.5 per cent). The most frequent outshoppers were under 30 years of age and two thirds of consumers that outshopped on a frequent basis were blue-collar workers.

The study compared the responses between the three main ethnic groups in Singapore; the Chinese, Malays, and Indians. It was found that there were some differences: the Chinese were the group that had the highest proportion of frequent and infrequent shoppers, but the Malays were four times more likely to be frequent than infrequent shoppers, and Indians were six times more likely to be frequent rather than infrequent shoppers. The survey demonstrated that the two main reasons why consumers outshopped were lower prices and the availability of parking spaces. The shoppers displayed low levels of ethnocentrism; they did not view their spending overseas, rather than at home, as inappropriate, immoral or unpatriotic.

A study of motives for Mexican nationals choosing to shop over the border in the USA indicated that four factors influenced their behaviour. The first was enhanced product quality, followed by better service quality, the availability of more extensive ranges for the fashion conscious, and a more fulfilling shopping experience. All of these features were positively related to consumers' frequency to outshop (Guo *et al.* 2006). Overseas shopping destinations are becoming more common among Chinese consumers, and as a result some luxury shops in Paris are employing Mandarin-speaking assistants. For most Chinese consumers however, Hong Kong continues to be the preferred destination (*Economist* 2004f). The development of new malls in India is a concerted effort to attract India's wealthy elite to local operators, rather than for them to continue to engage in outshopping in Singapore and Dubai (Ahmed 2005). Argentinians flock to outshop in the border towns of Bolivia to buy imported branded goods for half of the price that they would pay in Argentina. For those less well-off, there are fakes of designer products, inexpensive shoes from China and second-hand clothing from the USA. The trip is called Martyrdom because of the long drive it entails on terrible roads but to consumers heaven awaits and it is worth it (Classen 1996).

Ethnic outshopping

Ethnic aspects of outshopping in the same country have attracted less attention than the practice of crossing national boundaries. This aspect of outshopping has been investigated by Crockett and Wallendorf (2004) in relation to African-Americans living in Milwaukee in the USA. They found that some residents shopped in the predominantly black areas where they lived and others travelled to white areas. What is interesting is the different reasons that they gave for doing so and the ideology that underpinned their decisions. Crockett and Wallendorf define three distinct reactions to shopping, which they refer to as *exit, loyalty*, and *voice*. In this context exit refers to leaving an area or thinking about leaving an area, relationship or setting. Within the context of shopping *exit* can manifest itself in terms of outshopping, or outmigration, meaning moving house and leaving the area altogether. *Loyalty* involves giving public and private support to an organization, in this context a retailer, including being positive about prospects for improvement. *Voice* involves the active and constructive attempts to improve conditions, possibly by complaining about existing conditions.

Crockett and Wallendorf (2004) maintain that two distinctive political ideologies underpin consumers' shopping choices – traditional/disillusioned liberalism and Black Nationalism. Following Dawson they describe ideology as

> a world view readily found in the population, including sets of ideas and values that cohere, that are used publicly to justify political stances, and that shape and are shaped by society. Further, political ideology helps to define who are one's friends and enemies, with whom one would form political coalitions, and, furthermore, contains a causal narrative of society and the state.
>
> (Dawson 2001: 4–5)

Traditional black liberalism acknowledges that racial inequality is a feature of the black experience but is hopeful that full integration in public and private life will be achieved. Those that are disillusioned liberals are less likely to believe that full integration will occur and their emphasis has turned towards generating resources for the black community. Black nationalists on the other hand, focus on two main issues. The first feature is that race is the most important factor in which black social, political and economic life is operationalized. Second, that blacks should have some degree of autonomy from whites and white-controlled institutions as a form of social solidarity.

The ideological positions that consumers hold will impact on their shopping behaviour. For example, those holding liberal viewpoints would have no objections to moving out of black areas and living among whites and shopping in predominantly white areas. Consumers referred to enjoying shopping in white areas because they looked more middle class, had a better clientele, and seemed safer places to shop, the parking was close to the store, more security was around and the assistants were more helpful. Black working-class consumers living in black areas do not spend enough in the shops to keep them viable and allow them to flourish and their consumption patterns do not reflect a taste for cosmopolitan foods or luxuries. By contrast, black nationalists favour shopping in white areas in order to purchase the best quality produce at the lowest cost, even if that means clipping coupons out of newspapers and searching for sales. But outshopping is perceived as a more politically palatable option than outmigration. The participants did not want to demonstrate to their children that they had to live in white areas to have nice things. There was also a collective view that outmigration or outshopping was antagonistic to the black community since it channelled resources elsewhere. Black entrepreneurship was to develop a black parallel economy in the form of farmers' markets to compensate for lack of grocery stores in needy areas of the city. Absent from black nationalists was patronizing black owned stores on ideological grounds. Consumers made a judgment on criteria relating to product offerings rather than race, pride or issues of community development. The level of crime in the area had implications for the types of shops available. Stores in the worst areas were being drained of resources and had the worst managers, equipment, and this resulted in high food costs. There is also an influx of foreigners in the area from India and Pakistan which left a lot to be desired in terms of cleanliness, and for this reason blacks refused to shop in those stores.

What has attracted relatively little attention is the concept of ethnoscapes as outshopping experiences. Multicultural areas with their 'markets, festivals and other events in public spaces' are picturesque 'backdrops for consumption' (Shaw *et al.* 2004: 1983). Communities that once signified poverty and exclusion have been able to revitalize themselves by appealing to the sophisticated, cosmopolitan consumers wishing to experience the authentic 'other'. One of the earliest examples were Chinatowns that are now well established in North America and Europe. An appreciation of ethnic cuisine in all its varieties is a form of cultural capital and a marker of distinction (Warde 1995). In the UK, the city of Bradford has designed a guide entitled the *Flavours of Asia* that promotes Asian cuisine in the area, especially its famous curry houses, and sari centres. Indian takeaways have now outnumbered traditional fish and chip shops in Britain. Little Italy's have also become common in many North American and European cities as fine Italian dining.

A particularly famous area in the United Kingdom is Brick Lane in the East End of London that is home to the city's Bengali community. The place has reinvented itself with shops containing bright coloured sari fabrics, traditional music from the shops and the smells of the spices from the numerous Bangladeshi cafes and restaurants.

Alternative methods of retailing

One of the reasons for the restricted growth of international retailers is the persistence of local markets that are integrated more closely with the norms of local culture, including religion. European markets predated the rise of industrialism and in most parts of the Third World they existed before the penetration of European forms of mercantilism and colonialism (R.H.T. Smith 1978). Markets have attracted considerable attention from anthropologists especially in connection with market work being deemed as women's work although market work as women's work is culturally determined (see Seligmann 2001). Goldman *et al.* (1999) have also drawn attention to the continued importance of 'wet markets' in Hong Kong for purchasing fresh food. The term 'wet' refers to the constant wetness of the floor as a consequence of spraying produce and the cleaning of meat and fish stalls. They argue that a universal phenomenon in developed Asian countries is that supermarkets have achieved a lower market share of food retail sales compared with Europe and the USA. The vast majority of the population visit supermarkets at least once a week but fresh food continues to be purchased from wet markets. This observation is true of other Asian countries including Singapore, Taiwan and Thailand. The secret of the continued dominance of wet markets results from their ability to provide higher levels of personalized service to the customer, better quality products, deeper selection of narrower range of products than supermarkets, quantities tailored to the needs of the consumers and an environment that is conducive to social interaction. With simpler methods and lower costs they can offer customers cheaper prices. Because of their larger numbers and political clout they can secure priority and better terms from suppliers than supermarkets. And there is a preference among consumers to buy in Chinese weight measurements rather than the Western ones used in the supermarkets. These advantages outweigh some of the disadvantages of wet markets which include being dirty, slippery, crowded, smelly, noisy, with a lack of air conditioning and unhygienic conditions on some stalls.

There is an explicitly religious feel as Kapchan (2001) captures in the context of Islamic principles being applied to the sale of herbal remedies in a market in Morocco. Trust is an important aspect of market negotiations for Muslims and one should not be found to act in bad faith. In the following extract a woman herbalist calls attention to the relationship of trust with religious oaths to promote her products:

And whoever wants to prepare them by themselves, here they are. Whoever wants them already ground, I'll gather them up here. Bring them to your house and pound them and sift them.

Don't call me a liar or a daughter of a bitch.

And whoever of you doesn't know how or doesn't have honey or oil or the means to grind them

I'll give them to you prepared.

I gathered them and washed them and pounded them and sifted them and cooed the porcupine and shifted all of it.

If they have additions or subtraction, God subtract from my health, from here . . .

Whoever wants some from me give me a hundred [riyals].

By the truth of God!

If I've wasted your 100 riyals, tomorrow next to God – here, you are all more than twelve witnesses –

If I've wasted your 100 riyals, tomorrow next to God, you'll take a piece of my meat from here.

And whoever wants to taste a little, taste a little, here they are, mixed with honey and with oil.

If you eat some it's better than ghee or almonds or walnuts.

It's the sweetest thing to eat.

It's good for haemorrhage if it's in your head.

It's good for the person who has grief in his heart.

As the book said, it's good for stomach problems and pain.

These five herbs, use them for five days in a row as the book states.

(Kapchan 2001: 169–170).

The herbalist uses Islamic law that requires 12 witnesses in order for a testimony to become a legal fact. If she is found to be lying she will suffer in the next life and her customers will be able to take pieces of her flesh as payment. Accountability is promised and assured.

We know most about store retailing and rather less about aspects of non-store retailing. Informal aspects of retailing such as car boot sales, organic farmers' markets, house sales, and church jumble sales have attracted relatively little interest since they are not regarded as part of mainstream marketing. Yet it is important to recognize that what are perceived as alternative retailing strategies in advanced Western societies could constitute core activities in developing countries. The perception of Western retailing methods as constituting advanced and desirable developments in developing countries can have important implications for indigenous retailers. For example, Weismantel (2001) maintains that perception of development in Ecuador has had a negative effect on the perception of the country's mostly female market sellers who are treated by developers as dirty, out of place and morally suspect.

These forms of retail can best be regarded as informal retail and do not have the same characteristics as formal retailing. To a large extent studies of what might be described as informal retailing have taken something of a back seat while retailers have avidly marketed the propaganda in support of new goods, and the many other aspects are considered superfluous cultural relics of the modern retail environment (Sherry 1990). For example, informal retailing places a great deal of emphasis on consumers' disposal of goods rather than their acquisition. Young and Wallendorf (1989) have provided a useful categorization of disposition behaviours that includes selling, exchanging for other resources, giving away, recycling, throwing away in a societally approved manner, abandoning in a societally unacceptable manner, using up and destroying or intentionally damaging. The disposition process comprises two interrelated aspects. First is the physical separation or detachment from an object and second is the detachment from the meaning and emotion that a particular product may evoke. Systems of disposing for products have been developed and include garage sales, flea markets, church hall sales, auctions and so forth. Face-to-face events provide a forum where information can be shared about particular goods, for example, the way a chair has been handed down through the family and when it was originally bought and from where. In this context we can talk about a product biography, moving in and out of the market and from one consumer to another. The decision of what and how to sell or dispose of through these various channels is relatively under-researched (Hibbert *et al.* 2005), as are cultural differences in disposition behaviours (Price *et al.* 2000).

Nor do we know a great deal about buyer behaviour in the informal market. Car boot sales are a fairly common occurrence in Britain, especially at the weekend in summer. People fill up their cars with goods that they want to dispose of and meet at an allocated space, such as a farmer's field or a car park. Goods are sold from the boot or a small table. Gregson and Crewe (1997) challenge two commonly held myths about car boot sales: of being about 'shady rogues' disposing of volumes of dodgy gear on the unsuspecting public, or the preponderance of car boot sales being dominated by tat and disadvantaged sections of society. For Gregson and Crewe, people go to car boot sales to play; it is akin to theatre with participants performing roles. They argue that the conventions of retailing are suspended at these events. Of course there will be some commentators that argue that informal retailing such as car boot sales are unregulated and constitute an enterprise culture that is out of control. However, Gregson and Crewe (1997) maintain that this sentiment is not entirely true. Rather, car boot salespeople have developed their own code of conduct with respect to acceptable business practices. The American flea market has also been investigated as a distinctive 'retail ecology' by John Sherry (1990) and he came up with many of the same conclusions.

Concern over food safety has generated alternative systems of food supply that are different from conventional chains such as supermarkets (Freidberg 2004). The emphasis on shortening the food supply chains so that food origins can be traced has generated alternative distribution methods including farmers' markets, food shops, box deliveries, community supported agriculture and home deliveries (Ilbery and Maye 2005). The differences between conventional and alternative food supply systems often go beyond the distribution channels to include a range of other criteria, including quantity versus quality, the homogenization of foods as opposed to catering to the needs of regional palates. Sassatelli and Scott (2001) maintain that the reasons for the emergence of novel food markets and the promotional strategies attached to them such as 'buy local' are what they refer to as 'deficits in disembedded trust', where local supply systems, organic and environmentally friendly produce are considered more trustworthy.

In many societies the black economy is an important source of goods. In the former East Germany the scarcity of consumer goods meant that people had to spend huge amounts of time, attention and energy on acquiring the most basic goods. Social networks were a vital part of this process through which goods were bought and sold, and where rumours were exchanged about what might be on sale somewhere. Within this cultural context queues acted as a visible promotional tool since they signalled that something scarce and valuable was for sale (Veenis 1999).

Redlining

Redlining is a practice whereby organizations discriminate against providing services to individuals living in particular geographical locations. Organizations would use a map of their geographical market and draw a red line around those areas they had decided to exclude from their customer base. Redlining is therefore an example of place-based social exclusion (Aalbers 2005). The basis of their decisions would be justified as being an assessment of the costs of doing business in a particular area but sometimes were arbitrary as in the decline of credit. Redlining has been particularly associated with access to financial services, especially mortgages. The practice first emerged in the USA in the 1930s, when federal agencies encouraged lenders to rate neighbourhoods for mortgage risk. The denial of credit came to be viewed as discriminatory and this is how the term redlining first emerged. In Canada the term redlining did not become common currency until the late 1960s, but in practice was occurring in the area of mortgage finance in the 1950s as lenders learnt to discriminate against different types of residential districts (Harris and Forrester 2003).

At first sight it might seem that companies are entitled to deal with any consumers that they choose and therefore redlining is not an unethical business practice. What research on redlining has demonstrated is that some groups are discriminated against more than others based on their cultural characteristics. Very often these groups of consumers are perceived as a higher risk than the rest of the population and are indicative of poor quality consumers. However, these views are often not supported by research. In other words, individuals are being labelled as a bad risk when that is not necessarily the case. It is for this reason that redlining has been made illegal in some countries. Redlining has been associated with racial discrimination in the USA, more so than in Canada and the United Kingdom (Harris and Forrester 2003). Its existence in Europe has rarely been addressed (Aalbers 2005) and outside of north America and Europe discussions of redlining are very thin on the ground.

Although redlining is often associated with ethnic minority populations, it needs to be understood that racial discrimination is not integral to its definition.

In the USA, redlining is illegal in the financial service sector because it was demonstrated that ethnic minority communities were not able to obtain access to insurance, mortgage finance and other financial services that are regarded as essential features of living in a consumer society (Burton 2008). Cases of discrimination still do occur and find themselves in court from time to time. Another recent development is that ethnic minority consumers are being discriminated against and sold inferior products when their personal and economic characteristics would find this difficult to justify. A recent example is the case of mis-selling of sub-prime mortgages in the USA in areas with high levels of ethnic minority populations (Burton 2008).

Recent experiences in Canada seem to suggest, although hard data is often not available, that redlining is an issue in some Canadian cities and this has contributed to a decline in property prices in downtown areas (R. Harris 2003). A more detailed study has demonstrated that in Toronto within areas of immigrant settlement, few institutional mortgages are in evidence. However, these findings were attributed to the preferences of borrowers to fund their house purchases in a different way rather than because of discrimination at the hands of lenders (Murdie 1991). This said, often consumers can be put off applying for loans because of fear of being turned down.

Manual Aalbers (2005) has provided an interesting study of redlining in the two largest cities in the Netherlands: Amsterdam and Rotterdam over two time periods, 1999 and 2001. He found that redlining was a common practice in Rotterdam in 1999 but there were no signs of it in 2001. However, 'yellowlining' (lower loan-to-value ratios) were found to be common in some areas of Rotterdam. In Amsterdam, there was no evidence of redlining in 1999 and 2001, but in 1999 some areas were yellowlined. Aalbers suggests reasons for the findings are due to economic conditions, the state of the housing market, and the availability of mortgage finance in the system. At present, banks in the Netherlands are fully within their rights to refuse a mortgage application without providing a reason or making the information public, although the Dutch Association of Banks in a recent Code of Conduct has included redlining as 'no-go'. In declining neighbourhoods the decline of bank finance has led to the emergence of slum landlords, immigrant exploitation (through high rents) and the rise of an underworld drugs market (Aalbers 2006).

Retail redlining has not attracted the same level of attention and is legal in most countries. Large supermarkets have considerable discretion about where to locate their stores and some are avoiding areas with large ethnic minority populations. The charge against the supermarkets is that they are discriminating against people based on their ethnic and racial characteristics and not their ability to pay for goods. Retail redlining has some serious consequences for geographical areas that have been excluded by mainstream providers. These localities can become food deserts that lack basic retail outlets and the ones that do exist often provide an inferior and expensive range of products. This scenario is made worse because poor people often cannot afford the expenses incurred in travelling to more affluent areas where higher quality and better value for money retailers tend to be located.

D'Rozario and Williams (2005) argue that retail redlining is a dysfunction effect of retailing since it could cause markets to fail since there is a misallocation of the retailers' resources, loss of a potentially profitable market and, not being based on economically rational principles, may result in buyers and sellers not being able to buy and sell their products. They maintain that retail redlining is a highly complex and contentious issue and has resulted in multiple stakeholders holding their own, very different, views. D'Rozario and Williams identify several types of retail redlining:

Higher fees charged to franchisees operating in particular retail areas

Higher fees charged to franchisees operating in specific areas has it roots in higher fees and reductions for support activities such as marketing. This strategy is justified on the basis that there are often higher crime rates and insurance premiums payable in these areas. Furthermore, these higher risk areas are often locations that have a stagnant or declining population base as people move out to better areas. Thus investment could be made with uncertain levels of return in the medium to longer term. The result for the franchisee is that they have to pass on the higher costs to their customers resulting in less favourable trading conditions. Burger King was the subject of a lawsuit in the USA brought by ethnic minority franchisees based on this criterion.

Restricting minority franchisees only to minority-dominant retail areas

Restricting minority franchisees to ethnic minority areas is often aligned to the cultural familiarity in the franchisee–customer base relationship thus enhancing the service delivery. But this can often be detrimental to future businesses since, as discussed earlier, these tend to be the poor, less profitable areas.

Refusal by a service provider to service customers in a promising retail area

This form of retail redlining occurs when customers request a service in their community but are denied it despite other individuals in non-minority neighbour-hoods being served. In these cases it is usually the chain store's head office that gives reasons unrelated to race/ethnicity such as credit and delinquency risks for not serving them. Allegations against Domino's pizza and their refusal to deliver to areas within the predominantly African-American, American Beach area of Florida is an example of this form of redlining.

Removal of a successful store from an area by a chain

This type of redlining involves closing a store in one area while continuing to operate a less successful store in a non-minority area. A chain's head office regularly cites other reasons for the store closures including management problems. In their defence, companies often mention that they are opening new stores in minority areas. The car manufacturer Cadillac was criticized for just this reason in its decision to close a successful minority-owned dealership in a mostly minority neighbour-hood in the Bronx.

Denigrating the retailing potential of a promising geographic area

This aspect of redlining is the practice of retailing industry and local and state government officials resisting the potential of a specific area and instead favouring the cause of surrounding areas as more attractive retail locations. Retailers often find it convenient to blame the inadequacies of the local planning process and local government.

Questions

*   What does the history of the department store reveal about the development of retailing formats in different countries?
*   Why is it important to acknowledge the ethnic diversity of customers when developing marketing strategies for mall retailing in different countries?
*   What are some of the difficulties that direct marketing companies will face when operating in China?
*   What do you understand by the term international outshopping? Provide examples.
*   Why should retailers refrain from redlining?

Further reading

Benson, S.P. (1988) *Counter Cultures: Saleswomen, Managers and Customers in American Department Stores, 1890-1940*, Chicago: University of Illinois Press.

Coles, T. (1999) 'Department stores as innovations in retail marketing: Some observations on marketing practice and perceptions in Wilhelmine, Germany', *Journal of Macromarketing*, 19 (1): 34–47.

Crockett, D., Grier, S.A. and Williams, J.A. (2003) 'Coping with marketplace discrimination: An exploration of the experiences of Black men', *Academy of Marketing Science Review*, 4; available online at http://findarticles.com/p/articles/mi_qa3896/is_2003 01/ai_n9195211.

Crockett, D. and Wallendorf, M. (2004) 'The role of normative political ideology in consumer behavior', *Journal of Consumer Research*, 31 (3): 511–528.

D'Andrea, G., Lopez-Aleman, B. and Stengel, A. (2006) 'Why small retailers endure in Latin America', *International Journal of Retail and Distribution Management*, 34 (9): 661–763.

D'Rozario, D. and Williams, J.D. (2005) 'Retail redlining: Definition, theory, typology, and measurement', *Journal of Macromarketing*, 25 (2): 175–186.

Gordy, K. (2006) '"Sales + economy + efficiency = revolution"? Dollarization, consumer capitalism, and popular responses in special period Cuba', *Public Culture*, 18 (2): 383–411.

Michon, R. and Chebat, J. (2004) 'Cross-cultural mall shopping values and habits: A comparison between English- and French-speaking Canadians', *Journal of Business Research*, 57 (8): 883–892.

Piron, F. (2002) 'International shopping and ethnocentrism', *European Journal of Marketing*, 36 (1–2): 189–210.

Shaw, S., Bagwell, S. and Karmowsa, J. (2004) 'Ethnoscapes as spectacle: Reimaging multicultural districts as new destinations for leisure and tourism consumption', *Urban Studies*, 41 (10): 1983–2000.

6 Internet and mobile commerce

Introduction

The Internet has significant implications for cross-cultural marketing which can be contextualized in the wider frame of cyberculture in the networked society. Cyberculture is a concept developed by anthropologists to refer to the ways that information communications technology is used by individuals in daily life, and how the new replaces the old. The first section of this chapter outlines some of the key features of cyberculture in the context of network society. The second section of the chapter focuses on unequal access to the Internet in different parts of the world, which has considerable implications for marketers' ability to use the Internet as a method of distribution and promotion. The third part of the chapter discusses the important role that Internet cafés play in the cyberculture of developing countries that have low levels of access. Who uses Internet cafés, for what purpose, and the costs payable will be addressed. Another pertinent issue is the ethnic divisions that exist in Internet use and how it can be used to sustain or modify ethnic and racial identities. The fourth section addresses how transnational migrants use the Internet to maintain their cultural roots back 'home'.

The fifth section of the chapter emphasizes how the Internet is transforming the delivery of cultural products, including those associated with romance, entertainment and movies, and ancestry tracing for different cultural groups. An aspect of Internet use that has attracted relatively little attention, is the impact of language as a cultural variable. Yet, it has been argued that the dominance of English is contributing to a digital divide, especially with respect to developing countries. Language use on the Internet is a more complex phenomenon in the context of bilingual and illiterate consumers. The sixth section of the chapter addresses the issues of language and literacy on the Internet and their cultural implications. The penultimate part of the chapter focuses on crime and regulation on the Internet and more specifically how it can contribute to a culture of distrust in particular geographical location. The final part of the chapter relates to the use of mobile phones as a communication, advertising and market research tool in different countries.

Cyberculture and the network society

The Internet has been described as a super innovation and a super-diffusion technology. Super innovations are innovations that hold a position in the technological hierarchy above other innovations because of the speed, efficiency and effectiveness with which they 'transmit new ideas and technologies between individuals and cultures'. Previous super innovations have included sailing boats, maps and navigation instruments that allowed explorers to distribute new ideas and technologies to different cultures. In return, explorers would learn by seeing and doing and take their ideas back home. Other super-diffusion technologies have been the languages of Mandarin and Latin, that were imposed by conquerors to control and manage empires but which also speeded up the diffusion of new ideas and inventions; a further example is the printing press which took this process to another level (Dickson 2000). Escobar (1994: 215) suggests that technological deterministic arguments about the impact of computer and information technologies leading to 'worldwide homogenization and generalized acculturation', are too limited in their approach. Rather, a more appropriate line of enquiry is through the notion of 'interpretive flexibility' referring to the way different social groups interpret technological artefacts in various ways within different cultures. Particularly neglected are the effects of first world technologies on third world groups, especially in the context of cultural politics, including cultural destruction, hybridization, homogenization and the creation of new differences. The aim in the cyberculture domain is to understand the production and use of new technologies in different cultural settings; an examination of computer-mediated communities (virtual communities); the effect of new technologies on popular culture; the impact of computer mediated communication in connection to the relationship between language, communication, social structures and cultural identity; and finally, the political economy of cyberculture, in terms of the relationship between technology and capital, and the social relation between groups and nations. Slater and Tacchi (2004) have developed the concept of 'communicative ecology' to contextualize the complete range of media and information flows within a community, whether new communications displace old media, and whether they work within an existing communications network Panagakos and Horst note:

> Women living in slums in media saturated environments like Delhi, India are often restricted from answering ringing mobiles, or must request permission and assistance to make phone calls because mobile phones are viewed as men's domain . . . In Ghana, the reputations of many unmarried and unemployed women are placed on the line when they are seen with mobile phones because it is assumed that a man is paying for the phonecards needed to maintain a working phone in exchange for sexual favours.
>
> (2006: 119)

The role of new information and communications technologies has attracted considerable attention in marketing in connection with e-commerce, associated with online shopping, and m-commerce or mobile commerce via mobile phones and other hand-held devices (Dholakia and Dholakia 2004). However, largely absent from many discussions are the wider societal contexts in which these new technologies are used and developed. This is an important omission in the context of cross-cultural and multicultural marketing. An integrated and overarching theoretical approach to these new developments allows marketers to understand the dynamics of consumer and producer interaction over space. One such approach has been developed by Castells in his concept of the network society. Castells (2004: 3) defines the network society as 'a society whose social structure is made of networks powered by microelectonics-based information and communications technologies'. His reference to social structure includes 'the organizational arrangements of human relations of production, consumption, reproduction, experience, and power expressed in meaningful communication coded by culture'.

He maintains that networks have no centre but comprise an intersecting connection of nodes with some nodes having more relevance and importance to the network as a whole. The concept of network is not new to twenty-first-century societies or human organization since social networks have been at the heart of social interaction and the production of meaning for thousands of years. What sets the new era apart can be summarized by three features. First is the way that networks can be extended in terms of their processing and communicating capacity whether that is in connection with volume, complexity, or speed. Second, the network society is characterized by digital technologies that can combine and recombine information based on recurrent and active communication. One of the main features of the Internet is its ability to link up information from an enormous range of sources and feedback in real time or chosen time. The third feature of the new information and communication technologies is their flexibility that allows for processing ability in a variety of contexts whether that be in business-to-business communication, consumer nattering on the net, or engaging in cyber protests.

Castells maintains that digital networks are global, having little by way of barriers to reconfigure themselves. By the same token the network society is global in nature. However, this does not mean that everybody everywhere is included in the social network. Some countries are included more than others, as are some social groups. The imperfect globalization of network society is an important feature of its social structure as Castells notes:

> The coexistence of the network society, as a global structure, with industrial, rural, communal, or survival societies, characterizes the reality of all countries, albeit with a different share of population and territory on both sides of the divide, depending on the relevance of each segment for the dominant logic of each network. This is to say that various networks will have different geometries and geographies of inclusion and exclusion.
>
> (Castells 2004: 23)

Crucial for our analysis of cross-cultural marketing, network society develops in a range of cultural settings, reflecting the different historical context (economic, social, political) of each setting.

The concept of network society as a relatively novel mode of organizing social relations, is an important approach to understanding the environment in which cross-cultural marketing occurs. In 1999, over half the people on the planet had never received or made a telephone call (Castells 2001: 261). The Internet has certainly reduced the cost of transferring information from one place to another. Perrons (2004: 169) neatly illustrates this point when she notes 'e-mailing a 40 page document from Chile to Kenya costs less than 10 cents, faxing it about $10 and sending it by courier $50'. Likewise, Afemann (2000) notes that transmitting a 2,000 word document from Ghana to the Netherlands by telephone takes 10 minutes and costs $34, a fax takes 2 minutes and $7, and by email 7 seconds and costs 40 cents.

Often information and communication technologies are assessed in terms of new methods of promoting goods, and new delivery channels. The theory of network society provides a touchstone to think more widely in terms of marketing uses, ways consumers interface with technologies and the variations that exist within different cultural contexts. The characteristics of the network society have been addressed in the context of the USA and Finland (Himanen and Castells 2004), Russia (Vartanova 2004), China (Qiu 2004), Britain (Woolgar 2004) and in connection with different ethnic minority groups including African-Americans in Detroit (Baker and Coleman 2004) and ethnic groups in India (Chatterjee 2004).

Geography of Internet users

At the turn of the millennium approaching 200 countries were connected to the Internet (Rao 2002a and b). However, in reality, Internet access is very unequal in different parts of the world which has considerable implications for marketers' ability to use the Internet as a method of distribution. In 2003, 62 per cent of Internet users resided in Europe, Canada and the USA, yet only 16 per cent of the world's population lived in these areas. By stark contrast, only 1 per cent of Africa's population were Internet users but 13 per cent of the world's population resided in that continent. Some of the countries with the lowest levels of Internet access were Iran, India, Kenya, Botswana and Indonesia, where less than one per cent of the population were Internet users. Numerically, China has more Internet users than any other country except America, and over half of them have broadband (6.6 per cent in 2002). The number of Internet connected computers has doubled since the end of 2002, to 45.6 million and Internet users have risen by 75 per cent to 111 million (*Economist* 2006g). These statistics lead Perrons (2004) to suggest that information communications technologies have not resulted in the end of geography and the levelling of the playing field but that in some instances existing inequalities will be exacerbated.

Three preconditions are necessary for Internet use. The first is a phone connection, second a computer modem, and third an electricity supply. Purchasing a computer and modem in Third World countries is much more expensive than in the USA and other advanced countries. Many developing countries do not have a stable power supply and suffer from frequent power failures in cities, and in many rural areas there is a complete lack of a supply. One in three people in the Third World lacks access to electricity. Around 70 per cent of Africans live in rural areas without any power supply, this figure is around 50 per cent in the Indian sub-continent, which is similar to some countries in Latin America, for example Peru, Paraguay, and Bolivia (Afemann 2000). However, aggregate figures can mask considerable differences within various sections of the population. For example, Indonesia has 4.5 million Internet users but most were concentrated in the 10 largest cities, and most connections were made by those aged 26–35 (38 per cent), followed by 14–25 year olds (32 per cent) and those aged 36–55 (30 per cent). Users were also highly educated with nearly 40 per cent having a bachelor degree, a third were high school students and a further 25 per cent were a combination of undergraduate and postgraduate students (Rice and Sulaiman 2004). A young technologically minded population has also generated the considerable growth of broadband in South Korea. In 2002, nearly 70 per cent of homes were subscribing to a broadband Internet service compared with 15 per cent in America and 8 per cent in Western Europe. Part of the explanation for the depth of penetration is that 70 per cent of Korean households live in urban areas and 45 per cent live in apartment blocks, a situation that has enabled telecommunication companies to wire up households quickly and economically (*Economist* 2003a).

National statistics at the aggregate level also fail to reflect the development trajectories that indicate some of the poorer countries (Brazil, China and Malaysia) are rapidly increasing their Internet capabilities by developing cyber centres or cyber corridors at the forefront of technological developments. In some ways these initiatives bridge the digital divide between the rich and the poor, but often spatial disparities within the country are exacerbated. In Malaysia, a multimedia super corridor stretches from Kuala Lumpur City for a distance of 50 km to a new administrative capital at Putrajaya in the south of the country. Cyberjaya is a new city within Putajaya that acts as a site for IT companies and a similar arrangement exists in the north, near Penang, where Silicon Island hosts IT companies including Intel, Cisco and Seagate (Perrons 2004). A similar development has been brought to fruition in the United Arab Emirates with the construction of the Dubai Internet City, which exists as a free trade zone for the knowledge economy (Wheeler 2006). In other countries Internet users can be spatially concentrated in particular areas. For example, Rao (2002b) maintains that the Internet market in India is largely concentrated in the biggest four to eight cities.

In Africa, progress is being made but from a very low level of Internet connec-tions. Every capital city has been connected to the Internet, and cybercafés exist in smaller cities, towns and some villages. Even allowing for these developments, Africa has significant ground to make up with a ratio of one connection per 200 people, compared to one in three in North America and Europe. One of the main constraints in these poorer countries is the lack of a telecommunications infra-structure which can make connections prohibitively expensive (Perrons 2004). The cost of end user equipment in countries like Kenya and Nigeria has led individuals with professional jobs to seek Internet access in Internet cafés and other public places (Oyelaran-Oyeyinka and Nyaki Adeya 2004).

Within developing countries it is misleading to interpret Internet connection per household as a measure of Internet use. Wheeler's (2006) study of Internet access in the Middle East demonstrates significant numbers of Internet cafés in countries with low levels of connections per head of the population. For example, in Algeria there are low levels of Internet penetration as measured by the number of inhabitants that have Internet accounts (0.57 per cent). But the availability of Internet cafés is estimated to be 9.52 cafés per 100,000 inhabitants. A similar pattern repeats itself in Libya where per capita Internet penetration is around 0.24 per cent of the population but with an estimated 13.21 Internet cafés per 100,000 inhabitants. Wheeler argues that there is clearly sufficient Internet demand among the population in Algeria and Morocco to support 2,000 or 3,000 Internet cafés respectively. She maintains that parallels can be drawn with the availability of newspapers in coffee houses in the late nineteenth century, when low numbers of papers in circulation masked the numbers of people that actually read them. A further complicating factor is the rapid increase in mobile phone use. The lower setting up costs involved compared with the Internet (20–30 times less) and the existence of a secondhand phone market in many locations in the Arab world, has resulted in mobile phones being purchased for approximately half their original cost. Wheeler also suggests that mobile phones are more culturally compatible with Arab life where individuals communicate daily with family and friends and like the 24/7 availability.

The digital divide separating the 'knowledge rich' from the 'knowledge poor' continues to grow, thus exposing entire regions of the world to greater poverty and inequality. Globalization and technological innovation may result in widening the gap between the haves and the have-nots (Hill and Dhanda 2004). Some marketers view this as a problem that needs rectifying, others claim that the digital divide is not a problem and that people should be left alone to determine their own Internet participation (Block 2004).

Castells (2001) notes the information age is not blind to colour and the ethnic digital divide remains a feature of the cyberspace landscape. As soon as one aspect of discrimination within the technological divide seems to be diminishing, another emerges through differential access to high-speed broadband, cable modems and wireless-based Internet access. The most comprehensive account of multicultural access and use of the Internet are outside of marketing (see Go'mez-Pena 2001; Nakamura 2004). A significant benchmark study is that conducted by the Pew Foundation in America that examines the behaviour of white Anglos, African-Americans, Asian-Americans and Hispanics. Interestingly, considerable differences in patterns of use between the groups were found.

Ellen Arnould and Darcy Plymire (2000) make the important point that we know more about the behaviour of some ethnic groups in society than others. For example, they note that Native American Indians are rarely included in research on Internet use. They tend to be 'ghettoized' in what they term 'the vanishing Indian syndrome' (Arnould and Plymire 2000: 189). The start-up costs of Internet use remain comparatively high for this group who are the poorest minority group in the USA. Many members do not even have access to a telephone. Yet despite the lack of Internet access among native Indians, websites about them are numerous. Among the 550 recognized tribes of the USA and Alaska, 100 have active websites. The search term 'Cherokee Indians' yields thousands of pages. Web pages are a combination of political attempts to preserve their culture, to advertising reservation attractions for tourists, and selling 'authentic' native goods and services.

Bailey (2001: 342) notes that the sale and exchange of digitalized porn images caters increasingly to racial fetishes, with white and Asian women pictured in interracial scenarios carrying the highest currency. The narratives of interracial desire remain popular on porn BBSs, and even on African American porn BBSs like Ebony Shack, images of black male/white female scenarios sometimes outnumber all other configurations.

Nakamura (2004: 79) argues that future studies of the Internet 'must ask questions regarding people of color as *producers* of Internet content, not just as consumers of such content'. Tracking the extent to which racial minorities are availing themselves of the Internet's interactivity will tell us how much they are adding to the discourse rather than only describing which images, texts, and products they are consuming online – whether they are being *constructed* as markets and credit card holders as opposed to *constructing themselves* as authors, artists, community members, experts, interlocutors, and everyday online people.

Internet cafés

Understanding what happens online has been the focus of much marketing research but rarely have the 'microsociological' contexts of Internet use, including cybercafés or domestic spaces, been the subject of research (Miller and Slater 2000). This issue is of considerable significance to cross-cultural marketers since access to the Internet is highly differentiated around the globe. What follows is an assessment of the role of Internet cafés promoting Internet use in different countries.

Cybercafés are of relatively recent origin and have been traced to the launch of *Cyberia* in London. The number of cafés in existence worldwide is difficult to measure since there is little by way of an agreed definition or a definitive list. Furthermore, the fast moving nature of the sector raises the problem of keeping accurate data. In 1998, 1,908 cybercafés were listed in 109 countries, by March 2003 indicates 6,189 cybercafés were listed in 170 countries (http://www.cyber captive.com). In the UK, of the 53 per cent of the population who had accessed the Internet by October 2001, 10 per cent had done so via an Internet café, shop or library. In other countries, including Norway, Finland and the USA, the overall numbers of the population using Internet cafés may not be significant but for some specific groups in particular locations they may remain important. A positive attribute of the cybercafé is that they provide the sociability that is missing from other points of public access including libraries (Liff and Laegran 2003; Liff and Steward 2003).

In the UK, there has been a significant increase in the number of cybercafés. One of the most well known are those owned by easyJet, the budget airline. The first one opened in Victoria in 1999, and claimed to be the world's biggest Internet café comprising 400 terminals. The company tends to provide a cheaper service than independent rivals but the price does vary according to consumer demand. EasyJet has eight outlets in London and one each in Edinburgh, Glasgow and Manchester in addition to Europe and the USA. Other retailers involved with food or cafés with a presence on the high street are also moving into this area. For example, Starbucks has decided to locate high-speed, broadband wireless Internet access in some of its cafés. Some independent cybercafés have had difficulties making a profit, indeed easyJet had to inject £15 million to keep the Internet café business afloat (Liff and Laegran 2003).

Little research has centred on consumer use of the Internet in Internet cafés (Burton 2002). Yet it has been demonstrated that these social contexts, 'places of sociality' (Miller and Slater 2000), or technosocial space (Laegran and Stewart 2003) are important for marketers to understand since in some countries Internet café access is significant. There has been a small amount of work that has addressed the optimum layout for cybercafés and the relationship to Internet use but this area of scholarship is underdeveloped (Liff and Steward 2003). Moreover, there has been some discussion of the differences in not-for-profit and commercial cafés. Uotinen (2003) observes that commercial cafés seek a trendy look that is also reflected in the appearance of the staff, while community based initiatives tend to focus on promoting a healthy image. The charging structures for using the service can also differ. In the case of commercial enterprises the refreshments and Internet use are charged for, at least one of which is priced at the commercial rate. In community based activities such as the Joensuu Community Resource Centre in Finland, the use of computers is free of charge, and people are asked (although not required) to provide a donation for the refreshments they consume. There are no permanent price lists and the payments are not monitored. The centre attracts young people but also foreigners and middle-class women who are appreciative of the learning support that is on offer.

A cross-national examination of Internet cafés in Scotland and Norway identifies three main images that Internet cafés project; the trendy, the healthy, and the nerdy. Laegran and Stewart note that 'Trendy, healthy and nerdy images of Internet cafés shape the configuration of the clientele, computers, and the premises, in ways which facilitate different patterns of computer use in these spaces' (Laegran and Stewart 2003: 375). Wakeford's (2003) analysis of Internet cafés in London takes a different approach by suggesting that Internet cafés and the way they are used by consumers is a result of the complex interaction of technoscapes and ethnoscapes. In areas with high levels of ethnic minorities, Internet cafés are owned by migrants and efforts are made to market themselves to ethnic groups living in the area. Poetry readings and musical performances, offering training courses in the native language of migrants living in the area, and selling additional services such as mobile phone top-ups and international calling cards were all used as marketing strategies.

Most studies of cybercafés have been centred on advanced Western societies. Yet it is in developing countries where their potential to bring the Internet to the masses may be more valuable. Rao (2007) notes that in some countries in Latin America, Internet cafés have emerged as a response to the needs of tourists and are located close to tourist hotels, travel agencies and restaurants. This is particularly the case in Costa Rica and Ecuador, though less so in Columbia where the high cost of leased lines has been prohibitive causing some cafés to go out of business. Miller and Slater (2000: 72) found that in Trinidad cybercafés were 'largely unstable and in most cases unprofitable enterprises' that were spun off from other activities such as computer sales, maintenance and private IT tuition, and web design. The cafés also varied in their quality from scams charging high fees for sending emails, to dynamic community centres. One Internet café allowed the viewing of pornography, alone or in groups, another café disapproved of the practice, not on principle, but because it could be seen by other users who might be offended. In the café that did allow viewing, a group of gay Trinidadians regularly met in a back room to view sexually explicit material in privacy in a country that is renowned for its homophobia. Staff working in the café maintained that up to 70 per cent of Internet use focused on pornography. Griffiths (2003) argues that the pornography industry has tended to be the first to exploit new technologies and it would seem the Internet is no exception, even within developing countries. Some estimates have suggested that by the turn of the millennium the online pornography industry was worth $1 billion and over half of all spending on the Internet is related to sexual activity. It is interesting to note that the Chinese and Saudi Arabian governments have insisted on the use of software and proxy servers to screen out pornographic sites, or sites with subversive content (Dholakia *et al.* 2003).

The increase in Internet cafés in Turkey has been extraordinary. The first Internet café was opened in Istanbul in 1995, and there are currently around 15,000, making it one of the countries with the highest level of Internet cafés per head of the population. A reported 40 per cent of the population have used the Internet in an Internet café. Of those who use the Internet, 37 per cent connect from cafés and 40 per cent from home. A little over 70 per cent of Internet café users do not own a computer. The under 35s are the most frequent users and 80 per cent are men. Internet cafés do not generally collaborate with educational institutions. The main reason for use in order of preference include using and reading email, chatting, playing games that are often violent in nature, doing research, viewing pornography and engaging in online gambling (Gurol and Sevindik 2007).

Another issue relevant to the use of Internet cafés is whether they close the digital divide between rich and poor countries. Mwesige's (2004) research of Internet cafés in Kampala, Uganda found that they were mostly frequented by 'elites', those that were fairly well off, and the majority had access to Internet access elsewhere at home or work. Typical users were 25 year old single men, without children. The vast majority used Internet cafés for reading emails followed by emailing, surfing, research, chatting, reading online news, and significantly only 5 per cent engaged in shopping online. Wheeler (2006) makes similar remarks about the cost of Internet access in the Arab world which is prohibitive for many people. For example, in Jordan the average salary for a government employee is around 50 JD per month. An hour on the Internet at a café costs 1.5 JD ($2.10) which could buy a family of five a lunch in a restaurant. Internet access at home costs 15 JD for unlimited use which accounts for one-third of a monthly salary with additional access charges also needing to be factored into the equation.

Some dysfunctional effects of Internet café use have also been reported. In Turkey some Internet cafés have become associated with crime and undesirable behaviour among children, including smoking, alcohol abuse, and drug taking. Government regulation followed that limited the opening and closing hours, the age of users and a division between Internet cafés and playrooms (Gurol and Sevindik 2007). In Taiwan, online gaming has been associated with high levels of theft and fraud. Furthermore, the crime scene in 54.8 per cent of cases was an Internet café, presumably because it afforded a degree of anonymity (Chen *et al.* 2005). Computer 'addiction' and 'dependency' have been identified as a consequence of 'getting hooked on computers' (Shotton 1989). The net-addict is a contemporary manifestation of computer addiction as users reach out for an alternative, or compensate for a lack of social interaction (Shields 1996). These dysfunctional effects have not stopped some developing countries pushing ahead with creating Internet cafés. The Indian government plans to develop 1 million Internet cafés in the country by 2008 (Chopra 2006).

Internet and diaspora

In 'Welcome to Cyberia: notes on the anthropology of cyberculture' Escobar (1994) invites scholars to study cyberculture by assessing how the social construction of reality is changed and negotiated as new technologies emerge and become integrated into everyday life. The historical and cultural orientations shape the meaning of technologies for different social groups and subcultures. It also needs to be recognized that technology in its various guises is not always universally welcome. For example, the Amish in Pennsylvania, USA have banned the telephone from their homes since 1909 (Umble 1992). Escobar identified a number of themes ripe for investigation including the emergence of computer-mediated communities, language and cultural identity, and the political economy of cyberculture, amongst others.

A number of scholars have taken up some of the themes raised by Escobar to assess the ways in which transnational migrants use particular information communication technologies (ICT) to create and maintain their transnational lifestyles and support transnational networks. The concept of diasporic media studies as an academic domain, focuses on the production and circulation, and appropriation of symbolic and mediated messages whether in the form of telephone calls, letters, photos, newspapers, video letter, radio and television, popular music, the Internet and ICTs. In his discussion of diasporic media, Karim (2003) argues that because of their particular status and location, migrants are often at the leading edge of technological development in order to maintain contact with back home. Vertovec (2004) suggests that basic technologies such as cheap long-distance telephone calls have traditionally been one of the primary means that bind transnational migrants to their families, colleagues and friends located at home and abroad. The use of the Internet and mobile phones are further modes by which migrant communities can keep in touch.

These technologies are potentially important avenues by which cultures are produced and reproduced and are therefore important areas of research for cross-cultural marketers. Panagakos and Horst (2006: 118) argue that the Internet allows 'transnational migrants who share a common ethnicity, racial designation, religion and history of discrimination' to expand their social space and by so doing 'challenge the restrictive boundaries imposed by dominant host societies and the limitations of physical space and time'. Tyner and Kuhlke (2000) provide an interesting four-fold typology of diasporic Internet communications; *intra-diasporic*, *inter-diasporic*, *diaspora-host*, and *diaspora-homeland*. In this schema *intra-diasporic* refers to websites and Internet communications used by immigrants within the context of local communities in which they are residing. *Inter-diasporic* refer to websites and communications among immigrant populations in the same or different host countries. The *diaspora-host* category relates to diasporic communities and other ethnic or cultural groups within the host country. Finally, *diaspora-homeland* Internet communications involve websites and other communicative practices between the diasporic community and the hometown or home country.

Benitez (2006) has explored transnational dimensions of the digital divide among Salvadoran immigrants in the Washington DC metropolitan area of the USA. He describes how immigrants used the Internet to keep in touch with family and friends in different localities and access the Salvadoran mass media (newspapers, magazines, radio and television stations). A limiting factor was knowledge required to use a computer and access to the Internet, in other words cyber literacy. Some Salvadoran websites take the form of a cyber village connecting people that live in a specific village with people living abroad. This forum provides 'localized' exchanges about news, social events, history and culture along with photographs. One such website focuses on Intipuca city (http://www.intipucacity.com) which receives about 10,000 clicks a week and provides a good example of diaspora-homeland/hometown communication. Another example is of the *Centro Deportivo* (http://www.centrodeportivo.com) that originally began life as a soccer website but expanded to include social, cultural, political and musical activities. The site's popularity has been fuelled by the large number of photographs that are posted on the site each week which varies from 150–200. It is the visual aspects of cyber-culture which in this instance promotes transnational interactions or diaspora-homeland communications.

Mallapragada (2000) has provided a similar account of the Indian diaspora community. She highlights 'the politics of home, homeland and homepage' on the 'Indian-American' web – the section of the web that deliberately targets non-resident Indians and persons of Indian origin. Namaste.com focuses on selling the 'Indian look' to women in the context of clothes, hairstyles, make-up, and jewellery showing the slogan 'Bring India Home!' (Mallapragada 2000: 214). Indian World, the most widely known Indian website, has sections on the news, finance, cricket, cooking and matrimonials. Among its advertising are goods and services that are specifically aimed at the Indian diaspora living in the USA. For example, phone cards that offer competitive charges for calls from the USA to India, for sending cards and presents to friends and family in India, and for Internet banking and shopping online. Other websites take the form of community based bulletin boards such as http://www. bayareaundian.com for Indians living in the San Francisco Bay Area. Another form of Indian diasporic communication includes forums and chatrooms and can take the form of 'lighthearted conversations with fellow members, often bordering on the flirtatious, the discussion forums tend to be moderated arenas for the more heated struggle over cultural and political agendas' (Mallapragada 2000: 183). Matrimonial sections have emerged fairly recently as a legitimate way of finding a spouse and are arguably one of the most important uses of the Internet by the diasporic community. Discriminating between characteristics including age, caste, language and regional affiliation, these sites provide an example of how cybertechnology is being used to keep alive notions of community and group membership. Adams and Ghose (2003) argue that not only do Indian websites promote products, but they provide the example of specialized websites such as http://www.hindu.org and http://www.hindunet.org which assist in preserving 'Hindu spirituality and practices' among non-resident Indians (Adams and Ghose 2003: 429).

Androutsopoulos (2007) provides interesting insights about the differences that exist in the websites for German-based migrants from Afghanistan, Greece, India, India, Iran, Morocco, Pakistan, Poland, Romania, Russia, South East Asia and Turkey. He observes that most German-based diasporic websites are commercialized and display advertising banners for products and services that are likely to interest that particular ethnic group. This emergent online market largely comprises German-based young people from second and third generation migrants, but also includes first generation migrants and individuals from other ethnic groups.

Poster (1998) raises the issue of whether 'virtual ethnicity' can really exist and whether it constitutes a new way of viewing the relationship between the individual and community. Increasing attention is being paid to the role of the Internet in enhancing cultural identity and notions of home and belonging. Prior to developments in communications technologies, migration often meant a radical break from the place of origin and familiar ties that reinforced a sense of shared identity. This disruption is reflected in the terminology used to describe this process that includes 'uprooted', 'transplanted', and 'culture shock'. The notion of assimilation implies moving to unfamiliar environments and having to adapt to a new way of life, culture and customs. The concept of a transnational community has challenged the idea that migration need automatically necessitate a sharp break from the home community. Boundaries are now considered to be more permeable and simultaneously there has been an erosion of physical territory as the most important marker of community. The ability to travel and cross national boundaries has become much easier due to cheaper air travel, cheaper telephone calls, and the ability to maintain continuous contact via the Internet. Furthermore, the Internet allows individuals to blur the line between simulation and reality, what is real and what exists on the computer (Turkle 1996).

Miller and Slater's (2000: 85) ethnographic work on Internet use in Trinidad, discovered that in the case of diasporic Trinidadians, 'being Trini' and 'performing Trini', was a major reason why they were on the Internet in the first place – 'to lime, banter, talk music, food, drink and sex'. ('Lime' is the free-flowing sociability of chat sites). With respect to UK based Trinis, the banter, insult and flirting although common and acceptable online would be regarded as sexist and racist in their host country. They might use local dialect in their chat room conversations but would revert to more standard English in their private emails.

Hiller and Franz (2004) have provided an interesting assessment of the Internet use of migrants in three distinct phases: the *pre-migrant*, the *post-migrant*, and the *settled migrant*. They also maintain that during these three different phases individuals use search tools, email, bulletin board systems and chatrooms in different ways. The *pre-migrant* uses search tools to uncover information about the place to which they are moving. Exploring and discovering useful details about the new destination can assist with the adjustment process when they arrive. Email use during this phase tends to be focused on formal and informal contacts with people who are not personally known, as a way of extending their network of individuals that can provide an assessment of migration prospects and help. Bulletin boards are valuable for obtaining contacts about employment, housing and other areas of consumption. Further information can be elicited through formal postings. Chatrooms are valuable sources of informal knowledge from earlier migrants who have been in the same position.

In the *post-migrant* phase the search tools are directed towards learning more about the community of which they have become a member. For example, recreational events and groups that may bring them into contact with migrants sharing a similar background. Another function is to source information about the community that they have left, for example websites of local newspapers which some migrants view everyday. Others keep in touch with economic trends and the state of the job market to enable them to decide when might be an appropriate time for them to return home. The use of email shifts to remaining in contact with the community back home and establishing and retaining contact with other migrants. Email is quick, effective and cheap and migrants send group emails to members of their family, school classmates, neighbours and so forth. Bulletin boards are a proactive attempt to reconnect people whose ties have been broken as a result of migration. Finally, chatrooms are used for sustaining home ties as a way of substituting for real people.

In the *settled migrant* phase Internet use focuses on what Hiller and Franz term the 'backward gaze' and arises out of a desire to return home, homesickness, or the need to stay connected. Although this group may have adapted to their 'new' surroundings over a number of years, they are driven by the need to 'rediscover a lost or neglected connection or to sustain a connection to home that is driven more by nostalgia' (Hiller and Franz 2004: 742). Bulletin boards are useful ways of posting information and trying to generate contacts from the past, perhaps referring to people, places and events that happened many years ago. In this respect a new sense of being part of a community was developed among this group. Email was used to share life and personal histories and genealogies and the function of chatrooms was to create new friends and finding old ones based on a shared background.

Internet shopping

Online shopping is continuing to grow on a worldwide basis and this is particularly the case in emerging markets where consumers are shopping online for the first time. Organizations that wish to use online marketing on a global basis will increasingly have to understand the characteristics and motivations of online shoppers in different countries. Lynch, Kent and Srinivasan (2001) conducted a study across 12 nations and three geographical areas (North America, Latin America, and Western Europe) to assess the characteristics of websites that are important in increasing the likelihood that consumers will make a purchase and facilitate future loyalty. In each of the world regions they found that 'site quality, affect, and trust were important predictors of purchase intentions and site loyalty' (Lynch *et al.* 2001: 21). However, the degree of significance varied across regions and product categories which means that the adoption of one standard format to sell goods worldwide is probably not appropriate since different factors have to be enhanced in various markets.

Smith and Swinyard (2001) developed an 'Internet shopper Lifestyle' measurement instrument in order to segment American online shoppers from non-shoppers. Shoppers were defined as people who had made an online shopping purchase in the two months preceding the study. Internet shoppers were divided into three categories. *Shopping lovers* (11.1 per cent) are competent computer users, who enjoy online shopping and do so on a regular basis. *Internet explorers* (8.9 per cent) describe online shopping as fun and could be regarded as opinion leaders for online buying. *Suspicious learners* (9.6 per cent) form a group that is not particularly computer literate, however, they are open-minded when it comes to learning new things, but are extremely security conscious when it comes to handing over their credit card details. Internet nonshoppers were identified as *fearful browsers* (10.7 per cent) who are very computer literate and often engage in Internet 'window-shopping' but are aware of some of the disadvantages of online shopping such as those concerned with security, charges and the risks associated with not seeing products personally without purchasing. *Shopping avoiders* (15.6 per cent) are difficult to transform into online shoppers since they want the gratification associated with immediate purchase and want to see things in person before they buy. As the term suggests *technology muddlers* (13.6 per cent) are not particularly computer literate and do not spend a great deal of time online. Finally, *fun seekers* (12.1 per cent) like the fun element of surfing the Internet but are afraid of purchasing online. Furthermore, this group tend to be comprised of individuals that are less well educated and have lower incomes, leaving them little by way of purchasing power. Brengman *et al.* (2005) conducted an empirical study of consumers in the USA and Belgium using the same instrument to measure whether the same results would be found. They conclude that the segment profiles were very similar for the USA and Belgium. What follows is an assessment of two product categories sold on the internet; those concerned with romance an those concerned with ancestry tracing.

Romance

Few studies have been conducted on love communication whether cross-culturally or interculturally. Yet research suggests there are considerable cultural variations that are demonstrated by Wilkins and Gareis (2006) in exploring the expression 'I love you'. One respondent had this to say 'I love you is a more serious and committing term in other cultures. Middle Eastern girls who hear that from a guy automatically think marriage. Therefore, men of American culture should be very careful with their "I love you's"' (Wilkins and Gareis 2006: 58). Websites focusing on various aspects of romance are proliferating on the web from cyberflirting, to online romantic or sexual relationships, and finding a partner (Whitty and Carr 2003).

The mail-order bride concept has been around for many years but when the industry moved from a magazine format onto the Internet during the 1990s, the number of matchmaking services rapidly increased spreading from Russia and Asia into Latin America. Wheeler (2006) also observes that in Kuwait cyberdating, on Islamist websites is on the increase, a trend that would have been unthinkable a decade ago. Many accounts of matchmaking services emphasize the exploitation of poor women in developing countries by Western men, thus reproducing the binary relation between developing and Third World countries. Schaeffer-Grabiel's (2005) research of American men looking for Latin American brides, indicates that the incentives included marrying a younger, more beautiful woman than those in the USA, a woman who was willing to please as a sexual object for men's pleasure, and being less materialistic was another asset. Women on the other hand, wish to escape the dissatisfaction with their life and poverty. Men portray themselves as the heroes, the good guys rescuing women and giving them a taste of the American dream. In cyberculture, Latin American and other 'foreign' women are naturalized as having the right biological makeup and cultural grooming, making them appear more feminine, traditional, docile, and more closely aligned with the image of the ideal mother of the family. Unlike nineteenth-century constructions of racial mixing as degenerative, foreign genes, in the cyberbride context, are constructed as superior and regenerative.

Light-skinned *mestizas* are particularly in demand since they have the status of whiteness and the submissive attributes associated with developing countries. In website promotions women are often depicted in settings alongside nature which reflects an anti-capitalist orientation, free from corrupting forces such as materialism and feminism. Schaeffer-Grabiel (2005: 345) argues that the position of women in the cybermarriage market has a unique dynamic where African-American women, feminists, and white women fall to the bottom of the rung as the least desirable bodies, those who are imagined to be too outspoken, too demanding of their worth. However, the dream does not always come to fruition as a Latina wife describes in relation to her Anglo husband

> While men want a Latina because she is supposedly more passionate, when we have this passion, they don't know how to respond. Men prefer Internet pornography than to make love with us. They'd rather watch perfect women

than normal and real women. All of us agree that we can't compete with these unreal bodies, that don't fight, that don't get angry, who don't veer from the norm.

(Schaeffer-Grabiel 2005: 352)

In India, the matrimonial industry is worth an estimated $20 billion and the matchmaking element alone amounts to $300 million. The Internet has displaced the traditional matchmaker who went from door to door carrying armfuls of customer profiles. Shaadi.com is India's largest matrimony website and contains a database of 400,000 candidates and a global audience of nine million registered users. When it was first established the website was more popular among the Indian diaspora, whereas in 2007, 70 per cent of customers came from India and the rest from the USA, Britain, Australia, and the Gulf. With less than 5 per cent of the Indian population being online, there is considerable potential for expansion. For a premium fee of approximately $200, Shaadi will provide the enhanced service of publishing notices in newspapers and magazines and rank the candidate higher online. Approximately, 90 per cent of the consumers are parents rather than potential matches and thus online matchmaking continues the cultural traditional of parents arranging marriages. Most parents keen to make use of the service have no experience of using a computer and for this reason the linguistic codes in the language of matchmaking remain intact. For example, the phrase 'a well-settled family' refers to upper middle-class status and a 'simple woman' means no partying.

Adams and Ghose's (2003) study of Indian matrimonial websites discovered that caste remains an important feature included on online application forms and in some instances there is also a space to specify subcaste. One website they visited provided users with 520 options to choose from in the caste category. They note that although physical appearance on the Indian matrimonial sites is given far less prominence than in the USA, there is usually a space to describe complexion. Most applicants are registered as 'wheatish' which covers a variety of skin tones. The lower status associated with dark skin usually merits further explanation. One entry placed this information under negative points; 'NEGATIVE POINTS: My daughter is not of fair complexion. Of course she is not very dark, but with no amount of extrapolation she can be called as fair' (Adams and Ghose 2003: 432).

A different aspect of women, marriage and the Internet is provided by Jennifer Johnson-Hanks (2007) in her discussion of urban women in the Cameroon. She argues that at first sight the women in her study appear very much like women on other websites from Russia, the Philippines and the Ukraine as they advertise themselves on websites looking for a husband. However, she suggests that the looking for a European and North American husband has more to do with local history than global politics. She argues that women's respectability in the Cameroon has long been dependent on a 'proper marriage' based on romance, love, shared interests and self-control, as opposed to the 'performance of love'. Men in the Cameroon increasingly fall short where these traditional values are concerned and an inadequate marriage is considered worse than none at all. Thus women are using new transnational technologies to 'achieve old, local aims when the old, local methods for achieving those aims not longer suffice' (Johnson-Hanks 2007: 655). She maintains the importance of culture as a system even when radical changes are taking place in the context of cultural categories and practices. Transnational marriage via the use of the Internet is a new phenomenon in the Cameroon but 'its practice is grounded in old structures of gender, honor and marriage' (656).

Ancestry tracing

Tracing one's family history has been a long-standing pastime using publicly available archival material to trace relatives. Genealogy tracing was brought to the attention of the masses through Alex Haley's (1976) book *Roots*, in which Haley an African-American traced his roots to West Africa. The arrival of the Internet has contributed greatly to the development of these efforts via enquiries posted on notice boards, websites, discussion lists and exchanges of emails with online cousins and other relatives. In the USA, researching one's family tree is the second most popular hobby after gardening (Seabrook 2001). It is also popular in the Far East where respect for elders and ancestors is firmly embedded in these cultures. Chinese people have the oldest and richest genealogical history in the world, with detailed records dating back nearly three thousand years (Chao 2003). A similar tradition is evident in Korea (Paik 2000). Genealogical heritage-tourism is an emergent field of consumer behaviour. It has become a global pastime aided by the Internet, cheap air travel, and is an important revenue earner for numerous 'old' countries.

There are larger numbers of white people tracing their ancestry, commonly referred to as 'roots-tourism'. So significant has roots-tourism become in Scotland, that the Scottish Executive has identified it as an important niche market. Important consumers include US seniors, and Australian white-collar affluents from urban East Coast or Western Australia (Basu 2004). An estimated one in five Americans alive descended from the English, Irish, Scottish, or Welsh (http://www.ancestry.co.uk). In her study of Irish migrants tracing their ancestry Catherine Nash argues that 'old world ancestry reflects a nostalgia for an imagined time when place, identity, culture and ancestry coincided' (Nash 2007: 179). Personal genealogy projects comprise a complex network of interacting 'geographies of migration, origins and belongings' that sometimes reinforce the purity of ethnic identity, and sometimes offer contradictory interpretations. Irishness was perceived as a form of cultural capital among some middle and upper class Americans for whom the *whiteness* of their European roots was most prized. Likewise, Turner (1974) suggests that understanding roots-tourism is about *social drama*, finding one's people and one's place. It is engaging in crossing boundaries of familiar territory that can have a symbolic function. Pilgrims are often in possession of personal growth manuals including Frank MacEowen's (2002) *The Mist-Filled Path: Celtic Wisdom for Exiles, Wanderers, and Seekers* or Phil Cousineau's (1999) *The Art of Pilgrimage: The Seekers Guide to Making Travel Sacred*.

Seabrook (2001) maintains that ancestry tracing is an example of 'household genetics'. Genetic testing is a powerful tool in the genealogist's armory since it can provide data over much longer timescales than written records and in some developing countries it can compensate for their absence. It is estimated that more than 100,000 Americans, including celebrities like Oprah and Spike Lee have used genealogical DNA tests offered by commercial labs to learn about their ancestry. There are some fascinating discoveries that are helping to fuel commercial, web-based products. In 1997, Y-chromosome testing was used to determine the claims of families who believed they were descendants of Thomas Jefferson and his slave mistress Sally Hemings. Testing has also been used to provide evidence of genetic markers in the Lemba, a black southern African tribe whose tradition of oral history and customs have long denoted Jewish ancestry. Another example are the Melungeons, a mixed ancestry group who settled in the Appalachian mountains in eastern Tennessee and Virginia and whose ancestral origins had been unclear for centuries; genetic testing showed them as descendants of Sephardic Jews and Moors who fled the Spanish Inquisition. Other investigators have examined the relationship of DNA to identify membership of Indian tribes and castes (Kivisild *et al.* 2003). Elliot and Brodwin (2002: 1470–1471) maintain that 'Genetics can affect questions of ethnic identity (such as who counts as Cherokee or Maori), religious identity (who counts as Parsee or Jewish), family identity (who counts as a descendant of Thomas Jefferson), or caste (who counts as Brahman or Dalit)'. The commercialization of genetic ancestry tracing is a progression from academic research as the case study of spin-out company African Ancestry demonstrates.

Do you wonder what part of Africa you share ancestry with? We can tell you.

Would you like to develop a personal a connection with an African country? We can help you.

African Ancestry provides technology to help you trace your family history.

Trace your DNA. Find your roots.

http://www.africanancestry.com

The extract above is taken from African Ancestry's website that uses genetic testing to provide consumers with information about their family history. The Washington DC based company is one of the rapidly expanding number of organizations offering direct-to-consumer genetic testing. More than 3,000 people have taken African Ancestry's $349 genetic test. Alongside the testing kits the organization sells the African Ancestry Guide to West and Central Africa, African Ancestry baseball caps and gift vouchers. The site also includes a learning centre about the tribes in Africa and a news review section. Some 300,000 genes identified in the human genome contain 225 mutations called nucleotide polymorphisms that arose thousands of years ago and are linked to specific continents. The organization uses its African Lineage Database comprising 11,747 paternal and 13,690 maternal lineages from 160 ethnic groups. The data is 'a compilation of published sources, research collaboration and primary research'. DNA sequence data is sourced throughout the whole of Africa, although West and Central Africa are particularly well represented due to their participation in the Atlantic slave trade. The use of genetics to reveal ancestral history is of particular relevance to

African-Americans since they often have no other way of tracing their lineage. To a large extent, the slave trade severed their connection with Africa.

The organization's Patriclan Test uses the Y chromosome to trace the male line, father's father and so on, but does not include the father's mother. The Matriclan Test provides information about the equivalent female history. The tests comprise a swab kit with a few simple instructions and results are provided in six weeks. The results provide a country of origin analysis but not tribe-level data. Results are only provided on condition that a match of 90 per cent or higher can be identified.

African Ancestry has clearly identified a gap in the market for a new product in the form of a genetic test that meets the needs of one racial/ethnic group. However, there are concerns about the validity of the tests provided by African Ancestry and other similar DNA tests offered by commercial labs. As direct-to-consumer genetic testing becomes more commercialized the science becomes more simplistic, perhaps overly simplistic. Ancestry is not in perfect synchronicity, distributed in equal measure from relative to relative. For example, every person has four grandparents but 35 per cent of their genes may come from their maternal grandfather and 15 per cent from the other grandfather. Thus in some cases there may not be enough genes to show up in a test. There is also a criticism that tests demonstrate only a sliver of ancestry. If we go back 300 years we each have 1,000 ancestors but tests only provide data of about 1 in 1,000. There is a concern that some consumers may not be fully aware of the limitations of the science but nevertheless it may have a significant effect on their sense of identity, as revealed in some of the testimonials on the African Ancestry website.

Language and Internet use

An aspect of Internet use that has attracted relatively little attention is the impact of language as a cultural variable. Yet language choice and language use are an important way of signalling cultural identity in text-based computer-mediated communications, that transcend geographical boundaries and in which physical and social identifiers are reduced. To some extent this omission is beginning to be addressed with the publication of texts such as Danet and Herring's (2007) *The Multilingual Internet: Language, Culture and Communication Online*. Despite the worldwide use of the Internet the majority of websites are written in English. Castells (2001: 253) observes 'that 87 per cent of global websites are in English only'. This is even true of country websites where English is not the dominant language, such as the official websites of developing countries. In the mid-1990s, when 80 per cent of Internet users had English as their first language, the dominance of English language websites was not a serious issue. However, currently, less than half of people that browse the Internet have English as their first language. One view of the dominance of English is that it is a 'natural' benign extension of globalization. A radically different view is that the dominance of English is a form of 'linguistic imperialism' that threatens the status of smaller languages (Danet and Herring 2007: 3–4).

An important issue for the future is whether people from non-English-speaking communities will have to learn English in order to gain access to the services and information on the Internet, or conversely, whether the increase in users from non-English-speaking areas of the world will herald its decline. Some commentators have argued that Chinese may become the dominant language online as Internet penetration increases in China. Another debate is whether increase in global contact will create greater linguistic homogenization, or lead to linguistic diversity. The main sources of Internet user surveys tend to be marketing companies including Nielsen Net Ratings, Jupiter Research, and Global Reach, and government agencies, but much of this data is confidential. There are currently 6,000–7,000 living languages and the majority have less than 100,000 speakers. The most reliable data for the Internet indicates that it represents only 11 languages, all of which have numbers speaking in the tens or hundreds of millions (Paolillo 2007). From a commercial viewpoint, it is also important to note that secure servers are also dominated by English. A study conducted by the Organization for Economic Development (OECD 1999) discovered that 78 per cent of websites in OECD countries were in English, but that 91 per cent of websites on 'secure servers' were in English, and a higher proportion (96 per cent) of secure sites in the .com domain were in English.

Some commentators maintain that the dominance of English is contributing to a digital divide especially with respect to developing countries. Keniston (2004: 15) raises the case of India and notes that for 'Indians who speak no (or little) English, the barriers to the Information Age are almost insuperable'. A similar situation is evident in countries like Tanzania where more than a hundred minority languages are spoken, which are unrepresented online, and for the foreseeable future will remain so. A rather different issue is evident in the Arab world, where there is no uniform way of communicating in Arabic online, and many computers lack operating systems that can cope with Arabic. Another example is provided by the experiences of Uzbekistan, a country in Central Asia that was formerly part of the Soviet Union. Uzbek is the official language in that country replacing Russian. However, 17 per cent of Uzbekis who did have experience of using the Internet indicated that they used Russian, 70 per cent indicated that they used English, and only 13 per cent used Uzbek (Danet and Herring 2007).

The dominance of English is even apparent in countries that are highly multicultural such as the USA where there are large numbers of ethnic minorities for whom English is a second language (Luna *et al.* 2002). Furthermore, there are problems with treating English as a standardized language form. It is predicted that in the next decade or so the numbers of people who will speak English as a second language will exceed the number of native speakers. The centre of authority regarding the English language will shift from native speakers and evolve into a glocal language (Yano 2001). The form of English used in different countries or cultural groups might be very distinctive and not conform to that used in Anglo-Saxon countries.

Language and website design

Another important relationship between language and culture arises through the use of concepts, symbols and values that are embedded in language and are manifest in websites. Cultural congruity exists when linguistic forms are in synchronicity with the consumer's life experience. Incongruity exists when websites do not conform either linguistically or culturally to their expectations. Luna *et al.* (2002) maintain that cultural congruity can take two forms: *content congruity*, the inclusion of verbal and non-verbal content that resonates with different cultural groups; and *structural congruity*, denoting websites that conform to the thought processes within specific cultural groups which make them easier to navigate. Choices include flat or search-based sites and the importance attached to particular sections such as customer testimonials that reflect on their location within the stimulus. A fully integrated approach to website design would therefore provide consumers with a choice of language that would describe the technical aspects of a product and logistics of purchase, along with culturally appropriate content via symbols, values and rituals. In turn the marketers' use of the consumers' language may symbolize and be interpreted as appreciation for the visitors' culture. Without taking into account the culture of different groups of consumers, organizations will be engaged in designing ethnocentric websites that reflect their own cultural origins resulting in a production rather than a marketing orientation. Furthermore, websites that have low levels of congruity may be too difficult for consumers to process and result in negative evaluations. Conversely, websites that have very high levels of congruity maybe too predictable and boring and also result in negative evaluations albeit for different reasons.

In order to test their assumptions Luna *et al.* (2002) undertook a study of two groups of Spanish participants and one US sample all of which included Spanish-English bilinguals. They were asked to evaluate four different websites: (1) Spanish language and high-congruity graphics, (2) Spanish language and low-congruity graphics, (3) English language and high-congruity graphics, (4) English language and low-congruity graphics (Luna *et al.* 2002: 406). The results indicated the moderating effect of cultural congruity on language processing. High cultural and graphic congruity generated higher evaluations for second language sites rather than for first language sites. This finding suggests the extra cues and ease of navigation compensated for poorer language skills. This finding has important implications for marketers targeting cross-culturally and multiculturally since it suggests that if they produce websites with good graphics they may not need to translate their text into the customers' first language. This issue is particularly relevant for small and medium sized businesses for whom the costs of translating their websites into multiple languages may prove prohibitive.

Lynch and Beck (2001) surveyed 515 Internet buyers and their participants were drawn from 20 countries. They found significant variations between their three major regions: North America, Western Europe and Asia. North Americans were found to have the strongest preference for websites in their native language and were least satisfied with websites that were not designed for their world region.

However, it is unclear from the data whether their native language was presumed to be English. The North Americans were the group that had the highest degree of trust and the highest repeat purchase behaviour. Lynch and Beck maintain that building a standardized global web store on the US model may not be appropriate in other cultures given the different cultural characteristics of consumers. A case in point is Asia where consumers like to shop and have the strongest demand for branded products but they have the least favourable attitude to Internet shopping with respect to buying behaviour and the fear factor is the highest of all the regions. They found few differences between countries within different regions. A limitation of the study was that the sample was not a cross-section of the population or Internet buyers; 64 per cent were men, young (mean age 27), were well educated, had professional jobs and had travelled extensively.

Warden, Lai and Wu's (2002) study of Chinese consumers in Taiwan found that website language does affect consumer product evaluation. They argue that English is not a neutral communications medium, the international language of choice. It is preferable that organizations maintain websites in English, Chinese, Japanese in addition to various European languages, however the costs associated with this strategy are considerable. Warden *et al.* (2002) found that the use of native language does not necessarily lead to a higher product rating, and this was especially true of products with low levels of differentiation that were easy to understand. However, native language use did enhance attitudes towards differentiated products in low and high price categories. They maintain that the compromise position is for marketers to construct websites in English and augment them with product information in local languages. The Disney website in Asia is a good example of this local/global approach, whereby American Disney provide the main template and local offices are free to design pages focusing on local initiatives and items that are relevant to local consumers.

A related issue is that of literacy. Using the Internet requires basic levels of literacy since everyday conversation, including advice from sales people, is replaced by text. Marketers have yet to get to grips with this aspect of consumer behaviour in retailing and elsewhere (Wallendorf 2001). De Souza and Medeni's (2007) research of e-travel agents selling to Brazilian ethnic minority consumers (third largest foreign ethnic minority group 300,000) in Japan found that although Internet buying was useful, this group of customers preferred personal contact

> they prefer to look into the eyes of the person who is selling and be assured that the service will really be provided as promised . . . We clearly identified that because of the language barrier and cultural features, customers preferred to buy from, and maintain a relationship with, co-ethnic-owned travel agencies.
>
> (De Souza and Medeni 2007: 25)

Cyber crime and regulation

One of the biggest episodes in incidences of cyber crime occurred in 2003, when AOL the Internet company suffered a security breach that led to the theft of

92 million e-mail records. Ang and Lee (2002: 173) give the example of credit card fraud in Singapore. The company, Mustafa (http://www.mustafa.com.sg), which is well known for carrying a wide range of goods at low prices, had rung up sales of $1 million in June 1999 with very little advertising. Then, after it was hit by massive fraud, it stopped accepting credit card payments; sales plummeted to a few thousand dollars a month. In India Internet shopping is taking off with customers ordering groceries and cinema tickets but a problem is that payments made with credit cards need signature verification which is hampering progress (Rao 2002b).

Problems with credit cards have also caused problems with online gambling fraud. Credit cards are the preferred way to play since they are a convenient way to transfer money and for most payments transactions are made in US dollars. However, the controversy has occurred with charge-backs when customers indicate they have been charged for a service that they never received. To compensate for higher degrees of fraud associated with online gambling, credit card issuers charge higher rates to online-gambling sites, 4 per cent to an established firm and 9 per cent to a new site with no track record in credit card payments. These rates are two to three times greater than the norm for online retail transactions. Online gambling transactions are now identifiable by a special code that allows banks to decide whether they want to accept charges from a cardholder. Several lawsuits against banks and credit card companies along with higher security costs have limited the use of cards on some sites. As a consequence of the reluctance of credit card issuers to take what they view as unacceptable levels of risk, an alternative group of companies that specialize in electronic funds transfer have emerged as intermediaries (PayPal, FirePay and Citadel) (M. Wilson 2003).

Cybersquatting is another interesting development whereby private speculators seize valuable corporate brand names on the Internet and then attempt to sell them back for a huge amount of money to the organizations that carry those names.

There is recognition of the need for new policies to govern and regulate the new digital and media age in the public interest. The question of who will regulate is a pertinent issue as Poster (1995: 84) indicates: 'Nation-states are at a loss when faced with a global communications network. Technology has taken a turn that defies the power of modern governments'. Sassen (2000) maintains that there is regulation of Internet of sorts: technical standards of hardware and software, the protection of property rights and through aspects of the Internet address system and registry. Much of the work in developing instruments through which the state can exercise this authority is dominated by a limited number of countries, and in some respects the USA, which leaves other countries the task of catching up.

Indeed, it is the lack of regulation in cyberspace that has led to the emergence of new areas of business. In many advanced societies gambling is a regulated activity that creates regions, districts or specific locations where gambling may occur. For example, in the USA gambling sites are highly concentrated in the state of Nevada, Atlantic City and New Jersey, Zandvoort in the Netherlands, Brisbane in Australia, Seoul in Korea, and Estoril in Portugal. By contrast, some online gambling websites are registered in countries with questionable legal environments that undermine applying laws based on geographic boundaries (Wilson 2003).

Another area of concern is the advertising of pharmaceuticals on the Internet. Direct to consumer marketing of prescription drugs is illegal in most countries, although in New Zealand and the USA it has been permissible since 1981 and 1997 respectively. However, access to the sites is available to people living in other countries where direct to consumer advertising is illegal. In her analysis of antidepressant Internet marketing Woodlock (2005) found no preventative measures in this respect, which was worrying given that she found many of the websites seemed to be deliberately targeting vulnerable women.

Wiske and Schiller have discussed the issue of international Internet jurisdiction and they identify five main principles that shape international law and its relevance in cyberspace. First, the territoriality principle provides nation states with the right to control conditions under their jurisdiction which give government the authority to govern local web content and their link to computers elsewhere in the world. Second, the national principle enables states to regulate the behaviour of citizens at home and sometimes abroad. This would give the country or jurisdiction the right to prohibit residents from using particular types of websites such as gambling and pornography. Third, the effects principle can be used when there is a strong possibility of an act in one jurisdiction causing harm in another. Fourth, the protection principle allows government to protect its own functions when the activity takes place in another. For example, computer hacking and uncovering citizen's records. Fifth, the principle of universality applies to activities that are accepted as wrong across the world, such as abuses of human rights.

Yang (2007) reports that policies governing the Internet can be highly varied across different countries. He maintains that Hong Kong has a liberal policy, in China policies can be described as cautious and highly concentrated and Taiwan has taken a middle path.

Mobile commerce

'All the world seems to be on the move. Asylum seekers, international students, terrorists, members of the diasporas, holidaymakers, business people, sports stars, refugees, backpackers, commuters, the early retired, young mobile professionals, prostitutes, armed forces . . .' Internationally there are 700 million legal passenger arrivals compared with only 25 million in 1950 (Sheller and Urry 2006: 207). Sociology of mobility, how people travel from one destination to another, has been largely neglected in social science research, that has been described as static and trivialized the process of mobility and the methodological approaches that can be utilized to capture the process. Dholakia and Zwick (2003) have reviewed debates in the literature concerning the positive and negative effects of mobile technology. They conclude that 'mobile communications mean accessibility, and more importantly, the obligation to be accessible' (Dholakia and Zwick 2003: 10) and in so doing blur the boundaries between spaces for work, consumption and recreation.

The distinction between e-commerce and m-commerce is that e-commerce is fixed whereas m-commerce is characterized by 'novel, location-based services delivered by a variety of handheld terminals' (Dholakia and Dholakia 2004: 1391). The developments in e-commerce have largely been due to the Internet and the existence of web-browsers that are user-friendly. Preconditions for m-commerce take off, is that our mobile phones are data ready and are easily connected to digital communications networks. During the last few years other hand-held devices have emerged that widen the range of functions available. An interesting feature of mobile communications is that they do not closely relate to per capita income or existing patterns in Internet usage. The five countries that have the highest level of Internet users are Sweden, Finland, Denmark, Canada and the USA. Whereas the highest rates of mobile phone use are in Hong Kong, Finland, Sweden, Italy and Taiwan. In some countries there are stark differences between the penetration of mobile phones and Internet connections. For example, Canada and Australia have a strong Internet adoption record but are low in terms of mobile access. This is a similar pattern to that which is evident in the USA.

Mobile phones and landlines

Dholakia and Dholakia (2004) maintain that mobile technologies have some advantages over fixed voice or fixed PC-based data networks. Mobile phones also have considerable advantages over landlines. For example, in Jamaica around 86 per cent of the adult population (over the age of 15) own a mobile phone, compared to only 7 per cent of households that rely exclusively on landlines. In 2003, 75.9 per cent of all phone services were through mobile phones. By 2004, two million of the 2.6 million population were mobile phone subscribers comprising 80 per cent of the population (Office of Utilities Regulation 2004, cited in Horst 2006). This proportion of mobile phone use is much higher than in the USA at around 53.4 per cent, and 41.6 per cent in Canada. The percentage of users in Jamaica is on a par with that in the UK (Castells *et al.* 2005).

Horst's (2006) ethnographic account of the development of telephones and thereafter mobile phones in Jamaica, provides some interesting insights into the alternative trajectories that can be observed in different parts of the world. She makes the distinction between the *telephone box era*, the *house phone era* and the *mobile phone era*. Prior to 1995 the emphasis was on relatives living abroad to take responsibility for making telephone contact since few households had phones or access to phones. The density of phone ownership was very low comprising seven telephones in an area of 3,000 people in some locations. Making telephone calls from a phone box could be time consuming involving queuing for anything from 30 minutes to two to three hours in order to place a five minute telephone call. Another problem was the lack of privacy since other people could listen to what was said and this could be circulated as gossip. The late 1990s heralded the beginning of the house phone era when Cable and Wireless Jamaica Limited replaced Telecommunications of Jamaica Limited and made a concerted effort to extend phone lines to Jamaica's rural interior. Home phones provided a degree of privacy and much sharing of phones existed between neighbours and kin. However, high costs associated with calls and equipment in addition to the lack of security in connection with making international calls, meant that phones were used sparingly.

The mobile phone era began in 2001 when the company Digicel entered the market and placed mobile phone masts in many remote regions, along with supplying handsets for $30–50 (one week's wages for an individual engaged in domestic work). The costs of mobile phones could be controlled through prepayment phonecards, the company also charged per second rather than per minute like their competitor Cable and Wireless. In addition, phone calls abroad did not require the use of an operator and a degree of privacy could be maintained. Furthermore, the costs were perceived to be low since using the telephone to call overseas cost the same as a call to another company's mobile phone in Jamaica. Mobile phones facilitated a greater communication and intimacy between family members and loved ones. Moreover, families were able to check up on remittances (including emergency payments) that had been sent along with the arrival of 'barrels' that contained clothing, food, and other consumer items that had been purchased and shipped out. As Horst notes:

> The mobile phone became central to making specific requests to include special items in the "barrels", such as shoes and clothing, appliances, soap and detergents, as well as basic foodstuffs such as rice and cooking oil. It was easier to be involved in the day-to-day events of someone's life abroad.
>
> (Horst 2006: 154)

When it comes to bridging the divide between rich and poor countries it is the mobile phone and not the personal computer that is having the most impact. This development has prompted the view that emerging markets will be wireless-centric and not PC-centric. As noted above, mobile phones have become an important part of everyday life for many consumers in advanced societies. However, they are even more useful in developing societies where there is a lack of basic infrastructure and modes of communication such as roads, postal systems or land lines. In these contexts mobile phones have been used to very good effect. Fishermen and farmers are able to check on the latest prices before they sell their wares. Finding work becomes easier and quicker and the entrepreneurship is given a boost. Mobile phones can also be a convenient way of paying for goods and transferring money. Unlike fixed land lines, mobile phones are more flexible and can be easily shared by groups of people and even whole villages. Pre-paid phones do not require a bank account or credit check, which are further advantages.

Internet enabled mobile phone technology has increased in many markets following the first release of WAP (wireless application protocol) in 1998 when organizations began sending news alerts and location sensitive ads to mobile users (Okazaki and Taylor 2008) Japanese consumers are the most avid users of the mobile Internet which already exceeds the use of the stationary Internet. Funk (2005) maintains that m-Internet is based around the three cs – commerce, communication and contents. Commerce refers to activities including mobile banking and other forms of e-retailing. Communications include the use of web browsers and chatting. Contents comprise downloads, new and stock updates and other time-sensitive, location-based services. The annual spend via m-commerce is substantial. An analysis by category indicates that gambling, especially horse racing has the highest spend at US$ 2,370. Entertainment is the next most important category at $2,152, shopping follows closely at $2,001 and finally transactions including reservations and financial transactions at a much lower level of $474.

The attraction of mobile marketing for marketers and advertisers are the lower costs of reaching consumers compared to other media. Thousands of Japanese retailers, manufacturers and restaurants use the mobile Internet to send discount coupons, conduct surveys and offer free samples. In excess of 100,000 Japanese users redeem coupons (usually barcode-based coupons) with their mobile phones each month. Japan's leading video retailer, Tsutaya online, deals with several million redeemed coupons per month. Many restaurants also offer mobile-based coupons for discounts on nights when business is slow, thus offering potential to use mobile marketing as a form of dynamic pricing. Mobile phones are also used more generally as a points card for loyalty programmes instead of magnetic or paper points cards. Since small screens and keyboards make it difficult to search for products by using a search engine, many purchases are selected from personalized mail services for specific products that the users register for in advance. To some extent this process limits the product range sold over mobile phones. The fastest growing market segment is magazine advertising with fashions worn by celebrities on television programmes. Fashion-related magazines offer mobile alliances with large mobile shopping sites. Netprice is one of the leading providers in this market and its sales totaled $60 million in 2006.

SMS advertising

Research over many years has indicated that advertising can be at its most effective when it is delivered to the consumer at a time and place in which some need is salient. Within this context the mobile phone extends the traditional models of advertising. The mobile phone allows advertisers to increase the accessibility, speed and frequency of communication and as a result mobile ads can be delivered to consumers based on their socio-demographic profile and location. The short message service (SMS) or text messaging is the most widely used mobile application among some populations, and it has already been adopted as a direct marketing strategy. In 2005, around 36 per cent of marketers operating in Europe had used SMS ads for more than one year, and 39 per cent had begun to use it in the last 6–12 months. In the USA, mobile marketing and advertising expenditure reached $115 and $253 million respectively. In 2003, 56 per cent of mobile users received SMS ads in Germany, compared with 55 per cent in the UK, 47 per cent in Italy and France and 46 per cent in Spain (Okazaki and Taylor 2008).

The advantages of SMS advertising are that it can be highly tailored to individual consumers taking in contextual features including the customer's time, place and ads being delivered at the point of need. Consumer reactions to SMS advertising may be highly influenced by whether they already use the texting function on their mobile phones. There appear to be some cross-cultural differences in this respect. In France texting is very popular. In 2003, 9.8 billion SMS messages were sent, including 88 million on New Year's Day (Anis 2007). The context in the USA provides a sharp contrast, where 60 per cent of the population own a mobile phone, 90 per cent of phones are SMS capable but 80 per cent of mobile phone subscribers have never sent a text message. By contrast, in Korea 70 per cent of the Korean population own mobile phones and they are avid users of texting with only 3.8 per cent never having sent a text (Muk 2007).

One of the first trials of SMS advertising was in the UK. Respondents were paid cash incentives for receiving more than 100 messages in a six week trial period. Most responded that they were satisfied or very satisfied. Approximately, 81 per cent of the sample read all the messages, 63 per cent responded or took action, and 17 per cent forwarded at least one message. The respondents were positive about the experience of receiving SMS advertising with 84 per cent of the sample indicating that they are likely to recommend SMS advertising to friends, 24 per cent agreeing to receive them regularly and only 7 per cent likely to abandon the service. These positive findings have also been replicated in other SMS advertising research in which the majority of consumers liked receiving mobile advertising and it enjoyed a high level of recognition (Barwise and Strong 2002).

Not all studies of have reported positive results of the use of SMS advertising. Tsang, Ho and Liang (2004) were more cautious in their assessment of the potential of SMS advertising in Taiwan. The main findings of their study indicated that consumers have a negative attitude towards mobile phone ads unless they have consented to it in advance. Muk's (2007) investigation of intentions to opt in to SMS advertising by young Americans and Koreans indicated the intention to sign up was related to the extent they liked the new medium and the social pressure exerted on them to do so. Research in New Zealand has raised similar concerns. Carroll *et al.* (2007) found that mobile users were concerned that they had given their permission and had opted in before any mobile advertising messages of any kind were sent. Another important consideration was that the advertising was filtered by the service provider to ensure that it was advertising that the mobile phone user had specifically indicated that they would accept. Interestingly, the brand was of relatively little importance in these decisions. There was no preference for large well-known or local brands as long as the messages were filtered. Most consumers wanted a limit to the mobile advertising messages that they wished to receive and also some control over the time they were sent to prevent them being inundated at inconvenient times. Grant and O'Donohoe's (2007) research in the UK demonstrates that the motivation among young people for subscribing to mobile advertising was less positive. They found that mobile phones were used for convenient entertainment and social stimulation with or without friends around. The use of mobiles to obtain commercial information or advice did not even come on the radar.

Okazaki and Taylor (2008) have taken a rather different approach by questioning multinational companies in the USA, Europe and Japan about their reasons for using SMS advertising. They concluded that by far the most important factor was brand building. A second factor was the ability to offer location-based services which consumers perceive to be a major advantage. Location-based services can take a number of forms such as weather forecasts, restaurant guides, hotel maps, address finders, and traffic updates. New generation, real-time technologies will be able to advertise to consumers shopping in specific stores and in close proximity to retail outlets. The widespread availability of a suitable technological infrastructure in terms of a critical mass of mobile phone users was a third positive driver. The only negative factor was that consumers may have concerns about levels of privacy associated with SMS advertising.

For any company getting involved in m-commerce a decision that needs to be made is the appropriate language use. This issue was discussed in the previous chapter with reference to the Internet in connection with national languages. However, in m-commerce the issue is more complex given abbreviations in everyday use that are associated with short message services (SMS). Anis's (2007) study of linguistic neography (unconventional spelling) in France focuses on electronic messages sent by a French GSM (Global System for Mobile Communications) network. He notes a range of neographical transformations that deviate from the norms of standard French; including phonetic reductions, syllabograms (rebus writing b4 for 'before') and logograms such as symbols, abbreviations and acronyms (@ for 'at', or $ for 'dollar', f for 'female', IMHO 'In my humble opinion'). He notes that some cryptic messages need to be deciphered as though in a secret code that can only be unlocked by an 'in' group.

Market research

The previous section has addressed the issue of SMS advertising as a potentially important communications strategy of the future. Another use of SMS is as a market research tool. Web surveys are one of the fastest growing methods of data collection in advertising, accounting for approaching 40 per cent of all market research surveys conducted. It has also been reported that some market research agencies even consider web survey as a replacement, rather than a complementary technology to add to their portfolio. The benefits of web-based surveys are their ability to reach widely dispersed populations, within and between countries at a fraction of the cost of alternative methods and to do it more quickly (Schaefer and Dillman 1998; Couper 2000). The problems of web-based surveys are threefold. First, not all individuals have access to the Internet and users and non-users have different characteristics from each other. These differences are even more pronounced in less developed countries. Second, there tends to be a heavy reliance on non-probability, self-selected samples or individuals who have agreed to participate in online panels. It is very difficult to generate a random sample of email addresses and some anti-spamming legislation prohibits researchers from doing so. A third problem concerns low response rates in surveys and this is a particular problem for web-based surveys.

It has been suggested that the use of SMS technology can assist in the design and implementation of web surveys since the messages can be sent to mobile phones of large populations simultaneously, asking them to participate in web surveys. Balabanis, Mitchell and Heinonen-Mavrovouniotis (2007) have addressed this issue in their research in the UK. A text was sent to 200 randomly dialed UK mobile phone numbers. The eventual response rate was 36.5 per cent after three contacts. Of those that responded 56 per cent indicated that they would prefer to receive the survey via the web and 44 per cent via the telephone. The average age of those that agreed to participate was 32.2 years and 64 per cent of them were males. A noteworthy observation was that 44.5 per cent of all responses were received within five hours of the SMS being dispatched. The survey also demonstrated that interest or potential importance of the topic does not affect respondents' intentions to participate.

Questions

- Explain what you understand by the network society? What are the implications for cross-cultural marketers?
- What implications do geographical differences in Internet use have for cross-cultural marketers?
- Why might mobile commerce prove to be a more important marketing tool in some developing countries than ecommerce?
- What do you understand by the term cultural congruity in connection with language and web-site design?
- What does existing research reveal about the possibilities of using SMS advertising in cross-cultural marketing?

Further reading

Barwise, P. and Strong, C. (2002) 'Permission-based mobile advertising', *Journal of Interaction Marketing*, 16 (1): 14–24.

Castells, M. (2004) *The Network Society: A Cross Cultural Perspective*, Cheltenham: Edward Elgar, pp. 3–48.

Danet, B. and Herring, S.C. (2007) *The Multilingual Internet: Language, Culture, and Communication Online*, Oxford: Oxford University Press.

Dholakia, R.R. and Dholakia, N. (2004) 'Mobility and markets: Emerging outlines of m-commerce', *Journal of Business Research*, 57: 1391–1396.

Dholakia, R.R., Dholakia, N. and Khetri, N. (2003) 'Internet diffusion', in Bidgoli, H. (ed.) *The Internet Encyclopedia*, New York: Wiley.

Escobar, A. (1994) 'Welcome to Cyberia: Notes on the anthropology of cyberculture', *Current Anthropology*, 35 (3): 56–76.

Hiller, H.H. and Franz, T.M. (2004) 'New ties, old ties and lost ties: The use of the Internet in diaspora', *New Media and Society*, 6 (6): 731–752.

Liff, S. and Laegran, A.S. (2003) 'Cybercafes: Debating the meaning and significance of Internet access in a café environment', *New Media and Society*, 5 (3): 307–312.

Luna, D., Peracchio, L.A., and de Juan, M.D. (2002) 'Cross-cultural and cognitive aspects of web site navigation', *Journal of the Academy of Marketing Science*, 30 (4): 397–410.

Lynch, P.D. and Beck, J.C. (2001) 'Profiles of Internet buyers in 20 countries: Evidence for region-specific strategies', *Journal of International Business Studies*, 32 (4): 725–748.

Lynch, P.D., Kent, R.J. and Srinivasan, S.S. (2001) 'The global Internet shopper: Evidence from shopping tasks in twelve countries', *Journal of Advertising Research*, May/June: 15–23.

Panagakos, A.N. and Horst, H.A. (2006) 'Return to cyberia: Technology and the social worlds of transnational migrants', *Global Networks*, 6 (2): 109–124.

Wakeford, N. (2003) 'The embedding of local culture in global communication: iIndependent Internet cafés in London', *New Media and Society*, 5 (3): 379–399.

7 Pricing strategies

Introduction

Pricing is the area of the cross-cultural marketing mix that has been the most marginalized. One very innovative way to think about pricing is The Big Mac Index that was invented by *The Economist*'s economic editor in 1986, as a way of understanding exchange rates and comparative prices in different countries. The theory behind the Index is power, price, parity, denoting that over time 'exchange rates should move towards levels that would equalise the prices of an identical basket of goods and services in any two countries' (*Economist* 2006h: 94). The basket of goods is replaced by the Big Mac burger that McDonald's produce in 120 countries. The Big Mac power, price, parity is the exchange rate that would be required to enable consumers to purchase a Big Mac in their own currency as it would cost in US dollars in the USA. The Index was not designed to be a precise predictor of currency movements but over time burgernomics has proved reliable in forecasting the direction of foreign currency exchanges rates.

The first part of this chapter is to consider the relationship between price and consumer evaluations, and how these two variables can vary between cultures. Cultural differences and perceptions of price is the second theme of the chapter. Bargaining is not widely used in developed economies but is extensively used in emergent economies. Some of the strategies used in the bargaining process will be addressed in the third section of the chapter. Consumer tipping is more prevalent in some cultures than others. It can be an important factor in pricing decisions and consumer assessments of price. Consumer tipping will be addressed in the fifth section of the chapter. Price endings provide cues to customers about a whole range of product characteristics and this aspect of the marketing mix is discussed in the sixth section of the chapter. The perceptions of price endings also vary across cultures, for example superstition plays a part in Chinese culture in defining some numbers as unlucky.

The recycling of goods from the First to the Third World is one way that commodities can be priced so that they are affordable in subsistence economies. In the seventh section of the chapter two areas of recycling will be discussed: clothes and mobile phones. Low cost products specifically designed with developing countries in mind, are another way of pricing products that are affordable in different markets. In the eighth section of the chapter, three aspects of low cost products will be discussed: laptops, mobile phones, and cars. Free products are discussed in the penultimate section with respect to plastic surgery in Brazil. Consumers during crisis is the final theme to assess how consumers view prices in times of recession.

Price and consumer evaluations

A significant amount of research has demonstrated that consumers use price as an indicator of a product's or service's quality. Subjectivity plays a significant part in this process for a range of reasons:

- It is difficult to measure *quality* in an objective way. There is little systematic way of measuring the objective quality of a product or service.
- It is even more difficult to measure the *perceived quality* of a product or service. The concept of quality is subjective but it is not irrational and it is based on intrinsic product attributes such as physical characteristics, extrinsic product attributes that include branding, promotional strategies, and price.
- Perceived quality also combines with other evaluation criteria, monetary and non-monetary prices to form a perceived value that helps to shape a consumer's decision whether or not to buy a product or service.

A perceived monetary price means that consumers may not actually remember the exact price but that they have a general view of whether the price was cheap or expensive. There should be an alignment of the customer's perception of price in order for them to take the next step and buy. Consumers would be unlikely to make a purchase if they thought that a product was of poor quality but had a high price. However, customers have other agendas when evaluating prices. For example, in Western societies consumers make a trade off between time and money. Cash rich consumers who are time poor may buy lots of ready-made meals because they are too tired, or cannot be bothered to cook for themselves, despite the fact that ready made meals are expensive. Clearly, this example may not be relevant in all cultural contexts.

The relationship between price and objective quality has been measured through the use of consumer tests. For example, the *Which?* organization tests a range of goods and services and publishes them as a report which it distributes to its subscribers. Research has revealed that consumers often have a poor understanding of the relationship between price and objective quality. Furthermore, this observation extends across different countries. Usunier (2000: 361) indicates that 'it is not possible for consumers to assess clearly whether the Miele washing machine (from Northern Germany), three times more expensive than the Zanussi machine (from Italy, a subsidiary of the Swedish Electrolux group), lasts three times longer and is a considerably better performer in washing linen'.

Chung *et al.* (2006) conducted a study to examine cue utilization in assessing food product quality in the context of ready-made meals in India. The food market is worth $70 billion and processed meals account for $22.2 billion. The investigators compared the effects of *intrinsic cues,* such as taste and freshness, and *extrinsic cues*, such as price, packaging and brand name. Since there is an undifferentiated processed food market in India, consumers' use of cues is cultural and market specific. Indian consumers focus on price as the most important extrinsic cue in inferring product quality, whereas prestigious/famous brand names influence consumer perceptions of taste, but have no influence on freshness and nutrition. Despite some of the difficulties in the price/objective quality relationship, research demonstrates that price is a universal signal for quality across nations and culture.

Price-matching refund policies are strategies in which retailers indicate that they will not be undersold, and will have a refund policy, or will offer to match the lowest price available in the market. Conventionally, advertisements will state 'In the unlikely event that you find an identical item that you purchased here for a lower price at another store, we promise to refund the difference, or 'Our price-matching policy guarantees you the lowest price. If you find an item that you purchased here for a lower price elsewhere, we will gladly refund the difference'. Price matching policies have attracted relatively little research from academic researchers, and even less in the context of cross-cultural research. Research by Srivastava and Lurie (2001) on price-matching policies in the USA indicated that they do have a significant impact on consumer perceptions of store price and price search behaviour. When a store offered a price-matching policy, consumer perceptions of the store price were lower, and the likelihood of discontinuing the search was higher.

The internet has facilitated consumer evaluations of price and service quality, and is a prominent feature of what has become known as medical tourism. Some advanced countries including Britain and Canada, have long waiting lists for some medical procedures as supply has not kept up with demand. The market for low cost surgery abroad has developed as individuals opt to have their operations abroad at a time when it suits them, at a much lower cost than they would pay at home. It is largely developing countries that have been keen to tap into what has become a global market. For example, India attracted approximately 150,000 medical tourists in 2003, and it has been estimated that medical tourism could raise an additional 50–100 billion rupees ($1.1 to 2.2 billion) in annual revenue by 2012. However, in the international market India lags behind Thailand that attracts as many as a million medical tourists each year. Most of those arriving in India are from poor countries where some services are not available. Procedures that are currently on offer are wide-ranging and include disease management (joint replacements, heart bypasses and cataract operations) and elective treatments (cosmetic surgery and in-vitro fertilization). India is comparatively well qualified and cheap in most aspects of health care from new-drug discovery and testing, to surgery. India already offers what it refers to as health tourism including holidays that focus on aspects on Indian culture including yoga, massages, and traditional ayurvedic medicine.

In some cases the price differential of having procedures in developing countries can be significant. A hip replacement procedure that would cost around £10,000 in Britain, could be obtained in India for £6,000, and the price includes a four week stay. Chains of specialist hospitals around India perform heart bypass surgery which can be performed for one-third of the cost of a private operation in Britain.

The Indian diaspora is potentially a lucrative market. There are nearly 1.5 million people of Indian origin in Britain who may respond to advertising approaches that offer medical procedures in conjunction with a vacation to visit extended family. Potential future developments include charter flights with doctors and nurses onboard (*Economist* 2004a).

Cultural differences in perceptions of price

The impact of culture on price awareness is widely acknowledged (Ger and Belk 1996; Keegan and Schlegelmilch 2000) yet few studies have been undertaken specifically on cross-cultural aspects of consumer price knowledge. It is crucial that companies act globally and investigate how consumer price knowledge varies across countries and cultural groups (Aalto-Setala *et al.* 2006). Price is the least researched area within the cross-cultural and multicultural marketing mix. Some of the earliest literature focused on sales promotion and coupon usage among different ethnic groups (Green 1995a and b), information search behaviour between ethnic groups. Chin (2001) provides an interesting account of black kids and consumer culture that deals with some of the most pertinent issues associated with marketing in low income neighbourhoods, including price. Wallendorf's (2002) review of the impact of literacy on consumption is also relevant to pricing issues in a multicultural and cross-cultural marketing context. The consumption consequences of low levels of literacy can affect higher order, information processing functions, including discriminating on price (see Adkins and Ozanne 1998; Viswanathan and Harris 1999).The lower levels of internet access among some ethnic groups also means that they are disadvantaged in taking advantage of cheaper prices and keener rates offered by some online retailers (Hoffman and Novak 1998).

Estelami *et al.* (2001) conducted an analysis of 297 published articles on consumer price knowledge studies spanning 40 years, in order to document the effects of *inflation, unemployment, GDP growth, interest rates, country of study* and *passage of time*. It is noteworthy that 80 per cent of the studies were conducted in the USA. They found that economic expansion in the context of *GDP growth* decreases consumer price knowledge, seemingly prosperity reduces the need to pay attention to price inflation. *Inflation* was found to have a negative effect on price recall accuracy, since price instability could ensue. However, inflation had less of an effect on consumer price knowledge than economic growth. *Interest rates* had a relatively small impact on price recall accuracy as a result of interest rate information not being actively possessed, or easily processed by consumers. *Unemployment* did not have a significant effect on consumers' price knowledge.

Another study that compared the price knowledge of consumers in France and the USA demonstrated that frequent promotions increased consumers' ability to remember regular prices. Perhaps contrary to what might be expected, store switchers did not possess better price knowledge than other shoppers (Vanhuele and Dreze 2002). Another study that explored the differences between German and Finnish consumers, found that overall price knowledge was low among both groups. Approximately 31 per cent of Finnish consumers and 53 per cent of German consumers claim to have no knowledge of particular prices. Furthermore, there was substantial evidence of price estimation error between products. Finnish consumers gave price estimates more frequently than Germans but the estimates of German consumers were more accurate than those provided by the Finns.

Price is an important aspect of the marketing mix in developing countries such as those in Asia, and there can be significant differences in consumer price perception between Asian countries that, at face value, would appear to be culturally similar. For example, Sternquist, Byun and Jin (2004) have compared price perception among Chinese and Korean consumers. They found that price is generally not linked to quality by Chinese consumers, and they shop on the basis of price. For Korean consumers, value for money is an important issue in price perceptions. These findings may reflect cultural and historical realities in the two countries. There is a significant tradition of haggling in Chinese shopping behaviour that may be related to price consciousness and the need to be frugal. Furthermore, Chinese consumers have tended to be less brand-conscious than Korean consumers, especially in the context of goods that are used for private consumption. However, brands have started to gain more popularity in Chinese culture over the last few years.

Korean consumers have traditionally tended to be prestige oriented and unwilling to buy unknown or less prestigious brands. Thus it would seem that high price has operated as an indication of prestige. However, a number of foreign retailing discount stores have entered Korea over the last few years, which may have influenced the importance of the relationship between price and value in Korean shopping habits. Changes in the economy play an important role in consumer perceptions of price. In Korea the effects of the recession in 1997 had the observable effect of making consumers more price conscious. The same was also true of Japan, which witnessed little price competition until the recession of the 1990s. Now discount retailers in Japan emphasize low prices.

In many countries pricing strategies are designed to exploit human psychology and retail prices are set high in order that discounts can be offered. In this respect consumers believe that they have bagged a bargain. Islamic law prohibits this practice and disallows price changes that do not reflect related adjustments in product quantity and quality, since there is potential to intentionally deceive consumers for personal gain. Many consumers in Islamic countries are price sensitive, lack an appreciation of high quality, and have a limited understanding of value added. Thus drawing attention to core attributes as opposed to augmented attributes is a useful strategy when marketing in Islamic countries (Marinov 2007).

Food retailing in advanced Western societies is highly segmented but some of the largest retailers compete aggressively on price. A low cost pricing strategy is particularly suited to developing economies. Tesco has taken processes that work well in the United Kingdom and applied them in other countries, undertaking minimal amounts of research beforehand. The company's experience is that low prices are an important factor across Central Europe. Tesco engages in competitive pricing, uses regular special offer pricing, and price discounts. The company's 'value' and standard lines have been introduced in all Central European countries but the more expensive 'Finest' range have not because of consumer preferences for low prices. The emphasis on price has also kept facilities in the stores quite basic to keep costs down, so for example there were no café facilities available which have come to be the norm in more affluent countries (Rogers *et al.* 2005).

Wal-Mart the world's largest retailer that focuses on low price provides another example. How retailers market themselves on cost and value for money in different cultures provides some interesting insights into consumers' perceptions of price in various markets around the world. A very good example in this respect is Wal-Mart's attempts to consolidate its position in the Japanese market. Wal-Mart purchased a 51 per cent share of the Seiyu supermarket chain comprising 400 stores in 2005, at a cost of $1 billion. The theory behind the move was fear of overdependence in its US home market, which is potentially nearing saturation point. As the second largest economy in the world, a population of 127 million and one of the highest per capita incomes in the world, Japan was perceived to have all the hallmarks of a lucrative market. However, there have been some challenges in reconciling the price versus quality relationship.

In order to reduce overheads and keep prices competitive, the company was persuaded to dismiss 25 per cent of its headquarters' staff that included 1,500 employees and managers. Redundancy rarely happens on this scale in Japan where there is a premium on harmony in employee relations. When the dismissal is orchestrated by foreigners the fallout is particularly negative, and it created a climate of resistance which was interpreted by the media as an American company attempting to transfer a US operating model to Japan. A central problem is Wal-Mart's claim to offer 'always low prices'. This strategy has been successful in developing markets including China and Mexico but not so in countries similar to Japan where customers are happy to pay high prices for goods of the highest quality, and they are unlikely to discuss buying products at a discount. If Japanese consumers get a good deal they tend not to share information with others but would rather that people believe that they paid the full price (Sternquist *et al.* 2004). As one business publication observed of Wal-Mart, 'National-brand food prices have definitely come down, but high quality merchandise has disappeared from the shelves, and customers have left' (Holstein 2007: 52). Furthermore, Wal-Mart's strengths are in scouring the world for the best quality, cheapest source for a product. However, where food is concerned, Japanese consumers prefer Japanese-made products. Some commentators have even suggested that the company has got it so wrong that they should pullout of the country and focus on China (Holstein 2007).

D'Andrea *et al.* (2006c) provide a valuable insight into the role of promotions and other factors affecting overall store price image in Latin America. Their study was conducted in five major cities: Bogota, Buenos Aires, Mexico City, Santiago and São Paulo. They revealed five major consumer shopping segments in Latin American cities: *avid bargain hunters, high income bargain hunters, frustrated shoppers on a budget, range seekers on a budget, quality seekers and time savers.*

Avid bargain hunters were the consumers that were the most price sensitive of all; they shop a lot and are willing to visit a variety of stores in their search for a bargain. This group were the ones that most frequently compared prices, with 60 per cent indicating that they compare prices of goods often or very often. The consumers in this group are generally from the lower socio-economic groups, are male, and over 50 years of age. They spend the least on groceries of all the groups, 14 per cent less than average. They are the least loyal group, preferring to frequent modern discount stores. São Paulo and Buenos Aires had the highest proportion of consumers in these groups accounting for 40 and 30 per cent of the sample respectively. Bogota had by far the fewest numbers of consumers in this category.

High income bargain hunters are price sensitive and are willing to visit multiple stores to secure the best price. However, unlike the previous group they tend to shop in a narrower range of store notably modern supermarkets and hypermarkets. These consumers spend the highest proportion on goods, 15 per cent more than the average. There is no consistent pattern of loyalty behaviour in this group; some consumers are loyal to a particular store, others are not. There were similar proportions of consumers in these groups across the five cities ranging from 14–18 per cent. The only exception was in Bogota where this group accounted for 25 per cent of the sample.

Frustrated shoppers on a budget are low and middle earners who invest little time in shopping. They tend to be frustrated because they cannot afford many items they would wish to purchase and this explains their dislike of shopping. Their spending is 7 per cent less than the average and this group make less use of modern formats and shop in more traditional outlets. These shoppers tend to be concentrated in São Paulo, Buenos Aries, and Mexico City where this group accounts for between 20 and 26 per cent of the total.

Range seekers on a budget search out good quality produce but are constrained by a lack of spending power. Typically, this group are young, low income mothers, who live in larger households of six or more. Their spending is 4 per cent less than average and they tend to prefer to use hypermarkets. They are less loyal than other groups and tend to do one big shop per month. One quarter of shoppers in Santiago and Bogota were in this category.

Quality seekers and time savers are the most affluent with a monthly spend nearly 20 per cent higher than other groups. Consumer in this category will pay a premium in order to save time and have access to higher quality goods. They favour modern format stores and do not have the time to shop around for the best deal. Only 25 per cent of respondents indicated that they compared prices always or very often. Nearly one third of consumers in Mexico City, Santiago, and Bogota were in these categories but only 8 per cent in São Paulo.

When customers were asked whether they assessed store prices based on a few key products, most indicated that they did. The average number of prices that they memorized ranged from 3 to 5.1 per cent. The accuracy of price perceptions varied significantly with only 33 per cent of consumers in São Paulo correctly recognizing prices, compared with 79 per cent in Santiago.

Bargaining

Buying behaviour does not always revolve around retailer determined prices and non-bargainable products. Within developed societies there is less emphasis on bargaining than in developing countries. Regulation and consumer protection measures ensure that goods and services in advanced societies are appropriately priced and consumers have recourse to redress if they are not satisfied. In supermarkets and large stores, prices are non-negotiable, consumers make a decision to pay the price that is offered or not, it is a binary decision yes or no. However, in some local stores consumers do ask for a discount or for some extras to be provided for free. One example is the discount that some stores are willing to provide to senior citizens, especially at times of the week when business is slow. Another occasion might be when consumers offer cash for a purchase rather than paying by bank card. Bargaining does occur in some informal aspects of retailing such as car boot sales, swap meets and so forth, where negotiating a competitive price is part of the fun of the shopping experience. In developed countries bargaining occurs in specific purchasing contexts, especially with respect to large, occasional purchases such as cars, houses, and furniture. One study in the USA indicated that 35 per cent of durable goods retailers were willing to negotiate prices with consumers. A further study suggests that strength in numbers and a forceful communications style could contribute to getting a better deal (Dwyer 1984). With respect to organizational purchases, another range of factors offer bargaining opportunities, including customized products, services, order quantities, and delivery schedules.

Brucks and Schurr (1990: 409) define bargaining as 'a process by which two or more parties mutually define one or more attribute values for a product. From an information processing viewpoint, information uncertainty is what distinguishes a purchase involving bargainable attributes from a purchase involving fixed attribute values'. The buyer must acquire and evaluate information in order that they can make a choice among alternatives and place values on various attributes. Thus the final price achieved by the bargainer is dependent on the information search process and the bargaining process. In their study of consumers in the USA, they found that buyers reduce the amount of time they spend on information search activities when they have the option of bargaining.

In developing countries where markets and bazaars remain popular methods of shopping and financial resources are limited, bargaining is the norm, even for products of low value and low involvement products. Accurate information about prices is often the scarcest commodity because commodities are rarely standardized, the supply of some goods is extremely variable, prices are rarely marked on either the stall or product, and because bargaining is the usual way to negotiate a deal, prices can vary from transaction to transaction. From a Western standpoint, the lack of public knowledge about prices could be construed as a 'market failure', and symptomatic of an underdeveloped economic infrastructure. However, another interpretation is that inequalities in access to price information enable the traders to make a profit (Alexander and Alexander 2001). In some instances bargaining is an important survival strategy. Consumers are willing to invest time in bargaining in order to secure a better price. In developed countries consumers would make a trade-off between the time that the bargaining would take, the amount of discount achieved, and an assessment of whether the time could be better spent. In other words, there would be a calculated assessment of time versus money.

It would be incorrect to assume that bargaining and information search are unrelated in developing countries. Clifford Geertz has explored this aspect of pricing in the bazaar economy in Morocco. He notes that in the bazaar 'information is poor, scarce, maldistributed, inefficiently communicated, and intensely valued . . . The level of ignorance about everything from product quality and going prices to market possibilities and production costs is very high' (1978: 29). However, he makes the important point that these ignorances are *known* ignorances; it is not simply a matter of information that is lacking. As a consequence, information search in the bazaar is an art. Though price setting is the most obvious aspect of bargaining, the bargaining ethos can penetrate the whole transaction. Quantity and quality can be adjusted while keeping the price constant, credit arrangements can be varied, and bulk buying can lead to price adjustments. Thus bargaining can be a very intensive and detailed experience and having access to information is the key. In the bazaars there is a distinction made in the terminology between bargaining to *test the water* and bargaining to *conclude the purchase*. Furthermore, these two activities occur in different places. The first takes place with people with whom the customer has weak clientship ties, and the second with whom they have firm ties. The shops at the edge of the bazaar claim that they are 'rich in bargaining but poor in selling', in other words consumers do their market research in these places before going to their regular seller. Geertz concludes that 'Most bazaar "price negotiation" takes place to the right of the decimal point. But it is no less keen for that' (1978: 32)

In some cultures a ritual surrounds the practice of bargaining. In the Middle East, the interaction always begins with indications of respect, affection and trust in order to create an impression of friendliness and common bonds. When the consumer shows signs of interest and asks the price the seller might reply vaguely as follows:

> Between us there is no difference; we share the same interest, price is not what pleases me, what pleases me is to find out what pleases you; pay as much as you want; brothers do not disagree on price; for you it is free; it is a gift.
>
> (Usunier 2000: 356).

The next stage in the process is that the customer insists that a price is stipulated. The vendor then indicates a price after a lengthy preamble extolling the virtues of the product. It is bad practice for the customer to question the quality of the product because it could make him or her appear ignorant and thus vulnerable. Thereafter if the consumer decides to buy they agree a price and the transaction is concluded.

It can be disconcerting for a customer to ask the price of a product if the price is not displayed. However, in some cultures asking the price is considered indicative of behaviour of people in the lower classes that have low purchasing power. In the United Kingdom there is a saying which states, 'If you have to ask the price you can't afford it'. A similar sentiment is also true in Zambia as Roeber explains:

> Working people, I was told, were 'sufferers'. The meaning of that word was best explained by the man who stated vehemently, 'If you have to ask the price of something, you are automatically a sufferer'. . . there was another

category of people, the *apamwamba* or 'big shots', who did not have to ask for the price of commodities. They always had money to buy what they needed.

Some Avon ladies have even been known to negotiate and barter with consumers. One agent in Brazil exchanged a dozen eggs for a roll-on deodorant, and twenty pounds of flour for cologne (Klepacki 2005).

Differences in bargaining between different cultures is at its most obvious when they meet together, for example in the context of tourist exchanges. In Jamison's study of tourism in Kenya, Kikuyu hawkers in the Curio Village credited their knowledge of tourists and their ability to discern differences in tourist behaviour at a national level, as vital to their success (Jamison 1999). He notes that the British did not like to bargain and instead of gradually increasing the price, wanted an initial price that was close to the eventual price. The German tourists would quickly become frustrated with the bargaining process and an initially high price would cause them to move on. The Italians liked bargaining and would enjoy the process for as much as an hour before arriving at a final price and purchase. The hawkers factored these behaviours into their pricing structures, with the Italians being given the highest initial price, in anticipation of the bargaining that was to follow. For them bargaining was a value added part of the sales encounter. Although knowledge was incomplete and stereotypical it served as a basis for action – a rule of thumb for the hawkers.

Consumer tipping

In some cultures consumers give gifts of money, or tips to workers who have provided them with a service. The giving of tips is unlike most other economic transactions that have specified obligations regulating the exchange that are enforced in law. Customers who wish to purchase goods or services have to pay the specified price. The alternative is for individuals to refrain from the purchase, or steal the goods in question for which legal recompense is normally undertaken. However, there are relatively few rules concerning tipping, it is largely a matter that is governed by norms in different cultural contexts and/or a matter of individual conscience. Difficulties emerge when consumers contravene existing cultural norms governing tipping, by, for instance, failing to provide a tip when one was expected. Tipping is a topic of considerable economic importance in some countries. For example, in the USA consumer tips are worth many billions of dollars a year. Thus they provide an additional income for many low income service workers such as bar people, taxi cab drivers, porters, and beauticians. Furthermore, and of relevance to our discussions of pricing, tips are additional costs adding to the price of the service/product for consumers.

Tipping is also of significance to marketers since businesses that permit or actively promote the practice, allow consumers to set the price of the service, or at least a proportion of it. This in turn could have implications for overall business costs. For example, organizations could pay lower salaries in the knowledge that employees would make extra money on tips. This is especially the case in some developing countries in which taking a job in a hotel on low rates of pay is acceptable, because substantial tips from foreign guests are anticipated. In service contexts comprising intangible and highly customized services, employers are not always in the best position to assess the contribution of employees. Customers are in a better position to evaluate and reward employees' efforts. Not all organizations do permit tipping and have signs to inform consumers of this policy, others institutionalize tipping by introducing fixed service charges, yet others encourage consumers to provide tips on top of service charges. Despite the importance of consumer tipping in some cultural contexts it has rarely attracted attention in marketing and consumer research.

Lynn *et al.* (1993) have provided one of the few accounts of cross-country tipping. They suggest that a number of factors have been examined in the relationship between tip size and other variables, although it needs to be recognized that much of the literature is based on experiences in the USA. *Bill size* is the largest single predictor of tip size in restaurants, accounting for in excess of 50 per cent of the variance in tip size in many studies. Social norms in the USA dictate that tipping should account for 15–20 per cent of the total bill. *Server friendliness* is another strong predictor of tipping behaviour. Consumers give bigger tips when restaurant servers introduce themselves by name, smile at the customer, touch customers, and bend down next to the table when interacting with customers. *Server attractiveness* is another important feature, the higher the perceived attractiveness the bigger the tip. *Customer sex* is also a predictor of tip size, with men leaving larger tips than women. Why this occurs is unclear but suggestions have included differences between men's and women's income, familiarity with tipping norms and desire to impress the waitresses.

Cross-country differences in tipping behaviour have been documented by Nancy Star in her book entitled *The International Guide to Tipping* (1988). She describes the tipping practices of 38 service occupations in 34 countries. Lynn *et al.* (1993) used this data to examine the relationship between cross-cultural differences in values and tipping behaviour using Hofstede's framework. With respect to power difference, tipping appears to be more prevalent in countries with a high tolerance of status and power differences, than in countries whose tolerance of differences is low. Contrary to what they expected, tipping was more prevalent in communalistic countries than individualistic ones. Finally, tipping was less prevalent in so-called feminine countries that emphasize social relationships compared with countries with masculine values where the focus is on achievement and economic relationships.

The practice of tipping is one that would benefit from further research that emphasizes *cultural* differences surrounding the practice as opposed to *cross-national* differences. This approach would include ethnic and religious differences that could influence tipping behaviour in various countries.

Price endings

The presentation of price information in a globalizing world is an important consideration. A pivotal debate is whether organizations should use a standardization strategy, or adapt to local cultural conditions. In many Western countries certain digits occur more frequently than others in everyday life, and these tend to be 0 and 5. However, certain digits are likely to be perceived as the most appropriate right-most ones to use by marketers and consumer alike. Prices send out information to consumers about the *image of a product*. In the USA 99-endings tend to communicate a lower price image because 99-endings are perceived as lower prices. Consumers also learn from their marketplace interactions that 9-ending prices are used more for discount prices than for regular priced goods, and lower priced rather than higher priced retailers. Thus the 99-ending has been found to communicate a low price image. Price endings research has also been found to communicate an *unfavourable impression in relation to quality*. This observation may stem from a negative impression of the store and/or product quality because of the use of 99-endings and their low-price image. Because sometimes consumers use prices for judging quality, the idea of a low price may transfer to meaning lower quality. However, consumers may also learn from their marketplace interactions that retailers with an upmarket image tend to use prices that end in the digit 0 and avoid 9, and the reverse was true of retailers that had a more down market image like Wal-Mart. Schindler and Kibarian (2001) found that when the price in advertisements ended in 99 rather than 00, US consumers were more likely to regard it as the lowest price available and to consider it a discount price. Furthermore, advertisements of upmarket retailers that had 99-endings, decreased the customers' perception of the quality of the advertised item, and it also had wider negative implications relating to the overall quality of the merchandise and the classiness of the image *per se*.

Suri *et al.* (2004) studied the use of 9-ending prices in newspaper advertisements in the USA and Poland. They found that three quarters of advertised prices in the US sample, and 92.5 per cent of the Polish sample, did not have digits after the decimal place. No advertisements had just one digit after the decimal place and only 21.9 per cent of US and 6.8 per cent of Polish ads had two digits after the decimal point. Three digits were over-represented in the right-most digit position in both samples; these were 0, 5 and 9. In the US sample 12 per cent of right-end digits were 0, 22.7 per cent 5 and 43 per cent 9. The results for the Polish sample were very different; 44.4 per cent of the right-end digits were 0, 11.3 per cent 5, and 24.8 per cent were 9. In accounting for these differences, Suri *et al.* cite the bargaining culture that exists in Poland and having odd values at the end of a price would be considered something of a nuisance. A more wide-ranging study of prices posted on the internet in ten countries, found that price-endings varied between high and low context cultures. Consumers in non-Western cultures were not likely to be swayed by the illusion of cheapness or companies gain credit for model endings. To the contrary, consumers were more likely to be offended by perceived attempts to 'fool' them (Nguyen *et al.* 2007).

Cultural superstitions and price endings have attracted little attention. Simmons and Schindler (2003) have addressed this issue in the context of China. Price endings with the digit 9 are common in Western societies such as the UK and USA. However, this convention is not observed in China. In their assessment of 499 price ads, Simmons and Schindler observed that 8 is the most prominent non-zero ending and it is associated with prosperity and good luck. The digit 4 is avoided since it is associated with death. Within the sample, the end digit 8 was over-represented and the digit 4 was under-represented. The division between the use of the digits 8 and 4 was more pronounced in the context of lower priced items and less so in higher priced goods. These findings have suggested a Westernizing influence in higher priced goods.

Pricing of recycled goods

Within the consumer behaviour literature there has been an increase in attention paid to disposal rather than consumption. This is partly due to the criticisms of the consumer society as the throwaway society. Vance Packard was one of the first commentators to become a popular voice of the critique of the cycle of consumption and waste. In his trilogy of books *The Hidden Persuaders* (1957), *The Status Seekers* (1959) and *The Wastemakers* (1960) he accused large companies of encouraging disposability through several strategies, but particularly via planned obsolescence.

Most of this literature relates to disposal and second-hand use in developed economies and factors that increase or decrease an individual's willingness to purchase used goods. Some of these features include economic constraints and thriftiness, alongside demographic and behavioural contexts that affect purchasing decisions. Two aspects of recycling goods will be discussed in this section; clothes and mobile phones.

Clothing

Roux and Korchia (2006) have explored the symbolic meanings associated with second-hand clothing in France and note that there is often a taboo against re-using some types of clothes such as those with real or imagined body markings such as perspiration, stains or body odour. However, not all used clothing triggers aversion, such as mementoes from loved ones and wearing friends' clothes. Some consumers want the uniqueness that second-hand clothes can give them in order to separate them from the masses.

A rather different perspective on consumer disposal is how goods that are disposed of in advanced societies are 'consumed' in developing countries because of their low price. Worldwide trade in second-hand clothing increased six fold between 1980 and 1995. Sub-Saharan African countries are the largest importers. The USA is the world's largest exporter, followed by Germany, the Netherlands, Belgium and the United Kingdom. Used clothing is the sixth largest export from the USA to sub-Saharan Africa, accounting for nearly 40 per cent of the second-hand clothes market in the mid-1990s. Most of the clothing is sourced from charitable organizations that have excess capacity after choosing what to sell through their shops. They sell between 40 and 60 per cent of what they collect to recyclers or rag graders. The clothing is then sorted into different categories of garments and graded and placed in batches ready to be shipped. The category 'used clothing' also includes shoes, handbags, towels, sheets.

National culture affects whether second-hand clothes are imported, and what types of garment are allowed. For example, North Africa's Muslim influence is reflected in the fact that few second-hand clothes are imported. In Zaire an 'authenticity' code prohibits men from wearing Western coats and ties, and women from wearing jeans. In 1997, the new President of Congo banned women from wearing trousers, stretch leggings, and short skirts. In some cultures imported second-hand clothes were compared unfavourably with locally designed and manufactured clothes, yet in others they were considered far superior. Some countries have charged high import tariffs to protect their domestic textile industry (for example Mali) and others have at some time banned the import of second-hand clothes (Kenya, Nigeria, and Côte d'Ivoire).

Second-hand clothes are often given specific names in different cultures that sometimes have Western connotations. In Zaire they are called Vietnam, and in Ghana they are given a local name that means 'dead white men's clothes' (Stearns 2001). Karen Hansen (1999) sheds some light on the interplay between the local and the global with respect to second-hand clothing in Zambia. It has become common in Zambia since the mid-1980s, to refer to the term *salaula*, meaning second-hand clothing that has been imported from Western countries. *Salaula* within the Bemba language means 'to select from a pile in the manner of rummaging'. Hansen argues that this accurately reflects what goes on in urban and provincial markets throughout the country as consumers search through piles of imported clothing before selecting items that suit their needs, at a price they can afford to pay. By the 1990s, the *salaula* sections of outdoor markets had exceeded those devoted to food in both urban and regional markets. In the countryside, second-hand clothes are often exchanged for agricultural produce and foodstuffs. Most sections of society purchase second-hand clothes, apart from those in the highest social class that can afford to buy new designer clothes. Results of Hansen's survey demonstrated that approximately two thirds of surveyed households in high income areas satisfied their clothing needs from *salaula*, and more than half of these households also used a tailor on a frequent basis. Consumers in the lower socio-economic groups purchased most of their clothes via *salaula* apart from some items like children's school uniforms. Nurses who do not have the financial resources to buy a new uniform sort through *salaula* looking for lab coats and many young men buy their first suit in this way.

The process of shopping for clothes via *salaula* resembles that in Western societies. Hansen observes:

> When shopping for *salaula*, consumers have a number of things in mind, depending on whether they are covering basic clothing needs or satisfying specific desires. The scrutiny of *salaula* takes time. Colour co-ordination is keenly attended to, and there are issues of size and fit to consider. Regardless of income group, most consumers considered 'value for money' a major selection criterion, discerning 'good value' in terms of both quality and fashion/style. Low-income customers both in Lusaka and in the province paid attention to garment durability/strength, whereas young urban adults looked for 'the latest'. This is their own term, and it comprises influences from South

Africa, Europe and North America as well as from specific youth cultures. Because many men's trousers are too big and many women's dresses too tight for adult male and female Zambian bodies, young adults in fact have the best choice in the *salaula* markets.

(Hansen 1999: 356)

Consumers are unconcerned about how second-hand garments come to be sourced from overseas as long as they come from 'the West'. For many inhabitants of Third World countries the West is an imagined place, consumer societies where clothes are superior to anything that can be manufactured locally. The popularity of *salaula* has remained intact despite some negative publicity in the press. There have been instances were thieves have exhumed bodies to remove the clothes they were wearing. Indeed one grave robber confessed to visiting the funeral parlour before burial to observe what the deceased was wearing so they could make a decision on whether or not the garments were worth stealing. This practice raises the issue of authenticity in the second-hand clothes market. Consumers protected themselves by only buying clothes that look as though they have just come out of the bails and thus those having creases are regarded as authentic. Anything that looked nicely clean and ironed raised suspicion that it was *third-hand*, referring to the fact that it had been previously worn by a Zambian.

Mobile phones

Another approach to recycling to reduce prices is exporting mobile phones from advanced countries to the poorest countries that do not have a particularly well-developed telecommunications infrastructure. Over 130 million phones in the USA, and 105 million phones in Europe are thrown away each year. Increasing levels of product innovation, and the low unit value of second-hand phones makes them redundant for most consumers that are trading up to a new model. Canning (2006) has provided an assessment of two recovery/reuse/recycling schemes: one trial initiated by mobile phone manufacturers, and another as a commercially viable arrangement. The first trial was operated in Sweden and the UK and pioneered by Motorola and was joined by many other manufacturers (Ericsson, Nokia, Alcatel, Panasonic), and a group of retailers. The phones could be returned to nominated stores or in a pre-paid envelope to a collection centre. The batteries were removed and phones were shipped to a metal refiner in order to extract precious base metals in the phone. The plastic content, that made up around 45 per cent of the phone's weight after the battery was removed, was burned as fuel.

The commercially driven initiative known as Fonebank was orchestrated by Shields Environmental and builds on the model established by Motorola. Customers were asked to return old phones, including unwanted phones as part of an upgrade. In some cases cash incentives were offered in return for old phones with the refund being given to charity. Shields Environmental was responsible for documenting sales, reconditioning and recycling. As many as possible are sold to countries with less-developed cellular phone technology. Those that are not usable have their batteries recycled, with the nickel from batteries going to produce saucepans, irons and new batteries. An evaluation of the project raised concerns about the small number of consumers that participated in the recycling initiatives. In 2005 the proportion of phones recycled had increased but only to around 25 per cent.

Low cost products for developing countries

In some developed countries the introduction of low unit and low price products has been a strategy that has been deployed to appeal to a wider market. In India small-scale traders sell two or three sweets to children, single cigarettes, and tiny tobacco sachets (J. Elliot 2007). In some poor African countries like Mauritania, market traders sell sugar by the lump and carrots by the slice to make them affordable purchases for shoppers (Usunier 2000). Sadh and Tangirala (2003) have noted that in India a clear division has emerged between the purchasing power of the urban middle class that often make monthly purchases and have led to increases in large unit sizes. By contrast, the lower-middle classes and the poor that mostly live in rural areas have generated a demand in low cost sachets and *paise* (Indian coin) packs. Fifty per cent of product sales in the shampoo category measured by volume are derived from sachets. This trend is also observable in other product categories including toothpaste, chocolate, and soft drinks. The lower price of these products is leading to their increased usage and is simultaneously widening the customer base.

Consumers in developing countries tend to be highly polarized. There is often a huge difference between cities and large urban towns where the purchasing power is relatively high, and small provincial towns and villages where the population live on very low incomes and could not possibly afford to buy expensive Western products. Some organizations are responding to the needs of new groups of consumers in developing countries by developing low-cost versions of their products. For example, the mobile phone market is relatively mature in many advanced societies and therefore the prospect of encouraging new customers is extremely limited. By contrast there is huge potential for growth in emerging markets but the profit margins are likely to be much lower as a consequence of the need to provide low-cost, affordable products. In this section three low-cost products will be discussed: motor vehicles, personal computers, and mobile phones.

Motor vehicles

One of the growth markets in developing countries is for low-cost cars and this is how car manufacturers have prospered in emerging markets from Brazil to Thailand. Low-cost vehicles are likely to appeal to the rapidly expanding middle classes who aspire to own their first car. The low cost business model has been championed by Tata Motors in India, by manufacturing the Tata Nano, the 'People's Car'. The Nano is the cheapest car in the world priced at 100,000 rupees (£1,300 or US $2,500), the same price as the DVD player in a Lexus, and half the price of other low-cost models currently on the market. The company chairman has stated: 'I hope this changes the way people travel in rural India. We are a country of a billion and most are denied connectivity . . . This is a car that is affordable and provides all-weather transport for the family'. The standard version comes with the vital features: brakes, a four gear, manual transmission, seatbelts, locking, wind-down widows, a steering wheel and one windscreen wiper. The small boot is just large enough to store a duffle bag. The deluxe version will have air conditioning and optional extras including a radio and an airbag. The car is the result of five years of research from around the world, but the vehicle was designed and made in India. The company hopes to sell the car in other developing countries in Africa and Latin America. The car attracted huge attention when it was launched in January 2008; it had 4,000 hits on its website in the first week (O'Connor 2008).

Other motor manufacturers believe the mass adoption of small cars in India is some way off. Honda has taken a different view from Tata by suggesting that poor road conditions and high petrol prices will keep the population traveling on motorcycles for years to come. The company is developing new lines of motorcycles that will provide better fuel economy. That said, most of the major car manufacturers are developing lower cost, small cars. Honda's sub-Fit model would not be as low cost as the Nano because the vehicle would need to comply with the company's international environmental and safety standards. This type of car could sell between 500,000 to 700,000 units per year that reflects the sales of other global models like the Civic. The sub-Fit would be targeted at other developing countries including India, China, and other Asian countries and possibly Europe. Renault and Nissan are also working on a low-cost car to be priced at around $3,000. Toyota is also developing a low-cost car for Russia, India and other emerging markets. The company already has a car plant in St Petersburg and the low-cost model would be priced at $7,000–$10,000 (Reed and Simon 2008).

Whether the new low-cost cars will be a roaring success in all developing countries remains to be seen. Chinese consumers have already lost some of their enthusiasm for small, cheap vehicles. At the beginning of 2008, sales figures indicated that smaller engine vehicles fell sharply in 2007 in spite of an overall growth in the car market of about 24 per cent. Some commentators have argued that China is taking a different path to other developing economies. After starting out with small cars, consumers are trading up. In the first 12 months of 2007, sales of cars with an engine size of one litre or less, fell by 24 per cent. This trend occurred despite rising petrol prices and a tax policy that encouraged the purchase of cars with smaller engine sizes. Why this trend occurred is a point of conjecture but two factors appear relevant – rising wealth disparities and the link between cars and social status in China. The urban elite that want to buy the very best quality will buy a higher level car by borrowing from friends and family. Research by Volkswagen in 2007 found that the average Chinese car buyer spent twice his or her annual salary on the vehicle. Although low-cost cars are perceived as suitable for driving around town, socially they lack prestige. Driving to see business clients or turning up to a party in a low-cost car was perceived as a loss of 'face' (Dyer 2008).

Personal computers

How to bring internet access to remote parts of developing countries in a cost effective manner is a problem. The Jhai Foundation (http://www.jhai.org) was the first organization to bring internet access to remote communities through the bicycle-powered computer. The aim of the project was to provide internet access to a remote Laotian village, 30 kilometres from the closest telephone line and electricity. The main income of the villagers was from selling rice and other produce. They needed a way of sourcing the current prices before making the 30 kilometre journey to the nearest market to sell their goods. This information was valuable since they could wait until the prices were favourable before deciding to sell. The computer is a 486 operating on the Linux operating system that runs off a bicycle that subsequently stores energy on car batteries. A wireless internet card connects the computer to a solar-powered relay station which then passes the signals on to a computer in the nearest town that is connected to both the Lao phone system that provides for local calls, and to the internet.

A more recent development has been designing low-cost laptop computers for the developing world. In 2005, Professor Nicholas Negroponte from the Massachusetts Institute of Technology announced his project to design a US $100 laptop. The One Laptop per Child project had ambitions to provide laptops to school children in various countries around the developing world. Its partner Intel joined the venture to manufacture the laptops. Reports of the pilot studies were very positive with children enjoying and playing on their laptops. However, there were criticisms that hard evidence did not exist to demonstrate that the play and enjoyment was contributing to knowledge development and the intellectual growth of the child. Foreign governments were perceived as the main purchasers of the low cost laptops, but it soon became clear that the orders were not forthcoming. The millions of orders that were necessary to keep the price down never materialized. A dispute also emerged between Intel and Negroponte's group, about how a rival Intel product costing $250 would be marketed. As a result of the conflict, Intel eventually pulled out of the deal. Even though the $100 laptop may not materialize, the project did its job in generating a new, low-cost product for developing countries. There are currently many companies from Silicon Valley to East Asia making laptops for sale in developing countries that cost less than US $400 (Farivar 2008).

Mobile phones

Despite the considerable uses of mobile phones in developing economies, on average, only around 5 per cent of the population of India and sub-Saharan Africa own mobile phones. One of the main reasons for this lack of uptake has been the cost of the handset. Some of the largest network operators in those regions maintain that the numbers of users could double if the cheapest handsets were reduced in price from $30 to $60. Handset producers generate most of their profits from developing innovative designs for sale in comparatively wealthy, advanced societies where prices can average $200. However, as markets for mobile phones are nearing saturation in those countries, producers are looking to find alternative markets. Some of the main manufacturers are beginning to consider developing countries as lucrative emergent markets. Whereas the focus in advanced societies is on producing ever more sophisticated multi-functional models, the emphasis in developing countries is on manufacturing extremely cheap handsets to encourage wider product diffusion while maintaining a profitable business.

Several operators from developing countries came together in 2005 under the auspices of the GSM Association (GSM is the world's dominant mobile-phone standard). They orchestrated a contract to supply up to 6 million handsets for less than $40 each. The contract was eventually won by Motorola. The company maintains that its low costs are not due to cross-subsidies from high value-added sets sold in rich countries, or through corporate social responsibility funding but from being content with a smaller profit margin. The low-cost phones are not simply a budget version of existing phones. The design features are necessarily different; for example, they need to be very reliable and have considerable battery capacity since users very often do not have reliable sources of electricity. Motorola's handsets have a standby time of two weeks. Furthermore, the handsets have to be designed to conform to local languages and customs. For example, the handset sold in India includes a cricket game, whereas in Africa football is a more popular option. Although low cost the phones also have to look smart since consumers in developing societies have to spend a far larger proportion of their income to purchase even the cheapest handset. The visible attributes and brand of phones are much more of a status symbol in those societies. Consumers also appreciate added features such as music playback since they often cannot afford multiple devices such as an iPod, a PC and PlayStation and may require more from their mobiles. In 2005 Phillips, the Dutch electronics company, announced that it had developed a new range of low-cost chips that were designed to reduce the handset cost to below $20. Low-cost handsets are only one barrier to the adoption of mobile commerce in developing countries; other barriers are high government taxes and duties imposed on handsets.

Free products

Most of the cross-cultural discussions of pricing and pricing strategy focus on cultural perceptions of price and generating an appropriate price for goods and services. The discussion within this section is somewhat different, since it focuses on free cosmetic surgery for the poor in Brazil. The cosmetic surgery industry has become a global phenomenon. Initially practiced by the rich and famous it has now filtered down to a range of less well-off consumers who want to hold back the ravages of time. Television shows such as *Extreme Makeover*, *The Swan*, *Ten Years Younger* and many others, have popularized and normalized cosmetic surgery, along with magazine articles and websites. The main target group are working-class and lower middle-class women aged between 25 and 45 that increasingly reflect the audience for the television shows (Heyes 2007).

Despite its glamorous image, cosmetic surgery has less ostentatious roots. Cosmetic surgery emerged in the USA at the turn of the twentieth century. After the First World War surgeons realized that the improved techniques they had developed in the process of reconstructing the mutilated faces of soldiers, could be used for purely cosmetic purposes. The difficulty surgeons had to overcome was breaking the Hippocratic Oath since botched operations could harm otherwise healthy patients. Edmonds (2007) has noted that some of the earliest plastic surgeons referred to 'beauty doctors' as quacks. What prevented the peacetime growth of plastic surgery was a proper illness for which it could be diagnosed as a cure. The breakthrough was made, not in the area of medicine, but popular psychology. In the early twentieth century, psychology established a link between appearance and psyche that became widely accepted. The concept of 'inferiority complex' helped establish cosmetic surgery by giving it a therapeutic rationale.

In Brazil this therapeutic rationale has been extended to new territory by integrating it into the public health services and being provided for free. Over 35 years ago the first plastic surgery ward in a municipality was established. Dr Claudio was the surgeon that founded the facility and, here, provides an insight into why it was established:

> The public health system only paid for reconstructive surgery [in the past]. And surgeons thought cosmetic operations were vanity. But *plastica* has psychological effects, for the poor as well as the rich. We were able to show this and so it was gradually accepted as having a social purpose. We operate on the poor who have the chance to improve their appearance and it's a necessity not a vanity.
>
> (Edmonds 2007: 367)

Surgeons trained by Claudio have opened up surgeries around the country to meet the demands for *plastica* that keeps rising. In the private sector, aggressive price-cutting and the introduction of credit facilities to fund operations have brought plastic surgery within the reach of the aspirational middle class. Indeed in some quarters, the fact that more people in the country are having plastic surgery is interpreted as the country becoming more middle class. Finance companies have targeted the large number of women waiting for cosmetic surgery in public hospitals, a wait which can take up to three years. More than any other speciality, plastic surgeons are haunted by the patient complaining since defects can cause further psychological damage. In reality, post-operative reactions vary from 'depression and crises of regret to euphoria, exaggerated gratitude, and sexual invitations to surgeons' (Edmonds 2007: 367).

Plastic surgeons appear on talk shows, appropriately named, *Before and After*, take out ads in glossy monthlies in which the latest technological innovations are discussed alongside images of celebrities, and before and after images.

Patients' occupations were commonly cited as receptionists, elevator operators, maids, cooks, hotel employees, English teachers and secretaries. This list of occupations indicated three trends at work in Brazil: an increase in female opportunities, the feminization of the working class, and the rise of the service sector. Research has demonstrated that appearance is an important employee characteristic in service work and Brazil is no exception in this respect. Youth, beauty and sexual allure are important traits that can increase earnings and improve job prospects. In Brazil, good appearance is unofficially a requirement on the part of service personnel and although selection on the basis of colour is outlawed, in reality this often means white. Plastic surgery offers not only bodily change but a piece of First World modernity.

There is also an important racial and ethnic dimension to *plastica* in Brazil. Physical beauty has been integrated into the fantasies of northern Europeans for five centuries, from the letters of Portuguese sailors describing ardent Indians that met their ships to the contemporary online sex industry. The concept of racial mixture is integral to the culture identity of contemporary Brazil and this is linked to physical beauty. Edmonds (2007) spoke to one patient who reflected this sentiment: 'Our country is a country of pretty people. This miscegenation here gives us a different tone I think'. In contrast to the multicultural model of difference in Western societies that often views it as a threat, the model of racial mixing in Brazil has been central to national identity that eroticized and aestheticized beauty. Thus the racialized beauty myth dictates the ideal body comprises large hips, thighs, and buttocks, a narrow waist, with little attention to breast size. This image is widely marketed by the cosmetic surgery industry resulting in more operations to contour the body, as opposed to freshening the face. In Brazil, women use cosmetic surgery to correct traits that lie outside of the norm and in that respect cosmetic surgery can be viewed as a rite of passage. However, there are others who undertake one procedure after another to gain perfection. Edmonds concludes that when access to education is limited, the body relative to the mind becomes a more important basis for identity and social power.

Consumers during crisis

The majority of the consumer behaviour literature has focused on consumers that live above the poverty line in predominantly advanced Western society. These economies also tend to be economically stable and largely protected from protracted recession and huge levels of inflation. The majority of the existing literature is less relevant to developing societies that often suffer economic down turns on a regular basis and can be subject to high levels of inflation. Recessionary pressures have been felt in Japan since the 1990s, and as a result of global credit problems that began in 2007, have started to have an impact on consumer behaviour and consumption in many advanced, Western countries. In a declining economy the mood becomes bleak, the world looks drab, and people batten down the hatches and become suspicious (Borgmann 2000). Price sensitivity has become a more relevant issue and has had effects on marketing strategies in some areas. For example, at the beginning of 2008, supermarkets in the United Kingdom began moving away from using expensive celebrity-backed marketing strategies, and started focusing on price promotions ahead of a predicted slow down in consumer spending (Bokale 2008). Another strategy has been for manufacturers to reduce the size of branded goods, while keeping prices the same. Onken mousse pots recently shrank from 150g to 115g, but the price stayed the same. Kraft's standard pack of eight Dairylea slices became lighter. The box was the same, but the slices were thinner. The tactic known in the U.S. as 'grocery shrink ray' has been in operation for some time but has recently witnessed an increase.

How consumers adapt to different economic and social changes by changing their consumption patterns is an important addition to the cross-cultural consumer behaviour literature on pricing. Frugality has not received a great deal of discussion within marketing and consumer behaviour (Lastovicka *et al.* 1999), but it would seem that more attention in the direction is timely.

Since materialism and lifestyles are subject to significant international differences one might suspect that consumers could employ different strategies to deal with an economic downturn. Stagflation has been a significant economic, social and political phenomenon in the USA since the Depression, as it has in many countries around the world. The combination of a stagnant economy in a period of inflation became an important issue in the 1970s, and has currently returned to haunt Western economies. Sharma (1981) argued that stagflation bred a new breed of consumers in the USA during the 1970s that were different from pre-stagflation consumers. These consumers could be divided further into those that try harder to make ends meet, and those that change their lifestyles and values associated with conspicuous consumption and economic growth; 'The second group represents a totally new consumer, the voluntary simplifier' (Shama 1981; 120).

Sharma's research in New York demonstrated that stagflation affected most consumers negatively, psychological and economically. Real income was stagnant, or declining in real terms, and psychologically stagflation generated a more frustrated consumer who could no longer meet their material expectations. In marketing terms the non-voluntary simplifiers required an extension of the marketing mix, but the voluntary simplifiers required a different approach. Product messages needed to be congruent with the values of voluntary simplicity, an emphasis on appropriate technology, ecological responsibility, and marketing management should design or modify products to fit in with this philosophy. The price of products that voluntary simplifiers would wish to purchase, are usually more expensive because they require more expensive materials and labour which would result in higher prices. But the voluntary simplifiers were agreeable to purchasing the products, providing they fulfilled a need at a price that was acceptable. The charging of a premium price was unacceptable. Promotions that were thought most appropriate were informative or soft-sell images with less imagery because voluntary simplifiers are more interested in the characteristics of the product and how it functions rather than its symbolism to other. No frills packaging and cost-cutting distributing channels such as direct mail also came high up on the agenda.

Another account of consumers' responses in a crisis documented by Zurawicki and Braidot (2005) was in the context of the Argentinean economic crisis of 2001–2002. Economic reforms in Latin America liberalized markets and opened individual economies to the outside world. The welfare state diminished leaving Latin American families with a heavier burden of costs for basic social services. Zurawicki and Braidot argue that five factors have impacted on consumption patterns in Latin America. First, there was an avoidance of or postponement to big commitments such as cars, household appliances, and family vacations. Second, there was an overall reduction in consumer debt since consumers could not afford to service credit agreements, and thus had to return goods or declare themselves bankrupt. A decline in the penetration of credit cards occurred in the late 1990s. A third change was an increase in the level of expenditure given to basic commodities. Similar patterns were evident in Argentina, Brazil and Chile. Fourth, altered shopping habits were witnessed with self-service, discount stores, and large hypermarkets becoming more popular across all social groups. The volume of branded goods being purchased declined. A final change in behaviour was to seek out a favourable quality-to- price ratio. Unsurprisingly, price became a stronger determinant of choice providing that the quality was not compromised. However, this did not translate into a willingness on the part of customers to try newly introduced brands.

Over the period, total consumption of most items declined. However, there were some interesting variations on these trends. The purchase of beauty and personal care items such as toothpaste and deodorants declined substantially. Consumers also stopped eating out, going to the movies, the theatre, social and fitness clubs and purchasing newspapers and magazines. However, the demand for sweets and chocolates increased and beer consumption remained strong. Different product categories were affected in slightly different ways.

Similar observations to those in Latin America were observed in the Asian Pacific region (Japan, South Korea, Taiwan and Singapore), during the recessionary period at the end of the millennium. The recession had some profound marketing implications in the areas of market research, brand building and consumer behaviour. Tan and Lui (2002) found that many multinational companies reduced their market research spend in an attempt to reduce costs in a declining market. However, a minority of companies actually increased their budgets to help them understand a rapidly changing market in order to assist them to stand out from the crowd. More qualitative and tactical research was undertaken with a heightened emphasis on tracking consumer attitudes to promotion, packaging, and to cheaper versions of brands. Some products were more affected by tightening consumer budgets than others. The most resilient to changes in demand were personal care and baby products. Generic household products such as detergents and toilet paper were the most susceptible to substitution strategies. Unlike Latin America, chocolates, snacks, and fizzy drinks were considered luxuries in hard times. The main ways consumers reduced expenditure were by eating out less frequently and taking fewer weekend trips. Despite the economic downturn, the vast majority of middle-class Asian consumers did not become exclusively price conscious. Brand building was an important consideration for manufacturers and retailers. Brands needed to be repositioned from a pure quality image to one that included value for money.

Over the region as a whole, research indicated that a number of coping strategies were used by consumers:

- Downscaling on luxury items and recreational activities and cutting down on luxury products and services;
- The use of cheaper substitutes for expensive, specialized products;
- A more widespread set of multipurpose products, for example using laundry detergents to wash clothes, wash dishes, and clean the car;

- Switching from expensive imported brands to those that are cheaper and locally produced, especially clothes and fashion items;
- Buying products in smaller sizes to enable people to manage their cash flow better, particularly where detergents and shampoos were concerned;
- Using smaller amounts of products to make them last longer, e.g. shoes, clothes and toothbrushes;
- Using some products for special occasions rather than everyday use (this was particularly applicable in connection with wines, spirits and air fresheners)
- Giving up some products entirely was a last resort, although relatively few products came into this category.

(Tan and Lui 2002: 802)

Questions

- What are some of the differences in consumer perceptions of price within various Asian countries?
- Explain some of the cultural differences in the meaning of price endings.
- Assess why some companies are developing low priced products as an integral part of their cross-cultural marketing strategies.
- What does the free provision of plastic surgery in Brazil reveal about the cultural dynamics of Brazilian society?
- Why has cross-cultural marketing marginalized consumer behaviour in economic downturns?

Further reading

Edmonds, A. (2007) '"The poor have the right to be beautiful": Cosmetic surgery in neoliberal Brazil', *Journal of the Royal Anthropological Institute*, 13: 363–381.

Estelamin, H., Lehmann, D.R. and Holden, A.C. (2001) 'Macro-economic determinants of consumer price knowledge: A meta-analysis of four decades of research', *International Journal of Research in Marketing*, 18: 341–355.

Hansen, K.T. (1999) 'Second-hand clothing encounters in Zambia: Global discourses, Western commodities, and local histories', *Africa*, 69 (3): 343–363.

Simmons, L.C. and Schindler, R.M. (2003) 'Cultural superstitions and the price endings used in Chinese advertising', *Journal of International Marketing*, 11 (2): 101–111.

Zurawicki, L. and Braidot, N. (2005) 'Consumers during crisis: Responses from the middle class in Argentina', *Journal of Business Research*, 58: 1100–1109.

8 Marketing management practice

Introduction

A significant body of research has indicated that failure in cross-cultural businesses, whether in relation to joint ventures, global team effectiveness, and expatriation is not due to lack of managerial technical competence but as a consequence of the dynamics of the intercultural experience. These dynamics include differences in cultural perceptions in values and practices which influence understanding, and attitudinal satisfaction associated with living in a foreign culture. This chapter will focus on some of the variations in cross-cultural business practices in order to foster a degree of intercultural competence. The first part of this chapter considers whether globalization or glocalization are appropriate marketing management strategies. A range of different approaches have been advanced in connection to assessing national differences in the organization of marketing management. Most accounts of marketing as an organizational activity highlight the importance of culture that marketers need to accommodate. The second theme of the chapter is to assess the concept of marketer acculturation in aiding our understanding of the process of doing business at home or abroad. Peñaloza and Gilly (1999) have used the phrases 'the changer' and 'the changed' to denote how marketers learn from their interactions with consumers and in doing so become the changed. The third section of the chapter deals with the complex issue of intercultural competence. The fourth section assesses cross-cultural aspects of relationship marketing. Much has been written on the topic of relationship marketing over the last 20 years, but the cross-cultural aspect of this discourse has been limited.

The fifth section of the chapter focuses on cross-cultural aspects of corruption in organizations as a cultural phenomenon. There is a widely held assumption that corruption is more prevalent in emerging economies than it is in developed societies. This view will be critically evaluated. Corporate social responsibility (CSR) is the fifth theme to be addressed in this chapter. The emphasis will be on understanding how it is perceived in different cultural contexts, and whether differences in CSR policies vary within organizations from different countries. The penultimate section focuses on the process of cross-cultural negotiations that are central to industrial and consumer marketing. An assessment of what managers from different cultures bring to the negotiation table will be assessed. The final section highlights the role of ethics in cross-cultural business relations.

Globalization or glocalization of marketing management

The debate over the precise content of business education and the question of relevance in an international context has been debated for centuries. Malachy Postlethwayt's (1751) publication *The Universal Dictionary of Trade and Commerce* was published in the middle of the eighteenth century. This account demonstrated that abstract theory and practice were given much space, however, so were the international aspects of the curriculum that included 'foreign exchange and mercantile arithmetic', a general survey of trade and commerce of the world', 'language', 'geography and navigation', and 'public credit' (Norwood 1961: 52).

A debate has existed for a considerable number of years as to the 'universality' of managerial work worldwide, and the extent to which similarities can constitute a generic theory along the line of an administrative managerial science (Mintzberg 1973). The development of core managerial competences, and the convergence of managerial practices worldwide is driven by the desire to approach and complete tasks in the most cost effective and efficient ways. This common motivation is applicable regardless of social context and according to the convergence thesis, results in the universal concept of best practice. This view is one that has been perpetrated by international organizations involved with transferring managerial skills to developing countries (for example the United Nations and the World Bank, and the International Monetary Fund) that are based on diffusing Western management models (Kerrigan and Luke 1987).

Other reasons for the potential convergence of managerial values and beliefs across cultures are comparable administrative requirements, similar training, common technologies, or interaction with other cultures due to globalization. The proliferation of MBA programmes based on the US model of management and marketing administration generates a rather standardized education experience. Kwok, Arpan and Folks (1994) maintain that an important move towards internationalization in US business schools has been prompted by the accreditation standards of the American Assembly of Collegiate Schools of Business (AACSB) in which the internationalization of the curriculum is mandatory. Their global survey of the internationalization of the business school curriculum indicated that there was agreement that students should have at least minimal awareness of the global business environment, and this was particularly true at undergraduate level. However, despite good intentions the level of knowledge achieved was rather poor. The most favoured approach to internationalizing the curriculum was infusion whereby an international dimension was diffused in business core courses. Out of all the main business sub-disciplines it was in marketing where the curriculum was perceived as most internationalized, closely followed by management, finance and strategy.

While the globalization thesis, as it applies to management culture, might be appealing, in reality there is little research evidence to support this position. There is some evidence to suggest the gap is narrowing over time, and in some countries (Heuer *et al.* 1999). While managers may have to work in different cultural settings and learn new skills and behaviours, the task is made a little easier by the fact that there can often be considerable overlap between the job they do in a new culture, and the one they did in their own culture (Javidan and Carl 2005).

A rather different perspective is that cultural values provide scripts, or sequences of social action in the context of one's own culture (Shank and Abelson 1977). The literature on the comparative aspects of marketing activities within different cultural contexts has not received a great deal of attention from marketing scholars. Far more attention has been given to the process of standardization versus adaptation of international strategy, and adapting to the needs of consumers, than the differences between national marketing systems across time and space. Yet comparative marketing studies open up the possibility of identifying international generalizations of marketing concepts and developing theory, in addition to assisting firms understand and adapt their marketing programmes and processes to different environments. Deshpande and Webster (1989: 8) maintain that organizations need to know how to 'adapt management policies, programs, and structures to local personnel, channel institutions and organizations'. Culture does matter in organizational contexts. For example, American multinationals have lower control levels when there is a greater perceived social distance, since managers feel uncomfortable working in environments with different values and operating methods. Furthermore, there are important implications of the ethnic mix of managers, especially in countries that have a diverse ethnic population and have recently undergone consideration economic, social and political upheaval, like South Africa (Thomas and Bendixen 2000). A similar situation is apparent in North and South Vietnam that have long been divided by war. The North is traditionally more conservative and has operated under socialism since the 1940s. By contrast, the South experienced US dominance and Western influences for two decades until 1975 when the Americans withdrew (Ralston *et al.* 1999).

The lack of attention given to cross-cultural marketing practice has also served to generate some misunderstandings about marketing management practices. A case in point is Japanese marketing practice, which is often considered a textbook case of applying US methods. Marketing as a business tool was introduced into Japan in 1955 after top executives of large Japanese companies visited the USA under the sponsorship of the International Cooperation Administration (Hirata *et al.* 1961; Takahashi 2004). In Fullerton's terminology, this period coincided with the awareness stage of modern marketing in Japan (Herbig 1995). However, this interpretation is not an accurate representation of reality. Japanese marketing practice has its roots in a different orientation generated through a need to import most raw materials and export internationally from the outset. This is in contrast to the American model which was heavily dependent on the domestic market, and international aspects of marketing were developed later (Dunn 1994). Lazer *et al.* (1985) suggest that there has not been an Americanization of Japanese business methods but the Japanization of American marketing by modifying and adapting practices to adjust to Japanese culture that remains intact. The Soviet Union provides another distinctly different scenario to that of Japan and the USA. In the 1960s, M. I. Goldman (1961: 7) argued that the basic structure of the marketing operations in the Soviet Union was essentially the same as in the USA, although the Russian forms of organization were not as complex as those evident in the USA. The role of the government was the major distinguishing factor; in the USA the role of the government was minor, whereas in the Soviet Union the government owned and controlled every enterprise and outlet along the way to the consumer.

There are a number of factors present in the contemporary environment that require us to understand the way that the environment shapes, or is shaped by marketing processes. First, the shift towards the liberalization in what were planned economies as well as economies that had cultivated nationalistic, self-reliant economic development. Second, the regionalization of trade into different economic groupings throughout the world and the need to understand how these configurations work in practice. Third, the internationalization of activities that were once confined to the domestic economy, need to be rethought within the context of new and different environments. Fourth, the importance of social and political aspects of doing business which make the whole process more complex (Gopalkrishnan 1997).

An important issue that needs to be addressed is the basis on which comparisons can be made. A number of different approaches have been developed over the years. One approach is to assess the flow of *authority*, *communication* and *finance* and to compare how these are the same or different in various countries. Since many theories and models of marketing may be universal, the approach is centred on identifying universals or limited generalizations. However, this approach assumes a static theory of marketing and that systems can be readily compared. A rather different approach is to understand marketing practice as being diverse, open and in a constant state of flux. According to this interpretation, *marketing is a social system* as well as a *social process* that is subsumed under the forces of the market, economy society, and the nation. The study of marketing and its environment within different social contexts is proposed as the central concern of comparative marketing. Yet another approach is to focus on the *performance aspects* of marketing, including *inputs*, *outputs*, *constraints* and *efficiency*, thus understanding the impact of the environment on the firm, rather than the dynamic interaction between the two. Another way of understanding comparative marketing is by examining a wider range of features; functions, structures, processes, actors and environments that facilitate or mitigate marketing exchanges in various environments. These aspects would comprise a framework for understanding the *interaction between buyers and sellers within different marketing environments*. A penultimate approach is provided by the *institutional approach* to comparative marketing that suggests the term institution should be extended to include non-visible and non-formal methods of organization and governance. This view introduced the notion that institutions are social control mechanisms for facilitating economic and political interactions within a political economy. This approach differs from the alternative view of institutions as governance structures only; it offered the prospect of understanding politics as an institutional alternative. The final approach has been advanced by Scandinavian and Western European scholars, and emphasizes the role of *networks* in the studying of marketing systems (Gopalkrishnan 1997).

It is important to note that many of the approaches to marketing scholarship outlined above have been generated by scholars in Western countries, invariably from the standpoint of Western companies, and often based on experiences in advanced economies. The experience of emerging economies has largely been neglected within this discourse. Emerging economies present some interesting issues for marketing theory, practice, and relevance. Emerging economies have very different socio-economic, demographic, cultural, and regulatory environments from developed economies. These differences raise issues about whether theories and empirical generalizations developed in Western societies are applicable in radically different contexts. On a practical level, it is important that marketers research and learn from companies that have been successful in these markets since this will enhance the relevance of the marketing discipline (Burgess and Steenkamp 2006). A landmark study of the management literature in the 1980s (Kiggundu *et al.* 1983) demonstrated that Western-based theories were applicable to developing countries only where the organization's core functions were concerned, or technical issues were addressed. Other surveys have argued that regardless of the nature of research undertaken (empirical or theoretical), type of study (cross-sectional, longitudinal or historical), topics addressed, sector concerned (private or public), or geographical distribution of the regions covered by the studies – the degree of fit of Western theory to developing economies is very high (Hafsi and Farashahi 2005: 505; see also Darley and Johnson 1993)

Marketer acculturation

Many international business failures have been attributed to a lack of cross-cultural competence so the impact on the training and development of staff in companies is of considerable relevance to practitioners (Johnson *et al.* 2006). In his fascinating book *Blunders in International Business* David Ricks (1993: 2) notes that cultural differences are the most troublesome variables with which companies have to deal and the failure of managers to understand the differences between cultures has led to most international business blunders. An important concept to aid our understanding of marketers' interactions with culture within the marketplace is through the concept of *marketer acculturation*. This term was introduced by Peñaloza and Gilly (1999: 84) in the context of marketers understanding the behaviour of consumers from cultures other than their own, 'the general processes of movement and adaptation by marketers of one cultural market system to consumers of another cultural market system'. They point to some of the contradictions in the marketing literature concerning our understanding of the process by which consumers adapt to a new cultural environment, and yet the process of how marketers have learnt to accommodate the needs of different cultural groups has been neglected. The contemporary realities of the marketplace are such that consumers and marketers of multiple cultures adapt to each other simultaneously. They use the idea of the 'changers' and the 'changed'. The marketer in this context are the *changers* in seeking to attract consumers from different cultures to purchase their products, but in doing so they are also *changed* in the process as they learn new marketing strategies and accommodate other cultures. They argue the reason why this aspect of marketing management has not been given as much attention as it deserves, is because marketing managers who take strategic views about the future of the business are often some distance removed from the day-to-day interaction with consumers, but these opportunities are important sites of learning. Furthermore, marketing researchers often attempt to understand culture indirectly via marketer and consumer respondents, and far less emphasis has been placed on the 'generalized adaptation processes and their contexts'.

In order to assess the marketer acculturation process, Peñaloza and Gilly conducted an ethnographic study of an urban shopping street in San Pueblo in southern California. Retailers of multiple cultures were included – Latino, Asian, Middle Eastern, and Anglo – and the focus of the study was to uncover how they had adapted to an influx of Mexican immigrants. Marketers did this in a number of ways (1) by adapting products and services on offer, (2) constructing appropriate displays, (3) integrating sales support in the service delivery, (4) making an event of holiday celebrations and, (5) providing community support. In relation to products and services, stores had started stocking authentic Mexican foods and employing staff such as Mexican butchers that had the inside knowledge about consumer preferences for fresh meat, that was thinly sliced with the fat removed. Store owners also learnt from their competitors, for example bargaining had rapidly spread from one retailer to another. The displays included signs in Spanish and English that made it easier for people to shop.

Extra sales support including language competence in Spanish was an important strategic advantage for shopkeepers since there was often a consumer education element involved in transactions. Some customers did not know how to use goods with which they were unfamiliar, for example videocassette recorders, and explanations were necessary. The offer of credit 'easy payment, no money down' was something that immigrants were not used to, given that credit remained rather more inaccessible in Mexico, especially for working-class people. The prices were significantly lower than those available in Mexico and immigrants wages in the USA were much higher than in Mexico. Storekeepers were also adept at understanding the different characteristics various consumers wanted from the shopping experience. For example, Anglos shopped at stores for the quality of the goods on offer, and the service quality was of secondary importance. By contrast, the friendly service is more important for the Latino customers but only for some products. Where shopping for clothes was concerned, shopkeepers had learnt that Mexican women would take their husband or boyfriend with them to provide advice, so the help of the sales person was not required. By contrast, Korean women would welcome the salesperson's advice. Promoting the area through holiday celebrations, such as having a Mexican Independence Day parade, was good for business.

Peñaloza and Gilly have provided a very good example of marketer acculturation in a multicultural context in the USA. However, the same process of learning about consumers and other aspects of the marketing process are relevant, whether in the context of retail, or business-to-business marketing, at home or abroad.

Intercultural competence

Johnson *et al.* (2006: 534) argue that cross-cultural competence in organization has been dogged by a gap between 'antecedents ('knowing') rather than on its behavioral manifestations ('doing'). They argue that a model of cross-cultural competence includes a range of features. The first is what they term the *knowledge dimension* that is split between *culture-general knowledge* and *culture-specific knowledge*. Culture-general knowledge includes information about the different components of culture, frameworks for comparing and contrasting cultures, the cross-cultural environment and so forth. Culture-specific knowledge is very specific to knowledge about a particular culture and requires a wider range of information about 'geography, law, history, customs, hygiene, what to do, and what not to do' (Johnson *et al.* 2006: 531). Another aspect of the knowledge dimension in addition to those discussed above, concerns the cognitive aspect of knowledge acquisition relating to how individuals acquire, interpret and use cultural knowledge for the benefit of the organization.

A second main feature of cross-cultural competence is *the skills dimension*. A person's skill set will include behavioral competences, but also abilities and aptitudes such as foreign language expertise, adaptability, stress management, conflict resolution and so on. The third aspect of cross-cultural competence is the *personal attributes dimension*. This dimension includes traits such as ambition, courage, curiosity, integrity, judgement, loyalty, tolerance of ambiguity and so on, which are all at a premium in a cross-cultural business context. The fourth and final dimension relates *to moderating influences* such as institutional ethnocentrism, or ways of doing things which can affect the ability of individuals to respond to cultural differences in the workplace. An important issue in this respect is cultural distance, with respect to how far removed an individual's culture is from the one in which they are operating.

Cross-cultural business practices and cross-cultural markets are important aspects of knowledge in multinational companies, yet they are fraught with a variety of intercultural differences. Scholars who have investigated intercultural interaction suggest the concepts of *intercultural communication competence*, *intercultural effectiveness*, and *intercultural competence* are important factors in cognitive behavioral and affective dimensions required of cross-cultural managers. Anne Bartel-Radic (2006: 651) defines intercultural competence as 'the ability to understand the meaning of intercultural interaction and the ability to adapt one's behavior to these meanings in order to produce efficient behavior'. Personality traits such as empathy, open-mindedness and emotional stability have been associated with high levels of intercultural competence. However, it also needs to be recognized that intercultural competence can be learned. *Intercultural learning* can be gained through different practical experiences and a process of critical reflection. *Intercultural interaction* of this nature can be indirect, for example, through the media, and direct interaction, meeting people face-to-face, engaging in conversation. Some scholars have used the term *interculturation* to describe the process of interaction between individuals or groups from different cultures. In his article 'Over the wall: Experiences with multicultural literacy', Jones (2003) emphasizes the importance of the multicultural aspects of this learning process.

The intercultural communication is an incredibly complex aspect of business relations, nor is it confined to national cultural boundaries. For example, Spinks and Wells suggest that communications between executives based in Houston in the USA and Brussels in Belgium should present few difficulties, since culture and technology are shared. However, communicating with a branch office in the Amish area of the USA that was staffed by local Amish people that do not use technology, would be extremely difficult even though no national boundaries had been crossed. The different ways that contracts are viewed in different cultural contexts can be highly problematic. In the USA and most other advanced societies, contracts are final agreements between two or more parties and they are usually enforceable by law. Contracts guarantee that each side upholds their end of the agreement. Some cultures do not hold contracts in high esteem, violations do not matter and there are no negative consequences of not doing so. Furthermore, international legal systems are not inclined to enforce contracts which could prove costly if things go wrong. Social customs within the workplace can also vary. For example, in some countries in the Far East gifts must be taken into meetings otherwise it would be felt that the meeting was not being taken seriously enough, whereas in other cultures gifts are considered bribes. In some cultures gifts should be given in public and others in private. Informal dress is acceptable in some cultures but considered as showing lack of respect for the other business person in other cultures. Some countries are more forgiving than others when cultural norms are transgressed. Some cultures have a strict social hierarchy along the lines of class or caste that are transferred inside workplaces. Care should be exercised in dealing with culturally appropriate employees in business negotiations otherwise important cultural norms may be transgressed.

Opposition from the convergence approach to marketing management focuses on two factors: differences in culture, and the level of development of the host country. In order to empirically test this hypothesis Lubatkin, Ndiaye and Vengroff (1997) conducted research in Senegal in Africa, as an example of a nation that might have already converged, due to the influence of its French colonial heritage; and second Hungary, as a transitional, developing country that was considered progressive within the Eastern Bloc. The results indicated a substantial level of convergence and homogeneity between the two countries. However, there were some important differences. For example, dealing with inter-organizational politics via negotiating with representatives of other organizations/divisions was viewed as one of the most important skills by Hungarians. Furthermore, entrepreneurship defined as using whatever means to achieve organizational objectives, and action-oriented defined as one who initiates action, were ranked highly by Hungarian managers but not by the African managers. African managers ranked commanding respect from subordinates highly whereas this was ranked lowly by Hungarians.

National cultural differences

A question which needs to be addressed is how salient the differences are between various cultures where management styles are concerned, since this has important implications for the types of competences that need to be learned. Lenartowicz and Johnson (2002) addressed this issue by comparing managerial values of small retail stores in 12 Latin American countries. The values they assessed were civility (cheerful, helpful, loving, forgiving, clean, obedient and polite), self-direction (imaginative, independent, intellectual, open minded and logical), integrity (honest, responsible), and drive (responsiveness to customers needs). Integrity was ranked the highest in all of the 12 countries. The second most important value was civility which was ranked second or third in all countries except Bolivia. Drive was the third most important but no country ranked it as the most important. Self-direction was the characteristic that was ranked the lowest overall. Their study concluded that managers working for small companies are more likely to reflect local management values than those working for large companies, because they are more closely embedded within their communities. It also concluded that integrity and civility are likely to govern behaviour of Latin American managers, regardless of their country of origin. This relationship is bi-directional since managers treat their employees like they would expect to be treated themselves. Managers that do not display these values are perceived as aggressive and unnecessarily provocative. It was interesting to note, that managers in the sample put American and European expatriates in this category. Overall, the study concluded that there are differences in the values held by managers in different countries, thus Latin America should not be perceived as culturally homogeneous.

Sometimes the intercultural differences can be pronounced, as Sriussadaporn (2006) found when he interviewed an international group of managers who were working in Thailand. Books that are essentially guides of dos and don'ts are not sufficient, and sometimes manager ethnocentrism is a barrier, i.e. the belief that a manager's own culture is better than that of the host country. Managers reported that Thai employees were reluctant to think proactively, analytically and systematically and could not express themselves well. Problems in communicating main ideas spilled over into memos, reports and oral presentations. Part of the problem was attributed to the education system that is highly structured. Thai employees were also reluctant to express their own feelings and tended to say what they thought the boss wanted to hear. The view was also expressed that Thai employees did not have a strong commitment to assignments. They never indicated that they could not do the work or ask for help, they would leave it to the last minute to tell their superiors that they could not do the work or finish in the appropriate timescale. A big problem with Thai employees was their time management; there was little eagerness or commitment to meet deadlines, appointment times, or keep appointments for work meetings. Their pace of work is much slower than Europeans and Americans would expect and there was a need for expatriates to stay calm and be more patient than they would be working at home. Local Thai employees were not willing to communicate in English when they believed they could not speak English well and they needed considerable help with editing and rewriting reports. There were also problems with how personal/work relationships were understood. One manager took his female colleagues out for lunch one by one but this was considered inappropriate and he was labeled as a womanizer. A more appropriate strategy in that cultural environment was to go out in a group.

Regional differences

In a further study, Lenartowicz and Roth (2001) explored *regional* as opposed to *national* cultural differences, using the motivation and performance of owners of small kiosk businesses in Brazil as a case study. Kiosks are small retail businesses that carry an assortment of convenience goods. There was significant uniformity between them: they are all privately owned and operated, the demand for the goods is quite stable, purchase and sales prices are fixed by the government, and the supply system was uniform with manufacturers delivering goods weekly. The focus of the study was to investigate the existence of different sub-cultures among business owners in four regions of Brazil that supposedly had different cultures. As was noted in Chapter 1, the Brazilian population has a highly complex racial and ethnic mix. In the southern part of Brazil, where 70 per cent of the population live, four regional subcultures have been identified: Mineiros, Cariocas, Paulistas, and Gauchos, each supposedly exhibiting different cultural characteristics. The aim of the study was to assess the behaviour of these groups and identify any observable differences that could be identified as a result of regional culture differences.

The *Mineiros* are from the Minas Gerais state in the Central South of Brazil, a region noted for its mountainous terrain. There are a large number of gold mines in the area and it has traditionally attracted lots of newcomers and adventurers, along with the constant surveillance of tax collectors. The culture of this group reflects these characteristics. Mineiros are known for being 'tricky' and to protect themselves from outsiders they live in close family groups near to churches. Words used to describe Mineiros include 'austere, artful, quiet, laid back, introverted, reserved, suspicious modest, moderate and tolerant' (Lenartowicz and Roth 2001: 310). The *Cariocas* live in Rio de Janeiro which was the capital of the country and the capital of the Portuguese Empire in the seventeenth century. In this location there is a relaxed way of living and significant emphasis is placed upon arts, politics, and service industries. Descriptions of the Cariocas highlight characteristics such as 'easygoing, extroverted, liking music and parties, friendly, speculative, irreverent, indolent and appreciative of the "good life"' (Lenartowicz and Roth 2001: 310).

The third group, the *Paulistas*, live in São Paulo, a difficult to reach and inhospitable high plateau on the southern coast of Brazil. The first people to move to this area did so to escape legal prosecution and seek adventure. Due to the cold weather, it attracted European immigrants that saw it as a place in which to generate some wealth and subsequently move to a better place or return home. Words used to describe this group include 'restless, work oriented, attached to money and possessions, tenacious, formal, and directed to action' (Lenartowicz and Roth 2001: 310). Finally, *Gauchos* live in the extreme south on the pampas and were famous for their horsemanship and farming skills. The main immigrants were Italian and were noted for being extroverted and macho, but not for pursuing material gain since most were farmers. The descriptions of this group include 'authoritarian, opportunistic, extroverted, individualistic, courteous, and explosive' (Lenartowicz and Roth 2001: 310).

Given these very different subcultures, Lenartowicz and Roth wanted to find out whether they influenced business outcomes. Each manager's performance was measured in terms of achievement, enjoyment, restrictive conformity, security, self-direction, location, payment terms, and the assortment of goods they sold. They found that subculture performance patterns were closely related to what might have been predicted based on their knowledge of the different subcultures. The kiosks run by managers from Paulistas out-performed those run by managers from the Gaucho, Carioca and Mineiros subcultures. However, they also note that demonstrating a significant subculture effect does not necessarily negate the role of national culture, since every subculture had the same rank order domains. In short, each of the subcultures indicated that security followed by enjoyment was most important, and each ranked the lowest importance to self-direction and then restrictive conformity. They conclude that the concept of 'layers' of culture is an important one, and that cultural benchmarks should be undertaken at national and sub-cultural level.

Cross-cultural aspects of relationship marketing

Since the 1980s marketing researchers have identified a shift that has occurred in the ways industrial companies approach their customers and suppliers. A range of terms have been advanced to describe this shift including; 'relationship marketing, working partnerships, symbiotic marketing, strategic alliances, strategic partnerships, co-marketing alliances, channel partnerships, supplier partnerships, and just in time partnerships' (Morris *et al.* 1998). These orientations have developed as organizations have recognized that sustainable competitive advantage in the global economy requires being a trusted participant in a network, or set of strategic alliances. Relationship marketing activities are directed towards establishing, developing and maintaining successful relations. More recently, there has been further discussion of what constitutes relationship marketing. Studies of marital satisfaction and the quality of family life have indicated that relationships that provide more rewards than costs will generate mutual trust and attraction. It therefore follows, that within business-to-business relationships whether or not commitment and trust emerge between the partners is a function of the perceived costs and rewards of the exchange relationship.

Scholarship relating to buyer–seller exchanges in business-to-business marketing has proceeded through three main stages. The first generation of work developed the *interactive model* of business exchange relationships in institutions within industrial markets whereby both parties adapt to one another. The second generation of scholarship emphasized *buyer and seller networks*, thus the exchange relationship cannot be viewed in isolation from the pattern of relationships between firms that surround it. Relationships are embedded within systems of activity, resources, webs and of networks of actors. The final, and more recent work, has extended the idea of *networks and the environment* in which firms are embedded whether in relation to temporal, spatial, political, technological or social factors. An examination of contemporary marketing practice in the USA, Canada, Finland, Sweden and New Zealand found that transaction and interactive marketing dominated, whereas far less emphasis was placed on database and network marketing (Coviello *et al*. 2002). Welch and Wilkinson (2004) have assessed the political embeddedness of international business networks and found three distinct spheres of influence. *International business networks* are those in which government actors can play specific economic roles such as buyers, suppliers and intermediaries. *Policy-business networks* occur when governments and business interact with each other through policy communications and issues networks to develop influence and implement policy. Finally, *international government networks*, formed by actors, activities and resources – direct and indirect – from government, including ministries, departments, state and federal bodies and multilateral agencies.

Within international business relationships the issue of trust and commitment is made more complex due to language barriers and cultural differences which can prevent or complicate long-term relationships. For example, Aulakh *et al*. (1996) maintain that their sample of US organizations in the Fortune 500 who had foreign partnerships in Asia, Europe, Central/South America, found higher trust relationships with Asian and European firms, than those in Central/South America.

Friman *et al* (2002) have explored some of the important dimensions in cross-cultural business relationships in the international services sector (telecommunications, education, and temporary services) in Sweden, Australia, and the UK. Organizations were questioned about the reasons that led them to establish their business-to-business relationships and factors that were instrumental in their further development. Few of the organizations in the study indicated that they were driven by opportunism, although some admitted that they had initially acted with a high degree of self-interest. One of the companies admitted that the first meeting with their exchange partner was to steal ideas in order to make money from selling software around the world, developing relationships at that time was a secondary consideration. None of the entrepreneurs felt that they were guilty of being too greedy by attempting to maximize their own profits, indeed they were open about their intentions at the early stages of the relationship. Sharing information and communicating in an appropriate manner is a way of enhancing commitment and trust. Technical facilities, such as email, increased access to people and information, and the integration of communications systems served to bring partners closer together. One of the telecommunications firms did suffer from a lack of communication and the inability to provide information when it was requested, which damaged relationships with partners. Disclosing confidential information to the exchange partner exposes one's vulnerability, but it also facilitates trust.

All the companies indicated that shared values were crucial to their exchange relationships. Indeed some organizations stated that geographical location may be irrelevant in the context of corporate cultures that take a global perspective. There was an awareness of cultural differences and that they had to be managed effectively. The existence of a value system in partners was important even though it may have been based on a value system that did not necessarily reflect their own views. The values that were highly respected were based on integrity, respect, and trust. Relationship benefits were an important prerequisite for relational exchanges and when unsuitable people were involved it was usually to the financial detriment of the company. The termination costs of ending a relationship were not always of a monetary nature, the fear of failure can increase the interest in maintaining the relationship, and losing face was another factor.

Trust was identified as an important feature of all of the relationships, indeed some companies searched for quite a long time before they found a partner that they trusted. Personal bonds, and in some cases familial bonds were a prerequisite to some business relationships. The characteristics of competence, openness, honesty and personal liking were important attributes in defining trust. Finally, commitment was a time-dependent factor. One telecommunications manager indicated that it had taken 18 months to establish a sound relationship at all levels. Efforts at maintaining relationships were achieved through attending meetings and generally getting involved in the partner's business. Negotiations and signing contracts are important but alone they are not a sufficient basis for the continuance of business-to-business relationships – psychological commitment was also essential.

Most relationship marketing research has focused on developments in advanced, Western societies, marginalizing other cultures. However, even within the existing literature there are some doubts about the wholesale adoption of all aspects of relationship marketing. In their study of industrial firms in South Africa, Morris *et al.* (1998) found that the level of commitment to business relationships in practice was not as great as the marketing literature would have us believe. Respondents also indicated that their customers made even less of a commitment. Pels *et al.* (2004) have also noted low levels of marketing practice among some Argentinean firms compared with organizations in the USA and New Zealand, and the interactive marketing that was found in Argentina reflected the social environment in the country. Dadzie *et al.* (2008) have extended this work further by examining marketing practices in West Africa, Argentina and the USA. They investigated whether business-to-business marketing in West Africa was more or less trans-actional than in either the USA or Argentina. This study was also interesting because it distinguished between a small and large emergent economy. It was found that medium to high use of *transactional marketing*, where economic transactions are conducted at arms length, was used by 68 per cent of US firms, 59 per cent of West African and 52 per cent of Argentinean firms. Medium to high use of *database marketing*, which places little emphasis on personalization, occurred far more in US firms than those in West Africa and Argentina. The percentages were 67 per cent, 30 per cent, and 39 per cent respectively. *Interactive marketing* places a high reliance on face-to-face, complex personal interactions, and both the USA and Argentina scored highly with 90 per cent of firms indicating medium to high use, whereas for West Africa only 65 per cent of firms indicated this level of use. *Network marketing* is an understanding of the relationship in the context of other members in the market or industry. The use of network marketing was the highest in Argentina (76 per cent), West Africa (68 per cent) and the USA (64 per cent). Dadzie *et al.* concluded that in West Africa, transactional marketing is the norm and that pluralistic marketing is not that common. In contexts where marketing conditions were far less demanding, low levels of marketing practice were found.

A further study of the status and practice of relationship marketing in two former Yugoslavian markets, Serbia and Croatia, provided some highly varied results. Serbs more than Croats build relationships with buyers on the basis of values, trust and commitment. They respect the values of reliability, keeping promises, and honesty. Serbian mangers have respect for relationships despite the Balkan culture being considered risky and volatile and organizations being seen as untrustworthy. Personal ties are particularly important and business partners are considered 'one of us', which reflects a culture strong on collectivism and the importance of strong family ties. By contrast, Croatian companies are weak where respecting promises to partners are concerned, although firms did have the intention to keep relationships in the future. Thus wanting a longer term orientation was not necessarily supported by loyalty, trust and respect. Competition is more intense in Croatia than Serbia and therefore options for developing relationships are different. The role of business ethics is more problematic due to the current legal framework, the efficiency of the courts and low enforcement and the weakness of the economy (Zabkar and Brencic 2004).

As was learnt in Chapter 2 the essence of Chinese culture resides in the philosophical traditions of Confucianism and Taoism which is associated with the creativity of life, and harmony with nature. Traditional Chinese culture shapes the Chinese mentality in business and management in addition to interpersonal relationships. The concept of 'face' or 'public reputation' is an important value in Chinese culture in the context of interpersonal interaction and social exchange. 'Face' relates to an inner sense of worth which is experienced by the ego. The emotional impact of 'loss of face' is a real emotional dread, stronger than physical fear. Thus the protecting of 'face' comes high up on the agenda of interpersonal relations in China. The concept of losing face is not as strongly held in other cultures as it is in China as Ricks (1993: 62) points out: 'to be taken seriously in Italy, a person must try to win the argument. A person speaking precisely will be taken literally in Switzerland. The British prefer a much "softer sell" than the Germans'.

In the Chinese cultural context the granting of face and the maintenance of cordial *guanxi* has been highly practiced in the Chinese business community. The term *guanxi* refers to the special relationship that people have with each other that is based on reciprocity and connections. In Chinese culture a practical outcome of *guanxi* is that personal loyalty is often considered more important than organizational affiliation or legal standards. The view that loyalty is a virtue has been passed on through generations in Chinese culture. Loyalty to the family is particularly important. This emphasis is reflected in the service delivery since consumers tend to be very loyal to the same supplier. To engage in switching behaviour would cause loss of face to the provider which is something that the Chinese would tend to avoid (Jung and Au 2004). Interestingly, it has been found that superior performance occurs in organizations in China where managers have personal ties with government officials. Furthermore, personal ties have a more profound effect on performance than advertising, pricing, payment terms, or delivery.

By contrast, Fang (2001) maintains that trust and depth of relationships are not universal concepts in Chinese culture but are highly reciprocal, situational, dynamic, and context related. This has led to the view that China is a low-trust society, where trust is high inside among its members, but low outside in-group boundaries. He notes that 'Chinese business people can be both sincere and deceptive when dealing with their counterparts, depending on the level of trust and how favours are reciprocated. Therefore, the Chinese can use the 'coop-comp' (both cooperative and competitive) negotiation strategies in doing business' (Fang 2001: 54). It is therefore crucial that business relations take account of the principle of reciprocity in their handling of all kinds of business relationships.

A similar concept to *guanxi* in China has been identified in Africa. *Ubuntu* is a deeply embedded value of caring and community that fosters harmony, hospitality, humility and respect. The concept puts a great deal of emphasis on the group and it is embedded in kinship ties, linked to reward systems for group performance, and consensual decision-making. The concept has relevance in the context of consumer research with respect to understanding family decision-making, and word-of-mouth communication. In an organizational context, it has implications for developing organizational networks, and information sharing. Within the sales function, it relates to aligning organizational practices to *ubuntu* to provide competitive advantage linked to intrinsic motivation, loyalty, and long-run effectiveness.

Corruption

Over recent years there has been more interest in the relationship between international business and society. Rodriguez *et al.* (2006) maintain that recent events in political-economic history are responsible, and the trend has gathered pace since 1990, with the opening up of more countries and markets. A parallel discussion has focused on transnational crime, organized crime, money laundering and corruption that has taken on a distinctly international (see Beare 2003; Sheptycki and Wardak 2005; Williams and Vlassis 2005), and ethnic dimension (Bovenkerk 2005; Chin *et al.* 2005). Along with the expanding opportunities for business has come mounting criticism in the wake of corporate scandals and abuses of power. Ong (2000: 55–56) maintains that the rise of the Asian tiger, comprising countries in South East Asia, has been accomplished by submitting to the requirements of major global corporations, and in so doing has 'created new economic possibilities, social spaces and political constellations'.

Some of the recent adverse events have led to increased scholarly interest (one might also add public interest) in 'the diversity of social, economic, and political institutions that govern the behaviours of firms, and has heightened the importance of issues relating to politics, corruption and corporate social responsibility'. Recent accounts that have developed an explicit anti-capitalist agenda include Naomi Klein's (2000) *No Logo*, George Monbiots' (2000) *The Captive State: The Corporate Take over of Britain*, and Lasn's (1999) *Culture Jam: The Uncooling of America*. Furthermore, a whole host of anti-capitalist organizations are campaigning on the global stage. The importance of non-governmental organizations in global governance and value creation has become an important theme in international business and marketing (Doh and Teegen 2003; Teegen *et al.* 2004).

For example, Transparency International – a non-governmental organization which produces an index that rates countries according to their levels of corruption – found that some of the most corrupt countries were Bangladesh, Nigeria, Indonesia, Pakistan, Argentina and the Philippines. The least corrupt nations were Finland and New Zealand (*Economist* 2004b).

The World Bank defines corruption as the abuse of public power for private benefit. Likewise, the OECD refers to bribery as 'the offering, promising, or giving something in order to influence a public official in the execution of his/her official duties' (cf. Sanyal 2005: 139). However, it is important to recognize that corruption can also occur in the private sector. Bribes can take various forms including money, scholarships for a child's education, and favourable publicity. Bribery is certainly a significant problem in some countries. The World Bank has estimated that 5 per cent of exports to developing countries are appropriated by corrupt officials. Corruption is a fairly persistent problem and the successes of anti-corruption campaigns have been limited. In some countries, corruption is common in government procurement, in the provision of infrastructure services and in business licensing. At the individual level, relatively little is known about employees engaging in the practice. Most of what is known also relates to corruption that is outright illegal, and is most conspicuous in developing countries. Yet in practice, there is often a fine line between where corruption differs from *influence* over polices, for example lobbying (Rodriguez *et al*. 2006: 739). Different cultural contexts could position the goalposts in different places. Common views about corruption are that it discourages investors, and creates uncertainty about the costs of operating in a particular country, by acting as an irregular tax, increasing costs, and distorting incentives to invest. However, another perspective is that it has a positive effect on investment by helping along transactions in countries with excessive regulatory frameworks. Cuervo-Cazurra (2006) found that laws against bribery do act as a barrier to direct investment in some instances. However, they found that corruption is not a barrier to investors that have been exposed to bribery at home and thus it is embedded into the business culture, indeed they may deliberately seek out countries where corruption is prevalent.

Often countries in the East are portrayed as far more corrupt than those in the West. Khera (2001) maintains that stereotypical views exist in the West about businesses, officials and politicians in the East/Third World as being corrupt whereas the West is perceived as almost completely incorrupt. He argues that the reality is quite different, corruption exists everywhere and the major difference between East and West is that it is practiced so blatantly in the East that it makes the news headlines. Khera argues that there is one area in which the West has a claim to superiority of ethics, and that is in its effective investigative and judicial mechanisms to root out wrongdoers. Many Third World countries have cultures that have developed around feudal and paternalistic models, where power is concentrated in the cultural elite. In the Third World, transgressors and their families may be let off the hook, in advanced countries corrupt individuals rarely will be dealt with in such a way.

More recently, aspects of *guanxi* have been associated with aspects of corruption in China, or at the very least a set of ethical practices that differ from Western norms. As Millington *et al.* note:

> Although a culture of gift giving may be confused with or hide a system of corrupt or illegal payments for services, clear distinctions can be drawn between gift giving within *guanxi*, which is concerned with the building of relationships, and bribery which is targeted at illicit transactions.
>
> (2005: 256)

They argue that the influx of Western companies into China that have different ethical norms has weakened *guanxi* ties. In a society with a weak legal system, and a decline in standards of professional morality and social responsibility, *guanxi* has become an avenue for corruption. This observation is especially true in the public sector where bribes to state officials can be presented as *guanxi*. In some functions such as sales and purchasing, Millington *et al.* found that illicit payments in China were rife. Illicit payments were regarded as perks of the job by Chinese employees, especially when their salaries were poor. They suggest that the importance of *guanxi* in the networking and relationship building process is often overrated, with little emphasis on strong personal relationships being established, or socializing outside office hours. In one British company operating in China, steps were undertaken to reduce the number of illicit transactions in buyer–supplier relations by changing staff roles, introducing joint responsibilities, separating out different aspects of sourcing/purchasing, and increasing the involvement of senior staff.

Research has demonstrated that international companies engage in bribery for three reasons. First, it is a normal part of the culture in the country in which they are operating and deals cannot be struck or completed without conforming to cultural norms. Second, although a company might believe paying bribes is morally wrong, because every other company is doing it they just go along and equate it with the costs of doing business. Finally, a company may be so desperate for the business that they will do anything to obtain it, including bribery (Carmichael 1995). There have been numerous studies that have investigated the causes of corruption and they have generated a long list in doing so. Some of the factors involved include: 'political institutions, government regulations, legal systems, GDP levels, and salaries of public employees, to gender, religious cultural dimensions, and poverty, as well as the role of colonialism' (Di Rienzo *et al.* 2007: 321).

Access to information about the extent of corruption has not been extensively investigated but could have implications for reducing levels in the future. The anti-corruption group, Transparency International, maintains that Indian, Chinese, Russian, Turkish, and Taiwanese companies are the most prolific bribe payers when doing business abroad. The least affected businesses were those from Switzerland, Sweden, Australia, Austria, Canada and Britain (*Economist* 2006c). In countries like Russia, business people do not only do business with each other, but also compete with gangsterism. Practices such as favouritism, grease payments, price fixing and ignoring 'senseless' laws and regulations, are perceived as ethical in Russia, whereas they would be considered unethical in many advanced Western societies. Furthermore, Russian managers take the view that organizations doing business in Russia should fit in and act in the same way and not impose their cultural values on Russian managers (Jaffe and Tsimerman 2005).

Much of the existing literature on corruption has focused on how the institutional environment (country of operation) shapes the behaviour of multinational companies. In the 1970s there was considerable controversy about payments made to multinationals in developing countries. As a consequence, the USA introduced legislation to curb corrupt practices, although this lead was not followed by Europe. The US policy was a significant development for companies such as Unilever that had a considerable presence in developing countries. Unilever's company policy was never to bribe politicians and officials despite considerable pressure to do so, since it could damage the brand and that could be far more detrimental in the longer term. The company also gave its full support to those managers who enforced its policy on bribery, and indicated that there would be no ill-feeling if it meant losing business. During the 1980s, the company made the explicit 'distinction between bribery – which was absolutely prohibited – and 'facilitating payments'. Facilitating payments were defined as 'small payments made to minor officials to procure or expedite the legitimate performance of their normal functions' (Jones 2005).

Another strand to the debate is the effect of foreign direct investment (FDI) on the corruption environment. Kwok and Tadesse (2006) have addressed this issue by assessing the levels of corruption in countries that have benefited from relatively high levels of FDI, versus countries that have experienced low levels. The purpose of their study was to explore the relative importance of multinational companies having to adapt to the culture of their operating environment, while simultaneously adhering to the regulatory pressure from their home country, and to the international business community to which they belong. The results of the study demonstrated that levels of corruption were lower in countries that had received high levels of FDI. This outcome was persistent, regardless of whether FDI data from the 1970s, 1980s, or 1990s was used. They concluded that 'the harmful effects of culture on corruption are lower, and the beneficial effects of education on corruption are higher, in countries with higher FDI in the past' (Kwok and Tadesse 2006: 781). Of considerable relevance as far as marketers are concerned, is how corruption affects consumers. Di Rienzo *et al.* (2007: 329) argue that removing corruption will have consumer benefits. 'From an international business policy perspective, trust is critical between trading partners. If trust exists and bribes, kickbacks, and gifts do not, the cost of doing business internationally will be reduced and consumers will benefit'.

Corporate social responsibility

Corporate social responsibility has been given a high profile in the business environment in the last decade. Despite considerable discussion of corporate social responsibility, there has been a lack of a clear definition, its different dimensions, and the ways that it might be measured (Rowley and Berman 2000). Rodriguez *et al*. have proposed the following definition of CSR in relation to multinational organizations:

> We define CSR as instances where the company goes beyond compliance and engages in actions that appear to advance a social cause. Such actions might include adding social features or characteristics to products, or modifying production processes to signify that the firm is seeking to advance a social objective (e.g. selling cosmetics with ingredients that are not tested on animals, or adopting environmentally friendly technologies), or working closely with community organizations to ameliorate homelessness and indigence (e.g. the Society of St Vincent De Paul). In an international context, CSR may also involve avoiding operations in countries that commit human rights violations.
>
> (Rodriguez *et al*. 2006: 737)

The parameters of corporate social responsibility are culturally specific. At any one point in time, in any society there are generally accepted relationships, obligations and duties between the major institutions and society. Political theorists have referred to this relationship as the 'social contract'. Employees working outside of their own country need to be acculturated into the values in their work environment and understand how they should be integrated into marketing practice (Robin and Reidenbch 1987). There has not been a significant amount of attention given to CSR in the education of managers. Wilkie (2005) questioned a group of doctoral students about their exposure to CSR in their studies, and found that two thirds expressed a personal interest in the topic, but only 10 per cent had taken a single course on the subject.

Many CSR studies have assessed the relationship between company social performance and its financial performance. Multinational companies are more likely to be traded, are highly visible on radar of activists and NGOs, and are therefore vulnerable to pressure to improve their CSR agendas. It needs to be acknowledged, however, that research on the relationship between social performance and financial performance has not demonstrated strong associations. Businesses also need to be aware that business norms and standards, regulatory frameworks, political systems, corruption, and stakeholder demand for CSR can vary across nations, regions, and different parts of the business. A testament to how seriously some global companies view CSR is that they publish annual reports on social responsibility. McDonald's, Motorola, and Nike all publish social responsibility reports. At one level it could be construed as a good advertising ploy, little more than a public relations stunt and some consumers have criticised it as such, since all the information contained in the reports is filtered through senior management. From the company's viewpoint, CSR reports can be a useful competitive tool if aligned with a political strategy that harms competitors.

Studies that have assessed variations in company CSR images, have found considerable differences between those in the USA and Europe (UK, France, and the Netherlands) according to their motivation and content. Maignan and Ralston (2002) found that US and UK based organizations were more likely to discuss CSR issues than French and Dutch companies. The principles motivating CSR were also different. The US businesses were more likely to present CSR as an extension of their core values, whereas the Europeans had performance-related motivations, i.e. it was good for business. European firms also tended to introduce CSR initiatives in response to stakeholder scrutiny and pressure, from the community, customers, or regulators. There were also differences in the activities in which companies engaged as part of their CSR programmes. Of most importance for UK and US firms were philanthropic activities such as investment in cities and communities, but in France and the Netherlands the management of environmental impacts of business were paramount. Reasons for these differences were varied and included the role of the state, public opinion, religion, and the composition of investors.

The issue of whether global companies should standardize their CSR strategy or adapt to local conditions, is another ongoing debate. Some scholars have argued that companies should adapt their CSR strategies to local cultures, just as they adapt their products. Unfortunately, there is no definitive framework to distinguish between global and local CSR, although some tentative suggestions have been aired. One approach is to generate a set of universal principles around a set of core beliefs (religious, cultural, and philosophical), which comprise a set of hypernorms. Local community norms may differ from universal principles but are not allowed to contravene these hypernorms. A key differentiating feature between local and global CSR resides with the community that demands it. Universal principles contain rights and obligations to which all societies should be held accountable. By contrast, the local CSR community consists of self-defined groups whose members interact on the basis of shared tasks, values and goals, and who can establish their own norms of ethical behaviour. Thus local CSR is accountable to the demands of the local rather than global community. Husted and Allen (2006) found that multinational enterprises were more likely to adapt to local CSR strategies than global companies.

A high profile aspect of CSR has been workers rights in the Third World. Countries such as Indonesia, rarely protect workers by labour rights and they are often harassed by the military while working for sub-contractors producing goods for brand names such as Nike, Reebok, and Gap. Whenever a strike breaks out the army is used regardless of necessity, and army barracks are located adjacent to factories for this purpose (Ong 2000). In extreme cases, corporate social responsibility means pulling out of a country altogether resulting in loss of production and markets. One such case is Burma/Myanmar which has been ruled by a military elite since 1962. As a consequence, large American and Western European corporations have stopped operating and doing business in the country, since it was often not possible to do business without supporting the military junta and its poor record on human rights. In the early 1990s, Levi Strauss, Eddie Bauer, Liz Claibourne, Columbia Sportswear, Apple Computers, Motorola, Disney and PepsiCo all pulled out. In July 1996, the Danish brewer, Carlsberg, and Dutch brewer, Heineken, announced that they were shelving plans to invest in the country. Carlsberg had planned to invest $30 million in a bottling plant, and Heineken was involved in a half-built brewery. Heineken left with the words 'Every billboard in the country will come down . . . out is out' (Holliday 2005: 332). There have been codes of conduct in the sporting goods industry in an attempt to reassure consumers; however, very often compliance mechanisms are not well developed and rarely are sanctions given a mention (van Tulder and Kolk 2001). In India there is little chance of poor quality firms developing corporate governance as a sign of quality; it is not economically feasible in the context of family firms.

Some companies are developing environmentally responsible and sustainable production practices as part of their CSR strategy. Ikea's low cost, functional; design conscious products have found favour among consumers in Western Europe, and middle-class consumers in locations including China, Saudi Arabia, Malaysia, Romania and Russia. In 2006 the company estimated that 458 million consumers visited its stores, a figure equivalent to the population of the European Union. The company's products are manufactured in the Third World under conditions which are presented as 'responsible' towards the environment, which 'respect' the rights of workers and promote affluence through capital investment so that workers are able to purchase Ikea products for themselves. This combination of factors has allowed Ikea to promote itself as presenting a 'third way' paradigm of consumption:

> rebelliously undermining rigid, 'old' bourgeois, hierarchical assumptions that spending power, good taste, and class must be mutually dependent (through its celebration of minimalism and functionality for all), but also mediating between crass consumerism (getting as much as one can for as little as possible – effectively Ikea's modus operandi), and progressive ideals (global justice, environmental responsibility).
>
> (Hartman 2008: 485)

A contradiction in Ikea's sustainability strategy, is that their goods are so cheap that they are highly disposable and are often the first goods to be put in the rubbish when moving house or upgrading.

Ethical trade is concerned with sourcing, and specifically the conditions under which the workforce produces goods. In this respect it is unlike fair trade that explicitly attempts to challenge the unjust power relations between rich and poor countries. The demands of consumers in advanced societies have had an impact on the practices of wine producers in South Africa. However, some commentators maintain that supermarkets are hypocritical in their relationships with suppliers. On the one hand, they insist upon the introduction of various production standards from their suppliers, on the other, they simultaneously compromise these processes by insisting that suppliers should meet the cost of compliance. The increased downward pressure on prices leaves producers with very tight profit margins thus reducing the scope for improving the condition of workers (Hartman 2008: 315). In rural areas this process has led to a sharp polarization of the workforce between decreasing numbers of permanent workers whose social and working conditions are on the whole improving, and a sharp increase in temporary labour to provide the flexibility required to reduce costs (Bek *et al.* 2007).

Starbucks, the Seattle-based upmarket coffee company, has come under fire for exploiting Third World farmers who produce its organic products. In 2006, a pound of coffee had the price tag of $1.45 which taking into account fuel, bank interest, labour and transport costs netted the farmers less than $1. In the USA, the same pound of coffee sells for the considerably higher price of $26. Ethiopia's speciality coffee beans routinely retail in advanced economies for three times the price of ordinary coffee and this has led to the country wishing to trademark the names of three coffee-growing regions to ensure that companies selling its beans sign a licensing document to enable farmers to secure a higher price for their products. One region was Sidamo but when the country filed with the US Patent and Trademark Office, it found that Starbucks had got there first. In its defence, Starbucks maintained that it sourced 2 per cent of its beans from Ethiopia accounting for 2 per cent of the country's crop. It also maintains that since 2002, the company has invested $2.4 million in investments and loans, and also voluntarily sets minimum prices for green coffee which provides a buffer for farmers and allows them to ride out slumps in commodity prices. However, trademark status would not rely on the benevolence of the buyer and instead provide a better price for the coffee which would generate millions of dollars of extra revenue each year (Faris 2007).

The concept of product authenticity has different meanings within a cross-cultural CSR context. Boyle (2003: 44) argues that 'Authenticity doesn't just mean reliving the past: it means using it to find new ways of living – maybe even new kinds of progress. The most authentic isn't necessarily the most true to the past; it could be the most creative or the most human'. He suggests that organizations use different sorts of authenticity to market their products. The Body Shop sources many ingredients from the Amazonian rainforests, indigenous people in villages mix the potions, and they are paid a fair wage for their labour. The Body Shop has emphasized internationalism and given a high profile to ethical campaigns. Lush makes soaps from fresh fruits and vegetables that are sourced locally where possible, and made up in local shops. Lush presents itself as a local brand in Japan, the company is called Lush-Japan, products are given Japanese names, and 85 per cent are produced in Japan. By contrast, Brazilians want the Englishness associated with the products' source and in that market the company is called Lush-London.

Negotiation

Negotiations are part of daily life in consumer and industrial markets. It is therefore important that the process becomes more widely understood given a more connected-up global economy. The need to negotiate deals internationally, and therefore to understand the impact of culture on negotiating behaviour, distribution rules, biases and fairness judgements is essential for managers to appreciate (Buchan *et al.* 2004). Sometimes culture can have a considerable impact on negotiations which need to be understood in advance. A testament to its importance is the significant number of books that have been written of the topic of negotiating across cultures (Salacuse 1991; Foster 1992; Brett 2001; Sebenius 2002). For example, the Japanese may require several meetings before engaging in business whereas Americans and Northern European are quite happy to begin negotiations straightaway (Hollensen 2007). A high profile blunder occurred when an American salesman presented a Saudi Arabian client with a multimillion-dollar proposal in a pigskin binder. This was considered vile in Muslim culture and he was immediately thrown out. Furthermore, his company was blacklisted from working with Saudi companies in the future. How people greet and address one another, and the role of business cards, should be determined in advance. How silences are viewed – awkward, respectful, insulting – needs to be researched. Eye contact in negotiating is particularly important but it is also culturally specific. In dealing with the French it is important to look into the eyes of managers, whereas direct eye contact in Southeast Asia should be avoided until the deal is done (Sebenius 2002).

In their study of intercultural communications competence in sales and negotiation, Chaisrakeo and Speece (2004) identified three different aspects of intercultural competence: *cultural awareness*, *cultural sensitivity*, and *cultural adroitness*. Individuals who exhibit high levels of cultural awareness are better at predicting the effects of their behaviour on others and are more likely to modify their behaviour after learning something about other cultures. Cultural sensitivity relates to having the requisite values such as open-mindedness, high self concept, being non-judgemental, being socially relaxed in order to understand the value of different cultures, and the ability to become sensitive to verbal and non-verbal cues of people from different countries. Cultural adroitness relates to the ability to act effectively when in contact with a new cultural environment; knowing what to do and what to avoid in order to communicate more effectively without offending any parties. Managers with these positive characteristics become better cross-cultural negotiators.

Hollensen (2007: 617) suggests that even the language of negotiation can be culturally specific. For example, compromise for North Americans and Western Europeans equates to 'morality, good faith, and fair play'. But Mexicans and Latin Americans view compromise as losing dignity and integrity, and in Russia and in the Middle East, it is a sign of weakness. In their assessment concerning whether beliefs about fairness influence bargaining behaviour among buyers and sellers in the USA and Japan, Buchan *et al.* (2004) found that they did, but only up to a point. The comparison of USA and Japan is an interesting one, since the two cultures have a different understanding of the concept of power which is integral to negotiation situations. In Western societies, power can be viewed as coercive or noncoercive whereas in Japan, it is understood as less of a binary construct and more relational. The Japanese tend to view social power in a paternalistic context – a sign of authority or as nurturing an influence:

> Western views focus on the action and outcomes related to the power source, Japanese views concentrate on the type of negotiation relationship. In essence, from the perspective of Japanese culture, power is captured in the relationship between the negotiators. For Western cultures, power relates to the outcomes and ends of the negotiation.
>
> (Buchan *et al.* 2004: 184).

Buchan *et al*. also found that participants from the USA thought it fair that the party with the greatest power took a larger share of the wealth. In Japan, the reverse was true with participants believing that the party with the greater power should earn a smaller share of the wealth, thus sharing more of it with the weaker partner. However, an important exception was when fairness beliefs were aligned with self-interest. When beliefs about fairness conflict with self-interest, fairness beliefs do not have a significant influence on the bargaining behaviour of participants in the two countries.

The importance of time and timescales is particularly important in advanced cultures, as discussed in Chapter 2 in the context of consumer behaviour. Cultural perceptions of time are also important in business negotiations. For example, Arabs typically do not like deadlines and feel threatened by them, whereas many Americans try to speed up matters by setting deadlines as part of good practice. The same sort of conflict emerged in Greece where Americans tried to set time limits for meetings. The Greeks perceived this request as vulgar and insulting. This feature was compounded when the Americans wanted to agree the main principles of the deal and subsequently let subordinates deal with the details. The Greeks considered this a deceptive strategy and wanted senior people to deal with the whole contract, regardless of the time it would take. These cultural differences over perceptions in time led the Americans to lose the contract (Ricks 1993).

In their study of the dynamics of decision-making styles of US and Peruvian export managers, Marshall and Boush (2001) used the concept of in-group/out-group distancing. According to this approach or understanding, interpersonal relationships are defined by the extent to which a person treats members of their own group differently from outsiders. In-group/out-group distancing can have some important implications. For example, in-group members might compete with out-group members rather than co-operate, exploit rather than sacrifice, manipulate rather than help, and fight rather than accommodate. Partners at the start of international distribution arrangements are likely to be perceived as an out-group and their behaviour may reflect this. Marshall and Boush found that culture, personal preferences, and relationship history all played a part in the process to differing degrees and through different stages. Country-of-origin is influential at the start and Peruvians see the foreign importer as an out-group member. They maintain that country of origin is important early on in the relationship but that this factor's influence erodes fairly rapidly.

Ethics

A pertinent issue is whether cultural factors can affect the means by which multinational managers discharge their responsibilities ethically across cultures. An issue that has rarely been addressed is the appropriateness of formal codes, regardless of their content, for encouraging ethical behaviour in different cultural settings. Luo defines ethical codes as follows.

Ethical codes contain general precepts and mandate specific practices, providing provisions that deal with legalities and ethical concerns and detail sanctions. Hence, these codes make information and expectations about legal and ethical behaviors clearer. They also increase the likelihood of detection, ensure punishment of transgressions, reward desired behaviors, and discipline those who engage in offshore business illegalities . . . The codes help foreign employees' awareness of corporate policy and enlist their support in the fight against corruption in a host country . . . They also draw a distinction between the acceptable quid quo pro or networking, which is often necessary to develop business relationships in an emerging market, and corrupt practices.

(Luo 2006: 752)

Anthony Giddens's (1984, 1995) concept of structuration theory has been used in the context of understanding the ethical stance of individuals. He argues that an individual's political consciousness and social consciousness combined constitute what he termed 'practical consciousness' to help them navigate ethical issues in a reflexive way. Using this framework to understand the ethical behaviour of multinational companies operating in China, Luo found that when perceived corruption in the business sector increases, companies that focus more on ethics, tend to use arms-length bargaining to deal with the government. Whereas those that focus less on ethics, more frequently use social connections to deal with the government. So in this context ethics codes appear to work and this is important in the context of China which is ranked as one of the most corrupt countries in the world.

Ethics initiatives and programmes are often dominated by the application of American practices to non-American situations. The underlying philosophy is that a culture-free ethics management actually exists and can be applied unproblematically in diverse cultural settings. Ethics management takes the form of formal codes of business conduct; multinational companies are also advised to follow American practices by implementing formal ethics initiatives such as ethics committees and officers; and changing company cultures, and rewarding compliance, while simultaneously punishing non-compliance. The temptation for companies to follow the lead of American-style ethics codes is strong because they may wish to emulate more prominent and successful companies. Management consultancies also play their part and serve as agents for the diffusion of American business ideas and practices.

Various scholars have assessed international codes of conduct and how cultural content varies across cultures. European codes tend to focus on hierarchy and conservatism, whereas American codes emphasize liberal individualism. European codes appear to involve employees more in the design and implementation stages than American firms. European codes emphasize employees' responsibilities towards the organization more than American codes. Weaver (2001) uses Hofstede's framework to suggest that different countries require different ethics codes that fit with the dominant culture. Different combinations of cultural characteristics require culturally sensitive ways to encourage ethical behaviour. There are cultural differences in attitudes towards ethics along some of the lines highlighted above, but at the same time research has also indicated that as far as cross-cultural encounters are concerned, culture's reach is limited. For example, some employees have been found to adapt to the host culture when placed within a cross-cultural setting, putting to one side some of the norms and behaviours of their native culture. In effect, they play a role that is required of them in that particular cultural setting. However, they subsequently revert back to their native cultural norms when dealing with people from their own culture.

Over 30 empirical studies have been conducted on ethical attitudes and ethical behaviour in business relationships and most of them indicate the importance of national culture. Most of the studies are descriptive in nature, informing us about the similarities and differences in ethical attitudes and behaviour. However, largely absent from the discourse is *how* culture influences attitudes and behaviours (Christie *et al.* 2003). Also absent from the ethics literature is an understanding of sub-cultural investigations of ethical behaviour, for example those that focus on different ethnic groups. As argued elsewhere in the book, cross-cultural has often been defined as cross-national in ethics research and populations have been aggregated at the level of the nation. This situation has even occurred in instances where the ethnic population can be quite large as in the case of African-Americans in the U.S. (Swaidan *et al.* 2003). Yet research from around the world informs us that there can be differences in ethical beliefs between individuals within different ethnic groups living in the same country. For example, Tat (1981) found that ethical perceptions of African-Americans were different from the ethical perceptions of Caucasians. Sarwono and Armstrong (2001) also found significant differences in ethical behaviours and beliefs among the Javanese, Batak, and Indonesian-Chinese groups. By contrast, Tsalikis and Nwachukwu (1988) found that the ethical stance of ethnic groups in the USA was similar.

Business ethics has become an important issue in cross-cultural business settings and is highly complex since various marketing functions can be affected in different ways. Tadepalli *et al.* (1999) have addressed whether Mexican and American purchasing managers perceive ethical situations differently. Within Mexican culture, most business activities are concentrated in the hands of a few large families thus family connections and relationships are important. As a consequence, there are large power distances between those that run the business and their employees. The purchasing function has not evolved at anything like the extent as the USA. Purchasing managers are viewed as clerks who execute the orders of superior/family members and within this context uncertainty avoidance is strong. American organizations have made a point of stressing ethics in purchasing activities. The existence of 'perks' such as free lunches and tickets to football games have been curbed in order to reinforce the respectability of the purchasing profession and foster a reputation for quality and profitability.

Managers were provided with eleven statements relating to ethics and there were differences among seven of them. The statements on which there were differences were:

- Accepting free trips from salespeople is OK.
- It is acceptable to make exaggerated statements to a supplier to gain a concession.
- Accepting free entertainment from sales people in OK.
- Giving preferential treatment to suppliers who happen to be good customers is sound business.
- It is acceptable to obtain information about competitors by asking suppliers for that information.
- A salesperson's personality is an important part of the purchase decision process.
- Soliciting unnecessary quotations from new unused suppliers is okay even when selection procedures indicate a preference for existing suppliers.

Mexicans viewed accepting free trips and free entertainment as a perk of the job and this was a practice that was common all over Mexico. Mexico suffers from a dearth of good business information sources that are available in the US through outlets like Dunn and Bradstreet and *The Wall Street Journal*. With these advantages there are few problems for US companies sourcing information about suppliers. In Mexico there was little alternative but to strengthen relations with suppliers and solicit as much information from personal contacts in the market. Mexican purchase professionals saw no problems with choosing suppliers on the basis of personality, whereas in the USA the emphasis was on making sure everything was above board.

One of the few studies that have examined perceptions of business ethics in a multicultural society was undertaken in Malaysia. The focus was on three ethnic groups; the Malays that accounted for 60 per cent of the total population, the Chinese 30 per cent and the Indians 9 per cent. In such a diverse cultural setting one could have anticipated that there would be different cultural values with respect to what is considered right or wrong in one culture, and inappropriate in another. These misunderstandings can have a negative effect on business including failures in business deals and negotiations. For example, Rashid and Ho note:

> it is considered reasonable to a Chinese businessman to invite a Malay businessman to a drinking session as a business gesture and recognize their business relationships. To a Malay businessman, accepting such an invitation is acceptable, but since the Malay is generally a Muslim and does not consume alcoholic drink, the Chinese businessman may feel offended if the Malay businessman does not consume the alcoholic drink. The Chinese businessman could misinterpret the action of the Malay businessman as not giving 'face' to him in this situation. This could cause misunderstandings in business communication and relationships.
>
> (2003: 76)

Significant differences between the three ethnic groups were found among managers in the banking sector in connection with 'malpractice in sales', and the 'gaining of competitor information'. The Indian managers perceived both of these business situations more unethical than the Malays or Chinese. The Chinese perceived 'malpractice in sales' as more problematic than the Malays. The Chinese managers indicated that the 'gaining of competitor information' as less unethical than either the Malays or Indians (Zabid 1989). However, a more recent, wide-ranging survey of the ethical characteristics of the three groups suggested more of a cultural convergence. There was more of an adaptation to Chinese business ethics that dominate the business culture in Malaysia, which could be viewed as a form of acculturation and perhaps a strategy to ensure a continuous relationship with their business partners (Rashid and Ho 2003).

An interesting issue given the power of global companies, is how they are policed. Maynard (2001: 17) argues that 'There is a gray area of ethical judgment where the standards of the transnational's home country differ substantially from those of the host country'. He argues that in these situations the ethical practices of multinational companies will be policed by four policing authorities: the organization itself by virtue of the integrity of its own management following its own code of ethics; other competitor organizations that may offer a benchmark in ethical practice; governmental agencies including those of the host country; and public exposure including the media, non-governmental agencies, and watchdog groups.

Questions

- Does the globalization or glocalization of marketing management offer the most persuasive assessment of business-to-business marketing?
- What do you understand by the term 'marketer acculturation'?
- Why is it important to consider cross-cultural variations in marketing negotiation strategies?
- Why do marketers need to understand cross-cultural differences in corruption environments?
- Explain some of the differences in the cross-cultural ethical behaviour of marketing managers.

Further reading

Burgess, S.M. and Steenkamp, J.E.M. (2006) 'Marketing renaissance: How research in emerging markets advances marketing science and practice', *International Journal of Research in Marketing*, 23: 337–356.

Coviello, N.E., Brodie, R.J., Danaher, P.J. and Johnston, W.J. (2002) 'How firms relate to their markets: An empirical examination of contemporary marketing practice', *Journal of Marketing*, 66 (July): 33–46.

Gopalkrishnan, R.I. (1997) 'Comparative marketing: An interdisciplinary framework for institutional analysis', *Journal of International Business Studies*, 28 (3): 531–561.

Johnson, J.P., Lenartowicz, T. and Apud, S. (2006) 'Cross-cultural competence in international business: Toward a definition and a model', *Journal of International Business Studies*, 37 (4): 525–543.

Lazer, W., Murata, S. and Kosaka, H. (1985) 'Japanese marketing: Towards a better understanding', *Journal of Marketing*, 49 (Spring): 69–81.

Rodriguez, P., Siegel, D.S., Hillman, A. and Eden, L. (2006) 'Three lenses on the multinational enterprise: Politics, corruption, and corporate social responsibility', *Journal of International Business Studies*, 37 (6): 733–746.

Sebenius, J.K. (2002) 'The hidden challenges of cross-border negotiations', *Harvard Business Review*, March: 76–85.

Welch, C. and Wilkinson, I. (2004) 'The political embedding of international business networks', *International Marketing Review*, 21 (2): 216–231.

9 Marketing research

Introduction

The formal study of one group of people by another has existed for thousands of years in Eastern and Western civilizations (Mead 1967). Within the last century this interest has intensified given the substantial increase in business and economic transactions that cross national and geographic boundaries. The focus in this chapter is to consider the range of methods and approaches that can be undertaken to do this. It is probably true to say that there has been far more attention in cross-cultural marketing paid to the substantive content, prioritizing theoretical approaches and empirical findings, as opposed to discussing methodology and research practice. Over the last two decades there have been some important developments in the USA and Britain, across the social sciences and humanities with respect to the profile of scholars undertaking racial and ethnic research. New generations of ethnic minority scholars have a strong personal and political engagement that challenges the traditional White/Other dynamic of much research (Alexander 2006). Furthermore, they have introduced new research issues that have their roots in the wider social sciences such as discrimination and consumer racism.

There are a huge variety of methodological approaches that can be used in cross-cultural research designs. The focus of this chapter is to provide on overview of some of the possibilities along with examples used in the marketing literature. The chapter is divided into two main sections, one dealing with quantitative and the other emphasizing qualitative approaches to cross-cultural research. It is true to say that cross-cultural marketing traditionally has been dominated by quantitative methodological approaches, and research focusing on cultural values has had a particularly high profile. Some of the pertinent issues addressed in the quantitative section of the book include cross-cultural survey, content analysis, understanding the role of equivalence, and digitalizing cross-cultural research.

The qualitative section of the chapter provides an overview of the use of qualitative methods in cross-cultural research. Ethnography has a high profile since it is a well-established means of researching culture in many academic disciplines. Various aspects of ethnography are discussed here, including critical ethnography, corporate ethnography, online ethnography, netnography and the use of ethnography within the product design process. Ethnoconsumerism is a particular approach to undertaking cross-cultural research that borrows concepts from ethnography and sociology. This methodological approach views individuals as cultural beings as part of a sub-culture who have multiple affiliations. Textual analysis is a very flexible method of analysis in which images and words are analysed to cover hidden meanings. Critical approaches are also considered as a distinctive methodological domain. The final part of the chapter considers historical approaches to cross-cultural marketing.

Cross-cultural market research and diversity

Not so long ago Gerald Zaltman (2000) exalted consumer researchers to broaden their intellectual peripheral vision, and in so doing see relevance in seemingly distant fields and take 'ignorance as a friend'. His argument was that knowledge is transigent, today's knowledge contradicts what went before, and the half life of knowledge becomes shorter the more we have of it. It is in this context that he argues that we should become friends with ignorance for knowledge can only come from ignorance. This raises two important issues concerning ignorance: What do we know that is in error? And what do we fail to know because of perceived irrelevance? (Zaltman 2000: 423). Research questions originate in the minds of researchers or practitioners whether due to personal reflection, and/or as a result of available data using widely acceptable tools.

It is evident from the discussion in Chapter 1 about the high degree of cultural diversity in different countries, that marketing research is a complex and time-consuming activity that needs to be undertaken to obtain an accurate picture of the market. For global companies operating in several countries, the complexity is multiplied many fold. The availability and reach of different media and how they are embedded in the lives of consumers are all important considerations. Literacy rates have important implications for marketing research in a range of ways. Levels of literacy have implications for the research methods used for data collection. Cheaper methods such as mail and self-completion questionnaires, internet surveys, and mobile phone surveys are all excluded in populations with low levels of literacy. Another feature of marketing research diversity is rapid changes within countries that may make previous findings obsolete. Political turmoil, wars, and other forms of conflict are becoming important issues to affect marketing in some parts of the world, as previous chapters of the book have demonstrated.

The rate of product innovation is increasing the number of new models to con-tinually build, and test, and assess their suitability in different markets. Furthermore, the cultural composition of markets is becoming more diverse, given the increasing purchasing power of emerging markets in Latin America, India and China. At the turn of the millennium 90 per cent of marketing research was conducted in Europe, Japan, and the USA. However, with the desire of companies to extend their products into developing economies, this trend is likely to change, bringing new challenges for cross-cultural marketers (Craig and Douglas 2000). It also used to be acceptable to sell old models of products to emerging markets, but that is no longer the case. As a consequence of the globalization of advertising, consumers know the specifications they want from their products even though they may have limited purchasing power.

Emerging markets present some challenges for market research. These include absence of sampling frames, lack of reliable and fast transportation in parts of developing countries, unreliable mail delivery, and low penetrations of internet use. But there are some trade offs, for example it is much cheaper to collect primary quantitative data. For example, business-to-business interviews cost $200–400 in France and Japan, compared with about $40 in Thailand and Vietnam, and other developing countries. Furthermore, there are local research firms in many developing countries, and some global research organizations have agencies in these countries. Gallup International has member agencies in most developing countries including India, China, Indonesia, Vietnam, South Africa, Kenya, Nigeria, Zimbabwe, Argentina and Mexico (Burgess and Steenkamp 2006).

Recent developments in technological innovation could possibly reduce the costs of cross-cultural research further. In his article entitled 'Digitizing consumer research', Eric Johnson (2001) suggests that the impact of the Internet is likely to affect the research that marketers undertake, the respondents that are used, and types of measures that are employed. Increased validity of research may arise since web-based studies can actually capture actual consumer activity and purchasing decisions as they happen. The internet facilitates the globalization of research by recruiting respondents in diverse countries around the globe who would otherwise be extremely difficult to reach. Having reliable email addresses also makes it easier to recruit samples for the future, reduces costs of doing so, and allows respondents to be recruited on the basis of prior responses. As a consequence the end of the student subject that has dominated marketing research may also be in sight. Many researchers use students in their samples to save time and money, but they do represent a somewhat cohesive sample. In some respects this lessens the credibility of academic research among practitioners and policy makers. Larger samples are available via the internet, and there is also potential for much greater use of secondary data analysis. For example, some companies like MediaMetrix gather every click from panels of tens of thousands of internet users. A by-product is the ability to measure the time and order of consumer information acquisition.

Given such significant levels of diversity, the issue about how to approach researching cultural marketing issues is an important one. Companies enter international markets at their peril if they do not first undertake appropriate market research. There are many cases of organizations having disappointing results because they did not understand cultural differences. Ricks (1993) provides a significant number of examples of cultural problems and market research strategies.

No market research

A company in the USA on observing that ketchup was not available in Japan, dispatched a large quantity of its popular, brand-name product. One important oversight was that the company did not first make enquiries about why the product was not available and actively marketed in Japan. The reason why the company did not undertake research to identify the potential market was because it did not want to miss out on first mover advantages and let some other company win out. Unfortunately, this was an expensive mistake because the company learned to its cost that ketchup was not popular and that soy sauce was the product of choice. A similar problem occurred when a US cake mix company tried to market its 'add one egg' cake mixes in the United Kingdom. The company thought it was onto a winner by providing an opportunity for customers to bake the cake. Unfortunately, UK consumers did not like US style, spongy cakes and preferred something more substantial to eat with their tea.

Insufficient market research

A large US soft drinks company predicted a large market for its products in Indonesia. However, the size of the potential market was based on poor quality market research. The sample of consumers that were included in the study lived in Indonesian cities, and the results were projected to apply to the whole population. Not unlike many developing countries, there are major differences between the consumption pattern of consumers that reside in cities and rural areas. After the company had spent considerable sums of money setting up a large bottling plant and distribution network, they realized that the main consumers of soft drinks were tourists who only visited the cities, thus they were not representative of the population.

Lack of competitor analysis

Kentucky Fried Chicken saw potential in entering the Brazilian market, in the expectation that it would eventually open 100 stores. The company's first store was in São Paulo but after a short period of time it became evident that the sales were very disappointing. The reason why the sales were low was due to market competition from local suppliers that the company had not taken into account. Low-priced, charcoal-broiled chicken is an integral part of the fast food culture, and locals preferred it to the American company's recipe. In order to try and salvage the situation, Kentucky began offering hamburgers, Mexican tacos, and enchiladas. But this was not the road to profitability since these products were not embedded in Brazilian food culture and there was little interest from consumers.

Inappropriate market research

CPC International, the producer of dry Knorr soups, met with consumer resistance when it tried to market its products in the USA. The company's research prior to entering the market took the form of taste testing. The results came out well when consumers were given the final product to taste. However, when the soup was placed on the shelves in supermarkets, the sales were very low. The company was unaware that Americans tend to avoid purchasing dried soup. The taste testers were unaware that the soup was dry, and that it would require 15–20 minutes of cooking and stirring prior to serving. Had they known these things, they may not have said they would purchase when they tasted the product. Another example is in the case of governments sending milk powder to developing countries as aid. Significant quantities of the milk powder were distributed in South America. However, there were complaints that the product made consumers ill and they began to use it to whitewash their homes instead. Further research into the digestive problem proved that the indigenous people were correct. It seems that an enzyme required for the breakdown of milk in the stomach is retained by North Americans and European throughout their life. This is not so for many South Americans who only retain the enzyme while nursing, and it was for this reason they were unable to digest the milk, even though it was free.

Cross-cultural marketing research and equivalence

The complexity of consumer and industrial research is greatly increased when working in an international, multicultural and multilingual environment. The issue of establishing *equivalence* and *comparability* of data is particularly relevant since the same words and concepts may not have the same meaning in different countries. Far less emphasis has been given to cross-cultural marketing research than has been devoted to domestic markets. The classic distinction in cross-cultural research is between *emic* and *etic* approaches. The *emic* approach maintains that attitudinal or behavioral phenomena are expressed in a different way in each culture and therefore they need to be understood and interpreted in their own terms. According to this viewpoint measures need to be adapted to each cultural context, to demonstrate the similarities and differences since each measure is culturally specific. The *etic* approach is primarily concerned with identifying universal attitudinal and behavioral concepts and designing pan-cultural or culture-free measures. The use of such measures can give direct comparisons but the downside is that the measures may not actually be measuring the same thing in different cultures (Douglas and Craig 2000).

Usunier (2000) has identified six main types of cross-cultural equivalence involved in international market research: conceptual equivalence, functional equivalence, translation equivalence, measure equivalence, sample equivalence, data collection equivalence.

Conceptual equivalence

As already noted, conceptual equivalence relates to the issue of a particular construct meaning the same in different societies. Basic concepts including beauty, youth, wealth, the family, sex appeal are all used widely in retailing whether in the context of promotional, locational, or segmentation strategies. However, the key issue for retailers to address is whether each of these concepts has the same attributes in different countries. Essentially the question is 'Are we actually measuring the same thing?'. For example, the concept of the family is core to many retailing strategies and retailers need to know the internal dynamics of families and relationships in order that they can market themselves effectively. However, the family can mean different things in different countries. Many households in Britain come under the heading of nuclear families, with two parents and one or two children, although there is a growing trend of one and two person households. This is a very different scenario to the Indian subcontinent, the Middle East and Far East where extended families comprising grandparents and aunties and uncles are still very much in evidence. Market research designed to add value to retailing strategies needs to take into account these variations. Likewise, the concept of time or wasting time has a different connotation in different cultures. In Western, advanced societies the emphasis on individuals is to be time efficient and customers do not like waiting in queues, especially at lunch time. In societies that are less time conscious, waiting may not be such an issue.

Functional equivalence

Functional equivalence relates to similar products and services performing the same function in different societies. Functional equivalence will seriously affect the demand for a particular product and how marketers should approach developing marketing strategies. For example, a bicycle may be considered an important form of transportation in some countries, including the Netherlands and China, whereas in the UK or USA, bicycles are considered a leisure item. Likewise hot chocolate is viewed as a drink to consume in the evening before one goes to sleep in the UK and USA, whereas in France and much of Latin America it is a drink to be consumed in the morning. Functional equivalence highlights the importance of understanding the *social context* in which goods and services are bought and sold. Asking appropriate questions in these different contexts is crucial for retailers intending to enter new markets.

Translational equivalence

One of the most difficult areas for marketers is translational equivalence since language, culture, communication and translational techniques may produce data which is not entirely appropriate. *Lexical equivalence* is that provided by dictionaries. However, *idiomatic equivalence* is potentially more problematic since it relates to how words are translated in everyday language rather than their dictionary definition. For some expressions there are no translations. Billinguals often have groups of words and phrases that they use for translating non-equivalent phrases. Having the advantage of knowing both languages equally well is important in order to distinguish subtleties that exist between languages. In countries that have multilingual sub-groups different versions of the questionnaire may have to be translated which could prove expensive. *Grammatical-syntactical equivalence* refers to the ordering of words, how they are expressed in sentences and how meaning is expressed. English tends to be very direct and active beginning with the subject followed by the verb and the complement. Abstractions are avoided as are convoluted phrases and sentences. However, many other languages start by explaining the circumstances surrounding the main theme, and this appears convoluted to native English speakers. *Experiential equivalence* relates to what words and sentences mean for people in their everyday experience. Researchers can use back translation to identify probable translation errors.

Measure equivalence

Measure equivalence has been organized into four categories: perceptual equivalence, metric equivalence, calibration equivalence, and temporal equivalence. *Perceptual equivalence* varies across cultures. For example, colours are perceived differently in different cultures; they are not perceived as equivalent across the colour spectrum, and languages do not classify colours in the same way. The symbolic interpretation also varies widely between different cultures. When researching colours to be used for packaging they need to be perceived in similar ways between different cultures to ensure there is consistency in brand building. Yet we know that different colours generate different cues in different cultures and thus the use of the same colour is not perceptually equivalent. *Metric equivalence* refers to the cross-cultural equivalence of rating scales and the homogeneity of meaning within them. For example, there are often difficulties in finding direct equivalents for words in various languages to use in scales. Simply translating dictionary-equivalent words is not enough. A related issue is that there may not be equivalent differences in words (adjectives) used in scales in different languages. For example, studies have assessed the equivalence of a specified number of scale terms from excellent to very bad across eight languages. Some languages have few terms to express the graduation in differences whereas others have many. *Calibration equivalence* concerns the ability to design research instruments so that readings can be made in appropriate units, for example, differences in monetary units such as the pound, US dollar, yen, euro and so forth. This is especially the case in economies where there is a great deal of economic turbulence since it would be difficult to compare prices in a low inflation country with a high inflation country. Likewise, units of weight, volume and distance can also cause calibration problems. Temporal equivalence is closely related to calibration equivalence since it concerns the computation of dates and times, which are important in understanding development levels and technological advancement. For example, it was noted that retailing in developing countries is often compared to how it was in the USA several years previously.

Data collection equivalence

Norms and values within different societies can affect the ways in which consumers respond to questions which in turn raises the accuracy of data collected in different countries. There may be a reluctance to answer questions. This is particularly true of societies that are less democratic and where consumers fear potential reprisals. The secrecy and unwillingness to co-operate is indicative of *co-operation equivalence*. In her analysis of different response rates to cross-national industrial mail surveys, Harzing (2000) found that response rates varied considerably between different countries. Respondents who were geographically and culturally closer to the country sending the questionnaire, were more international in their outlook, countries with lower levels of power distance, and English language capacity were related to higher response rates. *Data collection context equivalence* relates to social context in which data are collected and the potential response biases that they might generate. For example, the use of nonverbal stimuli could be of considerable importance in cultural groups where literacy levels are low, such as Africa and the Far East. In these situations show cards with illustrated pictures might be usefully employed to help respondents comprehend the issues a little better. Advertisements might be shown, or packages of goods, or another strategy might be to use product samples, although in practice respondents can become agitated when they are removed for the next interview (Douglas and Craig 2000).

Response-style equivalence

This relates to the predisposition of consumers in different countries to provide different patterns of response, that are generated by the research process rather than reflecting the reality of consumer behaviour. For example, some cultures are more predisposed to giving positive responses and others to reporting negative responses. Social acquiescence or courtesy bias is prevalent in Asia where cultural values require that the interviewer is not distressed, disappointed or distressed in any way (Craig and Douglas 2000). There may also be bias in non-response with consumers in some cultures being persistently unwilling to answer certain questions. Finally, there are also patterns of extreme response bias. For example, respondents in the USA tend to be the most enthusiastic respondents and Japanese and Koreans the least. Webster's (1996) research with Anglos and Hispanics in the USA found that a higher response quality and more effective interviews were produced when the respondent's gender and ethnicity were matched. Respondents also significantly biased their responses to items pertaining to the interviewer's culture. For example, Hispanic men assigned themselves to a higher socio-economic status when interviewed by either Hispanic women or Anglo men. Women's response quality was relatively unaffected by the interviewer's sex, but men put more effort into a survey situation when there was a female interviewer. As Webster notes: 'This is especially true for Hispanic men, who tend to have a traditional sex-role orientation and be particularly susceptible to the opposite-sex attraction factor' (1996: 71).

Sample equivalence

In cross-national research, sample equivalence broadly relates to how similar matched samples are in two or more countries. In countries that are socially and economically similar, finding comparable samples is not generally problematic. However, this is not the case in countries that are very different in their composition. In her study of consumers' information search behaviour in the USA and China, Doran (2002) found that it was almost impossible to find a matched group of consumers because consumer characteristics in the two countries were so different.

She eventually chose consumers on the basis that they were representative of the average consumer in each country, as she explains: 'In China, this meant that respondents had access to consumer markets, and a standard of living high enough to actually be "consumers" . . . in north America the main concern was that respondents were representative of the "mainstream"' (Doran 2002: 825). Respondents in China were required to have an education level which could accommodate a literate information search. North Americans were required to be native English speakers who were born, and whose parents were born, in North America. Overall income and disposable income levels were very different between the two cultures. Furthermore, the salary differentials are extraordinary. A university professor earns less than a cleaner in McDonalds in Beijing. The educational qualifications required for specific jobs are also very different.

Sample equivalence is important for cross-national research but it is equally important in multicultural research with different ethnic minorities living in the same country. *Demographic equivalence* refers to the accuracy of using demographic indicators that are used unproblematically with the 'host' population to ethnic minorities, and with consumers in different countries. For example, social class is a problematic concept among the white population in Anglo-Saxon countries, but even more so among the ethnic minority community, where discrimination and racism in the labour market can often lead to individuals from ethnic minorities working in lower level occupations than might be predicted on the basis of their qualifications. Level of educational attainment may provide a better indicator than occupation, but even in instances where ethnic minorities have higher levels of education than the host population, they are often still more likely to be unemployed or underemployed (Sills and Desai 1996). Age may provide an approximate indication of first generation migrants and those born in the country of residence; however this assumption is not totally reliable since young people are still actively migrating in many countries. Classifications such as sex are simple to identify but gender needs further consideration with reference to ethnicity, household composition, paid and unpaid work and occupational status amongst others (Bell 1996; O'Hare 1998).

Another important feature is the pattern of inheritance across different ethnic groups. In the USA, intergenerational transfers of wealth have become an important feature, given the more widespread acquisition of pensions and property ownership. Lifetime inheritance is not just confined to wealth but can include intergenerational mobility of socio-economic status and the social reproduction of status and culture. There is some evidence which suggests that 'intergenerational correlations in consumption and wealth are stronger than intergenerational correlations in wages, earnings, or income' (Avery and Rendall 2002: 1303). Avery and Rendall's study of inheritance patterns amongst Anglos and blacks in the USA indicated that the mean, white baby boomers' lifetime inheritance was $125,000 at the age of 55, while the corresponding figure for black baby boomers will be $16,000. They conclude that 'white's much greater receipt of inheritances will work to counteract social policy successes in the domain of earnings inequality' (Avery and Rendall 2002: 1355).

Staeheli and Nagel (2006: 1605) in their research to assess our understanding of how Arab-American understandings of home affected their community activism in the USA, purposefully used a sample of respondents from three American cities – Los Angeles, Dearborn and Washington DC – because they offered very different contexts 'in terms of the size, duration, and national composition of Arab immigration'. Respondents came from Palestine, Lebanon, Jordan, Syria, Egypt, Saudi Arabia, Iraq, and Yemen with the purpose of understanding the diversity of Arab-American communities and 'the variety of outlooks and opinions within them'.

A rather different problem raised by Telles (2002) is the misidentification of racial categorization in Brazil. Unlike many Western societies, where many discrete ethnic categories exist, in Brazil there is a distinction between white, black and brown. Since the 1950s, the Brazilian Institute of Geography and Statistics has requested interviewers to code race in the decennial Census of Brazil according to the response that the subject gives them. However, the interviewers sometimes provide the response themselves because they believe they know the correct category, they are uncomfortable about asking about race, or rush interviews and provide insufficiently precise answers to questions that they feel are not crucially important. Telles' study was designed to assess the accuracy with which individuals and respondents in a 1995 national survey consistently classified race in Brazil, overall and in specific context. He found that overall classification as white, brown and black was consistent 79 per cent of the time. However, people at the dark end of the colour continuum were more consistently classified while the situation was more ambiguous for those at the lighter end of the continuum. Based on statistical estimation the consistency varies from 20 to 100 per cent dependent on a person's education, age, sex, and local racial composition.

Education had a whitening effect but mostly at the lighter end of the continuum and within predominantly non-white areas. Low levels of inconsistency for whites in white areas reflect low levels of racial mixing. For people classified white in non-white areas the situation is slightly different since they might be perceived to have a higher possibility of having non-white ancestors. Gender differences were found which demonstrated that women are likely to be categorized in a lighter category than men, and this was especially true at the darker end of the colour continuum. Among women that identify themselves as black, only 20 per cent are classified as black by interviewers. A potential reason for this finding is the term black is considered socially demeaning and 'nearly inconceivable in the case of a high status woman' (Telles 2002: 436). However, women self-classifying as black could be increasingly common due to the heightened cultural emphasis on black affirmation.

National culture as shared values

The predominant emphasis in the functionalist paradigm that has dominated cross-cultural marketing research is quantitative measurements of culture, with culture being characterized in terms of shared values (Schwartz 1994), with more recent attention turning towards shared beliefs, shared sources of guidance (see Smith 2006), and shared meanings (Earley 2006). This approach to researching cross-cultural differences is a legacy of the work of Hofstede who generated probably the most influential work in the field. The use of cultural indices or individual self-reports as measures of culture are subsequently converted into cultural distance scores that measure the extent to which the culture of one country is similar or different from another. A recent search on the Proquest Online Database, identified 90 articles that mentioned cultural distance scores, and 75 per cent of the articles were based on the dimensions developed by Hofstede (Ng *et al.* 2007).

Hofstede (1980: 260) describes culture as 'the collective programming of the mind' which refers to the way people think, feel and act. He maintains that not everyone within different countries has the same mental programming, but that national cultures are the dominant mental programmes that are shared by the indigenous middle class. Mental programmes are segmented into symbols, heroes, rituals and values. Within this schema symbols are the most specific and values are the most general mental programmes. In *Culture's Consequences*, the cultures of 40 countries were positioned on four dimensions:

1   power distance (unequal versus equal)
2   uncertainty avoidance (rigid versus flexible)
3   individualism (individual versus together)
4   masculinity versus femininity (tough versus tender).

A subsequent study increased the number of countries to 50 (Hofstede 1983) and a fifth dimension, long versus short term, was added (Hofstede 1991)

Hofstede's model has been extensively used by academics and by consultant and market researchers for commercial purposes. However, it needs to be recognized that some dimensions that Hofstede identified have been used more than others. The dimensions of individualism and power difference have been operationalized more widely than the rest (Smith 2006). A review of empirical research incorporating Hofstede's framework published in top-tier management, international management, and psychology journals demonstrated that his work has been replicated more than any other researcher working in the field. Between 1980 and 2002, 180 articles had been published using Hofstede's framework with the vast majority of scholars citing culture as the main factor in their findings (Kirkman *et al.* 2006). In marketing, it has been used in a wide-range of specialisms including advertising, website design (Singh and Matsuo 2004), and product diffusion (Dwyer *et al.* 2005).

An alternative to Hofstede's five dimensions of culture is Shalom Schwartz's cultural values framework (1992, 1994, 1999). Schwartz maintains that his value dimensions offer several potential advantages compared to Hofstede's framework: they are theoretically driven, they are more comprehensive, they have been tested with more recent data, and the samples were obtained across more diverse regions, for example former Eastern bloc countries. Schwartz's framework is based on needs derived from three sources: individuals' requirements as biological organisms, society's requirement for coordinated social interaction, and the group's requirement for survival and support (Schwartz 1992). The framework comprising 56 value items was developed and distributed to 87 teacher and student samples from 41 cultural groups in 38 nations between 1988 and 1992.

The data from these studies generated 10 individual level variables.

1 Power – social status and prestige, control or dominance over people and resources
2 *Achievement* – personal success through demonstrating competence according to social standards
3 *Hedonism* – pleasure and sensuous gratification for oneself
4 *Stimulation* – excitement, novelty, challenge in life
5 *Self-direction* – independent thought and action, choosing, creating, and exploring
6 *Universalism* – understanding, appreciation, tolerance and protection for the welfare of all people and for nature
7 *Benevolence* – preservation and enforcement of the welfare of people with whom one is in frequent personal contact
8 *Tradition* – respect for, commitment to, and acceptance of the customs and ideas that traditional culture or religion impose on the self
9 *Conformity* – restraint of actions, inclinations, impulses likely to upset or harm others and to violate social expectation or norms
10 *Security* – safety, harmony and stability of society, of relationships and of self

At a cultural level the mean scores for each value reflected the different solutions that cultures could deploy to resolve universal human problems. Seven cultural types were summarized into three dimensions: embededdness versus autonomy, hierarchy versus egalitarianism, and mastery versus harmony. The seven cultural types are

1 *Conservatism* – a society that emphasizes close knit harmonious relations, maintenance of the status quo while simultaneously avoiding actions that disturb the traditional order
2 *Intellectual autonomy* – a society that recognizes individuals as autonomous entities who are entitled to pursue their own intellectual interests and desires
3 *Affective autonomy* – a society where people are entitled to pursue stimulation and hedonism, interests and desire
4 *Hierarchy* – a society that emphasizes the legitimacy of hierarchical roles and resource allocation
5 *Mastery* – a society that facilitates the active mastery of the social environment and individual's right to do better than their peers
6 *Egalitarian commitment* – a society that emphasizes the transcendence of selfless interests
7 *Harmony* – a society that emphasizes harmony with nature[[/nl]]

Schwartz calculated national value scores for the seven cultural value types using samples from 26 nations and urban adult samples from seven nations. To further explore the cultural level value types Schwartz (1999) extended his methodology to 35,000 participants drawn from 122 samples in 49 nations. Schwartz maintains that his work incorporates Hofstede's dimensions and adds to them, although Schwartz tends to emphasize the differences, 'based on different theoretical reasoning, different methods, a different set of nations, different types of respondents, data from a later historical period, a more comprehensive set of values, and value items screened to be reasonably equivalent in meaning across cultures' (1994: 117). Ng *et al.* (2007) suggest that there is some evidence to suggest that the Schwartz framework captures more dimensions of culture than Hofstede's, but recognize that Schwartz's methodology has not been as extensively replicated. However, they also note that research on which both the frameworks are based is rather dated, 34 years in the case of Hofstede and 14 years with respect to Schwartz.

Hofstede's model of national culture has not gone without criticism, and it has been the subject of forceful, if not bitter, exchanges in which Hofstede reinforces the appropriateness of his methodology and others reinforce their criticisms (see Hofstede 2002; McSweeney 2002b; Williamson 2002). There are two distinctive ways of critiquing the concept of national culture: first, by saying that there are better methodological ways of measuring it, and second, by critiquing the methodology in its own terms. A main point of controversy is whether each nation does have a distinctive national culture. Hofstede holds this view, and also that national culture is a common core of a wider culture that contains elements of global and sub-national components. His approach is essentially a strong form of cultural determinism and one that is territorially unique, referring to a country or state, and not to a nation. Great Britain is a country but is comprised of three different nations –England, Scotland, and Wales – that each have distinctive aspects to their culture.

Critics have questioned the suitability of the IBM employee data on which the model was built. The sample comprised three discrete elements: organizational culture, occupational culture and national culture. Hofstede maintains that organizational culture was uniform, that it did not vary in different places. The same argument was presented with respect to occupational culture, that a laboratory clerk in the USA shared the same occupational culture as those in Germany and Bangladesh. Thus any differences were due to variations in national culture. McSweeney uses research evidence to suggest that this is highly unlikely, and that in organizations and occupations there are many different cultures operating at any one time, that may be contradictory and dissenting of the dominant culture. If we accept this version of reality, then we must question Hofstede's view that the differences he identified were due to differences in *national culture*.

A second factor concerns Hofstede's view that national culture is uniform and is held in the same regard by all individuals. If this were the case then there would not have been differences in consumer responses at intra-country level. However, the IBM survey demonstrated that there were significant differences within each country. In his acknowledgement of this fact Hofstede maintains that there was an 'average' or 'central tendency' in which a variety of responses were converted to a single score and labelled as the national culture difference. McSweeney argues that in any heterogeneous dataset there will, in principle, always be an average tendency. However, Hofstede argued that he found national tendencies or the relationship between them in single locations, i.e. IBM offices. But this reasoning suggests that the same average tendency would occur in every other organization, tennis club, political party, massage parlour and so forth. As McSweeney notes the average (national culture) tendency in the New York City Young Marxist Club, will be the same as the Keep America White Cheer-leaders Club in Smoky Hill, Kansas (2002a: 101). Furthermore, Hofstede underestimated the extent to which the recruitment and training, and personal contacts between subsidiary and international headquarters staff mean that they are not indicative of national populations but a very small sample. Furthermore, at the time that the survey was undertaken, working in high technology industries was more prevalent in some countries than others which further narrows the representativeness of the IBM sample. McSweeney (2002a: 102) concludes that Hofstede 'fails to satisfactorily justify his claim that an average tendency based on questionnaire responses from some employees in a single organization is also the national average tendency. His generalization to the national from the micro-local is unwarranted'.

McSweeney (2002a) also argues that it would have been unusual if Hofstede had not found different responses between individuals based on their national location. What is at issue is whether the observable differences are due to *national* differences, rather than other cultural differences such as religion, race, ethnicity and so forth. The dimensions of national culture generated by Hofstede have arisen because of subjective choices made by the researcher, and have not been empirically 'found' independently of the way the research process has been structured. Furthermore, it is entirely possible that if different questions had been used, a different reading of national culture may have emerged. The equivalence of variables used in the research has also been questioned since comparisons are relatively meaningless if equivalence of meaning has not been established. Hofstede did not establish conceptual equivalence and consequently it is not know whether the same questions measured the same concepts in exactly the same way in different national cultures.

There are other criticisms of Hofstede's work. Javidan *et al* (2006) maintain that Hofstede's survey was too US and IBM centred, since it was a consultancy project based on the company's needs. A rather different point is expressed by Smith (2002) when he suggests that the integrity and continuity of modern national cultures are being weakened by many contradictory trends and sources of influence. To suggest, as Hofstede does, that the same features characterize nations over time is not tenable, given the globalization processes discussed in Chapter 1. Some scholars have also argued that Hofstede fails to take into account gender differences as a consequence of his sample being dominated by predominantly, white, middle-class men (Moulettes 2007).

A newer approach is the GLOBE (Global Leadership and Organizational Behaviour Effectiveness) framework. GLOBE is a large scale programme conducted by 160 researchers from 62 cultures. The findings of the research programme were published as a book in 2004 entitled *Culture, Leadership, and Organizations: The GLOBE Study of 62 Societies* (House *et al.* 2004 and http://www.thunderbird. ed/wwwfiles/ms/globe). The GLOBE definition of culture made the distinction between *cultural vales* and *cultural practices,* since it took as its starting point that culture can be defined as values, beliefs, norms and behavioural patterns relating to a national group. This distinction between values and practices is useful, since individuals may have values but do not act them out in practice.

There is considerable ongoing debate between researchers working in the quantitative paradigm over the definition and measurement of culture. Hofstede (2006) suggests that the GLOBE framework presents too many dimensions that are too complex to operationalize and work with. Other scholars argue that what is at issue is not how many different aspects of cultural variation can be measured, since many dozen could potentially qualify. Rather, Smith (2006) argues that the emphasis should be on determining the extent to which the dimensions are independent of one another and are able to yield hypotheses that can be validly and differentially tested on readily available national samples. Advocating a more radical approach, Earley (2006) suggests that large-scale, value-based surveys have outlived their usefulness and more emphasis needs to be devoted to approaches that link culture to action, and developing alternatives to values as a basis for exploring culture in relation to action. However, it is unlikely that scholars wedded to traditional approaches will be swayed anytime soon as Schwartz and Ros (1995: 118) indicate:

> Resigning ourselves to unique, thick descriptions for each group would preclude the comparative approach to which many cross-culturalists are committed. The ultimate goal is to find a limited set of dimensions that captures the most prominent differences, integrates multiple culture features, and relates meaningfully to socio-historical variables.
>
> (1995: 118)

Content analysis

Content analysis is a well-established means of conducting research in many disciplines within the social sciences and humanities. One of the first accounts of its use in marketing was by Kassarjian (1977) in a paper published in the *Journal of Consumer Research* entitled 'Content analysis in consumer research' in which he set out its main features and explored some of its uses in marketing. According to Kassarjian (1977: 8) content analysis is a research technique for the 'objective, systematic, and quantitative description of the manifest content of communication'. It certainly has become an important method of analysing marketing images in advertising where it is used regularly in research designs. The researcher begins by constructing a set of hypotheses that they want to test, variables of interest are classified into categories, and a coding scheme is developed. The coding schemes are tested for reliability using judges to resolve any differences of opinion, and ensure that the data is as reliable as possible. Various types of statistical analyses are then used to analyse the data.

There are several very good articles that use content analysis to assess the impact of culture. How children's commercials differ between the USA and China was an issue addressed by Ji and McNeal (2001). Western advertisers are particularly eager to target younger people who are more likely to gravitate to Western lifestyles than their parents. Some large companies including McDonalds, Nabisco, KFC, M & M, Mars, and Kellogg's, have already spent significant amounts of money targeting this market. Although the number of babies born each year in China is restricted because of the one child policy, there are in excess of 27 million babies born each year which is equivalent to the population of Canada. The investigators analysed advertisements targeted at children in the two countries on five Chinese channels, and four US channels in one week in each of four months. The criteria for choosing the ads was two fold: (1) the products in the commercial were designed for children aged 12 and under, (2) the commercial itself was designed for children as the primary audience. The categories used were *activity* (scholastic versus athletic), *informational content* (quality and texture), *models* (gender and ethnic status), *spokesperson/character* (adult and gender), *style of display*, *values/appeals* (adventure, convenience, effectiveness, economy/price, education, fun/happiness, health, popularity, uniqueness) *voice-overs* (adult and gender). The content of the ads in the two countries was then compared. The conclusion of the study found that Chinese commercials reflect traditional cultural values and its social and economic stage of development.

Qualtitative research

Levy argues that the bias in favour of quantitative methods in marketing is not of recent origin but has been deeply embedded within the discipline over many years. He observes that qualitative researchers are often perceived as third class citizens.

> [G]enerally, the dominant paradigm people resist, show great hostility, and at many schools refuse to hire any faculty who are qualitatively oriented. They behave defensively, foolishly acting as though their livelihoods are threatened by the projective techniques and ethnographies that will replace surveys, regressions, and multivariate models.
>
> (Levy 2005: 342).

The discipline of marketing is not alone in this respect since it has also been a feature of research in the field of international business where qualitative studies are very much in the minority and marginalized (Lenartowicz and Roth 1999). International business scholars have even argued that carrying out qualitative research is a poor career move and for research students on that path the future could be particularly perilous (Marschan-Piekkari and Welch 2004). Moreover, qualitative researchers often have different research agendas than their quantitative colleagues. Nevid and Sta. Maria (1999) argue for more discussion of specific cultural characteristics in qualitative research including issues relating to gender, group communication, differences in values, cultural mistrust, and acknowledging one's own racial biases and how they impact on the research process. Qualitative research is particularly useful in the context of exploratory research and theory building, such as that directed at constructing new approaches to identity formation given the relatively immature nature of the field. It is important to remember this bias when reading research articles.

Few published articles use a qualitative approach comprising in-depth interviewing and ethnography (for those that do see Mehta and Belk 1991; Peñaloza 1994; Chung 1999; Thompson and Tambyah 1999; Peñaloza and Gilly 1999; Hirschman 2001). A classic article in the field of qualitative multicultural marketing research that should be required reading, is Nevid and Sta. Maria's (1999) paper entitled 'Multicultural issues in qualitative research'. Other texts include Stanfield and Dennis (1993) *Race and Ethnicity in Research Methods* and Marin and Marin (1991) *Research with Hispanic Populations*.

Mixing qualitative research methods is an option for researchers, and can often strengthen research findings. In *The Whiteness of Power: Racism in Third World Development and Aid*, Goudge (2003) combines in-depth interviews with aid workers, her own experiences, observations, and diaries to provide a richly textured and very perceptive account of the role of whiteness in Latin America. In their study investigating the glocalization of youth culture in Denmark and Greenland, Kjeldgaard and Askegaard (2006) asked their student participants to engage in three distinct phases of the research project. The first was to keep consumption diaries about how they spent their money, information about their favourite foods and clothes, and what their aspirations were for the future. The second stage involved giving some participants a disposable camera so that they could produce a photographic life description, taking pictures of their surroundings that could inform others about who they are. The third step included in-depth interviews partly based on the photographs they had taken, and other questions that dealt with important possessions in their lives and some of the material that was written in their diaries.

It is widely acknowledged that levels of acculturation can have important implications for consumption and consumer behaviour. Qualitative researchers also argue that acculturation is also relevant in cross-cultural research. Important features include the special considerations that researchers often have to negotiate when researching with minorities and the impact of the social and political context in which the research takes place (Rex 1996; Berry 1990). Varying levels of respondent acculturation have practical implications for research administration including language expertise (Peñaloza 1994; Bouchet 1995), the recruitment of participants (Sills and Desai 1996), choice of methods (Nevid and Sta. Maria 1999) and the use of translators or moderators (Edwards 1998). The acculturation of researchers relates to an in-depth understanding of culture, language, gender and social customs (Peñaloza 1994). Sills and Desai's (1996) work investigating the up-take of various public services within the ethnic populations in the London Borough of Newham in the United Kingdom, met with significant difficulties in operating focus groups. Recruiting Asians to participate was particularly problematic, and when they agreed they often arrived with their families. Some group members, especially older women, did not participate in group discussions. Language was a difficulty when the respondents did not speak any English, but also if there are varying levels of English spoken in the group (Robinson 1996). Because so few marketing academics are from ethnic minority backgrounds (Peñaloza 2000), the use of interpreters is usually necessary. Under these conditions, often the best strategy is to *work* with interpreters rather than *use* them as they may provide important culture-specific knowledge to the project (Edwards 1998).

Ethnic minority scholars have argued that they are more likely to generate questions that are different from those asked by majority researchers and are less likely to meet with distrust, hostility and exclusion. An 'insider' view through the advantage of lived experience may result in different interpretations of data from those generated by majority researchers, raising the issue about whose interpretation should be given prominence (hooks 1997). Due to the norms of professional community membership, even researchers of colour who study their own communities can be perceived as outsiders as a result of social class divisions (Stanfield 1993). The importance of lived experience in the conduct of multicultural research leads to the wider issue of the inclusion of ethnic minorities in the marketing academy where they are presently under-represented in a predominantly white, male, middle-class culture (Costa and Bamossy 1995; Peñaloza 2000). Penrose and Jackson summarize these dilemmas when they note:

> Developing a critical self-consciousness or reflexivity about our own positions as researchers is fraught with difficulty. We can write ourselves into our accounts in a variety of ways. But a simple statement of the 'as middle-class, White man/woman' kind is clearly inadequate. Our position is ascribed as much as it is chosen, and we may not be fully aware of how all the dimensions of our identities bear upon our research.

Ethnography

Ethnographic research has not attracted significant attention in marketing as compared with quantitative based approaches, but more studies are emerging using this methodological approach. Ethnography is arguably one of the most controversial forms of research and writing on culture. The level of trust and intimacy required in the research relationship is oppositional to the dominant research paradigm in marketing concerning what constitutes appropriate research, and the objective nature of the subject–researcher interface. At its broadest definition, ethnography has encompassed many forms of qualitative research, while in its 'pure' form it comprises participant observation. Ethnography has been shaped by the discipline of social anthropology as the study of people in their own natural environment, in an attempt to capture and represent the subjects' understanding of their world. In the 1960s, Winick (1961) argued that since anthropologists are specifically trained to study national and sub-cultural differences, language, symbols, taboos and consumption in everyday life using unobtrusive methodological approaches, their work was of relevance to marketers. He provides examples of how anthropologists have assessed markets in a variety of geographical contexts, from the introduction of central heating systems, designing appropriate styles of dress, and the packaging of confectionary and many more. A more recent reinvention of ethnography has been its use in the media as documentaries, films, reality TV and drama.

The ethnographer's humanistic commitment to giving 'voice' to participants has been particularly controversial: the status of what, or whom is being studied, the nature of the research process, and relationships, and the value and the implications of what is being advanced. Contemporary debates in ethnography have focused on its disciplinary boundaries, power inequalities in ethnographic production, its partiality and process of 'othering', that have both constrained and inspired creative engagement. The role of the visual in ethnographic research has always been controversial with respect to the status of the visual as 'real' or 'speaking for itself'. History has demonstrated that representations of colonized peoples in photographs assessed by ethnographers have overwhelmingly focused on negative inter-pretations by focusing on the black and not the white (Eves 2006). A rather different interpretation is that the visual, as far as possible, should be understood within and against an ethnographic narrative. Visuals may tell a story that may reflect or refute what is spoken, what it might add to a story, or whether it tells a different one. Recent ethnographic studies in consumer research have included how consumers shop for Christmas gifts in the USA (Otnes *et al.* 1993), the acculturation of Mexican immigrants in the USA (Peñaloza 1994), and the cultural meaning and memory at a stock show and rodeo (Peñaloza 2001),

Corporate ethnography

Economic anthropologists have a longstanding interest in the concept of reciprocity and exchange underpinning markets. Roberta Astroff provides an analysis of some of the similarities between marketing and anthropology:

> Both anthropology and marketing research can be seen as systems through which cultures are made knowable – that is, identified, defined and codified. Marketing, like anthropology, provides paradigms, theories, definitions, values and needs that are used to identify and produce cultures and markets. These processes in both anthropology and marketing make cultures into marketable goods according to their own disciplinary and economic structures.
>
> (Astroff 1997: 123)

Astroff suggests that anthropology has traditionally hidden its market economics in the process of striving to be an objective social science. Funding and other conditions of research are mentioned in acknowledgments but are not integrated into the text. Yet the relationship between the ethnographer and informant, the exchange of goods, money and status, are all exchanged for information. She refers to ethnography conducted for sale to marketers and advertisers, as para-ethnography (popular) in order to distinguish it in context, style and product from market research that presents itself as science.

Mazzarella (2003) argues that there has never been a time when advertising and anthropology have been closer aligned. Agencies that once favoured psychologists now regularly advertise for anthropologists. In turn, anthropologists are often delighted that their skills have a whole range of commercial applications, and the term corporate anthropologist has come into vogue. Corporate ethnography is undoubtedly an expanding area of research and this sentiment is reinforced by James Stengel, Proctor and Gamble's global marketing officer:

> Our research has changed a lot. We do much more immersion research, much more anthropological research. We really try to get at what we can do through our brands to make a difference in people's lives . . . We all go out and really spend time with consumers, especially those who are not like us. When I was in China the last time, I wanted to visit a very poor consumer and a very wealthy one, just to look at the differences in how they thought about brands, how they thought about media, what was important in their life.
>
> (Colvin 2007: 82)

Ethnographers favour long-term immersion, however, this is a luxury that marketers can often rarely afford, given the realities of rushed projects and strict deadlines. Very often they do not have the opportunity to make the distinction between what people say they do, and actually do in practice. Marketers need results not ivory tower contemplation and usually they work as a team rather than a lone anthropologist (Moeran 2004). Sunderland and Denny (2003) suggest that some clients say that they want an ethnographer when they want an anthropologist. Yet in many instances the issues that the client wishes to address are not anthropological, focusing on culture, but are designed to inform a deeper psychological under-standing of the target audience. A similar set of concerns has been raised by Stolzoff (2005) who maintains that although companies often request new approaches, they do not want to move out of their comfort zone. As a consequence they demand that ethnographic work is 'staged' so it resembles little more than a focus group. The holistic approach that includes participant observation is eliminated in the name of convenience.

One of the most recent uses of ethnography is in retailing, where people are watched as they go shopping through the use of sophisticated technological systems, supplemented with in-store ethnographers. Stores use the data to change the layout of their store, create new displays and adapt their staffing levels. In addition to providing data about consumer behaviour, some systems can determine each shopper's sex, age range and ethnic group with an 80 per cent accuracy rate. Some of the systems even provide a record of consumer conversations which they can search for key names and phrases. Inevitably these consumer monitoring systems raise issues about privacy, but the benefits of the ethnographic type systems in retailing look as though they are here to stay (*Economist* 2007b). In the following sections we take a closer look at market-oriented ethnography.

Macro, micro and meso market-oriented ethnography

Arnould and Price (2006) make the distinction between three approaches to market-oriented ethnography: *macro*, *micro* and *meso*. All of the three approaches have a degree of commonality in their 'aims to produce generative insights from the application of a broad and deep understanding of how cultures are organized, careful attention to the details of how culture plays out in everyday life, and disciplined curiosity about what people are up to' (Arnould and Price 2006: 251). Nevertheless, there are some differences. The *macro-level*, market-oriented approach emphasizes uncovering 'cultural templates' that consumers refer to, to give structure to their consumption patterns. Belk, Ger and Askegaard (2003) used this approach to uncover the dynamics of cross-cultural consumer desire or general consumption aspirations of men and women in North America, Northern Europe and Western Asia. Holt (2004) employs a similar approach to uncovering cultural templates and how they are sustained over time; he refers to this process as cultural branding. He maintains that cultural templates are often in tension with each other. For example, the rebel-man-of-action, mythical figure is at odds with another masculine template associated with the responsible, family man. Holt argues that a small number of brands, that he refers to as iconic brands, have been able to reconcile these differences over time. Using the example of the alcoholic drinks company, Mountain Dew, he demonstrates how the company has reconciled differences in masculinity through its 50 year history. Arnould and Price (2006) argue that a limitation of the macro-level approach is its emphasis on searching for cultural templates in the minds of consumers as opposed to emphasizing relational dynamics in social life that help us understand why consumers behave in the way they do.

The *micro-level*, market-oriented approach focuses on the relationship between a product, task, or application-specific process, and the consumer. For example, an ethnographic study of how people shower would be helpful for a plumbing firm to understand how products are used and potential for new product development. Another example might be Proctor and Gamble's interest in how people deal with spills as an example of products in use. Much design ethnography comes into this category and is discussed in more detail later in this section. Recent academic research in this area includes consumption communities and brands such as Harley Davidson HOGS (Fournier *et al.* 2000). The emphasis in this strand of research has been on the symbolic dimensions of brands, why people buy them, and what they mean. As a consequence, marketers can define market segments, develop more sophisticated product positioning in the market, and create innovative communication strategies. Arnould and Price (2006) argue that the main problem with the micro-level approach is that it does not adequately address why particular consumption patterns emerge, become embedded and are sustained.

The *meso-level* market-oriented approach, although closer in its characteristics to traditional ethnography, is less frequently used in applied marketing research. This approach is distinguished from the others in the following passage.

> Distinguishing our meso-level approach is an interest in consumers as intentional actors with personal projects that are embedded in their sociocultural

life worlds. From this springs a methodological focus on what people do, rather than what they say; and what they say about their goals and how they organize their everyday lives, rather than what they may say, when asked about specific brands, products, or tasks. We assert that customer-centricity is not understanding how customers feel about and use a firm's brand but instead is understanding how people use resources provided by firms in the culturally, socially situated practices of their everyday lives.

(Arnould and Price 2006: 254)

They illustrate the difference of the *micro* and *meso* approach to corporate ethnography by considering them in the context of home visits that have become a prominent approach in recent years. The *micro* approach focuses on a specific task and needs, such as the activities a housewife might undertake in her laundry or how a family use a computer. The *meso* approach views the home as a 'cultural field', where consumers undertake activities alone and within the context of a wider social network. In order to explore the meaning consumers give to family dinners, ethnographers spent significant amounts of time going shopping, looking after children, preparing, eating and washing up after the meal. Multiple members of the family were interviewed about family dinners. From this broad field of vision, they decided to select one subset of the industry focusing on providing family dinner the meal assembly services that provide set ingredients for the consumer to go home and cook themselves. In this respect self assembly services are a compromise between cooking a meal from scratch, and buying ready-made meals to heat up and serve. The cultural significance of providing homemade food provides an insight into why consumers use self-assembly services. Homemade food has strong associations with authenticity compared with the mass production food preparation. Preparing homemade food is an activity that has a symbolic function via looking after the family properly and providing a special meal for one's spouse. The concept of homemade also provides intergenerational continuity – food like grandma used to make.

Corporate ethnography and the design process

Observing people going about their daily business is not a new activity within marketing. Designers have examined the ways that consumers use products and services, and interpret the meaning they have in people's lives. However, changes have occurred in the way that companies view these methods in opposition to the more traditional quantitative approaches. Many businesses are of the opinion that understanding consumers in context is a competitive necessity and thus value the 'texture, sophistication and depth' in the data (Suri and Howard 2006: 246). Suri and Howard argue that ethnography is being used in a variety of organizations in different ways, in order to provide fresh insights. They emphasize a variety of ways that they are using ethnography for their clients. The first relates to the generation of *non-linear interpretations*. They provide an example of improving the design of ATMS. By observing people using the machines they noticed that people looked over their shoulder to ensure nobody was looking and their security was being compromised. A mirror was incorporated as a design feature to allow consumers to view people that may have been standing behind them. They argue that this is an example of a linear interpretation comprising observation, insight and solution. They argue that the importance of ethnographic research relies on non-linear interpretations such as those associated with strategic insights on complex issues including lifestyle, identity and meaning. For example, assessing the future of mobile communications in South Asia, how might product packaging be made more luxurious while maintaining a company's values concerning sustainability, how might educational tools be designed for children in Bangladesh compared with the USA? The intention is that researchers should look deeper and at less obvious patterns to inspire their thinking.

Zooming out for context is the second of Suri and Howard's categories. They provide an example of being asked by a company to take one of their existing products and design a more upmarket version. Rather than focusing on designing alternatives that might be appropriate for the new target group, zoning out would be to explore wider issues such as the meaning of luxury within the target group. Once the parameters of luxury have been generated the company has a much stronger understanding of possibilities and how they might be incorporated into the product.

Understanding *multiple layers of subjectivity* is their third use of ethnography in a commercial context. Within traditional, quantitative market research a great deal of emphasis is placed on objectivity in the research process. In ethnographic work the focus is on subjectivity: 'By listening to people's language, watching and learning about their activities, their relationships, their culture, and their behaviors, we do our best to understand their world as they do' (Suri and Howard 2006: 247). This approach does not involve understanding just one person's worldview but multiple views simultaneously, that may be overlapping. Comparing and contrasting different views allows researchers to uncover patterns in the data.

Incorporating individuals at the *extremes* and *analogies* are part and parcel of ethnographic work whereas mainstream research focuses on individuals that are representative of particular groups and settings. Individuals at the extremes in research designs concern those that might be regarded as marginal or insignificant in mainstream research, or who are at the margins of society. Suri and Howard provide an example of a research project that they undertook on the future of beauty care. In their sample they included transvestites and Goths who had different views of beauty than the mainstream, to provide a broader view of the phenomenon. Equally, this approach could be usefully applied in a cross-cultural setting and findings incorporated into marketing campaigns targeted at different cultural groups. Analogous cases are those that have some similarities with the context of interest and which provide a wider frame of reference that might highlight new areas of interest that might otherwise have been overlooked.

Another characteristic of ethnographic research is *synthesizing multiple sources*. Ethnographic research is small scale and in-depth focusing on understanding consumers and their lifestyles intimately. As part of the process researchers can use other information sources, such as market research, focus groups, and surveys. The process of using a variety of approaches is called triangulation and it allows researchers to use different data sources to check out consistency. If all the data point to the same outcome, then this is a firm basis for developing strategy. Ethnographic work facilitates *open-source interpretation* by allowing other business departments and collaborators to be included in interpreting data, providing a platform for unifying and motivating teams. Another feature of ethnographic work is that it facilitates *collaboration with consumers*, treating them as creative participants as opposed to passive recipients of researchers' commercially motivated interpretations. In this respect, the research process is generating more of a two-way dialogue, rather than a one-way conversation. Thus the research design is reflecting the co-production of products and services and web-based dialogue about their merits. Another use of ethnographic research is to *turn the lens inside*. While ethnographic research can provide valuable insights about the behaviour of consumers, it can also be used to provide information about employees and their needs, motivations and as a way of narrating organizational culture. Crucially, ethnographic work can also explore how employees will use research data and how it is affected by their own worldview.

Online ethnography

An expanding area of interest is online ethnography and this is potentially a significant development for cross-cultural research, since it cuts down the cost and time of undertaking in-depth research in geographically distant places. Online ethnography can take a number of forms. Ishmael and Thomas (2006) advocate the use of multiple methods including participants keeping diaries, either on-, or off-line, to provide an account of their behaviour and thoughts. Participants are encouraged to take digital pictures that relate to the focus of the project, for example a kitchen, lounge and so forth. Sometimes customers are asked to take photographs of other household members and describe who they are, and what they are doing, and what the activity means to them. Projective techniques are sometimes used for example selecting a photograph that represents the personality of the brand. Ishmael and Thomas describe a project on the use of health and beauty products among men and women in the USA, United Kingdom and France. Respondents were asked to take digital photographs in their storage places and then describe what was in the picture. Other components of the methodological procedure were recording daily diaries of their morning/evening health and beauty routines, descriptions of their shopping trips to purchase health and beauty products, and a log of the advertisements they observe of beauty and health products during a specified period. Follow-up, in-depth interviews were used to add to the overall interpretation. Ishmael and Thomas argue for the importance of pictures over words, suggesting that pictures offer a deeper level of analysis, reflecting that a picture is worth more than a thousand words in understanding the consumer's mind.

Netnography

Another approach to online ethnography has been termed netnography. The Sage *Dictionary of Social Research Methods* defines netnography as 'qualitative, interpretive research methodology that adapts the traditional, in-person ethnographic research techniques of anthropology to the study of the online cultures and communities formed through computer-mediated communications' (Jupp 2006). Netnography provides a way to study e-tribes and virtual communities of consumption. The naturally occurring communication of consumers on the web provides the raw data for netnography, and because contributors are often from different cultural groups, the method is an interesting addition to the cross-cultural researcher's armory. Netnography is less expensive than traditional ethnography and it can provide an up-to-the minute assessment of consumer culture with respect to consumer segmentation, brand perception, brand meanings and preferences.

According to Kozinets (2006: 282), the core features of netnography are the same as ethnography; by providing insights into the cultural realities of consumer groups as they 'live their activities: local language, the history, the players, the practices and rituals, the enculturation, education, and eventual burn out of members in a life cycle of membership'. Consumers volunteer information online that they may not wish to reveal in face-to-face interaction. Netnography is being used on a commercial basis by specialist market research agencies to scan online communities in order to gather information that might inform company marketing strategy. A number of published academic studies have also included netnography of personal web pages and what they reveal about the consumption patterns of the author (Schau and Gilly 2003). De Valck (2005) has explored Dutch and Flemish food cultures online. Nelson and Otnes (2005) have analysed intercultural wedding message boards for the advice they provide to brides-to-be and their helpers. Brides from one culture marrying into another in a foreign country need to navigate online sites to provide them with advice and information in planning the big day. Nelson and Otnes found that message boards were structured around resolving issues of cross-cultural ambivalence and were used to solicit advice, opinions, obtain information, social comparison and camaraderie. Themes that occurred were where to obtain bilingual invitations, priests, or DJs, international postage arrangements, and ways of incorporating elements of each of the marriage partner's cultures into the ceremony.

Other projects have included analysing Danish cosmetic surgery bulletin boards (Langer and Beckman 2005), American and Chinese digital camera discussion groups (Fong and Burton 2006) and the fan base of *Star Trek* and the *X-Files* as online communities (cf. Kozinets 2002, 2006). *Star Trek* sites provided a wealth of data that could have the potential to generate new products. For example, Kozinets describes one contributor who enjoyed 'ripping', meaning criticizing the movies for their continuity errors. This data could have laid the foundations for a new book for enthusiasts. There were also plenty of suggestions for additional customized services for fans including 'specialized fan chat rooms, targeted online videogame and role-playing access, online conventions, and *Star Trek* fan dating services' (Kozinets 2006: 286). In the ensuing period some of these suggestions were brought to commercial fruition. The blending of consumer understanding and marketer understanding via netnography generates a different model of marketer–consumer interaction.

Ethnoconsumerism

Ethnoconsumerism was developed by Alladi Venkatesh (1995) to provide a distinctive cross-cultural methodological approach that forces researchers to view individuals as cultural beings, as part of a culture, sub-culture, and who have other group affiliations. He argues that the marketing discipline, and the social sciences more generally, are premised on theories and philosophies that are influenced by Western thought. Much social science that originates outside Europe and America has not achieved a high status, and as a consequence the Western version dominates. He argues that Euro-American theories and practices cannot be transferred unproblematically to other cultures, since they may not reflect the realities of consumers living in other places. In other words, it is important to frame questions concerning marketing and consumer research from within different cultural settings, rather than their being imposed from the outside, to ensure that they are meaningful and relevant within specific cultural contexts. Many Western concepts such as 'class', 'authority', 'rules', 'values' and so on, are alien in other cultures.

The ethnoconsumerist approach is multi-layered. At one level is an examination of 'the cultural', including symbolic and belief systems, norms and ritualistic practices. At the next level is 'the social', manifest in social organizations and institutions. At the final level is 'the individual', comprising personality, cognition and behaviour. Venkatesh provides some general guidelines to follow in order to conduct ethnoconsumer research. The first step is to identify the *cultural framework* which is the theoretical structure that is based on cultural categories. *Cultural categories* have two sources, those that are generated in the *field* when investigators describe practices, collect first-hand statements from people about their experiences, and draw impressions about the cultural setting. The second aspect is information that is generated by *texts* that provide archival sources of culture, novels, diaries, company accounts, which can be especially useful for highlighting trends over time. Thus the direction of the study is bottom up, rather than top down. Steps three and four, concern interpreting the *meanings* for cultural categories and establishing the *relationship* between them. Step five is to identify relevant cultural practices, and socio-economic trends to provide more context for the study. Step six focuses on identifying *cultural objects* and establishing their *meanings*. The final two steps include *describing* consumer environments and specific consumer behaviours, and *interpreting* consumer environments and behaviours. Crucially, the findings need to be interpreted in such a way that the reader is aware that the interpretation is based on the researcher's own perspective, since they were the filter through which knowledge about the cultural context was generated.

Venkatesh provides a range of examples using this approach and others have been published since (Arnould 1989) but one of the most interesting is provided by De Pyssler (1992) in his analysis of the motor scooter in India. De Pyssler begins by providing a historical overview of the technology, design, and its cross-cultural semiotics. He then discusses the meaning of the motor cycle in different cultural settings – Italy, Britain, and India. The article provides a narrative that considers what the motor scooter meant to various groups of Indians. Thus DePyssler took the indigenous consumers' point of view about what the motor scooter meant when it was introduced as a new technology 30 years previously. The next part of the study focused on the contemporary significance of the motor scooter and how Indians have adopted their lifestyles and cultural practices to accommodate it. The meaning given to the motor scooter in India is then compared to Britain and Italy, where it is very different. In Italy the motor scooter is a feminine icon, in Britain it is associated with rebel groups like the mods, and in India it is used as a useful family vehicle. Thus, the cultural categories of meaning are generated within the cultural context and not imposed from the outside to provide a rich description of meaning. It is vital for marketers to understand this since it is the basis upon which marketing, especially advertising, strategies are developed. It is interesting to note that the debate about the motor scooter in India has returned in the wider context of low-cost cars in developing countries.

Textual analysis

The discussion so far in this chapter has focused on the mechanics of undertaking empirical research, using individuals as subjects in research samples. A rather different approach to undertaking cross-cultural research is textual analysis, in which images and words are analysed to uncover their hidden meanings. Literary texts such as novels and poetry have been an important source of information about cross-cultural differences, especially within a historical context, since they have been written for centuries, long before a range of marketing texts were widely available. Prior to the introduction of mass media, novels about far away places were the source of information about 'the other'. The analysis of a discipline's or an industry's texts can provide insights into the ideological spaces they inhabit, blind spots, and instances of missed opportunities (Eagleton 1991; Stern 1998). Textual analysis has been widely used in consumer and advertising research for this purpose (Stern 1989a, 1989b, 1990, 1993). Barbara Stern (1989b: 322) maintains that analysing advertising text is an additional way of learning about consumers 'for ads simultaneously reflect and influence behavior. They reveal information about consumers and their values, as well as about advertisers, firms, products, media, and messages'. Advertisements are texts that can be read and interpreted as cultural products. The 'reading' of ads can vary according to reader characteristics, including social class, gender race/ethnicity, sexuality and historical context.

A rather different approach to reading culture can be achieved by examining cultural artefacts such as cookbooks. Tobias (1998: 3) argues that 'Cookbooks contain not only recipes, but hidden clues and cultural assumptions about class, race, gender and ethnicity. They reflect many of the dramatic transformations that have come to define the boundaries of the modern public sphere'. In particular, he argues that cookery books published in eighteenth-century America positioned women as homemakers, and defined their role in society. Zafar (1999) has undertaken a similar study by exploring how African-American cookbooks record the cultural aspects of African-American consumption. Hewer and Brownlie (2007: 175) have studied cookbooks and the recipes they contain to understand what they tell us about 'where we have been, who we are and where we maybe going'. They argue that cookbooks allow consumers to experience and practice local global- ization, recipes from far away places cooked up in the comfort of one's own home. Consumers can take a culinary journey – cultural tourism – around the world in a matter of a few short pages.

Arnesen (2001) maintains that the cultural turn with its emphasis on language, word play, discourse analysis, the interpretation of texts, including literary ones, has been an instrumental feature in the growth of literature on whiteness. Whiteness becomes a strategic resource through language (Nakayama and Krizek 1999), a mechanism by which ideologies of whiteness have been produced, reproduced and become synonymous with power (Wetherell and Potter 1992; Steyn 2005; Taylor 2005). In their article entitled 'Postcolonialism, identity, and location: Being white Australian in Asia', Schech and Haggis (1998) explore the way Australians have imagined themselves in relation to Asia since the 1960s. They undertake this task by analysing Christopher Koch's two novels *The Year of Living Dangerously* and *Highways to a War*. Both novels are set in Southeast Asia in the1960s and 1970s, and follow the experiences of journalists in war-torn settings. They examine how a postcolonial reading of the white self and its place in Asia has influenced Australian overseas-aid policies.

A rather different approach has been to investigate 'extreme' whiteness. The behaviour of white supremacists amounts to white racism and oppression, from which most 'normal' everyday whites distance themselves. Interviews with white supremacist leaders (Ware and Back 2002), assessing white supremacist newsletters (Ferber 1998), analysing Internet-based white, racialist women's organizations (Mothers of the Movement (MOM); see Fluri and Dowler 2004) are ways that researchers have investigated extreme whiteness. There are also important spatial dimensions to extreme whiteness nationally (Flint 2004) and internationally (Hague *et al.* 2005). How white supremacists vary from 'regular' whites, and how move- ments in different countries vary from each other, and the indigenous population in their consumer behaviour are interesting issues.

Critcal approaches to cross-cultural research

It is important to recognize how different theoretical approaches can inform our research methodology. To illustrate this point we can differentiate between *whiteness theory* and *critical race theory* as distinctive methodological approaches since both are separate but parallel discourses situated within the critical research tradition. Both theories investigate whiteness albeit it in different ways. Critical race theory is longer established and has its roots in critical legal scholarship dating from the 1970s. It was developed by people of colour as an alternative narrative grounded in the experiences of people of colour themselves (Ladison-Billing 1994; Baldwin 2000). Critical race theory is not a united theory but a collection of theories including

LatCrit (Latina/o Critical Race Theory) and TribalCrit (Tribal Critical Race Theory) reflecting the ethnic ancestry and epistemological standpoint of the researcher. Critical race feminists have also argued that gender is a distinctive strand of critical race theory due to their additional standpoint of women of colour (Wing 2004).

These various strands of critical race theory are also associated with particular methodological traditions including storytelling, folklore counter-stories, ethnic autobiography, ethnography, oral history, and participatory action research (Ladison-Billing 1994). One purpose of critical race theory is to make whites think about racism and thus they centre race, but they may do so in a way that troubles white privilege. Examples of critical race theory in consumer research include Peñaloza's (1994) account of Latino assimilation, and Crockett and Wallendorf's (2004) account of political ideology and consumption within the African-American community.

Whiteness theory has been developed predominantly, although not exclusively, by white scholars since the early 1990s as a way to explore their particular epistemological standpoint. Non-white 'readings' of whiteness by people of colour have provided an important contribution to this debate albeit from a different epistemological standpoint. The focus of this methodological approach is to uncover whiteness by analysing power, privilege and rewards of whiteness and it is intimately associated with anti-racist discourse (Aal 2004). Current scholarship is overwhelmingly of US origin. However, this is changing with the publication of texts that take an international perspective (Bonnett 2000; Levine-Rasky 2002) and more interest within Europe (Bonnett 1998; Jackson 1998), South Africa (Steyn 2005), Australasia (Wetherell and Potter 1992), and the Far East (Ashikari 2005).

Investigators have explored how whiteness is depicted in the cinema via the relationships between characters, the context in which the movies are set, and what are deemed appropriate roles for whites and people of colour (Giroux 1997; Dyer 1988; Seshadri-Cooks 2000; Foster 2003). Labour historians have been the most prolific authors during the first decade of whiteness scholarship using a variety of archive media to construct accounts of whiteness (Roediger 1991, 1994; Kolchin 2002). Consumer researchers may be interested in historical aspects of whiteness in retailing and links between art history, whiteness and commodities (Rosenthal 2004).

Visual images (painting, postcards, and photographs) have also provided important insights about how dominant populations, such as colonists, have depicted the indigenous population. Barthes argues that the photograph simultaneously offers a neutral objective view of the world, and also value-laden ideological view. Photographs are a collusion of the natural and the cultural that are at the heart of bourgeois mythical systems. Another example is the historical depiction of ethnicity on postcards, such as the master–slave relationship, as in the case of the American south during slavery in the late nineteenth century (Mellinger 1994). Art history provides interesting insights into the cultural significance of white skin and its commodification (see Chapter 1). Sociologists have engaged in in-depth interviewing and ethnographic work in their quest to uncover contemporary manifestations of whiteness. Frankenberg's (1993) seminal work *White*

Women, Race Matters is a landmark text in this methodological tradition. However, many scholars report difficulties when requesting white respondents to critically reflect on their whiteness. Giroux and McLaren (1989) argue that for whites to think about what it means to be white is a radical move. When white consumers have been questioned they are often reluctant to identify the range of available options, or discuss the process of labelling for fear of being considered racist (McIntyre 1997; Martin *et al.* 1999; Best 2003). Barrett's (2001) experience suggests that when people take the concept seriously they find it a liberating experience, an invitation to critically reflect on an issue they had always held to be natural. An alternative epistemological position is to engage with the non-white reading of whiteness. There is a rapidly expanding research base upon which consumer researchers can draw in this respect (see hooks 1997; Roediger 1998; Knadler 2002; Yancy 2004). Non-white readings of whiteness have the potential to open up some fascinating insights on whiteness and provide new avenues of research inquiry.

Historical approaches

History has not had a high profile in marketing discourse, despite attempts by marketing historians to raise the profile of the sub-specialism. Indeed the teaching of marketing history has been on something of a downward spiral compared with the 1950s and 1960s, when it was an integrated part of the marketing curriculum (Burton 2005). In this respect, marketing is not unlike many other business school specialisms, where there has been a decline in the teaching of history (Van Fleet and Wren 2005). Methodological difficulties of undertaking historical research in marketing have occurred because of the traditions of mainstream, international research that remains predominantly based on statistically modelling, especially multiple regressions. Qualitative research including history was regarded as non-rigorous in this quantitative dominated environment. The published output of historians was also at odds with mainstream management research. Historical works often comprise large detailed monographs that often examine one firm or phenomenon in detail. Their size and level of detail can be off-putting for non-specialists.

The lack of attention to the historical aspects of international business has recently been raised as an issue that needs to be addressed in the future. Jones and Khanna (2006) maintain that the use of history in international business has four main benefits. First, they argue that historical variation is at least as good as contemporary cross-sectional variation in illustrating conceptual issues and, one might add, in theory building. Cross-sectional (contemporary) studies can be complemented with historical (time series) approaches to give a richer 'reading' of the phenomenon in question. In this respect using historical examples is as valuable for teaching students as it is for educating executives in the workplace.

A second important use of history is in the identification of dynamics, environments, organizations, and consumers change over time. Studying history within an international context facilitates an understanding of the central dynamics of change over time and why changes happen in the way that they do. It helps us to understand that the world has not always been the way that we know it, and that not everything labelled as novel and new turns out to be so. Strasser (2003: 376) maintains that incorporating historical perspectives in discussions of consumer culture has a range of advantages. 'Historical accounts illuminate the abundance of our choices, help us understand that to be human is not necessarily to be like us, it provides insights into other cultures that facilitate a process of self-reflection and an awareness of alternative futures'. Furthermore, Jones and Khanna (2006) argue that very influential international business forms have existed in the past but have since disappeared, yet they could teach us some important lessons. They draw attention to government-charted corporations, including the European East Indian Companies of the seventeenth and eighteenth centuries, which grew into massive international trading organizations but also diversified and played a pivotal role in running South Asia. Giant international cartels that are now pretty much extinct were another organizational form that by the 1930s controlled at least 40 per cent of world trade. Historians have also demonstrated that these organizations played an important role in cross-border flows of knowledge. Understanding a range of possibilities enables us to widen our frames of reference and alerts us to the fact that these organizational forms may re-occur in the future.

A third reason why historical approaches are valuable in cross-cultural marketing is that they allow for an investigation of the core competencies of organizations and how they develop over time. A fourth role for history is developing the domain of enquiry. Specifically, historical examination enables us to consider and assess the effect of particular choices over time, often long periods of time. This approach is valuable in some contexts more than others. For example, the impact of international business in the context of foreign direct investment on country development is an issue that has moved further up the agenda, given the heightened interest in corporate social responsibility. Other aspects of countries being 'opened up' by foreign companies include the effects on indigenous markets, industrial organization and labour policies. Long-run historical evidence is likely to produce a much clearer picture of the effects of multiple changing factors and processes and potentially the different outcomes in various countries. The methodological approaches of business historians favour assessing the inter-dependence of variables and their interconnectedness over time. This may mean deploying methodologies 'that accept and explore chaos and complexity' (Jones and Khanna 2006: 463). This approach is very different from many international researchers employing quantitative methodological approaches that typically seek to distinguish dependent from independent variables.

Questions

- What types of deficiencies in cross-cultural marketing research have contributed to marketing blunders?
- What are the different types of cross-cultural equivalence? Explain with examples.
- How persuasive is McSweeney's critique of Hofstede's work?

- Why has qualitative market research generated such opposition among some marketing academics?
- Why is it important to engage with critical approaches to cross-cultural marketing research?

Further reading

Burgess, S.M. and Steenkamp, J.E.M. (2006) 'Marketing renaissance: How research in emerging markets advances marketing science and practice', *International Journal of Research in Marketing*, 23 (4): 337–356.

Craig, C.S. and Douglas, S.P. (2001) 'Conducting international marketing research in the twenty-first century', *International Marketing Review*, 18 (1): 80–90.

Crockett, D., Grier, S.A. and Williams, J.A. (2003) 'Coping with marketplace discrimination: An exploration of the experiences of Black men', *Academy of Marketing Science Review*, 4; available online at http://findarticles.com/p/articles/mi_qa3896/is_2003 01/ai_n9195211.

Crockett, D. and Wallendorf, M. (2004) 'The role of normative political ideology in consumer behavior', *Journal of Consumer Research*, 31 (3): 511–528.

Doran, K.B. (2002) 'Lessons learned in cross-cultural research of Chinese and North American Consumers', *Journal of Business Research*, 55 (10): 823–829.

Peñaloza, L. (1994) 'Atravesando fronteras/border crossings: A critical ethnographic exploration of the consumer acculturation of Mexican immigrants'. *Journal of Consumer Research* 21 (June): 32–54.

Stern, B.B. (1989b) 'Literary criticism and consumer research: Overview and illustrative analysis', *Journal of Consumer Research*, 16 (December): 322–334.

Stern, B.B. (1993) 'Feminist literary criticism and the deconstruction of ads: A postmodern view of advertising and consumer response', *Journal of Consumer Research*, 19 (March): 556–566.

Bibliography

Aaker, J., Brumbaugh, A. and Grier, S. (1998) 'Non-target markets and viewer distinctions: The impact of target marketing on advertising attitudes', *Journal of Consumer Psychology*, 9 (3): 127–140.

Aal, W. (2004) 'Moving from guilt to action: antiracist organizing and the concepts of whiteness for activism and the academy', in B.B. Rasmussen, E. Klinenberg, I.J. Nexica, and M. Wray, *The Making and Unmaking of Whiteness*, Durham: Duke University Press, pp. 294–310.

Aalbers, M.B. (2005) 'Place-based social exclusion: Redlining in the Netherlands', *Area*, 37 (1): 100–109.

Aalbers, M.B. (2006) '"When the banks withdraw, slum landlords take over": The structuration of neighbourhood decline through redlining, drug dealing, speculation and immigrant exploitation', *Urban Studies*, 43 (7): 1061–1086.

Aalto-Setala, V., Evanschitzky, H., Kenning, P. and Vogel, V. (2006) 'Differences in consumer price knowledge between Germany and Finland', *International Journal of Retail Distribution and Consumer Research*, 16 (5): 591–599.

Abaza, M. (2001) 'Shopping malls, consumer culture and the reshaping of public spaces in Egypt', *Theory, Culture and Society*, 18 (5): 97–122.

Acton, T.A. (1999) 'Globalization, the pope and the gypsies', in Brah, A., Hickman, M.J. and Mac an Ghaill (eds) *Global Futures: Migration, Environment and Globalization*, Macmillan Press: Basingstoke.

Adams, C.A. and Zutshi, A. (2006) 'Corporate disclosure and auditing', in Harrison, R., Newholm, T. and Shaw, D. (eds) *The Ethical Consumer*, London: Sage, pp. 207–217.

Adams, P.C. and Ghose, R. (2003) 'India.com: The construction of a space between', *Progress in Human Geography*, 27 (4): 414–437.

Adkins, N.R. and Ozanne, J.L. (1998) 'Between functional literacy and consumer literacy', paper presented at the Association of Consumer Research, Montreal.

Adkins, N.R. and Ozanne, J.L. (2005) 'The low literate consumer', *Journal of Consumer Research*, 32 (June): 93–105.

Afemann, M. (2000) Internet and developing countries – pros and cons, International workshop on the social usage of the internet in Malaysia, 22–25 March.

Agrawal, J. and Kamakura, W.A. (1995) 'The economic worth of celebrity endorsers: An event study analysis', *Journal of Marketing*, 59 (July): 56–62.

Agrawal, M. (1995) 'Review of a 40-year debate in international advertising: Practitioner and academician perspectives to the standardization/adaptation issue', *International Marketing Review*, 12 (1): 26–48.

Agustin, L. (2006) 'The disappearing of a migration category: Migrants who sell sex', *Journal of Ethnic and Migration Studies*, 32 (1): 29–47.

Ahmad, S. (2005) 'In defense of brands', *NyenrodeNow*, March: 14–17.

Ahmed, Z. (2005) 'India readies for shopping mall boom', BBC News, available online at http://news.bbc.co.uk/2/hi/business/4286020.stm (accessed 23 April 2008).

Aiyer, A. (2007) 'The allure of the transnational: Notes on some aspects of the political economy of water in India', *Cultural Anthropology*, 22 (4): 640–658.

Alashban, A.A., Hayes, L.A., Zinkhan, G.M. and Bulazs, A.L. (2002) 'International brand name standardization/adaptation: Antecedents and consequence', *Journal of International Marketing*, 10 (3): 22–48.

Al-Azmeh, A. (1991) 'Barbarians in Arab eyes', *Past and Present*, 134: 3–18.

Alderson, W. and Cox, R. (1948) 'Toward a theory of marketing', *Journal of Marketing*, 13 (October): 137–152.

Alexander, C. (2006) 'Introduction: mapping the issues', *Ethnic and Racial Studies*, 29 (3): 397–410.

Alexander, J. and Alexander, P. (2001) 'Markets as gendered domains: The Javanese *Pasar*', in Seligmann, L.J. (ed.) *Women Traders in Cross-Cultural Perspective*, Stanford: Stanford University Press, pp. 47–72.

Alford, W.P. (1985) *To Steal a Book is an Elegant Offense: Intellectual Property Law in Chinese Civilization*, Stanford: Stanford University Press.

Ali, A.J. and Al-Kazemi, A. (2005) 'The Kuwaiti manager: Work values and orientations', *Journal of Business Ethics*, 60 (1): 63–73.

Allen, R.C. (1995) *To Be Continued. . . Soap Operas Around the World*, London: Routledge.

Alvarez, R.R. (2005) *Mangos, Chiles and Truckers: The Business of Transnationalism*, Minneapolis: University of Minnesota Press.

Amine, L. and Cavusgil, S.T. (1990) 'Marketing environment in the Middle East and North Africa: the forces behind market homogenization', in Thorelli, H. and Cavusgil, S.T. (eds) *International Marketing Strategy*, Oxford: Permagon Press, pp. 229–247.

Amine, L.S., Chao, M.C.H. and Arnould, M.J. (2005) 'Anti-American feeling and the war against Iraq', *Journal of International Marketing*, 13 (2): 114–150.

Anderson, B. (1983) *Imagined Communities: Reflections on the Origin and Spread of Nationalism*, London: Verso.

Androutsopoulos, J. (2007) 'Language choice and code switching in German-based diasporic web forums', in Danet, B. and Herring, S.C. (2007) *The Multilingual Internet: Language, Culture, and Communication Online*, Oxford: Oxford University Press, pp. 340–361.

Ang, P.H. and Lee, B. (2002) 'Wiring an intelligent island: the internet in Singapore', in Rao, S and Klopfenstein, B.C. (eds) *Cyberpath to Development in Asia*, Westport: Praeger, pp. 159–182

Ang, S.H., Jung, K., Kau, A.K., Leong, S.M., Pompitakpan, C. and Tan, S.J. (2004) 'Animosity towards economic giants: What the little guys think', *Journal of Consumer Marketing*, 21 (3): 190–207.

Anis, J. (2007) 'Neography: Unconventional spelling in French SMS messages', in Danet, B. and Herring, S.C. (ed.) *The Multilingual Internet: Language, Culture, and Communication Online*, Oxford: Oxford University Press, pp. 87–115.

Appadurai, A. (1990) 'Disjuncture and difference in the global cultural economy', in Featherstone, M. (ed.) *Global culture: Nationalism, Globalization and Modernity*, London: Sage, pp. 195–311.

Appadurai, A. (1996) *Modernity at Large: Cultural Dimensions of Globalization*, Minneapolis: University of Minneapolis Press.

Arnesen, Eric (2001), "Whiteness and the historians' imagination", *International Journal of Labor and Working-Class History*, 60 (Fall): 3–32.

Arnould, E. (1989) 'Towards a broadened theory of preference formation and the diffusion of innovations: Cases from Zinder Province, Niger Republic', *Journal of Consumer Research*, 16 (September): 239–266.

Arnould, E. and Plymire, D. (2000), 'in Gauntlett, D. (ed.) 'The Cherokee Indians and the internet', *Web Studies: Rewiring Media Studies for the Digital Age*', Arnold: London, pp. 186–193.

Arnould, E.J. and Price, L.L. (2006) 'Market-oriented ethnography revisited', *Journal of Advertising Research*, September: 251–262.

Arnould, E., Price, L. and Zinkhan, G. (2004) *Consumers*, Boston, MA: McGraw-Hill/Irwin.

Ashikari, M. (2005) 'Cultivating Japanese whiteness: The "whitening" cosmetics boom and the Japanese identity', *Journal of Material Culture*, 10 (1): 73–91.

Askegaard, S., Arnould, E.J. and Kjeldgaard, D. (2005) 'Postassimilationist ethnic consumer research: Qualifications and extensions', *Journal of Consumer Research*, 32 (June): 160–170.

Aslam, M.M. (2006) 'Are you selling the right colour? A cross-cultural review of colour as a marketing cue', *Journal of Marketing Communications*, 12 (1): 15–30.

Aspinall, P.J. (2003) 'The conceptualisation and categorisation of mixed race/ethnicity in Britain and North America: Identity options and the role of the State'. *International Journal of Intercultural Relations*, 27 (3): 269–296.

Astroff, R.J. (1997) 'Capital's cultural study: Marketing popular ethnography of US Latino culture', in Nava, M., Blae, A., MacRury, I. and Richards, B. (eds) *Buy This Book*, London: Routledge, pp. 120–138.

Atkinson, R. and Flint, J. (2003) 'Fortress UK? Gated communities, the spatial revolt of the elites and time–space trajectories of segregation', Keynote paper presented at Gated Communities Conference, Glasgow, 19 September.

Aulakh, P.S., Kotabe, M. and Sahay, A. (1996) 'Trust and performance in cross-border marketing partnerships: A behavioral approach', *Journal of International Business Studies*, 27 (5): 1005–1032.

Avery, R.B. and Rendall, M.S. (2002) 'Life-time inheritances of three generations of whites and blacks', *American Journal of Sociology*, 107 (5): 1300–1346.

Back, L. (2002) 'Aryans reading Adorno: cyber-culture and twenty-first-century racism', *Ethnic and Racial Studies*, 25 (4): 628–651.

Bailey, C. (2001) 'Virtual skin: Articulating race in cyberspace', in Trend, D. (ed.) *Reading Digital Culture*, Oxford: Blackwell Publishing Limited, pp. 334–346.

Bailey, S.R. (2002) 'The race construct and public opinion: Understanding Brazilian beliefs about racial inequality and their determinants', *American Journal of Sociology*, 108 (2):406–439.

Baker, W.E. and Coleman, K.M. (2004) 'Racial segregation and the digital divide in the Detroit Metropolitan Region', in Castells, M. (ed.) *The Network Society: A Cross Cultural Perspective*, Cheltenham: Edward Elgar, pp. 249–270.

Balabanis, G., Diamantopoulos, A., Mueller, R.D. and Melewar, T.C. (2001) 'The impact of nationalism, patriotism and internationalism on consumer ethnocentric tendencies', *Journal of International Business Studies*, 32 (1): 157–175.

Balabanis, G. and Diamantopoulos, A. (2004) 'Domestic country bias, country-of-origin effects, and consumer ethnocentrism: A multidimensional unfolding approach', *Journal of the Academy of Marketing Science*, 32 (1): 80–95.

Balabanis, G., Mitchell, V, and Heinonen-Mavrovouniotis, S. (2007) 'SMS-based surveys: strategies to improve participation', *International Journal of Advertising*, 26 (3): 369–385.

Baldwin, J. (2000) 'White man's guilt', in *Black on White: Black Writers on What it Means to be White*, ed. Roediger, D., New York: Shocken Books.

Banerjee, A. (1994) 'Transnational advertising development and management: An account planning approach and a process framework', *International Journal of Advertising*, 13: 95–124.

Banerjee, S.B. and Linstead, S. (2004) 'Masking subversion: Neocolonial embeddedness in anthropological accounts of indigenous management, *Human Relations*, 57 (2): 221–247.

Barboza, D. (2005) 'China, new land of shoppers, builds malls on gigantic scale', *New York Times*, 25 May.

Barnett, C., Cafaro, P. and Newholm, T. (2006) 'Philosophy and ethical consumption', in Harrison, R., Newholm, T. and Shaw, D. (eds) *The Ethical Consumer*, London: Sage, pp. 11–24.

Barrett, J.R. (2001) 'Whiteness studies: Anything here for historians of the working-class?', *International Journal of Labor and Working Class History*, 60 (Fall): 33–42.

Bartel-Radic, A. (2006) 'Intercultural learning in global teams', *Management International Review*, 46 (6): 647–677.

Barth, F. (1969) *Ethnic Groups and Boundaries: The Social Organization of Cultural Differences*, Boston: Little, Brown.

Barwise, P. and Strong, C. (2002) 'Permission-based mobile advertising', *Journal of Interaction Marketing*, 16 (1): 14–24.

Basu, P. (2004) 'Route Metaphors of "Roots-Tourism" in the Scottish Highlands Diaspora', in Coleman, S. and Eade, J. (2004) *Reframing Pilgrimage Cultures in Motion*, London: Routledge, pp. 150–190.

Bayly, C.A. (1999) 'The origins of swadeshi (home industry): cloth and Indian society, 1700–1930', in Appadurai, A. (ed.) *The Social Life of Things: Commodities in Cultural Perspective*, Cambridge: Cambridge University Press, pp. 285–323.

Bazerman, M.H. (2001), 'Consumer research for consumers,' *Journal of Consumer Research*, 27 (March): 499–504.

BBC (2003) 'US babies get global brand names', 13 November; available online at http://news.bbc.co.uk/1/hi/world/americas/3268161.stm (accessed 24 April 2008).

Beard, F.K. (2005) 'One hundred years of humor in American advertising', *Journal of Macromarketing*, 25 (1): 54–65.

Beare, M.E. (2003) *Critical Reflections on Transnational Organized Crime, Money Laundering, and Corruption*, Toronto: University of Toronto Press.

Beck, R.M. (2006) 'Popular media for HIV/AIDS prevention? Comparing two comics: Kingo and the Sara communications initiative', *Journal of Modern African Studies*, 44 (4): 513–541.

Bek, D., McEwan, C. and Bek, K. (2007) 'Ethical trading and socioeconomic transformation: critical reflections on the South African wine industry', *Environment and Planning A*, 39: 301–319.

Belk, R.W. (1983) 'Worldly possessions: issues and criticisms', *Advances in Consumer Research*, 10: 514–519.

Belk, R.W. (1985) 'Materialism: Trait aspects of living in the material world', *Journal of Consumer Research*, 12 (December): 339–361.

Belk, R.W. (1987) 'Material values in the comics: A content analysis of comic books featuring the themes of wealth', *Journal of Consumer Research*, 14 (June): 26–42.

Belk, R.W. (1988) 'Third world consumer culture', in Kumcu, E. and Firat, A.F. (eds) *Marketing and Development: Towards Broader Dimensions*, London: Jai Press Inc., pp. 133–128.

Belk, R.W. (1992) 'Moving possessions; An analysis based on personal documents from the 1847–1869 Mormon migration', *Journal of Consumer Research*, 19 (3): 339–361.

Belk, R.W. and Costa, J.A. (1998) 'The mountain man myth: A contemporary consuming fantasy', *Journal of Consumer Research*, 2 (3): 218–240.

Belk, R.W., Ger, G. and Askegaard, S. (2000) 'The missing streetcar named desire', in Ratneshwar, S., Mic, D.G. and Huffman, C. (eds) *The Why of Consumption*, London: Routledge, pp. 98–119.

Belk, R.W., Ger, G. and Askegaard, S. (2003) 'The fire of desire: A multisided inquiry into consumer passion', *Journal of Consumer Research*, 30 (3): 326–362.

Belk, R.W. and Pollay, R.W. (1985) 'Images of ourselves: The good life in twentieth century advertising', *Journal of Consumer Research*, 11 (March): 887–897.

Bell, C.S. (1996) 'Data on race, ethnicity and ender: Caveats for the user', *International Labor Review*, 135: 535–551.

Benitez, J.L. (2006) 'Transnational dimensions of the digital divide among Salvadoran immigrants in the Washington DC metropolitan area', *Global Networks*, 6 (2): 181–199.

Benson, A. (ed.) (2000) *I Shop Therefore I Am: Compulsive Shopping and the Search for Self*, Northvale, NJ: Jason Aronson Inc.

Benson, S.P. (1988) *Counter Cultures: Saleswomen, Managers and Customers in American Department Stores, 1890–1940*, Chicago: University of Illinois Press.

Berger, P.L. (2002) 'Introduction: The cultural dynamics of globalization', in Berger, P.L. and Huntington, S.P. (eds) *Many Globalizations: Cultural Diversity in the Contemporary World*, Oxford: Oxford University Press, pp. 1–16.

Bernstein, A. (2002) 'Globalization, culture, and development: Can South Africa be more than an offshoot of the West?', in Berger, P.L. and Huntington, S.P. (eds) *Many Globalizations: Cultural Diversity in the Contemporary World*, Oxford: Oxford University Press, pp. 185–249.

Berry, J.W. (1990) 'Psychology of acculturation', in Berman, J.J. (ed.) *Cross-Cultural Perspectives*: Proceedings of the Nebraska Symposium on Motivation, pp. 201–234.

Best, A.L. (2003) 'Doing race in the context of feminist interviewing: Constructing whiteness through talk', *Qualitative Inquiry*, 9 (6): 895–914.

Bhabha, H.K. (1990) 'Introduction: narrating the nation', in Bhabha, H.K. (ed.) *Nation and Narration*, London: Routledge, pp. 1–7.

Bianchi, C.C. and Ostale, E. (2006) 'Lessons learned from unsuccessful internationalization attempts: Examples of multinational retailers in Chile', *Journal of Business Research*, 59: 140–147.

Biggart, N.W. (1988) *Charismatic Capitalism*, Chicago: University of Chicago Press.

Billig, M. (1995) *Banal Nationalism*, London: Sage.

Binnie, J., Holloway, J.J,. Millington, S. and Young, C. (2006) 'Introduction; grounding cosmopolitan urbanism, approaches, practices and policies', in Binnie, J., Holloway, J.J,. Millington, S. and Young, C. (eds) *Cosmopolitan Urbanism*, London: Routledge, pp. 1–34

Biswas, D., Biswas, A. and Das, N. (2006) 'The differential effects of celebrity and expert endorsements on consumer risk perceptions', *Journal of Advertising*, 35 (2): 17–31.

Block, W. (2004) '"The digital divide is not a problem in need of rectifying', *Journal of Business Ethics*, 53 (4): 393–406.

Blum, K. and Noble, E.P. (1994) 'The Sobering D2 Story', *Science*, 265: 1346–1347.

Blunt, A. (2005) *Domicile and Diaspora: Anglo-Indian Women and the Spatial Politics of Home*, Oxford: Blackwell Publishing.

Boddewyn, J.J. (1982) 'Advertising regulation in the 1980s: The underlying global forces', *Journal of Marketing*, 48 (Winter): 27–35.

Bokale, J. (2008) 'Supermarkets to shun star ties for price focus', *Marketing*, 27 February, p. 1.

Bonnett, A. (1998) 'How the British working class became White: The symbolic (re)formulation of racialized capitalism', *Journal of Historical Sociology*, 11 (3): 316–340.

Bonnett, A. (2000) *White Identities: Historical and International Perspectives*, New York: Prentice Hall.

Bonnett, A. (2006) 'The Americanization of anti-racism? Global power and hegemony in ethnic equity', *Journal of Ethnic and Migration Studies*, 32 (7): 1083–1103.

Borgmann, A. (2000) 'The moral complexion of consumption', *Journal of Consumer Research*, 26 (March): 418–422.

Bornman, E. (2006) 'National symbols and nation-building in post-apartheid South Africa', *International Journal of Intercultural Relations*, 30: 383–399.

Bouchet, D. (1995) 'Marketing and the redefinition of ethnicity', in Costa, J.A. and Barmossy, G. J., *Marketing in a Multicultural World*, London: Sage, pp. 68–104.

Bourdieu, P. (1984) *Distinction: A Social Critique of the Judgment of Taste*, Cambridge, MA: Harvard University Press.

Bovenkerk, F. (2005) 'Organized crime and ethnic minorities: Is there a link?', in Williams, P. and Vlassis, D. (eds) *Combating Transnational Crime: Concepts, Activities and Responses*, London: Frank Cass, pp. 109–126.

Boyle, D. (2003) *Authenticity: Brands, Fakes, Spin and the Lust for the Real Life*, London: Harper Collins.

Bradshaw, A., McDonagh, P. and Marshall, D. (2006) 'No space – New blood and the production of brand culture colonies', *Journal of Marketing Management*, 22 (5–6): 579–599.

Brama, A. (2006) '"White flight"? The production and reproduction of immigrant concentration areas in Swedish cities, 1990–2000', *Urban Studies*, 43 (7): 1127–1146.

Braziel, J.E. and Mannur, A. (2003) *Theorizing Diaspora*, Oxford: Blackwell Publishing.

Brengman, M., Geuens, M., Weijters, B., Smith, S.M. and Swinyard, W.R. (2005) 'Segmenting internet shoppers based on their web-usage-related lifestyle: A cross-cultural validation', *Journal of Business Research*, 58 (1): 79–88.

Brennan, T. (1990) 'The national longing for form', in Bhabha, H.K. (ed.) *Nation and Narration*, London: Routledge, pp. 44–70.

Brett, J.M. (2001) *Negotiating Globally*, New York: Jossey Bass.

Brettell, C. (2003) *Anthropology and Migration*, Oxford: Altamira Press.

Brewis, J. and Jack, G. (2005) 'Pushing speed? The marketing of fast and convenience food', *Consumption, Markets and Culture*, 8 (1): 49–67.

Brown, A. (1998) '"Doing time": The extended present of the long-term prisoner', *Time and Society*, 7 (1): 93–104.

Brown, S., Kozinets, R.V. and Sherry, J.F. (2003) 'Teaching old brands new tricks: Retro branding and the revival of brand meaning', *Journal of Marketing*, 67 (July): 19–33.

Brucks, M. and Schurr, P.H. (1990) 'The effects of bargainable attributes and attribute range knowledge', *Journal of Consumer Reseaarch*, 16 (March): 409–419.

Brumbaugh, A.M. and Grier, S.A. (2006) 'Insights from a "failed" experiment: Directions for pluralistic, multiethnic advertising research', *Journal of Advertising*, 35 (3): 35–46.

Buchan, N.R., Croson, R.T.A. and Johnson, E.J. (2004) 'When do fair beliefs influence bargaining behavior? Experimental bargaining in Japan and the United States', *Journal of Consumer Research*, 31 (1): 181–190.

Burgess, S.M. and Steenkamp, J.E.M. (2006) 'Marketing renaissance: How research in emerging markets advances marketing science and practice', *International Journal of Research in Marketing*, 23: 337–356.

Burke, T. (1996) *Lifebuoy Men, Lux Women: Commodification, Consumption, and Cleanliness in Modern Zimbabwe*, London: Leicester University Press.

Burke, T. (2002) '"Our mosquitoes are not so big": Images and modernity in Zimbabwe', in Landau, P.S. and Kaspin, D.D. (eds) *Images and Empires: Visuality in Colonial and Postcolonial Africa*, Berkley: University of California Press, pp. 41–55.

Burton, D. (2002) 'Postmodernism, social relations and remote shopping', *European Journal of Marketing*, 36 (7/8): 792–810.

Burton, D. (2005) 'Marketing theory matters', *British Journal of Management*, 16: 5–18

Burton, D. (2008) *Credit and Consumer Society*, London: Routledge.

Bush, A.J., Smith, R. and Martin, C. (1999) 'The influence of consumer socialization variables on attitude towards advertising: A comparison of African-Americans and Caucasians', *Journal of Advertising*, 28 (3): 13–24.

Cabezas, A.L. (2004) 'Between love and money: Sex, tourism, and citizenship in Cuba and the Dominican Republic', *Signs: Journal of Women in Culture and Society*, 29 (41): 987–1015.

Canavan, O., Henchion, M. and O'Reilly, S. (2007) 'The use of the internet as a marketing channel for Irish speciality food', *International Journal of Retail and Distribution Management*, 35 (2): 178–195.

Canning, L. (2006) 'Rethinking market connections: Mobile phone recovery reuse and recycling in the UK', *Journal of Business and Industrial Marketing*, 21 (5): 320–329.

Cannon, H.M. and Yaprak, A. (2002) 'Will the real-world citizen please stand up! The many faces of cosmopolitan consumer behavior', *Journal of International Marketing*, 10 (4): 30–52.

Carey, J. (1997) 'Reflections on the project of (American) cultural studies' in Ferguson, M. and Golding, P. (eds) *Cultural Studies in Question*, London: Sage.

Carmichael, S. (1995) *Business Ethics: The New Bottom Line*, London: Demos.

Carroll, A., Barnes, S.J., Scornavacca, E. and Fletcher, K. (2007) 'Consumer perceptions and attitudes towards SMS advertising: Recent evidence from New Zealand', *International Journal of Advertising*, 26 (1): 79–98.

Cashmore, E. (1996) *Dictionary of Race and Ethnic Relations*, London: Routledge.

Castells, M. (2001) *The Internet Galaxy: Reflections on the Internet, Business and Society*, Oxford: Oxford University Press.

Castells, M. (2004) 'Informationalism, networks, and the network society: A theoretical blueprint', in Castells, M. (ed.) *The Network Society: A cCross Cultural Perspective*, Cheltenham: Edward Elgar, pp. 3–48.

Castells, M., Fernandez-Ardevol, M, Qui, J.L. and Sey, A. (2005) 'The mobile communication society: A cross-cultural analysis of available evidence on the social uses of wireless communication technology', *International Workshop on Wireless Communication Policies and Prospects: A Global Perspective*, held at the Annenberg School for Communication, University of Southern California, Los Angeles, 8–9 October 2004.

Castles, S. (2007) 'Twenty-first-century migration as a challenge to sociology', *Journal of Ethnic and Migration Studies*, 33 (3): 351–371.

Castles, S. and Davidson, A. (2000) *Citizenship and Migration*, London: Macmillan Press.

Castree, N. (2006) 'Geographical knowledges, universities, and academic freedom', *Environment and Planning A*, 38 (9): 1189–1394.

Caws, P. (1994) 'Identity: Cultural, transcultural, and multicultural', in Goldberg, D.T. (ed.) *Multiculturalism: A Critical Reader*, Oxford: Blackwell.

Cayla, J. (2006) 'Domesticating the Indian imagination', Special Session Summary, *Advances in Consumer Research*, 33: 459.

Cayla, J. and Peñaloza, L. (2006) 'The production of consumer representations', Special Session Summary, *Advances in Consumer Research*, 33: 458–9.

Chao S. (2003) 'Chinese genealogical research: Coordination and resource-sharing with a global perspective', *Library Collections, Acquisitions, and Technical Services*, (27): 225–240.

Chaisrakeo, S. and Speece, M. (2004) 'Culture, intercultural communication competence and sales negotiation: A qualitative research approach', *Journal of Business and Industrial Marketing*, 19 (4): 267–282.

Chapman, M. (1997) 'Social anthropology, business studies, and cultural issues', *International Studies of Management and Organization*, 26 (4): 3–29.

Charavat, F.J. (1961) *Supermarketing*, New York: The Macmillan Company.

Chatterjee, A. (2004) 'Globalization, identity, and the television networks: Community mediation and global responses in multicultural India', in Castells, M. (ed.) *The Network Society: A Cross Cultural Perspective*, Cheltenham: Edward Elgar, pp. 402–419.

Cheah, P. and Robbins, B. (1998) *Cosmopolitics: Thinking and Feeling beyond the Nation*, Minneapolis: University of Minneapolis Press.

Chen, Y.C., Chen, P.S., Hwang, J.J., Korba, L., Song, R. and Yee, G. (2005) 'An analysis of online gaming crime characteristics', *Internet Research*, 15 (3): 246–261.

Cherlow, J.R. (1981) 'Measuring values of travel time savings', *Journal of Consumer Research*, 7 (March): 360–371.

Childers, T.L. and Roa, A.R. (1992) 'The influence of familial and peer-based reference groups on consumer decisions', *Journal of Consumer Research*, 19 (2): 198–211.

Chin, E. (2001) *Purchasing Power: Black Kids and Consumer Culture*, Minneapolis: University of Minneapolis Press.

Chin, K., Zhang, S. and Kelly, R.J. (2005) 'Transnational Chinese organized crime activities: Patterns and emerging trends', in Williams, P. and Vlassis, D. (eds) *Combating Transnational Crime: Concepts, Activities and Responses*, London: Frank Cass, pp. 127–154.

Choi, S.M., Lee, W. and Kim, H. (2005) 'Lessons from the rich and famous: A cross-cultural comparison of celebrity endorsement in advertising', *Journal of Advertising*, 34 (2): 85–98.

Chopra, R. (2006) 'Global primordialities: Virtual identity politics in online Hindutva and online Dalit discourse', *New Media and Society*, 8 (2): 187–206.

Christie, P.M.J., Kwon, I.G., Stoerl, P.A. and Baumhart, R. (2003) 'Cross-cultural comparison of ethical attitudes of business managers: India, Korea and the United States', *Journal of Business Ethics*, 46 (3): 263–287.

Chung, E. (1999) 'Navigating the primodial soup: Charting the lived worlds of the migrant consumer', *Journal of Consumer Marketing*, 17: 36–54.

Chung, J., Yu, J.P. and Pysarchik, D.T. (2006) 'Cue utilization to assess food product quality: A comparison of consumers and retailers in India', *International Review of Retail Distribution and Consumer Research*, 16 (2): 199–214.

Clarke, A.J. (1999) *Tuperware: The Promise of Plastic in 1950s America*, London: Smithsonian Institution Press.

Clarke, I and Honeycutt, E.D. (2000) 'Color usage in international business to business print advertising', *Industrial Marketing Management*, 29: 255–261.

Clarke, I. and Honeycutt, E.D. (2000) 'Color usage in international business-to-business print advertising', *Industrial Marketing Management*, 29: 255–261.

Classen, C. (1996) 'Sugar cane, Coca-Cola and hypermarkets: Consumption and surrealism in the Argentine Northwest', in Howes, D. (ed.) *Cross-cultural Consumption: Global Markets Local Realities*, London: Routledge, pp. 39–54.

Clegg, A. (1998) 'Colour blind', *Marketing Week*, 19 (13): 38–41.

Clifford, J. (1988) *The Predicament of Culture: Twentieth-century Ethnography, Literature and Art*, Cambridge, MA: Harvard University.

Clifford, J. (1997) *Routes: Travel and Translation in the Late Twentieth Century*, Cambridge MA: Cambridge University Press.

Clifford, J. (1998) 'Mixed feelings', in Cheah, P. and Robbins, B. (eds) *Cosmopolitics: Thinking and Feeling beyond the Nation*, Minneapolis: University of Minnesota Press, pp. 362–70.

Cohen, L. (2004) *A Consumers' Republic*, New York: Vintage Books.

Cohen, R. (1997) *Global Diaspora: An Introduction*, London: UCL Press.

Coles, T. (1999) 'Department stores as innovations in retail marketing: Some observations on marketing practice and perceptions in Wilhelmine, Germany', *Journal of Macromarketing*, 19 (1): 34–47.

Colvin, G. (2007) 'Selling P and G', *Fortune*, 17 September, 81–87.

Cook, I. and Harrison, M. (2003) 'Cross over food: Re-materializing postcolonial geographies', *Transactions of the Institute of British Geographers*, New Series, 28: 296–317.

Cooke, B. (2005) 'The managing of the (Third) World', in Grey, C. and Willmott, H. (eds) *Critical Management Studies*, Oxford: Oxford University Press, pp. 244–271.

Costa, J.A. and G.J. Bamossy (eds) (1995) *Marketing in a multicultural world*, London: Sage.

Cotte, J., Ratneshwar, S. and Mick, D.G. (2004) 'The times of their lives: Phenomenological and metaphorical characteristics of consumer timestyles', *Journal of Consumer Research*, 31 (September): 333–345.

Couper, M. (2000) 'Web surveys: a review of issues and approaches', *Public Opinion Quarterly*, 64: 464–494.

Coviello,N.E., Brodie, R.J., Danaher, P.J. and Johnston, W.J. (2002) 'How firms relate to their markets: An empirical examination of contemporary marketing practice', *Journal of Marketing*, 66 (July): 33–46.

Craig, C.S. and Douglas, S.P (2000) *International Marketing Research*, New York: John Wiley and Sons.

Craig, C.S. and Douglas, S.P. (2001) 'Conducting international marketing research in the twenty-first century', *International Marketing Review*, 18 (1): 80–90.

Craig, C.S., Greene, W.H., Douglas, S.P. (2005) 'Culture matters: Consumer acceptance of US films in foreign markets', *Journal of International Marketing*, 13 (4): 80–103.

Crockett, D., Grier, S.A. and Williams, J.A. (2003) 'Coping with marketplace discrimination: An exploration of the experiences of Black men', *Academy of Marketing Science Review*, 4; available online at http://findarticles.com/p/articles/mi_qa3896/is_2003 01/ai_n9195211.

Crockett, D. and M. Wallendorf (2004) 'The role of normative political ideology in consumer behavior', *Journal of Consumer Research*, 31 (3): 511–528.

Cross, G. (1998) 'Toys and time: Playthings and parents' attitudes toward change in early 20th-century America', *Time and Society*, 7 (1): 5–24.

Cuervo-Cazurra, A. (2006) 'Who cares about corruption?', *Journal of International Business Studies*, 7 (6): 807–822.

Cui, G. (2001) 'Marketing to ethnic minority consumers: A historical journey (1932–1997)', *Journal of Macromarketing* 21 (1): 23–31.

Cuneo, A. (2004) 'Marketers dial into message', *Advertising Age*, 1 November, p. 18.

D'Andrea, G., Lopez-Aleman, B. and Stengel, A. (2006a) 'Why small retailers endure in Latin America', *International Journal of Retail and Distribution Management*, 34 (9): 661–763.

D'Andrea, G., Ring, L.J., Lopez-Aleman, B. and Stengel, A. (2006b) 'Breaking the myths on emerging consumers in retailing', *International Journal of Retail and Distribution Management*, 34 (9): 674–687.

D'Andrea, G., Schleicher, M. and Lunardini, F. (2006c) 'The role of promotions and other factors affecting overall store price image in Latin America', *International Journal of Retail and Distribution Management*, 34 (9): 688–700.

D'Rozario, D. (2004) 'A tale of two 'cities': ("It was the worst of times"; "It was worse at times"): Shoppers in Montgomery County, MD and Washington, DC during the recent sniper attacks', *Advances in Consumer Research*, 31: 630–631.

D'Rozario, D. and Williams, J.D. (2005) 'Retail redlining: Definition, theory, typology, and measurement', *Journal of Macromarketing*, 25 (2): 175–186.

Dadzie, Q., Johnston, W.J. and Pels, J. (2008) 'Business-to-business marketing practices in West Africa, Argentina and the United States', *Journal of Business and Industrial Marketing*, 23 (2): 115–23.

Danet, B. and Herring, S.C. (2007) *The Multilingual Internet: Language, Culture, and Communication Online*, Oxford: Oxford University Press.

Darley, W. and Johnson, D.M. (1993) 'Cross-national comparison of consumer attitudes toward consumerism in four developing countries', *The Journal of Consumer Affairs*, 27 (1): 37–54.

Das, V. (1995) 'On soap opera: What kind of anthropological object is it?', in Miller, D. (ed.) *Worlds Apart: Modernity through the Prism of the Local*, London: Routledge, pp. 169–189.

Daswani, C. (2001) 'Issues of literacy development in the Indian context', in Olson, D.R. and Torrance, N. (eds) *The Making of Literate Societies*, Oxford: Blackwell Publishers, pp. 284–295.

Davila, A. (2001) *Latinos Inc: The Making and Marketing of a People*, Berkeley: University of California Press.

Daviron, B. and Ponte, S. (2005) *The Coffee Paradox*, London: Zed Books Ltd.

Davis, T. (2003) 'Creolization or prodigalization? The many avatars of an Indo-Singaporean food consumptionscape', *Advances in Consumer Research*, 30: 284–288.

Davis, T. (2005) 'Creolized and modernized: Religious consumption in the South Indian church', *Advances in Consumer Research*, 32: 80.

Davis, T. and Yip, J. (2004) 'Reconciling Christianity and modernity: Australian youth and religion', *Advances in Consumer Research*, 31: 113–117.

Dawson, M.C. (2001) *Black Visions: the Roots of Contemporary African-American Political Ideology*, Chicago: University of Chicago Press.

De Mauro, T. (1996) 'Linguistc variety and linguistic minorities', in Forgacs, D. and Lumley, R. (eds) *Italian Cultural Studies*, Oxford: Oxford University Press, pp. 88–101.

de Mooij, M. and Hofstede, G. (2002) 'Convergence and divergence in consumer behavior: Implications for international retailing', *Journal of Retailing*, 78 (1): 61–69.

De Pyssler, B. (1992) 'The cultural and political economy of the Indian two-wheeler', in Sherry, J.F. and Sternthal, B. (eds) *Advances in Consumer Research*, 19: 437–442.

De Souza, E.G.M. and Medeni, T. (2007) 'E-travel agents selling to ethnic customers', in Ammi, C. (ed.) *Global Consumer Behavior*, London: ISTE, pp. 3–25.

De Valck, K. (2005) *Virtual Communities of Consumption: Networks of Consumer De Waal Malefyt, T. and Moeran, B. (2003)* Advertising Cultures, Oxford: Berg.

De Wit, J.W. (1996) *Poverty, Policy and Politics in Madras Slums*, London: Sage. Knowledge and Companionship, Rotterdam: Erasmus Research Institute of Management.

Denton, N.A. and Tolnay, S.E. (eds) (2002) *American Diversity: A Demographic Challenge*, New York: State University of New York Press.

Denzin, N.K. (2001) 'The seventh moment: Qualitative inquiry and the practices of a more radical consumer research', *Journal of Consumer Research* 28 (September): 107–115.

Desai, J. (2004) *Beyond Bollywood: The Cultural Politics of South Asian Diasporic Film*, New York: Routledge.

Deshpande, R., Hoyer, W.D. and Donthu, N. (1986) 'The intensity of ethnic affiliation: A study of the sociology of Hispanic consumption', *Journal of Consumer Research* (13): 214–220.

Deshpande, R. and Webster, F.E. (1989) 'Organizational culture and marketing: Defining the research agenda', *Journal of Marketing*, 53 (January): 3–15.

Dholakia, N. and Zwick, D. (2003) 'Mobile technologies and boundaryless spaces: Slavish lifestyles, seductive meanderings, or creative empowerment?'; available online at http://ritim.cba.uri.edu/wp2003/pdf_format/HOIT-Mobility-Technology-Boundary-paper-v06.pdf.

Dholakia, R.R. and Dholakia, N. (2004) 'Mobility and markets: Emerging outlines of m-commerce', *Journal of Business Research*, 57: 1391–1396.

Dholakia, R.R., Dholakia, N. and Khetri, N. (2003) 'Internet diffusion', in Bidgoli, H. (ed.) *The Internet Encyclopedia*, New York: Wiley.

Dholakia, R.R., Sharif, M. and Bhandari, L. (1988) 'Consumption in the Third World: Challenges for marketing and development', Kumcu, E. and Firat, A.F. (eds) *Marketing and Development: Towards Broader Dimensions*, London: Jai Press Inc., pp. 129–148.

Di Rienzo, C.E., Das, J., Cort, K.T., Burbridge, J. (2007) 'Corruption and the role of information', *Journal of International Business Studies*, 38: 320–332.

Dichter, E. (1962) 'The World Consumer', *Harvard Business Review*, 40 (July/August): 113–122.

Dicken, P. (2000) *Global Shift: Mapping the Changing Contours of the World Economy*, London: Sage.

Dickson, P.R. (2000) 'Understanding the trade winds: The global evolution of production, consumption, and the internet', *Journal of Consumer Research*, 27 (June): 115–122.

Dimofte, C.V., Forehand, M.R. and Deshpande, R. (2004) 'Ad schema inconginuity as elicitor of ethnic self awareness and differential ad response', *Journal of Advertising*, 32 (4): 7–17.

Dittmar, H. and Drury, J. (2000) 'Self-image- is it in the bag? A qualitative comparison between "ordinary" and "excessive" consumers', *Journal of Economic Psychology*, 21: 109–142.

Do Campo, S.B. (2007) 'Adios to poverty, hola to consumption', *The Economist*, 18 August, 22–24.

Doh, J.P. and Teegen, H. (2003) *Globalization and NGOs: Transforming Business, Government and Society*, Westport: Praeger.

Dolnicar, S. and Jordaan, Y. (2007) 'A market-oriented approach to responsibility managing information privacy concerns in direct marketing', *Journal of Advertising*, 36 (2): 123–49.

Domosh, M. (1996) 'The feminized retail landscape: Gender, ideology and consumer culture in nineteenth-century New York City', in Wrigley, N. and Lowe, M. (eds) *Retailing, Consumption and Capital: Towards the New Retail Geography*, Harlow: Longman Group Limited, pp. 257–70.

Domzal, T.J. and Kernan, J.B. (1993) 'Mirror, mirror: Some postmodern reflections on global advertising', *Journal of Advertising*, XXII (4): 1–20.

Dominguez, V.R. (1994) 'A taste for "the other": Intellectual complicity in racializing practices', *Current Anthropology*, 35 (4): 333–348.

Donnelly, J.H. (1970) 'Attitudes towards culture and approach to international advertising', *Journal of Marketing*, 34 (July): 60–68.

Donthu, N. and Cherian, J. (1994) 'Impact of strength of ethnic identification on Hispanic shopping behaviour', *Journal of Retailing*, 70: 383–93.

Doran, K.B. (2002) 'Lessons learned in cross-cultural research of Chinese and North American Consumers', *Journal of Business Research*, 55: 823–829.

Douglas, S.P. (1976) 'Cross-national comparisons and consumer stereotypes: A case study of working and non-working wives in the US and France', *Journal of Consumer Research*, 3 (1): 12–20.

Drazin, A. (2002) 'Chasing moths: Cleanliness, intimacy and progress in Romania', in Mandel, R. and Humphrey, C. (eds) *Markets and Moralities: Ethnographies of Postsocialism*, Oxford: Berg, pp. 101–126.

Duncan, T. and Ramaprasad, J. (1995) 'Standardized multinational advertising: the influencing factors', *Journal of Advertising*, XXIV (3): 55–68.

Dunn, S.W. (1994) 'Early days of international advertising education in the U.S.', *Journal of Advertising*, XXIII (1): 111–113.

Durakbasa, A. and Cindoglu, D. (2002) 'Encounters at the counter: Gender and the shopping experience', in Andiyoti, D. and Saktanber, A. (eds) *Fragments of Culture: The Everyday of Modern Turkey*, London: I.B.Tauris and Co, pp. 73–89.

Durgunoglu, A.Y. and Verhoeven, L. (1998) *Literacy Development in a Multilingual Context: Cross-cultural Perspectives*, New Jersey: Lawrence Erlbaum Associates Inc.

Dwyer, F.R. (1984) 'Are two better than one: Bargaining behavior and outcome in an asymmetrical power relationship', *Journal of Consumer Research*, 11 (September): 680–693.

Dwyer, S., Mesak, H. and Hsu, M. (2005) 'An exploratory examination of the influence of national culture on cross-national product diffusion', *Journal of International Marketing*, 13 (2): 1–27.

Dyer, G. (2008) 'Chinese lose enthusiasm for small, cheap vehicles', *Financial Times*, 14 January, p. 22.

Dyer, R. (1988) 'White', *Screen*, 29 (4): 44–64.

Eagleton, T. (1991) *Ideology*, London: Verso.

Earley, P.C. (2006) 'Leading cultural research in the future: A matter of paradigms and taste', *Journal of International Business Studies*, 37 (6): 922–931.

Eckhardt, G.M. (2005) 'Local branding in a foreign product category in an emerging market', *Journal of International Marketing*, 13 (4): 57–79.

Eckhardt, G.M. and Houston, M.J. (2002) 'Cultural paradoxes reflected in brand meaning: McDonalds in Shanghai, China', *International Journal of Marketing*, 10 (2): 68–82.

Eckhardt, G.M. and Mahi, H. (2004) 'The role of consumer agency in the globalization process in emerging markets', *Journal of Macromarketing*, 24 (2): 136–146.

Economist (2003a) 'Seriously wired', 19 April, p. 7.

Economist (2003b) 'Special report: Counterfeiting', 17 May, pp. 69–71.

Economist (2003c) 'Special report: The Beauty Business', 24 May, pp. 71–73.

Economist (2004a) 'Medical tourism to India: Get well away', 9 October, pp. 49–50.

Economist (2004b) 'The uncorrupt', 23 October, p. 118.

Economist (2004c) 'Political food', *Economist*, 30 October, p. 37.

Economist (2004d) 'Consumer goods in India', 6 November, p. 77.

Economist (2004e) 'Middle class amid the shanties', 15 May, p. 53.

Economist (2004f) 'Luxury's new empire', 19 June, pp. 69–70.

Economist (2005a) 'The silent majority', 9 April, p. 76.

Economist (2005b) 'If only the adults would behave like children', 23 April, p. 31.

Economist (2005c) 'Business China: Still off the doorstep', XXXI, 13, pp. 1–2.

Economist (2005d) 'Warfare in the aisles', 2 April, pp. 6–8.

Economist (2006a) 'When markets melt away', 11 February, p. 66.

Economist (2006b) 'Rich pickings', 19 August, p. 63.

Economist (2006c) 'Bribery', 14 October, p. 130.

Economist (2006d) 'Trouble at the till', 4 November, p. 18.

Economist (2006e) 'Migrants remittances', 25 November, p. 134.

Economist (2006f) 'Coming to market', 15 April, p. 75.

Economist (2006g) 'The party, the people and the power of cyber-talk', 29 April, p. 27.

Economist (2006h) 'McCurrencies', 27 May, p. 94.

Economist (2007a) 'Let 1,000 titles bloom', 17 February, p. 73.

Economist (2007b) 'Watching as you shop', 8 December, pp. 25–36.

Economist (2008) 'Emerging-market multinationals', 12 January, 61–63.

Edmonds, A. (2007) '"The poor have the right to be beautiful": Cosmetic surgery in neoliberal Brazil', *Journal of the Royal Anthropological Institute*, 13: 363–381.

Edwards, R. (1998) 'A critical examination of the use of interpreters in the qualitative research process', *Journal of Ethnic and Migration Studies*, 24 (1): 197–208.

Ehrkamp, P. (2006) '"We Turks are no Germans": Assimilation discourses and the dialectical construction of identities in Germany', *Environment and Planning A*, 38 (9): 1673–1692.

Ehrkamp, P. and Leitner, H. (2006) 'Rethinking immigration and citizenship: new spaces of migrant transnationalism and belonging', *Environment and Planning A*, 38 (9): 1591–1598.

Elias, N. and Greenspan, L. (2007) 'The honey, the bear and the violin: The Russian voices of Israeli advertising', *Journal of Advertising Research*, March: 113–122.

Elliot, C. and Brodwin, P. (2002) 'Identity and genetic ancestry tracing', *British Medical Journal*, 325 (21 December): 1469–1471.

Elliott, J. (2007) 'Retail Revolution', *Fortune*, 9 July, 14–16.

Elliot, R. (1994) 'Addictive consumption: Function and fragmentation in postmodernity', *Journal of Consumer Policy*, 17: 159–179.

Elliot, R., Eccles, S. and Gournay, K. (1996) 'Man management? Women and the use of debt to control personal relationships', *Journal of Marketing Management*, 12: 657–669.

Ellis, E. (2007) 'Iran's Cola War', *Fortune*, 19 February, 32–36.

Erikson, E. and Bearman, P. (2006) 'Malfeasance and the foundations of global trade: The structure of English trade in the East Indies, 1601–1833', *American Journal of Sociology*, 112 (1): 195–230.

Escobar, A. (1994) 'Welcome to Cyberia: Notes on the anthropology of cyberculture', *Current Anthropology*, 35 (3): 56–76.

Estelamin, H., Lehmann, D.R. and Holden, A.C. (2001) 'Macro-economic determinants of consumer price knowledge: A meta-analysis of four decades of research', *International Journal of Research in Marketing*, 18: 341–355.

Ettenson, R. (1993) 'Brand name and country of origin effects in the emerging market economies of Russia, Poland, and Hungary', *International Marketing Review*, 10 (5): 14–36.

Everson, M. (2006) 'Legal constructions of the consumer', in Trentmann, F. (ed.) *The Making of the Consumer: Knowledge, Power and Identity in the Modern World*, Oxford: Berg, pp. 99–124.

Eves, R. (2006) '"Black and white, a significant contrast 2: Race, humanism and missionary photography in the Pacific', *Ethnic and Racial Studies*, 29 (4): 725–748.

Eyben, R. (2000) 'Development and anthropology: A view from inside the agency', *Critique of Anthropology*, 21 (1): 7–14.

Fahy, J., Hooley, G., Cox, T., Beracs, J., Fonfara, K. and Snoj, B. (2000) 'The development and impact of marketing capabilities in Central Europe', *Journal of International Business Studies*, 31 (1): 63–81.

Falk, P. (1994) *The Consuming Body*, London: Sage.

Fallon, I. (1988) *The Brothers*, London: Hutchinson.

Fang, T. (2001) 'Culture as a driving force for interfirm adaptation: A Chinese case', *Industrial Marketing Management*, 30: 51–63.

Faris, S. (2007) 'Starbucks vs. Ethiopia', *Fortune*, 5 March, 19–21.

Farivar, C. (2008) 'Laptop project for developing countries hits snag', *NPR*, 23 February; available online http://www.npr.org/templates/story/story.php?storyId=17894663.

Featherstone, M. (1992) *Consumer Culture and Postmodernism*, London: Sage.

Featherstone, M. (1995) *Undoing Culture: Globalization, Postmodernism and Identity*, London: Sage.

Featherstone, M. (2000) 'Archiving cultures', *British Journal of Sociology*, 51 (1): 161–184.

Feeny, A., Vongpatanasin, T. and Soonsatham, A. (1996) 'Retailing in Thailand', *International Journal of Retail and Distribution Management*, 24 (8): 38–44.

Feinberg, R.A. and Meoli, J. (1991) 'A brief history of the mall', *Advances in Consumer Research*, 18: 426–427.

Fendley, A. (1995) *Saatchi and Saatchi the Inside Story*, New York: Arcade Publishing.

Ferber, A.L. (1998) 'Constructing whiteness: The intersections of race and gender in US white supremacist discourse", *Ethnic and Racial Studies* 21 (1): 48–62.

Firat, A.F. and Dholakia, N. (1998) *Consuming People: From Political Economy to Theatres of Consumption*, London: Routledge.

Fine, B. (2006) 'Addressing the consumer', in Trentmann, F. (ed.) *The Making of the Consumer: Knowledge, Power and Identity in the Modern World*, Oxford: Berg, pp. 291–311.

Finkler, K. (2005) 'Family kinship, memory and temporality in the age of the new genetics', *Social Science and Medicine*, 61: 1059–1071.

Finnstrom, S. (2001) 'In and out of culture: Fieldwork in war-torn Uganda', *Critique of Anthropology*, 21 (3): 247–258.

Firat, A.F. and Venkatesh, A. (1995) 'Liberatory postmodernism and the reenchantment of consumption', *Journal of Consumer Research*, 22 (December): 239–267.

Flint, C. (2004) *Spaces of Hate: Geographies of Discrimination and Intolerance in the USA*, London: Routledge.

Fluri, J. and Dowler, L. (2004) 'House bound: Women's agency in white separatist movement' in Flint, C. (ed.) *Spaces of Hate: Geographies of Discrimination and Intolerance in the USA*, London: Routledge, pp. 69–85.

Foner, N. (1997) 'What's new about transnationalism? New York migrants today and at the turn of the century', *Diaspora* (6): 355–75.

Fong, J. and Burton, S. (2006) 'Online-word-of-mouth: A comparison of American and Chinese discussion boards', *Asia Pacific Journal of Marketing and Logistics*, 18 (2): 146–156.

Forster, P.G., Hitchcock, M. and Lyimo, F.F. (2000) *Race and Ethnicity in East Africa*, London: Macmillan.

Fortun, K. and Fortun, M. (2007) 'Editors' introduction to the "Coke Complex"', *Cultural Anthropology*, 22 (4): 616–620.

Foster, D.A. (1992) *Bargaining across Borders*, London: McGraw-Hill.

Foster, G.A. (2003) *Performing Whiteness: Postmodern Re/constructions in the Cinema*, New York: State of University of New York Press.

Fournier, S. (1998) 'Consumers and their brands: Developing relationship theory in consumer research', *Journal of Consumer Research*, 24 (March): 343–373.

Fournier, S., Sensiper, S., McAlexander, J. and Schouten, J. (2000) 'Building a brand community on the Harley-Davidson posse ride', Multimedia case, Cambridge, MA: Harvard Business School Cases.

Fox, K.F. and Kotler, P. (1980) 'The marketing of social causes: The first 10 years', *Journal of Marketing*, 44 (Fall): 24–33.

Franco, J. (1996) 'Globalization and the crisis of the popular', in Salman, T. (ed.) *The Legacy of the Disinherited, Poplar Culture in Latin America: Modernity, Globalization, Hybridity and Authenticity*, Amsterdam: Cedla.

Frank, R. (1974) Editorial, *Journal of Consumer Research*, 1, June.

Frankenberg, R, (1993) *White Women, Race Matters: The Social Construction of Whiteness*, Minneapolis: University of Minnesota Press.

Freake, D. (1995) 'The semiotics of wristwatches', *Time and Society*, 4 (1): 67–90.

Freidberg, S. (2004) *French Beans and Food Scares: Culture and Commerce in an Anxious Age*, Oxford: Oxford University Press.

Freitas, R.F. (1996) *Centres commerciaux: îles urbaines de la post-modernité*, Paris: L'Harmattan.

French, J.D. (2000) 'The missteps of anti-imperialist reason: Bourdieu, Wacquant and Hanchard's *Orpheus and Power*', *Theory, Culture and Society*, 17 (1): 107–128.

Frey, W.H. (1998) 'The diversity myth', *American Demographics*, 20: 38–43.

Friedman, M. (1985) 'The changing language of a consumer society: Brand name usage in popular American novels in the postwar era', *Journal of Consumer Research*, 11 (March) 927–938.

Friese, S. (2000) *Self-concept and Identity in a Consumer Society: Aspects of Symbolic Product Meaning*, Marburg: Tectum.

Friman, M., Garling, T., Millett, B., Mattsson, J. and Johnston, R. (2002) 'An analysis of international business-to-business relationships based on the commitment-trust theory', *Industrial Marketing Management*, 31: 403–409.

Frosh, P. (2007) 'Penetrating markets, fortifying fences: Advertising consumption and violent national conflict', *Public Culture*, 19 (3): 461–482.

Freyre, G. (1959) *New World in the Tropics: The Culture of Modern Brazil*, New York: Knopf.

Funk, J.L. (2005) 'The future of the mobile phone internet: An analysis of technological trajectories and lead users in the Japanese market', *Technology in Society*, 27 (1): 69–83.

Gabaccia, D.R. (2000) *Italy's Many Diasporas*, London: UCL Pess.

Gage, J. (1995) *Colour and Culture: Practice and Meaning from Antiquity to Abstraction*, London: Thames and Hudson.

Gainer, B. and Fischer, E. (1991) 'To buy or not to buy? That is not the question: Female ritual in home shopping', *Advances in Consumer Research*, 18: 597–602.

Gamble, J. (2006) 'Consumers with Chinese characteristics? Local customers in British and Japanese multinational stores in contemporary China', in Trentmann, F. (ed.) *The Making of the Consumer: Knowledge, Power and Identity in the Modern World*, Oxford: Berg, pp. 175–198.

Ganesh, K. and Thakkar, U. (2005) *Culture and the Making of Culture in Contemporary India*, London: Sage.

Gao, Z. (2005) 'Harmonious regional advertising regulation?', *Journal of Advertising*, 34 (3): 75–87.

Geertz, C. (1995) *After the Fact: Two Countries, Four Decades, One Anthropologist*, Cambridge, MA: Harvard University Press.

Geertz, C. (1978) 'The bazaar economy: Information and search in peasant marketing', *Economics and Anthropology*, 68 (2): 28–32.

Geertz, C. (1973) *The Interpretation of Cultures*, Basic Books: New York.

Gentile, M. and Tammaru, T. (2006) 'Housing and ethnicity in the post-Soviet city: Ust'-Kammenogorsk, Kazakhstan', *Urban Studies*, 43 (10): 1757–1778.

Gentry, J.W., Jun, S. and Tansuhaj, P. (1995) 'Consumer acculturation processes and cultural conflict: How generalizable is a North American model for marketing globally?', *Journal of Business Research*, 32: 129–139.

Ger, G. (2005) 'Religion and consumption: The profane sacred', *Advances in Consumer Research*, 32 (1): 79–81.

Ger, G. and Belk, R.W. (1996) 'Cross-cultural differences in materialism', *Journal of Economic Psychology*, 17 (1): 55–77.

Ger, G. and Belk, R.W. (1999) 'I'd like to buy the world a Coke: Consumptionscapes of the "Less Affluent World"', *Journal of Consumer Policy*, 19: 271–304.

Ger, G. and Wilk, R. (2005) 'Religious material culture: Morality, and Aesthetics', *Advances in Consumer Research*, 32: 80–81.

Gerriysen, M., Korzilius, H., van Meurs, F. and Gusbers, I. (2000) 'English in Dutch commercials: Not understood and not appreciated', *Journal of Advertising Research*, 40 (4): 17–31.

Giddens, A. (1984) *The Constitution of Society: Outline of the Theory of Structuration*, Berkeley, CA: University of California Press.

Giddens, A. (1991) *Modernity and Self-Identity*, Cambridge: Polity Press.

Giddens, A. (1995) *Politics, Sociology and Social Theory*, Stanford University Press: Stanford.

Gillespie, K., Riddle, L., Sayre, E. and Sturges, D. (1999) 'Diaspora in homeland investment', *Journal of International Business Studies*, 30 (3): 623–634.

Gilley, B. (1996) 'Lure of the West', *Far Eastern Economic Review*, 159: 70.

Gilly, M.C., Peñaloza, L.N. and Kambara, M. (1998) 'The role of American identity in expatriates' consumer adjustment', *Advances in Consumer Research*, 25: 46.

Giroux, H.A. (1997) 'Racial politics and the pedagogy of whiteness', in M. Hill (ed.) *Whiteness: A Critical Reader*, New York: New York University Press.

Giroux, H.A. and McLaren, P. (1989) *Critical Pedagogy, the State and Cultural Struggle*, Albany: SUNY Press.

Gladney, D.C. (2007) 'Islam in China: Beijing's Hui and Uighur challenge', *Global Dialogue*, 9 (1–2): 89–95.

Glasze, G. and Alkhayyal, A. (2002) 'Gated housing estates in the Arab world: Case studies in Lebanon and Riyadh, Saudi Arabia', *Environment and Planning B: Environment and Design*, 29: 321–336.

Gobineau, J.A. de (1853) *The Inequality of Human Races*, New York: G.P. Putnam.

Golding, H. (1998) 'Racial integration', *Marketing Week*, July 16, 1–4.

Goldman, A. (1974) 'Growth of large food stores in developing countries', *Journal of Retailing*, 50 (2): 50–60.

Goldman, A. (1975/6) 'Stages in the development of the supermarket', *Journal of Retailing*, 51 (4): 49–64.

Goldman, A. (1982) 'Adoption of supermarket shopping in a developing country: The selective adoption phenomenon', *European Journal of Marketing*, 16 (1): 17–26.

Goldman, A., Krider, R. and Ramaswami, S. (1999) 'The persistent competitive advantage of traditional food retailers in Asia: Wet markets' continued dominance in Hong Kong', *Journal of Macromarketing* 19 (2): 126–139.

Goldman, M.I. (1961) 'The marketing structure in the Soviet Union', *Journal of Marketing*, 25 (5): 7–14.

Gomez-Pena, G. (2001) 'The virtual barrio@ the Other frontier (or the Chicago Interneta), in Trend, D. (ed.) *Reading Digital Culture*, Oxford: Blackwell Publishing, pp. 281–286.

Gopalkrishnan, R.I. (1997) 'Comparative marketing: an interdisciplinary framework for institutional analysis', *Journal of International Business Studies*, 28 (3): 531–561.

Gordy, K. (2006) '"Sales + economy + efficiency= revolution"? Dollarization, consumer capitalism, and popular responses in special period Cuba', *Public Culture*, 18 (2):383–411.

Goudge, P. (2003) *The Whiteness of Power: Racism in Third World Development and Aid*, London: Lawrence and Wishart.

Gould, S.J. (1996) *The Mismeasure of Man*, New York: Norton.

Gould, S.J. and Gupta, P.B. (2006) '"Come on down": How consumers view game shows and the product placed in them', *Journal of Advertising*, 35 (1): 65–81.

Gould, S.J., Gupta, P.B. and Grabner-Krauter, S. (2000) 'Product placements in movies: A cross-cultural analysis of Austrian, French and American consumers' attitudes toward this emerging, international promotional medium', *Journal of Advertising*, XXIX (4): 39–49.

Grabosky, P.N. (2005) 'Crime in Cyberspace', in Williams, P. and Vlassis, D. (eds) *Combating Transnational Crime: Concepts, Activities and Responses*, London: Frank Cass, pp. 195–208.

Graham, R.J. (1981) 'The role of perception of time in consumer research', *Journal of Consumer Research*, 7 (March): 335–342.

Grant, I. and O'Donohoe, S. (2007) 'Why young consumers are not open to mobile marketing communication', *International Journal of Advertising*, 26 (2): 223–246.

Gray, B. (2004) *Women and the Irish Diaspora*, London: Routledge.

Green, C.L. (1995a) 'Media exposure's impact on perceived availability and redemption of coupons by ethnic consumers', *Journal of Advertising Research* 35 (2): 56–64.

Green, C.L. (1995b) 'Differential responses to retail sales promotion among African-American and Anglo-American consumers', *Journal of Retailing* 71 (1): 83–92.

Gregson, N. and Crewe, L. (1997) 'The bargain, the knowledge and the spectacle: Making sense of consumption in the space of the car boot sale', *Society and Space: Environment and Planning D*, 15: 87–112.

Grier, S.A. and Brumbaugh, A.M. (1999) 'Noticing cultural differences: Ad meanings created by target and non-target markets', *Journal of Advertising*, XXVIII: 81–93.

Grier, S.A., Brumbaugh, A.M., and Thornton, C.G. (2006) 'Crossover dreams: Consumer responses to ethnic-oriented products', *Journal of Marketing*, 70 (2): 35–51.

Griffin, M., Babin, B.J. and Christensen, F. (2004) 'A cross-cultural investigation of the materialism construct: Assessing the Richens and Dawson's materialism scale in Denmark, France and Russia', *Journal of Business Research*, 57 (8): 893–900.

Griffith, M. and Wolch, J. and Lassiler, U. (2002) 'Animal practices and the racialization of Filipinas in Los Angeles', *Society and Animals*, 10: 221–48.

Griffiths, M. (2003) 'Sex on the internet: Issues, concerns, and implications', in Turow, J. and Kavanaugh, A.L. (eds) *The Wired Homestead*, Cambridge: MIT Press, pp. 261–281.

Grimaud, E. (2005) 'Maps of audiences: Bombay films, the French territory and the making of an "oblique" market', in Assayag, J. and Fuller, C.J. (eds) *Globalizing India: Perspectives from Below*, London: Anthem Press, pp. 165–184.

Grunenberg, C. and Holein, M. (2002) *Shopping: A Century of Art and Consumer Culture*, Berlin: Hatje Cantz Publishers.

Gubar, S. (1997) R*ace Changes: White Skin, Black Face in American Culture*, London: Oxford University Press.

Guirat, R.B. (2007) 'The gender approach to understanding time-saving durables buying: Tunisian women in 2000', Ammi, C. (ed.) *Global Consumer Behavior*, London: ISTE, pp. 87–108.

Gunew, S. (2004) *Haunted Nations: The Colonial Dimensions of Multiculturalisms*, London: Routledge.

Guo, C., Vasquez-Parraga, A.Z. and Wong, Y. (2006) 'An exploratory study of motives for Mexican nationals to shop in the US: More than meets the eye', *Journal of Retailing and Consumer Services*, 13 (5): 351–362.

Gupta, P.B. and Lord, K.R. (1998) 'Product placement in movies: The effect of prominence and mode on audience recall', *Journal of Current Issues and Research in Advertising*, 20 (Spring): 47–59.

Gurol, M. and Servindik, T. (2007) 'Profile of internet café users in Turkey', *Telematics and Informatics*, 24 (1): 59–68.

Hafsi, T. and Farashahi, M. (2005) 'Applicability of management theories to developing countries: A synthesis', *Management International Review*, 45 (4): 483–511.

Hague, E., Giordano, B., and Sebesta, E.H. (2005) 'Whiteness, multiculturalism and nationalist appropriation of the Celtic Culture: The case of the League of the South and the Lega Nord', *Cultural Geographies*, 12 (2): 151–173.

Hale, G.E. (1998) *Making Whiteness: The Culture of Segregation in the South, 1890-1940*, New York: Pantheon Books.

Hall, E.T. (1959) *The Silent Language*, New York: Doubleday.

Hall, S. (1992) 'The rest and the West: Discourse and power', in Hall, S. and Gieben, B. (eds) *Formation of Modernity*, Cambridge: Polity Press.

Hall, S. (2000) 'Old and new identities, old and new ethnicities', in L. Black and J. Solomos (eds) *Theories of Race and Racism*, London: Routledge.

Hall, S. (2002) 'Multiple belonging in a world of multiple identities' in Vertovec, S. and Cohen, R. (eds) *Conceiving Cosmopolitanism*, Oxford: Oxford University Press, pp. 25–31.

Halter, M. (2000) *Shopping for Identity: The Marketing of Ethnicity*, New York: Shocken Books.

Hanna, T. and Palepu, K.G. (2004) 'Globalization and convergence in corporate governance: Evidence from Infosys and the Indian software industry', *Journal of International Business Studies*, 35 (6): 484–507.

Hannerz, U. (1990) 'Cosmopolitans and locals in a world culture', *Theory, Culture and Society*, 7 (June): 237–251.

Hannerz, U. (1992) *Cultural Complexity: Studies in the Social Organization of Meaning*, New York: Columbia University Press.

Hannerz, U. (1996) *Transnational Connections: Culture, People, Places*, London: Routledge.

Hansen, K.T. (1999) 'Second-hand clothing encounters in Zambia: Global discourses, Western commodities, and local histories', *Africa*, 69 (3): 343–363.

Hardin, T.S. (1976) *The Popular Practice of Fraud*, New York: Amo Press.

Harding, T.S. (1976) *The Popular Practice of Fraud*, New York: Amo Press.

Harris, G. (1994) 'International advertising standardization: What do the multinationals actually standardize?, *Journal of International Marketing*, 2 (4): 13–30.

Harris, R. (2003) 'From "black-balling" to "marking": The suburban origin of redlining in Canada, 1930–1950s', *The Canadian Geographer*, 47 (3): 338–350.

Harris, R. and Forrester, D. (2003) 'The suburban origins of redlining: A Canadian case study, 1935–54', *Urban Studies*, 40 (13): 2661–2686.

Harrison, R., Newholm, T. and Shaw, D. (2006) *The Ethical Consumer*, London: Sage.

Hart, S. and Young, R. (2003) 'Introduction', in Hart, S. and Young, R. (eds) *Contemporary Latin American Cultural Studies*, London: Arnold.

Harzig, C. and Juteau, D. (2003) Introduction, in Harzig, C., Juteau, D. and Schmitt, I. (eds) *The Social Construction of Diversity: Recasting the Master Narrative of Industrial Nations*, New York: Berghahn Books, pp. 1–12.

Harzing, A. (2000) 'Cross-national industrial mail surveys: Why do response rates differ between countries', *Industrial Marketing Management*, 29: 243–254.

Haley, A. (1976) *Roots*, London: Vintage.

Harsman, B. (2006) 'Ethnic diversity and spatial segregation in the Stockholm region', *Urban Studies*, 43 (8): 1341–1364.

Hartman, T. (2008) 'On the Ikeaization of France', *Public Culture*, 19 (3): 483–499.

Hassan, L.M., Walsh, G., Shui, E., Hastings, G. and Harris, F. (2007) 'Modeling persuasion in social advertising', *Journal of Advertising*, 36 (2): 15–32.

Hendrickson, C. (1996) 'Selling Guatemala: Maya export products in US mail-order catalogues', Howes, D. (ed.) *Cross-Cultural Consumption: Global markets, local realities*, London: Routledge, pp. 106–124.

Herbig, P. (1995) *Japanese Style*, Westport, CT: Quorum Books.

Heuer, M., Cumming, J.L. and Hutabarat, W. (1999) 'Cultural stability or change among managers in Indonesia?, *Journal of International Business Studies*, 30 (3): 599–610.

Hewer, P. and Brownlie, D. (2007) 'Consumer culture matters: Insights from contemporary representations of coking', *Advances in Consumer Research*, 34: 175–179.

Heyes, C.J. (2007) 'Cosmetic surgery and the televisual makeover: Foucauldian feminist reading', *Feminist Media Studies*, 7 (1): 17–33.

Hibbert, S., Horne, S. and Tagg, S. (2005) 'Charity retailers in competition for merchandise: Examining how consumers dispose of used goods', *Journal of Business Research*, 58 (6): 819–828.

Hill, R.P. and Dhanda, K.K. (2004) 'Globalization and technological achievement: Implications for macromarketing and the digital divide', *Journal of Macromarketing*, 24 (2): 147–155.

Hiller, H.H. and Franz, T.M. (2004) 'New ties, old ties and lost ties: the use of the internet in diaspora', *New Media and Society*, 6 (6): 731–752.

Himanen, P. and Castells, M. (2004) 'Institutional models of the network society: Silicon Valley and Finland, in Castells, M. (ed.) *The Network Society: A Cross Cultural Perspective*, Cheltenham: Edward Elgar, pp. 49–83.

Hirata, J., Fukushima, A., Omuro, T., Shiosaki, M. and Takeda, K. (1961) 'Marketing research practices and problems in Japan', *Journal of Marketing*, 25 (4): 34–37.

Hirschman, E.C. (1981) 'American Jewish Ethnicity'. *Journal of Marketing*, 45 (Summer): 102–10.

Hirschman, E.C. (1985) 'Primitive aspects of consumption in modern American society', *Journal of Consumer Research*, 12 (September): 142–155.

Hirschman, E.C. (1993) 'The consciousness of addiction: Toward a general theory of compulsive consumption', *Journal of Consumer Research*, 19 (Sept): 155–179.

Hirschman, E.C. (2001) 'Ethnicity, racism, and the colonization of consumption', *American Marketing Association Conference Proceedings*, Summer: 236–244.

Hobsbawm, E.J. (1990) *Nations and Nationalism since 1780: Programme, Myth, Reality*, Cambridge: Cambridge University Press.

Hoffman, D.L. and Novak, T.P. (1998) 'Bridging the racial divide on the internet', *Science*, 280 (April 17): 390–391.

Hofstede, G. (1980) *Culture's Consequences: International Differences in Work-related Values*, Beverly Hills, CA: Sage.

Hofstede, G. (1983) 'Dimensions of national cultures in fifty countries andthree regions', in Deregowski, J.B., Dziurawiec, S. and Annis, R.C. (eds) *Expiscations in Cross-cultural Psychology*, Lisse, Netherlands: Swets and Zetlinger, pp. 335–355.

Hofstede, G. (1991) *Cultures and Organizations: Software of the Mind*, London: McGraw-Hill.

Hofstede, G. (2002) 'Dimensions do not exist: A reply to Brendan McSweeney', *Human Relations*, 55 (11): 1355–1361.

Holbrook, M.B. and Lehmann, D.R. (1981) 'Allocating discretionary time: Complementarity among activities', *Journal of Consumer Research*, 7 (March): 395–406.

Holland, J. and Gentry, J.W. (1999) 'Ethnic consumer reaction to targeted marketing: A theory of intercultural accommodation', *Journal of Advertising*, 28: 65–78.

Hollander, S.C. (1974) 'Cosmopolitanism and chauvinism in American retail trade', *Journal of Retailing*, 50 (1): 3–8.

Hollensen, S. (2007) *Global marketing*, Harlow: Prentice Hall.

Holliday, I. (2005) 'Doing business with rights violating regimes corporate social responsibility and Myanmar's military junta', *Journal of Business Ethics*, 61 (4): 329–342.

Holloway, S.L. (2003) 'Outsiders in rural society? Constructions of rurality and nature-society relations in the racialisation of English gypsy-travellers, 1869–1934', *Environment and Planning D: Society and Space*, 21 (6): 695–715.

Holstein, W.J. (2007) 'Why Wal-Mart can't find happiness in Japan', *Fortune*, 6 August, 51–55.

Holt, D.B. (2004) *How Brands Become Icons*, Cambridge, MA: Harvard University Press.

Holt, D.B., Quelch, J. and Taylor, E. (2003) *Managing the Transnational Brand*, Harvard: Harvard University Business School.

Hood, J.N. and Logsdon, J.M. (2002) 'Business ethics in the NAFTA countries: A cross-cultural comparison', *Journal of Business Research*, 55: 883–890.

hooks, B. (1997) 'Representing whiteness in the black imagination', in R. Frankenberg (ed.) *Displacing Whiteness*, London. Duke University Press.

Hooper, B. (2000) 'Globalisation and resistance in post-Mao China: The case of foreign consumer products', *Asian Studies Review*, 24: 439–70.

Hornik, J. and Schlinger, M.J. (1981) 'Allocation of time to the mass media', *Journal of Consumer Research*, 7 (March): 343–355.

Horst, H.A. (2006) 'The blessings and burdens of communication: Cell phones in Jamaican transnational social fields', *Global Networks*, 6 (2): 143–159.

Horst, H. and Miller, D. (2005) 'From kinship to link-up: Cell phones and social networking in Jamaica', *Current Anthropology*, 46 (5): 755–778.

House, R.J., Hanges, P.J., Javidan, M., Dorfman, P. and Gupta, V. (2004) *Culture, Leadership, and Organizations: The GLOBE Study of 62 Societies*, Thousand Oaks, CA: Sage.

Hou, F. (2006) 'Spatial assimilation of racial minorities in Canada's immigrant gateway cities', *Urban Studies*, 43 (7): 1191–1213.

Howell, S. (2003) 'The house as analytic concept: A theoretical overview', in Sparkes, S. *The House in Southeast Asia*, London: Routledge, pp. 16–34.

Hroch, M. (1996) 'From national movement to the fully formed nation: The nation building process in Europe', in Eley, G. and Suny, R.G. (eds) *Becoming National: A Reader*, New York: Oxford University Press, pp. 60–77.

Huang, S. (2004) '"Times" and images of others in an Amis village, Taiwan', *Time and Society*, 13 (2/3): 321–338.

Hung, K., Gu, F.F. and Tse, D.K. (2005) 'Improving media decisions in China: A target ability and cost–benefit analysis', *Journal of Advertising*, 34 (1): 49–63.

Hunter, J.D. and Yates, J. (2002) 'In the vanguard of globalization: The world of American globalizers', in Berger, P.L. and Huntington, S.P. (eds) *Many Globalizations: Cultural Diversity in the Contemporary World*, Oxford: Oxford University Press, pp. 323–358.

Husted, B.W. and Allen, D.B. (2006) 'Corporate social responsibility in the multinational enterprise: strategic and institutional approaches', *Journal of International Business Studies*, 37 (6): 838–849.

Ilbery, B. and Maye, D. (2005) 'Alternative (shorter) food supply chains and specialist livestock products in the Scottish-English borders', *Environment and Planning A*, 37 (5): 823–844.

Ilkucan, A. and Sandikci, O. (2005) 'Gentrification and consumption: An exploratory study', *Advances in Consumer Research*, 32: 474–479.

Inglis, D. and Holmes, M. (2000) 'Toiletry time: defecation, temporal strategies and the dilemmas of modernity', *Time and Society*, 9 (2/3): 223–246.

International Organization for Migration (2000) *World Migration Report 2000*, IOM and the United Nations.

Ishmael, G.S. and Thomas, J.W. (2006) 'Worth a thousand words', *Journal of Advertising Research*, September: 274–278.

Jack, G. and Westwood, R. (2006) 'Postcolonialism and the politics of qualitative research', *Management International Review*, (4): 481–501.

Jackson, P. (1998) 'Constructions of "Whiteness" in the Geographical Imagination', *Area*, 30: 99–106.

Jackson, P. (2004) 'Local consumption cultures in a globalizing world', *Institute of British Geographers*, New Series 29: 165–178.

Jackson, P., Crang, P. and Dwyer, C. (2004) *Transnational Spaces*, London: Routledge.

Jackson II, R.L. and Heckman, S.M. (2002) 'Perceptions of white identity and white liability: An analysis of white student responses to a college campus racial hate crime', *Journal of Communication*, 52 (2): 434–443.

Jackson-Beeck, M. and Robinson, J.P. (1981) 'Television nonviewers: An endangered species', *Journal of Consumer Research*, 7 (March): 356–359.

Jacobs, L., Samli, A.C. and Jedlik, T. (2001) 'The nightmare of international product piracy: Exploring defensive strategies', *Industrial Marketing Management*, 30: 499–509.

Jacobson, M.F. (1998) *Whiteness of a Different Color: European Immigrants and the Alchemy of Race*, Cambridge, MA: Harvard University Press.

Jacoby, J., Szybillo, G.J. and Berning, C.K. (1976) 'Time and consumer behavior: An interdisciplinary overview', *Journal of Consumer Research*, 2 (March): 320–339.

Jae, H. and DelVecchio, D. (2004) 'Decision-making by low-literacy consumers in the presence of point-of-purchase information', *Journal of Consumer Affairs*, 38 (2): 342–54.

Jaffe, E.D. and Martinez, C.R. (1995) 'Mexican consumer attitudes towards domestic and foreign-made products', *Journal of International Consumer Marketing*, 7 (3): 7–27.

Jaffe, E.D. and Tsimerman, A. (2005) 'Business ethics in a transition economy: Will the next Russian generation be any better?', *Journal of Business Ethics*, 62 (1): 87–97.

Jain, S. (2003) *Handbook of Research in International Marketing*, Edward Elgar: Cheltenham.

James, A. (2001) 'Making sense of race and racial classification', *Race and Society* (4): 235–247.

Jamison, D.J. (1999) 'Masks without meaning: Notes on the processes of production, consumption, and exchange in the context of first world-third world tourism', *Journal of Macromarketing*, 19 (1): 8–19.

Javidan, M. and Carl, D.E. (2005) 'Leadership across culture: A study of Canadian and Taiwanese Executives', *Management International Review*, 45 (1): 23–44.

Javidan, M, House, R.J., Dorfman, P. Hanges, P.J. and de Luque, M.S. (2006) 'Conceptualizing and measuring cultures and their consequences: a comparative review of GLOBE's and Hofstede's approaches', *Journal of International Business Studies*, 37 (6): 897–914.

Jenks, C. (1993) *Culture*, London: Routledge.

Jerolmack, C. (2007) 'Animal practices ethnicity and continuity: the Turkish pigeon handlers of Berlin', *American Sociological Review*, 72 (6): 874–894.

Ji, M.F. and McNeal, J.U. (2001) 'How Chinese children's commercials differ from those of the United States: A content analysis', *Journal of Advertising*, 30 (3): 79–92.

Jimeno, M. (2001) 'Violence and social life in Columbia', *Critique of Anthropology*, 21 (3): 221–246.

Johansson, J.K. (1994) 'The sense of "nonsense": Japanese TV advertising', *Journal of Advertising*, XXIII (1): 17–27.

Johnson, E.J. (2001) 'Digitizing consumer research', *Journal of Consumer Research*, 28 (September): 331–336.

Johnson, J.P., Lenartowicz, T. and Apud, S. (2006) 'Cross-cultural competence in international business: Toward a definition and a model', *Journal of International Business Studies*, 37 (4): 525–543.

Johnson, N. (1995) 'Cast in stone: Monuments, geography, and nationalism', *Environment and Planning D: Society and Space*, 13: 51–65.

Johnson-Hanks, J. (2007) 'Women on the market: Marriage, consumption, and the Internet in urban Cameroon', *American Ethnologist*, 34 (4): 642–658.

Jones, G. (2005) *Renewing Unilever: Transformation and Tradition*, Oxford: Oxford University Press.

Jones, G. and Khanaa, T. (2006) 'Bringing history (back) into international business', *Journal of International Business Studies*, 37 (4): 453–468.

Jones, W.H. (2003) 'Over the wall: Experiences with multicultural literacy'. *Journal of Marketing Education*, 25 (3): 231–240.

Joppke, C. and Lukes, S. (1999) *Multicultural Questions*, Oxford: Oxford University Press.

Jung, K. and Au, A.K. (2004) 'Culture's influence on consumer behaviors: Differences among ethnic groups in a multiracial Asian country', *Advances in Consumer Research*, 31: 366–372.

Jupp, V. (2006) *The Sage Dictionary of Social Research*, London: Sage.

Kahle, L.R. and Homer, P.M. (1985) 'Physical attractiveness of the celebrity endorser: A social adaptation perspective', *Journal of Consumer Research*, 11 (March): 954–961.

Kalra, V.S., Kaur, R. and Hutnyk, J. (2005) *Diaspora and Hybridity*, London: Sage.

Kapchan, D.A. (2001) 'Gender on the market in Moroccan women's verbal art: Performative spheres of feminine authority', Seligmann, L.J. (ed.) *Women Traders in Cross-Cultural Perspective*, Stanford: Stanford University Press, pp. 169–184.

Kapfer, J. (2008) *The New Strategic Brands Management*, London: Kogan Page.

Kaplan, M. (2007) 'Fijian water in Fiji and New York: Local politics and a global commodity', *Cultural Anthropology*, 22 (4): 621–639.

Karim, K.H. (2003) *The Media of Diaspora*, London: Routledge.

Kaufman-Scarborough, C. and Lindquist, J.D. (2003) 'Understanding the experience of time scarcity: Linking consumer time-personality and marketplace behavior', *Time and Society*, 12 (2/3): 349–370.

Keegan, W.J. and Schlegelmilch, B.B. (2000) *Global marketing management*, Englewood Cliffs, NJ: Prentice Hall.

Kemper, S. (2003) 'How advertising makes its object', De Waal Malefyt, T. and Moeran, B. (eds) *Advertising Cultures*, Oxford: Berg, pp. 35–54.

Kendall, G. and Wickham, G. (2001) *Understanding Culture: Cultural Studies, Order, Ordering*, London: Sage.

Keniston, K. (2004) 'Introduction: The four digital divides', in Keniston, D. and Kumar, D. (eds) *IT Experience in India: Bridging the Digital Divide*, Sage: New Delhi, pp. 11–36.

Kerrigan, J.E. and Luke, J. (1987) *Management Training Strategies for Developing Countries*, Boulder, CO: Lynne Rienner Publishers.

Khatri, N., Tsang, E.W.K. (2006) 'Cronyism: A cross-cultural analysis', *Journal of International Business Studies*, 37 (1): 61–75.

Khera, I.P. (2001) 'Business ethics east vs. west: Myths and realities', *Journal of Business Ethics*, 30 (1): 29–39.

Kiggundu, M.., Jorgensen, JJ. and Hafsi, T. (1983) 'Administrative theory and practice in developing countries: A synthesis', *Administrative Science Quarterly*, 28: 66–84.

Kilbourne, W.E. (2004) 'Globalization and development: An expanded macromarketing view', *Journal of Macromarketing*, 24 (2): 122–135.

Kim, E. (2002) 'Race sells: Racialized trade cards in 18th-century Britain', *Journal of Material Culture*, 7 (2): 137–165.

King, A.D. (2004) *Spaces of Global Cultures: Architecture, Urbanism, Identity*, London: Routledge.

Kirkman, B.L., Lowe, K.B. and Gibson, C.B. (2006) 'A quarter century of culture's consequences: A review of empirical research incorporating Hofstede's cultural values framework', *Journal of International Business Studies*, 37 (3): 285–320.

Kivisild, T., Rootsi, S., Metspalu, S., Kaldma, K., Parik, J., Metspalu, E., Adojaan, M., Tolk, H-V., Stepanove, V., Golge, M., Usanga, E., Papiha, S.S., Cinnioglu, C., King, R., Cavalli-Sforza, L., Underhill, P.A., Villems, R. (2003) 'The genetic heritage of the earliest settlers persists both in Indian tribal and caste populations', *American Journal of Human Genetics*, (72): 313–332.

Kjeldgaard, D. and Askegaard, S. (2006) 'The glocalization of youth culture: The global youth segment as structures of common difference', *Journal of Consumer Research*, 33 (2): 231–247.

Klaufus, C. (2006) 'Globalization in residential architecture in Cuenca, Ecuador: Social and cultural diversification of architects and their clients', *Environment and Planning D: Society and Space*, 24 (1): 69–89.

Klein, J.G. (2002) 'US versus them, or us versus everyone? Delineating consumer aversion to foreign goods', *Journal of International Business Studies*, 33 (2): 345–363.

Klein, J.G., Ettenson, R., and Morris, M.D. (1998) 'The animosity model of foreign product purchase: An empirical test in the People's Republic of China', *Journal of Marketing*, 62 (January): 89–100.

Klein, J.G., Smith, N.C. and John, A. (2004) 'Why we boycott: Consumer motivations for boycott participation', *Journal of Marketing*, 68 (July): 92–109.

Kleinman, P. (1987) *The Saatchi and Saatchi Story*, London: Weidenfeld and Nicolson.

Klepacki, L.L. (2005) *Avon: Building the World's Premier Company for Women*, New Jersey: John Wiley and Sons Inc.

Kishwar, M. (2001) 'Blackmail, bribes and beatings: Lok Sunwayi of Delhi's street vendors', *Manushi*, 124, May–June.

Knadler, S.P. (2002) *The Fugitive Race: Minority Writer Resisting Whiteness*, Jackson: University of Mississippi Press.

Kobrin, S. J. (2001) 'Territoriality and the governance of cyberspace', *Journal of International Business Studies*, 32 (4): 687–704.

Kofman, E. (2004) 'Family-related migration: A critical review of European studies', *Journal of Ethnic and Migration Studies*, 30 (2): 243–262.

Kolchin, P. (2002) 'Whiteness studies: The new history of race in America', *Journal of American History*, 89 (1): 154–173.

Koser, K. (2003) *New African Diasporas*, London: Routledge.

Koslow, S., Shamdasani, P.N. and Touchstone, E.E. (1994) 'Exploring language effects in ethnic advertising: A sociolinguistic perspective', *Journal of Consumer Research*, 20 (4): 575–585.

Kowinsi, W.S. (1985) *The Malling of America*', New York: William Morrow and Company, Inc., 2005.

Kozinets, R.V. (2002) 'Can consumers escape the market? Emancipatory illuminations from Burning Man', *Journal of Consumer Research*, 29 (1): 20–38.

Kozinets, R.V. (2006) 'Click to connect: Netnography and tribal advertising', *Journal of Advertising Research*, September: 279–289.

Kozinets, R.V. and Handelman, J.M. (2004) 'Adversaries of consumption: Consumer movements, activism, and ideology', *Journal of Consumer Research*, 31 (December): 691–704.

Krotz, E. (1997) 'Anthropologists of the South: Their rise, their silencing, their characteristics', *Critique of Anthropology*, 17 (3): 237–251.

Kumar, A. (2002) *The Black Economy of India*, New Delhi: Penguin Books.

Kumcu, E. and Firat, A.F. (eds) (1988) *Marketing and Development: Towards Broader Dimensions*, London: Jai Press Inc.

Kwok, C.C.Y., Arppan, J. and Folks, W.R. (1994) 'A global survey of international business education in the 1990s', *Journal of International Business Studies*, 25 (3): 605–623.

Kwok, C.C.Y. and Tadesse, S. (2006) 'The MNC as an agent of change for host-country institutions: FDI and corruption', *Journal of International Business Studies*, 37 (6): 767–785.

Kwong, P. (1997) 'Manufacturing ethnicity', *Critique of Anthropology*, 17 (4): 365–387.

Kyle, D. and Koslowski, R. (2001) *Global Human Smuggling: Comparative Perspectives*, London: John Hopkins University Press.

La Ferle, C. and Lee, W. (2005) 'Can English language media connect with ethnic audiences/ethnic minorities' media use and representation perceptions', *Journal of Advertising Research*, March: 140–153.

La Ferle, C. and Edwards, S.M. (2006) 'Product placement: How brands appear on television', *Journal of Advertising*, 35 (4): 65–86.

Ladison-Billing, G. (1994) 'Racialized discourses and ethnic epistemologies', in *Handbook of Qualitative Research*, Denzin, N.L.K. and Lincoln, Y.S. (eds), London: Sage, pp. 257–276.

Laegran, A.S. and Stewart, J. (2003) 'Nerdy, trendy or healthy? Configuring the internet café', *New Media and Society*, 5 (3): 357–377.

Laitin, D.D. (1999) 'National revivals and violence', in Bowen, J.R. and Petersen, R. (eds) *Critical Comparisons in Politics and Culture*, Cambridge: Cambridge University Press, pp. 21–30.

Lambert, D. (2001) 'Liminal figures: poor whites, freedmen, and racial reinscription in colonial Barbados', *Environment and Planning D: Society and Space*, 19: 335–350.

Landau, P.S. and Kaspin, D.D. (2002) *Images and Empires: Visuality in Colonial and Postcolonial Africa*, Berkley: University of California Press.

Landau, P.S. (2002) 'Empires of the visual: Photography and colonial administration in Africa' in Landau, P.S. and Kaspin, D.D. (eds) *Images and Empires: Visuality in Colonial and Postcolonial Africa*, Berkley: University of California Press, pp. 141–171.

Lang, T. and Gabriel, Y. (2006) 'A brief history of consumer activism', in Harrison, R., Newholm, T. and Shaw, D. (eds) *The Ethical Consumer*, London: Sage, pp. 39–54.

Langer, R. and Beckman, S.C. (2005) 'Sensitive research topics: Netnography revisited', *Qualitative Market Research*, 8 (2): 189–203.

Lankshear, C. and McLaren, P.L. (1993) *Critical Literacy: Politics, Praxis, and the Postmodern*, New York: State University of New York Press.

Larkin, M. (1998) 'Global aspects of health and health policy in Third World Countries', in Kiely, R. and Marfleet, P. (eds) *Globalisation and the Third World*, London: Routledge, pp. 91–112.

Laroche, M., Kirpalani, V.H., Pons, F. and Zhou, L. (2001) 'A model of advertising standardization in multinational corporation', *Journal of International Business Studies*, 32 (2): 249–266.

Larsson, J. and Sanne, C. (2005) 'Self-help books on avoiding time shortage', *Time and Society*, 14 (2/3): 213–230.

Lash, S. and Lury, C. (2007) *Global Culture Industry: The Mediation of Things*, Cambridge: Polity Press.

Lash, S. and Urry, J. (1994) *Economies of Signs and Spaces*, London: Sage.

Lassiler, U. and Wolch, J. (2005) 'Changing attitudes towards animals among Chicanas and Latinas in Los Angeles', in Hise, G. and Deverell, W. (eds) *Land of Sunshine: The Environmental History of Metropolitan Los Angeles*, Pittsburgh: University of Pittsburgh Press, pp. 267–87.

Lastovicka, J.L., Bettencourt, L.A., Hughner, R.S. and Kuntze, R.J. (1999) 'Lifestyle of the tight and frugal: Theory and measurement', *Journal of Consumer Research*, 26 (June): 85–98.

Latham, A. (2006) 'Sociality and the cosmopolitan imaginary: national, cosmopolitan and local imaginaries in Auckland, New Zealand', in Binnie, J., Holloway, J.J. and Millington, S., Young, C. (eds) *Cosmopolitan Urbanism*, London: Routledge, pp. 89–111.

Lazer, W., Murata, S. and Kosaka, H. (1985) 'Japanese marketing: Towards a better understanding', *Journal of Marketing*, 49 (Spring): 69–81.

Le Vine, R.A. and Campbell, D.T. (1972) *Ethnocentrism: Theories of Conflict, Ethnic Attitudes, and Group Behaviour*, New York: John Wiley and Sons Inc.

Lavin, M. (1995) 'Creating consumers in the 1930s: Irna Phillips and the radio soap opera', *Journal of Consumer Research*, 22 (June): 75–89.

Leamer, E.E. and Storper, M. (2001) 'The economic geography of the internet age', *Journal of International Business Studies*, 32 (4): 641–665.

Ledeneva, A. (1998) *Russia's Economy of Favours: Blat, Networking and Informal Exchange*, London: Cambridge.

Lee, M. and Faber, R.J. (2007) 'Effects of product placement on on-line games on brand memory', *Journal of Advertising*, 36 (4): 75–90.

Lehtonen, T. (1999) 'Any room for aesthetics? Shopping practices of heavily indebted consumers', *Journal of Material Culture*, 4 (3): 243–262.

Leistikow, N. (2008) 'Indian women criticize 'Fair and Lovely' ideal', *Women's enews*, 22 March, http://www.womensenews.org.

Lemanski, C. (2006) 'Spaces of exclusivity or connection? Linkages between a gated community and its poorer neighbour in a Cape Town master plan development', *Urban Studies*, 43 (2): 397–420.

Lenartowicz, T. and Johnson, J.P. (2002) 'Comparing managerial values in twelve Latin American countries: An exploratory study', *Management International Review* (3): 279–307.

Lenartowicz, T. and Roth, K. (1999) 'A framework for culture assessment', *Journal of International Business Studies*, 30 (4): 781–798.

Lenartowicz, T. and Roth, K . (2001) 'Does subculture within a country matter? A cross-cultural study of motivational domains and business performance in Brazil', *Journal of International Business Studies*, 32 (2): 305–325.

Levine, R. (1997) *A Geography of Time*, New York: Basic Books.

Levine-Rasky, C. (ed.) (2002) *Working Through Whiteness: International Perspectives*, Albany: State University of New York Press.

Ley, D. (2004) 'Transnational spaces and everyday lives', *Transactions of the Institute of British Geographers*, New Series 29: 151–164.

Lie, J. (2001) *Multiethnic Japan*, Cambridge, MA: Harvard University Press.

Lopez, L.E. (2001) 'Literacy and intercultural bilingual education in the Andes', in Olson, D.R. and Torrance, N. (eds) *The Making of Literate Societies*, Oxford: Blackwell Publishers, pp. 201–224.

Lee, H. and Liebenau, J. (2000) 'Time and the Internet at the turn of the Millennium', *Time and Society*, 9 (1): 43–56.

Lenartowicz, T. and Roth, K. (2001) 'Does subculture within a country matter? A cross-cultural study of motivational domains and business performance in Brazil', *Journal of International Business Studies*, 32 (2): 305–325.

Lessinger, J. (2001) 'Inside, outside, and selling on the road: Women's market trading in South India', in Seligmann, L.J. (ed.) *Women Traders in Cross-Cultural Perspective*, Stanford: Stanford University Press, pp. 73–100.

Levitt, T. (1983) 'The globalization of markets', *Harvard Business Review*, 88 (3): 92–102.

Levy, S.J. (2005) 'The evolution of qualitative research in consumer behavour', *Journal of Business Research*, 58 (3): 341–347.

Lichtenstein, N. (2006) 'Wal-Mart: A template for twenty first century capitalism', in Lichtenstein, N. (ed.) *Wal-Mart the face of twenty-first-century capitalism*, London: The New Press, pp. 3–30.

Liff, S. and Laegran, A.S. (2003) 'Cybercafes: debating the meaning and significance of internet access in a café environment', *New Media and Society*, 5 (3): 307–312.

Liff, S. and Steward, F. (2003) 'Shaping e-access in the cybercafe: networks, boundaries and heterotopian innovaton', *New Media and Society*, 5 (3): 313–334.

Light, E. (1997) 'Understanding ethnicity', *Marketing Magazine – Auckland*, 16: 36–42.

Lipson, H.A. and Lamont, D.F. (1969) 'Marketing policy decisions facing international marketers in the less-developed countries', *Journal of Marketing*, 33 (November): 24–31.

Lin, C.A. (2001) 'Cultural values reflected in Chinese and American television advertising', *Journal of Advertising*, XXX (4): 83–94.

Lopez, A.J. (ed.) (2005) *Postcolonial Whiteness: A Critical Reader on Race and Empire*, New York: State University of New York Press.

Love, J.F. (1987) *McDonald's Behind the Arches*, Toronto: Bantam Press.

Lowe, M. and Wrigley, N. (1996) 'Towards the new retail geography', in Wrigley, N. and Lowe, M. (eds) *Retailing, Consumption and Capital: Towards the New Retail Geography*, Harlow: Longman Group Limited, pp. 3–30.

Lubatkin, M.H., Ndiaye, M. and Vengroff, R. (1997) 'The nature of managerial work in developing countries: A limited test of the universalist hypothesis', *Journal of International Business Studies*, 28 (4): 711–733.

Luke, C. and Luke, A. (1998) 'Interracial families: Difference within difference', *Ethnic and Racial Studies*, 21: 728–753.

Luna, D., Peracchio, L.A., and de Juan, M.D. (2002) 'Cross-cultural and cognitive aspects of web site navigation', *Journal of the Academy of Marketing Science*, 30 (4): 397–410.

Luo, Y. (2006) 'Political behavior, social responsibility, and perceived corruption: a structuration perspective', *Journal of International Business Studies*, 37 (6): 747–766.

Luo, Y. and Shenkar, O. (2006) 'The multinational corporation as a multilingual community: Language and organization in a global context', *Journal of International Business Studies*, 37 (3): 321–339.

Lury, C. (1996) *Consumer Culture*, Polity Press: Cambridge.

Lynch, P.D. and Beck, J.C. (2001) 'Profiles of internet buyers in 20 countries: Evidence for region-specific strategies', *Journal of International Business Studies*, 32 (4): 725–748.

Lynch, P.D., Kent, R.J. and Srinivasan, S.S. (2001) 'The global internet shopper: Evidence from shopping tasks in twelve countries', *Journal of Advertising Research*, May–June: 15–23.

Lynn, M., Zinkhan, G.M. and Harris, J. (1993) 'Consumer tipping: A cross-country study', *Journal of Consumer Research*, 20 (3): 478–488.

McCracken, G. (1986) 'Culture and consumption: A theoretical account of the structure and movement of the cultural meaning of consumer goods', *Journal of Consumer Research*, 13 (June): 71–84.

McCracken, G. (1989) 'Who is the celebrity endorser? Cultural foundations of the endorsement process', *Journal of Consumer Research*, 16 (December): 310–321

McFerson, H.M. (2002) *Mixed Blessings*, London: Greenwood Press.

McGuigan, J. (1999) 'Whither cultural studies?', in Aldred, N. and Ryle, M. (eds) *Teaching Culture: The Long Revolution in Cultural Studies*, Leicester: NIACE, pp. 79–94.

McIntyre, A. (1997) *Making Meaning of Whiteness: Exploring Racial Identity with White Teachers*, Albany: State of New York Press.

McLaren, P. (1994) 'White terror and oppositional agency: Towards a critical multiculturalism', in D. T. Goldberg (ed.) *Multiculturalism: A Critical Reader*, Oxford: Blackwell.

McSweeney, B. (2002a) 'Hofstede's model of national cultural differences and their consequences: A triumph of faith- a failure of analysis', *Human Relations*, 55 (1): 89–118.

McSweeney, B. (2002b) 'The essentials of scholarship: A reply to Geert Hofstede', *Human Relations*, 55 (11): 1363–1372.

Maheswaran, D. and Chen, C.Y. (2006) 'Nation equity: Incidental emotions in country-of-origin effects', *Journal of Consumer Research*, 33 (3): 370–376.

Mai, N.T.T., Jung, K., Lantz, G. and Loeb, S.G. (2003) 'An exploratory investigation into impulse buying behaviour in a transitional economy: A study of urban consumers in Vietnam', *Journal of International Marketing*, 11 (2): 13–35.

Maignan, I. and Ralston, D.A. (2002) 'Corporate social responsibility in Europe and the US: Insights from businesses' self-presentations', *Journal of International Business Studies*, 33 (3): 497–514.

Makhotra, N.K., Agarwal, J. and Peterson, M. (1996) 'Methodological issues in cross-cultural marketing research: A state-of-the-art review', *International Marketing Review*, 13: 7–43.

Mallapragada, M. (2006) 'Home, homeland, homepage: belonging and the Indian-American web', *New Media and Society*, 8 (2): 207–227.

Mallapragada, M. (2000) 'The Indian diaspora in the USA and around the web', in Gauntlett, D. (ed.) *Web Studies; Rewiring media studies for the digital age*', London: Arnold, pp. 179–185.

Mangaliso, M.P. (2001) 'Building competitive advantage from ubuntu: Management lessons from South Africa', *Academy of Management Executive*, 15 (3): 23–34.

Manning, P. and Uplisashvili, A. (2007) '"Our Beer": Ethnographic brands in postsocialist Georgia', *American Anthropologist*, 109 (4): 626–641.

Marcus, E. (1961) 'Selling the tropical African market', *Journal of Marketing*, 25 (5): 25–31

Marin, G. and Marin, B.V. (1991) *Research with Hispanic Populations*. London: Sage.

Marinov, M.A. (2007) *Marketing in the Emerging Markets of Islamic Countries*, Basingstoke: Palgrave Macmillan.

Marlatt, G.A., Baer, J.S., Donovan, D.M. and Kivlahan, D.R. (1988) 'Addictive behaviors: Etiology and treatment', *Annual Review of Psychology*, 39: 223–252.

Marschan-Piekkari, R. and Welch, C. (2004) *Handbook of Qualitative Research Methods for International Business*, Edward Elgar: Cheltenham.

Marshall, R.S. and Boush, D.M (2001) 'Dynamic decision-making: A cross-cultural comparison of US and Peruvian export managers', *Journal of International Business Studies*, 32 (4): 873–893.

Martin, J.N., Krizek, R.L., Nakayama, T. and Bradford, L. (1999) 'What do white people want to be called? A study of self-labels for white Americans', in Nakayama, T.L. and Martin, J.N. (eds) *Whiteness: the Communication of Social Identity*, London: Sage.

Mastenbroek, W. (1999) 'Negotiating as emotion management', *Theory, Culture and Society*, 16 (4): 49–73.

May, S. (1999) 'Critical multiculturalism and cultural difference: Avoiding essentialism', in S. May (ed.) *Critical Multiculturalism: Rethinking Multicultural and Antiracist Education*, London: Falmer Press.

Maynard, M.L. (2001) 'Policing transnational commerce: Global awareness in the margins of morality', *Journal of Business Ethics*, 30 (1): 17–27.

Mazzarella, W. (2003) 'Critical publicity/public criticism: Reflections on fieldwork in the Bombay ad world', in De Waal Malefyt, T. and Moeran, B., *Advertising Cultures*, Oxford: Berg, pp. 55–74.

Mazzucato, V., Kabki, M. and Smith, L. (2006) 'Transnational migration and the economy of funerals: Changing practices in Ghana', *Development and Change*, 37 (5): 1047–1072.

Mead, M. (1967) *Cooperation and Competition among Primitive People*, Boston, MA: Beacon.

Mehta, R. and Belk, R.W. (1991) 'Artifacts, identity, and transition: Favorite possessions of Indians and Indian immigrants to the United States', *Journal of Consumer Research*, 17 (March): 398–411.

Mellinger, W.M. (1994) 'Towards a critical analysis of tourism representations', *Annals of Tourism Research*, 21 (4): 756–779.

Mensah, J. (2003) 'Transnationalism and new African immigration to South Africa', *The Canadian Geographer*, 47 (3): 356–357.

Michon, R. and Chebat, J. (2004) 'Cross-cultural mall shopping values and habits: A comparison between English- and French-speaking Canadians', *Journal of Business Research*, 57 (8): 883–892.

Mick, D.G. (1996) 'Are studies of dark side variables confounded by socially desirable responding? The case of materialism', *Journal of Consumer Research*, 23 (September): 106–119.

Mihailova, A. and Schofield, A. (2007) 'More bad news in the post', *The Sunday Times*, 25 November, p. 13.

Miller, D. (2001) *The Dialectics of Shopping*, Chicago: University of Chicago Press.

Miller, D. (2002) 'Coca-cola: A black sweet drink from Trinidad', in Buchli, V. (ed.) *The Material Culture Reader*, Oxford: Berg, pp. 245–263.

Miller, D. (2003) 'Advertising, production and consumption as cultural economy', in De Waal Malefyt, T. and Moeran, B., *Advertising Cultures*, Oxford: Berg, pp. 75–89.

Miller, D., Jackson, P., Thrift, N., Holbrook, B. and Rowlands, M. (1998) *Shopping, Place and Identity*, London: Routledge.

Miller, P. and Rose, N. (1997) 'Mobilizing the consumer: Assembling the subject of consumption', *Theory, Culture and Society*, 14 (1): 1–36.

Miller, D. and Slater, D. (2000) *The Internet: An Ethnographic Approach*, London: Routledge.

Millington, A., Eberhardt, M. and Wilkinson, B. (2005) 'Gift giving, *guanxi* and illicit payments in buyer-supplier relations in China: Analyzing the experience of UK companies', *Journal of Business Ethics*, 57 (3): 255–268.

Minority Groups International (2007) *State of the World's Minorities 2007*, London: Minority Groups International.

Mintzberg, H. (1973) *Managerial Work*, New York: Harper and Row.

Mittelstaedt, J.D. (2002) 'A framework for understanding the relationships between religion and markets', *Journal of Macromarketing*, 22 (1): 6–18.

Moeran, B. (2003) 'Imagining and imagining the Other: Japanese Advertising International, in De Waal Malefyt, T. and Moeran, B., *Advertising Cultures*, Oxford: Berg, pp. 91–112.

Moeran, B. (2004) 'Marketing ethnography: Disciplines and practices', in Garsten, C. and de Montoya, M.L. (eds) *Market Matters: Exploring Cultural Processes in the Global Marketplace*, Basingstoke: Palgrave, pp. 23–45.

Money, B., Shimp, T.A. and Sakano, Y. (2006) 'Celebrity endorsements in Japan and the United States: Is negative information all that harmful', *Journal of Advertising Research*, March: 113–123.

Monga, Y.D. (2000) 'Dollars and lipstick: The United States through the eyes of African women', *Africa*, 70 (2): 192–207.

Morris, M.H., Brunyee, J. and Page, M. (1998) 'Relationship marketing in practice: Myths and realities', *Industrial Marketing Management*, 27: 359–371.

Morrison, T. (1992) *Playing in the Dark: Whiteness and the Literary Imagination*, Cambridge, MA: Harvard University Press.

Mouer, R. (2004) 'Globalization and Japan after the bubble', in Davies, G. and Nyland, C. (eds) *Globalization in the Asian Region*, Cheltenham: Edward Elgar, pp. 164–184.

Moulettes, A. (2007) 'The absence of women's voices in Hofstede's *Cultural Consequences*;: A postcolonial reading', *Women in Management Review*, 22 (6): 443–455.

Muk, A. (2007) 'Consumers' intensions to opt in to SMS advertising: A cross-national study of young Americans and Koreans', *International Journal of Advertising*, 26 (2): 177–198.

Mukhija, V. (2003) *Squatter as Developers: Slum Redevelopment in Mumbai*, Aldershot: Ashgate Publishing Limited.

Mukhopadhyay, B. (2006) 'Cultural studies and politics in India today', *Theory, Culture and Society*, 22 (7–8): 279–292.

Murdie, R.A. (1991) 'Local strategies in resale home financing in the Toronto housing market', *Urban Studies*, 28 (3): 465–483.

Murray, J.B. (2002) 'The politics of consumption: A re-inquiry on Thompson and Haytko's (1997) "Speaking of Fashion"', *Journal of Consumer Research*, 29 (3): 427–441.

Mwesige, P.G. (2004) 'Cyber elites: a survey of internet café users in Uganda', *Telematics and Informatics*, 21 (1): 83–101.

Mycoo, M. (2006) 'The retreat of the upper and middle classes to gated communities in the poststructural adjustment era: The case of Trinidad', *Environment and Planning A*, 38: 131–148.

Nakamura, L. (2001) 'Race in/for cyberspace: Identity tourism and racial passing on the internet', in Trend, D. (ed.) *Reading Digital Culture*, Oxford: Blackwell Publishing Limited, pp. 226–235.

Nakamura, L. (2004) 'Interrogating the digital divide: The political economy of race and commerce in new media', in Howard, P.N. and Jones, S. (eds) *Society oOnline: The Internet in Context*, London: Sage, pp. 71–84.

Nakashima, C.L. (1996) 'Voices from the movement: Approaches to multiraciality', in M. Root (ed.) *The Multiracial Experience: Racial Borders as the New Frontier*, Sage Publications, Thousand Oaks, California.

Nakayama, T.L. and Krizek, R.L. (1999) 'Whiteness as a strategic rhetoric', in Nakayama, T.L. and Martin, J.N. (eds) *Whiteness: the Communication of Social Identity*, London: Sage.

Nakazawa, D.J. (2003) *Does Anybody Else Look Like Me?*, Cambridge, MA: Da Capo Lifelong Books.

Narayan, U. (2000) 'Undoing the "package picture" of culture', *Signs*, 25 (4): 1083–1086.

Nash, J. (2007) 'Consuming interest: Water, rum and Coca-cola from ritual propitiation to corporate expropriation in highland Chiapas Mexico', *Cultural Anthropology*, 22 (4): 621–639.

Nava, M. (1997) 'Modernity's disavowal: Women, the city and the department store', in Falk, P. and Campbell, C. (eds) *The Shopping Experience*, London: Sage, pp. 56–91.

Nava, M. (2002) 'Cosmopolitan modernity: Everyday imaginaries and the register of difference', *Theory, Culture and Society*, 19 (1–2): 81–99.

Nelson, M.R. and Otnes, C. (2005) 'Exploring cross-cultural ambivalence: A netnography of intercultural wedding message boards', *Journal of Business Research*, 58 (1): 89–95.

Nelson, M.R., Deshpande, S., Devanathan, N. and Lakshmi, C.R. (2005) 'If the table for McWorld has been set by Hollywood, What is served by Bollywood', *Advances in Consumer Research*, 33 (1): 473.

Nelson, M.R., Yaros, R.A. and Keum, H. (2006) 'Examining the influence of telepresence on spectator and player processing of real and fictitious brands in a computer game', *Journal of Advertising*, 35 (4): 87–100.

Nevid, J.S. and Sta Maria, N.S. (1999) 'Multicultural issues in qualitative research', *Psychology and Marketing*, 16: 305–325.

Ng, S.I., Lee, J.A., and Soutar, G.N. (2007) 'Hofstede's and Schwartz's value frameworks congruent?', *International Marketing Review*, 24 (2): 164–80.

Nguyen, A., Heeler, R.M. and Taran, Z. (2007) 'High-low context cultures and price-ending practices', *Journal of Product and Brand Management*, 16 (3): 206–214.

Nordstrom, C. (2000) 'Shadows and sovereigns', *Theory, Culture and Society*, 17 (4): 35–54.

Norwood, B.J.S. (1961) 'An 18th century plan for business education', *Journal of Marketing*, 26 (6): 52–55.

Nuttall, S. (2006) 'The politics of the emergent cultural studies in South Africa', *Theory, Culture and Society*, 22 (7–8): 263–278.

O'Barr, W.M. (1994) *Culture and the Ad: Exploring Otherness in the World of Advertising*, Boulder: Westview Press.

O'Connor, A. (2008) 'Tata Nano: World's cheapest new car is unveiled in India', *The Times*, 11 January.

Office of Utilities Regulation (2004) *Towards a Universal Access Obligation for Telecommunications Services in Jamaica*, Kingston: Jamaica.

O'Hare, J. (1998) 'Managing multiple race data', *American Demographics*, 20: 42–44.

Okazaki, S. and Taylor, C.R. (2008) 'What is SMS advertising and why do multinationals adapt it? Answers from an empirical study in European markets?', *Journal of Business Research*, 61 (1): 4–12.

Okazaki, S., Taylor, C.R. and Zou, S. (2006) 'Advertising standardization's positive impact on the bottom line', *Journal of Advertising*, 35 (3): 17–33.

Okechuku, C. and Onyemah, V. (1999) 'Nigerian consumer attitudes toward foreign and domestic products', *Journal of International Business Studies*, 30 (3): 611–622.

Olsen, B. (1995) 'Consuming Rastafari: Ethnographic research in context and meaning', *Advances in Consumer Research*, 22: 481–485.

Olson, D.R. and Torrance, N. (2001) *The Making of Literate Societies*, Oxford: Blackwell Publishing.

Olumide, J. (2002) *Raiding the Gene Pool: The Social Construction of Mixed Race*, London: Pluto Press.

Ong, A. (2000) 'Graduated sovereignty in South-East Asia, *Theory, Culture and Society*, 17 (4): 55–75.

Organization for Economic Development (1999) *Default Language*, Paris: OECD.

Oropesa, R.S. (1993) 'Female labor force participation and time-saving household technology: A case study of the microwave from 1978 to 1989', *Journal of Consumer Research*, 19 (1): 567–594.

Osman, K.M. and Suliman, M. (1996) 'Spatial and cultural dimensions of the houses of Omdurman, Sudan', *Human Relations*, 49 (4): 395–428.

Oswald, L.R. (1999) 'Culture swapping: Consumption and the ethnogenesis of middle-class Haitian immigrants', *Journal of Consumer Research*, 21 (June): 32–54.

Otnes, C., Lowrey, T.M. and Kim, Y.C. (1993) 'Gift selection for easy and difficult recipients: A social roles interpretation', *Journal of Consumer Research*, 20 (2): 229–244.

Ouellet, J. (2007) 'Consumer racism and its effects on domestic cross-ethnic product purchase: An empirical test in the United States, Canada, and France', *Journal of Marketing*, 71 (1): 113–128.

Oushakine, S.A. (2000) 'The quantity of style: Imaginary consumption in the New Russia', *Theory, Culture and Society*, 17 (5): 97–120.

Oyelaran-Oyeyinka, B. and Nyaki Adeya, C. (2004) 'Internet access in Africa: Empirical evidence from Kenya and Nigeria', *Telematics and Informatics*, 21 (1): 67–81.

Oza, R. (2001) 'Showcasing India: Gender, geography, and globalization', *Signs: Journal of Women in Culture and Society*, 26 (4): 1066—1095.

Ozaki, R. and Lewis, J.R. (2006) 'Boundaries and the meaning of social space: A study of Japanese house plans', *Environment and Planning D: Society and Space*, 24 (1): 91–104.

Ozden, C. and Schiff, M. (2006) *International Migration, Remittances and the Brain Drain*, Basingstoke: Palgrave Macmillan.

Paasi, A. (2005) 'Globalisation, academic capitalism, and the uneven geographies of international journal publishing spaces', *Environment and Planning A*, 37 (5): 769–789.

Packard, V. (1957) *The Hidden Persuaders*, Harmondsworth: Penguin.

Packard, V. (1959) *The Status Seekers*, Harmondsworth: Penguin.

Packard, V. (1960) *The Wastemakers*, Harmondsworth: Penguin.

Paik S. (2000) 'The formation of the united lineage in Korea', *The History of the Family: An International Quarterly*, 5 (1): 75–89.

Panagakos, A.N. and Horst, H.A. (2006) 'Return to cyberia: technology and the social worlds of transnational migrants', *Global Networks*, 6 (2): 109–124.

Paolillo, J.C. (2007) 'How much multilingualism? Language diversity on the internet', in Danet, B. and Herring, S.C. (eds) *The Multilingual Internet: Language, Culture, and Communication Online*, Oxford: Oxford University Press, pp. 408–430.

Parekh, B. (2000) *Rethinking Multiculturalism: Cultural Diversity and Political Theory*, Basingstoke: Macmillan.

Parker, D. and Song, M. (2001) *Rethinking Mixed Race*, London: Pluto Press.

Parloff, R. (2007) 'China's newest export: Lawsuits', *Fortune*, 23 July, p. 17.

Pastina, A.C. (2006) 'Product placement in Brazilian telenovelas: Selling soaps and social causes', *Advances in Consumer Research*, 33: 135–136.

Pels, J., Brodie, R.J. and Johnston, W.J. (2004) 'Benchmarking business to business marketing practices in emerging and developed economies: Argentina compared to the USA and New Zealand', *Journal of Business and Industrial Marketing*, 19 (6): 386–396.

Peñaloza, L. (1994) 'Atravesando fronteras/border crossings: A critical ethnographic exploration of the consumer acculturation of Mexican immigrants'. *Journal of Consumer Research* 21 (June): 32–42.

Peñaloza, L. (2000) 'Have we come a long way, baby? Negotiating a more multicultural feminism in the marketing academy in the USA', in Catterall, M., Maclaran, P., Stevens, L., *Marketing and Feminism*, London: Routledge.

Peñaloza, L. (2001) 'Consuming the American west: Animating cultural meaning and memory at a stock show and rodeo', *Journal of Consumer Research*, 28 (December): 369–398.

Peñaloza, L. and Gilly, M.C. (1999) 'Marketer acculturation: The changer and the changed', *Journal of Marketing* 63: 84–104.

Pendakur, M. (2003) *Indian Popular Cinema: Industry, Ideology and Consciousness*, New Jersey: Hampton Press Inc.

Penn, R. (2000) 'British population and society in 2025: Some conjectures'. *Sociology* 34 (1): 5–18.

Pepper, D. (2007) 'Matchmaking Indian-style', *Fortune*, 19 March, 14–15.

Perkins, M. (1998)'Timeless cultures: The "dreamtime" as colonial discourse', *Time and Society*, 7 (2): 335–351.

Perrons, D. (2004) *Globalization and Social Change: People and Places in a Divided World*, London: Routledge.

Pervan, S.J. and Martin, B.A.S. (2006) 'Soap operas in New Zealand and the US: Product placement strategy and consumption imagery', *Advances in Consumer Research*, 33: 134–137.

Pfeiffer, K. (2003) *Race Passing and American Individualism*, Amherst and Boston: University of Massachusetts Press.

Philo, C. and Wilbert, C. (2000) *Animal Spaces, Beastly Places*, Routledge: New York.

Pieke, F.N., Van Hear, N. and Lindley, A. (2007) 'Beyond control? The mechanics and dynamics of "informal" remittances between Europe and Africa', *Global Networks*, 7 (3): 348–366.

Piekkari, R. and Welch, C. (2006) 'Guest editors' introduction to the focused issue: Qualitative research methods in international business', *Management International Review* (4): 391–396.

Pieterse, J.N. (2002) 'Globalization as hybridization', in Featherstone, M., Lash, S. and Robertson, R. (eds) *Global Modernities*, London: Sage, pp. 45–68.

Piron, F. (2002) 'International shopping and ethnocentrism', *European Journal of Marketing*, 36 (1–2): 189–210.

Polegato, R. and Bjerke, R. (2006) 'The link between cross-cultural value associations and liking: The case of Benetton and its advertising', *Journal of Advertising Research*, September: 263–272.

Pollay, R.W., Lee, J.S. and Carter-Whitney, D. (1992) 'Separate, but not equal: Racial segmentation in cigarette advertising', *Journal of Advertising*, XXI (1): 45–71.

Polonsky, M.J. and Hyman, M.R. (2007) 'A multiple stakeholder perspective on responsibility in advertising', *Journal of Advertising*, 36 (2): 5–14.

Portes, A., Guarnizo, L. and Landolt, P. (1999) 'The study of transnationalism: Pitfalls and promise of an emergent research field', *Ethnic and Racial Studies*, 22 (2): 217–237.

Poster, M. (1995) *The Second Media Age*, Cambridge, MA: Polity Press.

Pyong, G.M., and Kim, R. (2000) 'Formation of ethnic and racial identities: Narratives by young Asian-American professionals', *Ethnic and Racial Studies*, 23: 735–760.

Poster, M. (1998) 'Virtual ethnicity: Tribal identity in an age of global communications', in Jones, S.G. (ed.) *Cybersociety 2.0*, London: Sage, pp. 184–211.

Potter, R.B. and Phillips, J. (2006) 'Both black and symbolically white: The "Bajan-Brit" return migrant as post-colonial hybrid', *Ethnic and Racial Studies*, 29 (5): 901–927.

Poulsen, M. and Johnston, R. (2006) 'Ethnic residential segregation in England: Getting the right message across', *Environment and Planning A*, 38 (12): 2195–2199.

Poulter, S. (2008) 'Treasure island UK', *Daily Mail*, 30 January, p. 28.

Prahalad, C. and Hammond, A. (2002) 'Serving the world's poor profitably', *Harvard Business Review*, September: 48–55.

Prasso, S. (2007) 'India's pizza wars', *Fortune*, 1 October, 31–34.

Prendergast, M. (2000) *For God, Country and Coca-Cola*, London: Thomson.

Price, L.L., Arnould, E.J. and Curasi, C.F. (2000) 'Older consumers' disposition of special possessions', *Journal of Consumer Research*, 27 (September): 179–201.

Pringle, H. (2004) *Celebrity Sells*, London: John Wiley and Sons Ltd.

Pryer, J. (2003) *Poverty and Vulnerability in Dhaka Slums*, Ashgate: Aldershot.

Qiu, J.L. (2004) 'The internet in China: Technologies of freedom in a Satist society', in Castells, M. (ed.) *The Network Society: A Cross Cultural Perspective*, Cheltenham: Edward Elgar, pp. 99–124.

Rajan, G. (2006) 'Constructing-contesting masculinities: Trends in South Asian cinema', *Signs: Journal of Women in Culture and Society*, 31 (4): 1099–1124.

Ralston, D.A. , Van Tang, N. and Napier, N.K. (1999) 'A comparative study of the work values of North and South Vietnamese managers', *Journal of International Business Studies*, 30 (4): 655–672.

Rao, M. (2007) 'Bringing the net to the masses: Cybercafes in Latin America', available online at http://www.cybersociology.com/files/4_CyberCafesLatinAmerica.html (accessed 10 October 2007).

Rao, S. (2002a) 'Introduction: The cyberpath to development in some Asian countries', in Rao, S and Klopfenstein, B.C. (eds) *Cyberpath to Development in Asia*, Westport: Praeger, pp. 1–13.

Rao, S. (2002b) 'The skills route to cyberspace: India's internet experience', in Rao, S and Klopfenstein, B.C. (eds) *Cyberpath to Development in Asia*, Westport: Praeger, pp. 85–105.

Rapport, N. and Dawson, A. (1998) *Migrants of Identity*, Oxford: Berg.

Rashid, M.Z.A. and Ho, J.A. (2003) 'Perceptions of business ethics in a multicultural community: The case of Malaysia', *Journal of Business Ethics*, 43 (1/2): 75–87.

Raybeck, D. (1992) 'The coconut-shell clock: Time and cultural identity', *Time and Society*, 1 (3): 323–340.

Reed, J. and Simon, B. (2008) 'Honda disputes cheap car logic', *Financial Times*, 14 January, p. 22.

Renan, E. (1990) 'What is a nation?' in Bhabha, H.K. (ed.) *Nation and Narration*, London: Routledge, pp. 8–22.

Renne, E.P. (2007) 'Mass producing food traditions for West Africans abroad', *American Anthropologist*, 109 (4): 616–625.

Rex, J. (1994) 'Ethnic mobilisation in multi-cultural societies', in Rex, J. and Drury, B. (eds) *Ethnic Mobilisation in a Multi-cultural Europe*, Avebury: Aldershot, pp. 3–12.

Rex, J. (1996) 'National identity in the demographic multi-cultural state', *Sociological Research Online* 1 (2); http://www.socresoline/1/4/rex.html.

Riano, Y. and Wastl-Walter, D. (2006) 'Immigration policies, state discourses on foreigners, and the politics of identity in Switzerland', , *Environment and Planning A*, 38 (9): 1693–1713.

Ribeiro, G.L. (2006) 'World anthropologies: Cosmopolitics for a new global scenario in anthropology', *Critique of Anthropology*, 26 (4): 363–386.

Rice, R.C. and Sulaiman, I.F. (2004) 'Globalization and the Indonesian economy: Unrealized potential, in Davies, G. and Nyland, C. (eds) *Globalization in the Asian Region*, Cheltenham: Edward Elgar, pp. 80–91.

Richards, G. (1998) 'Time for a holiday: Social rights and international tourism consumption', *Time and Society*, 7 (1): 145–160.

Richins, M.L. (1994) 'Valuing things: The public and private meanings of possessions', *Journal of Consumer Research*, 21 (December): 504–521.

Richins, M.L. and Dawson, S. (1992) 'A consumer values orientation for materialism and its measurement: Scale development and validation', *Journal of Consumer Research*, 19 (December): 303–316.

Ricks, D.A. (1993) *Blunder in International Business*, Oxford: Blackwell Publishers Limited.

Ricks, D.A., Arpan, J.S. and Fu, M.Y. (1974) 'Pitfalls in advertising overseas', *Journal of Advertising Research*, 14 (6): 47–51.

Rindfleisch, A., Burroughs, J.E. and Denton, F. (1997) 'Family structure, materialism, and compulsive consumption', *Journal of Consumer Research*, 23 (March): 312–325.

Ritson, M. (2008) 'Panda's prowess is a lesson to us all', *Marketing*, 5 March, p. 25.

Ritzer, G. (1993) *The MacDonaldization of Society*, Thousand Oaks, CA: Pine Forge Press.

Ritzer, G. (1999) *Enchanting a Disenchanted World: Revolutionizing the Means of Consumption*, Thousand Oaks, CA: Pine Forge Press.

Ritzer, G. (2004) *The Globalization of Nothing*, London: Sage.

Robertson, J. (1997) 'Empire of nostalgia: Rethinking "internationalization" in Japan today', *Theory, Culture and Society*, 14 (4): 97–122.

Robertson, R. (1990) 'Mapping the global condition: Globalization as the central concept', in Featherstone, M. (ed.) *Global Culture: Nationalism, Globalization and Modernity*, London: Sage.

Robertson, R. (2002) 'Glocalization: Time–space and homogeneity–heterogeneity', in Featherstone, M., Lash, S. and Robertson, R. (eds) *Global Modernities*, London: Sage, pp. 25–44.

Robin, D.P. and Reidenbach, R.E. (1987) 'Social responsibility, ethics and marketing strategy: Closing the gap between concept and application', *Journal of Marketing*, January: 44–58.

Robinson, C. (1996) 'Asian culture: The marketing consequences', *Journal of the Market Research Society*, 38 (1): 55–62.

Rockhill, K. (1993) 'Gender, language and the politics of literacy', in Street, B. (ed.) *Cross-cultural Approaches to Literacy*, Cambridge: Cambridge University Press, pp. 156–175.

Rockquemore, K.A. (1998) 'Between black and white: Exploring the biracial experience', *Race and Society* 1 (2): 197–212.

Rodriguez, P., Siegel, D.S., Hillman, A. and Eden, L. (2006) 'Three lenses on the multinational enterprise: Politics, corruption, and corporate social responsibility', *Journal of International Business Studies*, 37 (6): 733–746.

Roediger, D.R. (1991) *The Wages of Whiteness: Race and the Making of the American Working Class*, London: Verso.

Roediger, D.R. (1994) *The Abolition of Whiteness. Essays on Race, Politics, and Working Class History*, London: Verso.

Roediger, D.R. (1998) *Black on White: Black Writers on What it Means to be White*, New York: Schocken Books.

Rofe, M.W. (2003) 'I want to be global: Theorizing the gentrifying class as an emergent elite global community', *Urban Studies*, 40: 2511–2526.

Rogers, H., Ghauri, P.N. and George, K.L. (2005) 'The impact of market orientation on the internationalization of retailing firms: Tesco in Eastern Europe', *International Review of Retail Distribution and Consumer Research*, 15 (1): 53–74.

Rook, D. (1985) 'The ritual dimension of consumer behavior', *Journal of Consumer Research*, 12 (Dec): 251–264.

Root, M. (ed.) (1994) *Racially Mixed People in America*, Thousand Oaks, CA: Sage Publications.

Root, M. (ed.) (1996) *The Multiracial Experience: Racial Borders as the New Frontier*, , Thousand Oaks, CA: Sage Publications.

Rose, M. (1993) *Authors and Owners: The invention of Copyright*, Cambridge, MA: Harvard University Press.

Roseman, C.C., Laux, H.D. and Thieme, G. (1996) *EthniCity*, Maryland: Rowman and Littlefield Publishers.

Rosenthal, A. (2004) 'Visceral culture: Blushing and the legibility of whiteness in eighteenth-century British portraiture', *Art History*, 27 (4): 563–592.

Rossiter, J.R. and Chan, A.M. (1998) 'Ethnicity in business and consumer behavior', *Journal of Business Research*, 42: 127–134.

Roux, D. and Korchia, M. (2006) 'I am what I wear? An exploratory study of symbolic meanings associated with second hand clothing', *Advances in Consumer Research*, 33: 28–35.

Rowley, T. and Berman, S. (2000) 'A brand new brand of corporate social performance', *Business and Society*, 39 (4): 397–418.

Rugimbana, R. and Nwankwo, S. (2003) *Cross-Cultural Marketing*, London: Thomson Learning.

Russell, D.W. (2007) 'Cultural identity salience as a catalyst of consumer resistance', *Advances in Consumer Research*, 34: 149.

Ryan, M. (1990) *Contemporary Soviet Society: A Statistical Handbook*, Aldershot: Edward Elgar.

Saad, G., Gill, T. and Nataraajan, R. (2005) 'Are later borns more innovative and nonconforming consumers than first borns? A Darwinian perspective', *Journal of Business Research*, 58 (7): 902–909.

Sadh, A. and Tangirala, S. (2003) 'The rhetoric and reality of marketing in India', in Kitchen, P.J. (ed.) *The Rhetoric and Reality of Marketing: An International Managerialist Approach*, Basingstoke: Palgrave Macmillan, pp. 146–174.

Said, E.W. (1994) *Culture and Imperialism*, New York: Vintage Books.

Sajor, E.E. (2003) 'Globalization and the urban property boom in Metro Cebu, Philippines', *Development and Change*, 34 (4): 713–741.

Salacuse, J.W. (1991) *Making Global Deals*, London: Times Business.

Samiee, S., Jeong, I., Pae, J.H. and Tai, S. (2003) 'Advertising standardization in multi-national corporations: The subsidiary perspective', *Journal of Business Research*, 56 (8): 613–626.

Sandikci, O. (2001) 'Mysterious sights: Consumption creolization and identity construction in a postmodern world', Special Session Summary, *Advances in Consumer Research*, 28: 143–5.

Sandikci, O. and Ger, G. (2002) 'In-between modernities and postmodernities: Theorizing Turkish consumptionscapes', *Advances in Consumer Research*, 29: 465–470.

Sandikci, O. and Ger, G. (2006) 'Representing the Islamist consumer: Transformation of the market', Special Session Summary, *Advances in Consumer Research*, 33: 459–60.

Sandor, G. and Larson, J. (1994) 'The "other" Americans'. *American Demographics*, 16 (6): 36–42.

Sanyal, R. (2005) 'Determinants of bribery in international business: The cultural and economic factors', *Journal of Business Ethics*, 59 (1/2): 139–145.

Saporito, B. (1994) 'Behind the tumult at P & G', *Fortune*, 7 March, 74–82.

Sar, S. (2007) 'Comparative content analysis of Thai and Vietnamese ads, 1994 and 2004', *Advances in Consumer Research*, 34: 428–433.

Sarwono, S.S. and Armstrong, W. (2001) 'Microcultural differences and perceived ethical problems: An international perspective', *Journal of Business Ethics*, 31 (1): 41–56.

Sassatelli, R. and Scott, A. (2001) 'Novel food, new markets and trust regimes: Responses to the erosion of consumers' confidence in Austria, Italy, and the UK', *European Societies*, 3: 213–244.

Sassen, S. (1991) *The Global City. New York, London, Tokyo*, Princeton: Princeton University Press.

Sassen, S. (2000) 'Digital networks and the State: Some governance questions', *Theory, Culture, and Society*, 17 (4): 19–33.

Schaefer, D.R. and Dillman, D.A. (1998) 'Development of a standard email methodology: Results of an experiment', *Public Opinion*, 62 (3): 378–390.

Schaeffer-Grabiel, F. (2005) 'Planet-love.com: Cyberbrides in the Americas and the transnational routes of US masculinity', *Signs*, 31 (2): 327–345.

Schau, H.J. and Gilly, M.C. (2003) 'We are what we post? The presentation of self in personal webspace', *Journal of Consumer Research*, 30 (3): 385–404.

Schech, S. and Haggis, J. (1998) 'Postcolonialism, identity, and location: Being white Australian in Asia', *Environment and Planning D: Society and Space*, 16: 615–629.

Schelling, V. (1998) 'Globalisation, ethnic identity and popular culture in Latin America', in Kiely, R. and Marfleet, P. (eds) *Globalisation and the Third World*, London: Routledge, pp. 141–162.

Scherhorn, G., Reisch, L.A. and Raab, L.A. (1990) 'Addictive buying in West Germany: An empirical investigation, *Journal of Consumer Policy*, 13: 155–189.

Schindler, R.M. and Kibarian, T.M. (2001) 'Image communicated by the use of 99 endings in advertised prices', *Journal of Advertising*, XXX (4): 95–99.

Schmidt, P.R. and Mosenthal, P.B. (2001) *Reconceptualizing Literacy in the New Age of Multiculturalism and Pluralism*, Connecticut: Information Age Publishing.

Schmitt, B.H., Pan, Y. and Tavassoli, N.T. (1994) 'Language and consumer memory: The impact of linguistic differences between Chinese and English', *Journal of Consumer Research*, 21 (4): 419–431.

Schouten, J.W. and McAlexander, J. (1995) 'Subcultures of consumption: An ethnography of the New Bikers', *Journal of Consumer Research*, 22 (June): 43–61.

Schroeder, J.E. (2002) *Visual Consumption*, London: Routledge.

Schutte, H. and Ciarlante, D. (1998) *Consumer Behaviour in Asia*, Basingstoke: Macmillan Press.

Schwartz, S.H. (1992) 'Universals in the content and structure of values: Theoretical advances and empirical tests in 20 countries', *Advances in Experimental Social Psychology*, 25: 1–65.

Schwartz, S.H. (1994) 'Beyond individualism/collectivism: New cultural dimensions of values', in Kim, U., Triandis, H.C., Kagitcibasi, C., Choi, S.C. and Yoon, G. (eds) *Individualism and Collectivism: Theory, Method and Applications*, Thousand Oaks, CA: Sage, pp. 85–119.

Schwartz, S.H. (1999) 'Cultural value differences: some implications for work', *Applied Psychology: An International Review*, 48: 23–48.

Schwartz, S.H. and Ros, M. (1995) 'Values in the West: A theoretical and empirical challenge to the individualism–collectivism cultural dimension', *World Psychology*, 1 (2): 91–122.

Scully, E. (2001) 'Pre-cold war traffic in sexual labour and its foes: Some contemporary lessons', in Kyle, D. and Koslowski, R. (eds) *Global Human Smuggling: Comparative Perspectives*, London: John Hopkins University, pp. 74–106.

Seabrook, J. (2001) 'The tree of me', *The New Yorker*, 26 March, 58–71.

Sebenius, J.K. (2002) 'The hidden challenges of cross-border negotiations', *Harvard Business Review*, March, 76–85.

Segrave, K. (2004) *Product Placement in Hollywood Films: A History*, London: McFarland and Company.

Seligmann, L.J. (1993) 'Between worlds of exchange: Ethnicity among Peruvian market women', *Cultural Anthropology*, 8 (2): 187–213.

Seligmann, L.J. (2001) *Women Traders in Cross-Cultural Perspective*, Stanford: Stanford University Press.

Seshadri-Cooks, K. (2000) *Desiring Whiteness: A Lacanian Analysis of Race*, London: Routledge.

Shabbir, H. and Thwaites, D. (2007) 'The use of humor to mask deceptive advertising', *Journal of Advertising*, 36 (2): 75–86.

Shanahan, K.J. and Hopkins, C.D. (2007) 'Truths, half-truths and deception', *Journal of Advertising*, 36 (2): 33–48.

Shank, R.C. and Abelson, R.P (1979) 'Scripts, plans, goals, and understanding: An inquiry into human knowledge structures', *American Journal of Psychology*, 92 (1): 176–178.

Sharma, A. (1981) 'Coping with stagflation: Voluntary simplicity', *Journal of Marketing*, 45 (3): 120–134.

Sharma, S., Shimp, T.A. and Shin, J. (1995) 'Consumer ethnocentrism: A test of antecedents and moderators', *Journal of the Academy of Marketing Science*, 23 (1): 26–37.

Shatkin, G. (2004) 'Planning to forget: Informal settlements as "forgotten places" in globalizing Metro Manila', *Urban Studies*, 41 (12): 2469–2484.

Shaw, D. (2006) 'Modelling consumer decision making Fair Trade', in Harrison, R., Newholm, T. and Shaw, D. (eds) *The Ethical Consumer*, London: Sage, pp. 137–154.

Shaw, S., Bagwell, S. and Karmowsa, J. (2004) 'Ethnoscapes as spectacle: Reimaging multicultural districts as new destinations for leisure and tourism consumption', *Urban Studies*, 41 (10): 1983–2000.

Sheller, M. (2003) 'Creolization in discourses of global culture', in Ahmed, S. *et al.* (eds) *Uprooting/Regrounding: Questions of Home and Migration*, Oxford: Berg, pp. 273–289.

Sheller, M. and Urry, J. (2006) 'The new mobilities paradigm', *Environment and Planning A*, 38 (2): 207–226.

Sheptycki, J. and Wardak, A. (2005) *Transnational and Comparative Criminology*, London: Glasshouse Press.

Sherry, J.F. (1990) 'A sociocultural analysis of a midwestern American flea market', *Journal of Consumer Research*, 17 (June): 13–30.

Shields, R. (1996) 'Introduction: Virtual spaces, real histories and living bodies', in Shields, R. (ed.) *Cultures of the Internet: Virtual Spaces, Real Histories, Living Bodies*, London: Sage, pp. 1–10.

Shimizu, T. (2004) 'Consumption and marketing in Japan', *Journal of Business Research*, 57 (3): 268–276.

Shimp, T.A. and Sharma, S. (1987) 'Consumer ethnocentrism: construction and validation of the CETSCALE', *Journal of Marketing Research*, XXIV, August: 280–289.

Shirin, M. (2004) 'Bangalore: Internal disparities of a city caught in the information age', in *The Cybercities Reader*, London: Routledge.

Shoham, A., Davidow, M., Klein, J.G. and Ruvio, A. (2006) 'Animosity on the home front: The intifada in Israel and its impact on consumer behavior', *Journal of International Marketing*, 14 (3): 92–114.

Shome, R. (1999) 'Whiteness and the politics of location', in Nakayama, T.L. and Martin, J.N. (eds), *Whiteness: the Communication of Social Identity*, London: Sage.

Shotton, M.A. (1989) *Computer Addiction? A Study of Computer Dependency*, London: Taylor and Francis.

Shultz, C.J. (2001) 'Have-not's in a world of haves: Disenfranchised nations and their consumers in an increasingly affluent and global world', Special Session Summary, *Advances in Consumer Research*, 28: 277.

Shultz, C.J., Burin, T.J., Grbac, B. and Renko, N. (2005) 'When policies and marketing systems explode: An assessment of food marketing in the war-ravaged Balkans and implications for recovery, sustainable peace, and prosperity', *Journal of Public Policy and Marketing*, 24 (1): 24–37.

Sikin, L. (2001) 'Traditional medicines in the marketplace: Identity and ethnicity among female vendors', in Seligmann, L.J. (ed.) *Women Traders in Cross-Cultural Perspective*, Stanford: Stanford University Press, pp. 209–225.

Sills, A. and Desai, P. (1996) 'Qualitative research amongst ethnic minorities in Britain', *Journal of the Market Research Society*, 38 (3): 251–265.

Simmons, L.C. and Schindler, R.M. (2003) 'Cultural superstitions and the price endings used in Chinese advertising', *Journal of International Marketing*, 11 (2): 101–111.

Simon-Barouh, I. (2003) 'Assimilation and ethnic diversity in France', in Harzig, C., Juteau, D. and Schmitt, I. (eds) *The Social Construction of Diversity: Recasting the Master Narrative of Industrial Nations*, New York: Berghahn Books, pp. 15–39.

Sinclair, J. and Irani, T. (2005) 'Advocacy advertising for biotechnology: The effect of public accountability and corporate trust and attitude toward the ad', *Journal of Advertising*, 34 (3): 59–74.

Singh, N. and Matsuo, H. (2004) 'Measuring cultural adaption on the web: a content analyticstudy of U.S. and Japanese web sites', *Journal of Business Research*, 57 (8): 864–872.

Slater, D. and Tacchi, J. (2004) *Research: ICT Innovations for Poverty Reduction*, New Delhi: UNESCO.

Smith, P.B. (2002) 'Culture's consequences: Something old and something new', in *Human Relations*, 55 (1): 119–134.

Smith, P.B. (2006) 'When elephants fight, the grass gets trampled: The GLOBE and Hofstede projects', *Journal of International Business Studies*, 37 (6): 915–921.

Smith, R.A. and Lux, D.S. (1993) 'Historical method in consumer research: Developing causal explanations of change', *Journal of Consumer Research*, 19 (1): 595–610.

Smith, R.H.T. (1978) *Market-place Trade: Periodic Markets, Hawkers, and Traders in Africa, Asia, and Latin America*, Vancouver: University of British Columbia Press.

Smith, S.M. and Swinyard, W.R. (2001) 'The identification of shopping behaviors among Internet users', World Marketing Congress, Cardiff Business School. Available online at http://www.cf.ac.uk/carbs/conferences/wmc/wmcprog1.pdf.

Soderstrom, O. (2006) 'Studying cosmopolitan landscapes', *Progress in Human Geography*, 30 (5): 553–558.

Sojka, J.Z. and Tansuhaj, P.S. (1995) 'Cross-cultural consumer research: A twenty-year review', *Advances in Consumer Research*, 22: 461–474.

Srinivas, T. (2002) '"A tryst with destiny" The Indian case of cultural globalization', in Berger, P.L. and Huntington, S.P. (eds) *Many Globalizations: Cultural Diversity in the Contemporary World*, Oxford: Oxford University Press, pp. 89–116.

Sriussadaporn, P. (2006) 'Managing international business communication problems at work: A pilot study in foreign companies in Thailand', *Cross Cultural Management an International Journal*, 13 (4): 330–344.

Srivastava, J. and Lurie, N. (2001) 'A consumer perspective on price-matching refund policies: Effect on price perceptions and search behavior', *Journal of Consumer Research*, 28 (September): 296–307.

Staeheli, L.A. and Mitchell, D. (2006) 'USA's Destiny? Regulating space and creating community in American hopping malls, *Urban Stu*dies, 43 (5/6): 977–992.

Staeheli, L.A. and Nagel, C.R. (2006) 'Topographies of home and citizenship: Arab-American activists in the United States', *Environment and Planning A*, 38 (9): 1599–1614.

Stanfield, J.H. (1993) *A History of Race Relations Research*, London: Sage.

Stanfield, J.H. and Dennis, R.M. (1993) *Race and Ethnicity in Research Methods*, Newbury Park, CA: Sage.

Star, N. (1988) *The International Guide to Tipping*, New York: Berkley.

Stearns, P.N. (2001) *Consumerism in World History: The Global Transformation of Desire*, London: Routledge.

Steele, T. (1999) 'Marginal occupations: Adult education, cultural studies and social renewal', in Aldred, N. and Ryle, M. (eds) *Teaching Culture: The Long Revolution in Cultural Studies*, Leicester: NIACE, pp. 7–21.

Steenkamp, J.E.M. (2001) 'The role of national culture in international marketing research', *International Marketing Review*, 18 (1): 30–44.

Steenkamp, J.E.M (2005) 'Moving out of the US Silo: A call to arms for conducting international marketing research', *Journal of Marketing*, October: 8–9.

Stengel, J. (2007) 'Selling P & G', *Fortune*, 17 September, 81–87.

Stern, B.B. (1989a) 'Literary explication: A new methodology for consumer research', in Hirschman, E. (ed.) *Interpretive Consumer Research*, Provo: Association for Consumer Research, pp. 48–59.

Stern, B.B. (1989b) 'Literary criticism and consumer research: overview and illustrative analysis', *Journal of Consumer Research*, 16 (December): 322–334.

Stern, B.B. (1990) 'Literary criticism and the history of marketing thought: A new perspective on "reading" marketing theory', *Journal of the Academy of Marketing Science*, 18 (4): 329–336.

Stern, B.B. (1993) 'Feminist literary criticism and the deconstruction of ads: a postmodern view of advertising and consumer response', *Journal of Consumer Research*, 19 (March): 556–566.

Stern, B.B. (1995) 'Consumer myths: Frye's taxonomy and the structural analysis of consumption text', *Journal of Consumer Research*, 22 (September): 165–185.

Stern, B.B. (1998) 'Deconstructive strategy and consumer research: Concepts and illustrative exemplar', *Journal of Consumer Research*, 23 (September): 136–147.

Stern, B.B. (1998) 'Deconstructing consumption text: A strategy for reading the (re)constructed consumer', *Consumption, Markets and Culture*, 1 (4): 361–392.

Stern, B.B. (1999) 'Gender and multicultural issues in advertising: Stages on the multicultural research highway', *Journal of Advertising* 28 (4): 31–46.

Stern, B.B. and Russell, C.A. (2004) 'Consumer responses to product placement in television sitcoms: Genre, sex, and consumption', *Consumption, Markets and Culture*, 7 (4): 371–394.

Sternquist, B., Byun, S. and Jin, B. (2004) 'The dimensionality of price perceptions: A cross-cultural comparison of Asian consumers', *International Review of Retail Distribution and Consumer Research*, 14 (1): 83–100.

Stevenson, T.H and Swayne, L.E. (1999) 'The portrayal of African-Americans in business-to-business direct mail: A bench mark study', *Journal of Advertising*, 28: 25–36.

Steyn, M. (2005) '"White Talk": White South Africans and the management of diasporic whiteness', in Alfred J. Lopez (ed.) *Postcolonial Whiteness: A Critical Reader on Race and Empire*, New York: State University of New York Press.

Stirrat, R.L. (2000) 'Cultures of consultancy', *Critique of Anthropology*, 20 (1): 31–46.

Stolzoff, N. (2005) 'What's anthropological about corporate ethnography? Lessons from the field', *Advances in Consumer Research*, 32: 347.

Strasser, S. (2003) 'The alien past: Consumer culture in historical perspective', *Journal of Consumer Policy*, 26: 375–393.

Strasser, S. (2006) 'Woolworth to Wal-Mart: Mass merchandising and the changing culture of consumption', in Lichtenstein, N. (ed.) *Wal-Mart the Face of Twenty-first-century Capitalism*, London: New Press, pp. 31–56.

Street, B. (1993) *Cross-cultural Approaches to Literacy*, Cambridge: Cambridge University Press.

Striffler, S. (2007) 'Neither here nor there: Mexican immigrant workers and the search for home', *American Ethnologist*, 34 (4): 674–688.

Sumner, W.G. (1906) *Folkways*, New York: Dover Publications, 1959.

Sunderland, P.L. and Denny, R.M. (2003) 'Psychology vs anthropology: Where is culture in marketplace ethnography', in De Waal Malefyt, T. and Moeran, B. (2003) *Advertising Cultures*, Oxford: Berg, pp. 187–200.

Suri, J.F. and Howard, S.G. (2006) 'Going deeper, seeing further: Enhancing ethnographic interpretations to reveal more meaningful opportunities for design', *Journal of Advertising Research*, September: 246–250.

Suri, R., Anderson, R.E. and Kotlov, V. (2004) 'The use of 9-ending prices: contrasting the USA with Poland, *European Journal of Marketing*, 38 (1/2): 56–70.

Swaidan, Z., Vitell, S.J. and Rawwas, M.Y.A. (2003) 'Consumer ethics: Determinants of ethical beliefs of African Americans', *Journal of Business Ethics*, 46 (2): 175–186.

Szerszynski, B. and Urry, J. (2002) 'Cultures of cosmopolitanism', *The Sociological Review*, 50 (4): 461–481.

Tadepalli, R. Moreno, A. and Trevino, S. (1999) 'Do Mexican and American purchasing managers perceive ethical situations differently?', *Industrial Marketing Management*, 28 (2): 369–380.

Takahashi, I. (2004) 'Theory and research on marketing in Japan: An introduction', *Journal of Business Research*, 57 (3): 266–267.

Taher A. (2005) 'British genes are invasion proof', *Sunday Times*, 5 June, p. 6.

Talavera, A.F. (2002) 'Trends towards globalization in Chile', in Berger, P.L. and Huntington, S.P. (eds) *Many Globalizations: Cultural Diversity in the Contemporary World*, Oxford: Oxford University Press, pp. 250–295.

Tan, T.W.T. and Lui, T.J. (2002) 'Globalization and trends in international marketing research in Asia', *Journal of Business Research*, 55: 799–804.

Tansey, R. and Hyman, M.R. (1994) 'Dependency theory and the effects of advertising by foreign-based multinational corporations in Latin America', *Journal of Advertising*, XXIII (1): 27–42.

Tat, P.K. (1981) 'Minority student perceptions of the ethics of marketing practices', *Southern Marketing Association Proceedings*: 214–216.

Tatla, D.S. (1999) *The Sikh Diaspora: The Search for Statehood*, London: UCL Press.

Taylor, C.R and Stern, B.B. (1997) 'Asian-Americans: Television advertising and the "model minority" stereotype', *The Journal of Advertising*, 26: 47–62.

Taylor, G. (2005) *Buying Whiteness: Race, Culture and Identity from Columbus to Hip Hop*, New York: Palgrave Macmillan.

Teegen, H., Doh, J.P. and Vachani, S. (2004) 'The importance of nongovernmental organizations (NGOs) in global governance and value creation; an international business research agenda', *Journal of International Business Studies*, 35 (6): 463–483.

Telles, E.E. (2002) 'Racial ambiguity among the Brazilian population', *Ethnic and Racial Studies*, 25 (3): 415–441.

Tesser, P.T.M., Merens, J.G.F. and van Praag, C.S. (1999) *Rapportage Minderheden 1999* (Report Minorities 1999), Rijswijk: Sociaal en Cultured Plambureau.

Thapan, M. (2005) *Transnational Migration and the Politics of Identity*, London: Sage.

Tharp, M.C. (2001) *Marketing and Consumer Identity in Multicultural America,* London: Sage.

Thelen, S.T. and Honeycutt, E.D. (2004) 'Assessing national identity in Russia between generations using the national identity scale', *Journal of International Marketing*, 12 (2): 58–81.

Thomas, A. and Bendixen, M. (2000) 'The management implications of ethnicity in South Africa', *Journal of International Business Studies*, 31 (3): 507–519.

Thomas, E.R. (2006) 'Keeping identity at a distance: Explaining France's new legal restrictions on the Islamic headscarf', *Ethnic and Racial Studies*, 29 (2): 237–259.

Thomas, K.W. and Tymon, W.G. (1982) 'Necessary properties of relevant research: Lessons from recent criticisms of the organizational sciences', *Academy of Management Review*, 7 (July): 345–352.

Thompson, C.J. and Arsel, Z. (2004) 'The Starbucks brandscape and consumers' (anticorporate) experiences of glocalization', *Journal of Consumer Research*, 31 (December): 631–643.

Thompson, C.J. and Tambyah, S.K. (1999) 'Trying to be cosmopolitan', *Journal of Consumer Research*, 26 (December): 214–241.

Thorelli, H.B. (1968) 'South Africa: Its multi-cultural marketing system', *Journal of Marketing*, 32 (April): 40–48.

Tilly, C. (2006) 'Wal-Mart in Mexico: The limits of growth', in Lichtenstein, N. (ed.) *Wal-Mart the Face of Twenty-first-century Capitalism*, London: New Press, pp. 189–209.

Tippu, S. (2007a) 'Now streaming: Bollywood movies', *Fortune*, 1 October, p. 19.

Tippu, S. (2007b) 'The malling of Bangalore', *Fortune*, 14 May, pp. 14–15.

Tobias, S.M. (1998) 'Early American cookbooks and cultural artifacts', *Papers on Language and Literature*, 34 (1): 3–18.

Trappey, C.V. and Lai, M.K. (1996) 'Retailing in Taiwan: Modernization and the emergence of new formats', *International Journal of Retail and Distribution Management*, 24 (8): 31–37.

Triebel, A. (2001) 'The roles of literacy practices in the activities and institutions of developed and developing countries', in Olson, D.R. and Torrance, N. (eds) *The Making of Literate Societies*, Oxford: Blackwell Publishers, pp. 19–53.

Trompenaars, F. and Woolliams, P. (2004) *Marketing Across Cultures*, Chicester: Capstone.

Tsalikis, J. and Nwachukwu, O. (1988) 'Cross-cultural business ethical beliefs between blacks and whites', *Journal of Business Ethics*, 7 (10): 745–754.

Tsang, M.M., Ho, S.C. and Liang, T.P. (2004) 'Consumer attitudes toward mobile advertising: An empirical study', *International Journal of Electronic Commerce*, 8 (Spring): 65–78.

Tumari, T. (2006) 'Reflections on the development of cultural studies in Japan', *Theory, Culture and Society*, 7–8 (22): 293–304.

Turkle, S. (1996) *Life on the Screen: Identity in the Age of the Internet*, London: Weidenfeld and Nicholson.

Turner, V. (1974). *Dramas, Fields, and Metaphors: Symbolic Action in Human Society*, Ithaca: Cornell University Press.

Tylor, E. (1964) 'Culture defined', in L.A. Coser and B. Rosenburg (eds) *Sociological Theory: A Book of Readings*, West Drayton: Collier-Macmillan, pp. 18–21.

Tylor, E.B. (1871) *Primitive Culture: Researches into the Development of Mythology, Philosophy, Religion, Language, Art and Custom*, New York: H. Holt.

Tyner, J. and Kuhlke, O. (2000) 'Pan-national identities: Representations of the Philippine diaspora on the World Wide Web', *Asian Pacific Viewpoint*, 41: 231–52.

Umble, D.Z. (1992) 'The Amish and the telephone: Resistance and reconstruction', in Silverstone, R. and Hirsch, E. (eds) *Consuming Technologies: Media and Information in Domestic Spaces*, London: Routledge, pp. 183–194.

Uotinen, J. (2003) 'Involvement in (the information) society: The Joensuu Community Resource Centre netcafe', *New Media and Society*, 5 (3): 35–356.

Usunier, J.G. and Valette-Florence, P. (1994) 'Perceptual time patterns ("time-styles"): A psychometric scale', *Time and Society*, 3 (2): 219–241.

Valence, G., d'Astous, A., Fortier, L. (1988) 'Compulsive buying: Concept and measurement', *Journal of Consumer Policy*, 11: 419–433.

Valsh, V. (2005) 'A peripherist view of English as a language decolonization in post-colonial India', *Language Policy*, 4 (2): 187–206.

Van Fleet, D.D. and Wren, D.A. (2005) 'Teaching history in business schools: 1982–2003', *Academy of Management Education and Learning* (4): 1: 44–56.

Vanhuele, M. and Dreze, X. (2002) 'Measuring the price knowledge shoppers bring to the store', *Journal of Marketing*, 66 (October): 72–85.

Vann, E.F. (2006) 'The limits of authenticity in Vietnamese consumer markets', *American Anthropologist*, 108 (2): 286–296.

Van Tulder, R. and Kolk, A. (2001) 'Multinationality and corporate ethics: Codes of conduct in the sporting goods industry', *Journal of International Business Studies*, 32 (2): 267–283.

Vartanova, E. (2004) 'The Russian network society', in Castells, M. (ed.) *The Network Society: A Cross Cultural Perspective*, Cheltenham: Edward Elgar, pp. 84–98.

Veeck, A., Yu, H. and Burns, A.C. (2005) 'Maintaining family identity through meals in post-Mao urban China', *Advances in Consumer Research*, 32: 481.

Veenis, M. (1999) 'Consumption in East Germany', *Journal of Material Culture*, 4 (1): 79–112.

Venkatesh, A. (1995) 'Ethnoconsumerism: A new paradigm to study cultural and cross-cultural consumer behavior', in Costa, J.A. and Bamossy, G.J. (eds) *Marketing in a Multicultural World*, London: Sage.

Veronis, L. (2006) 'The Canadian Hispanic Day Parade, or how Latin American immigrants practise (sub)urban citizenship in Toronto', *Environment and Planning A*, 38 (9): 1653–1671.

Vertovec, S. (2004) 'Cheap calls: the social glue of migrant transnationalism', *Global Networks*, (4): 219–24.

Vertovec, S. and Cohen, R. (2002) 'Introduction: Conceiving cosmopolitan', in Vertovec, S. and Cohen, R. (eds) *Conceiving Cosmopolitanism. Theory Context and Practice*, Oxford: Oxford University Press, pp. 1–22.

Vicziany, M. (2004) 'Globalization and *Hindutva*: India's experience with global economic and political integration', in Davies, G. and Nyland, C. (eds) *Globalization in the Asian Region*, Cheltenham: Edward Elgar, pp. 92–116.

Viswanathan, M. and Harris, J. (1999) 'Functional illiteracy: The dark side of information processing', in Arnould, E.J. and Scott, L.M., *Advances in Consumer Research*, 26, Provo, UT: Association for Consumer Research.

Viswanathan, M., Rosa, J.A. and Harris, J.E. (2003) 'Towards understanding functionally illiterate consumers', unpublished working paper, Department of Marketing, University of Illinois, Urbana-Champaign, IL 61820.

Vom Bruck, G. (2005) 'The imagined "consumer democracy" and elite (re)production in Yemen', *Royal Anthropological Institute*, 11: 255–275.

Waitt, G. and Head, L. (2002) 'Postcards and frontier mythologies: Sustaining views of the Kimberley as timeless', *Environment and Planning D: Society and Space*, 20: 319–344.

Wakeford, N. (2003) 'The embedding of local culture in global communication: Independent internet cafés in London', *New Media and Society*, 5 (3): 379–399.

Wald, G. (2000) *Crossing the Line*, Durham: Duke University Press.

Waldinger, R. and Fitzgerald, D. (2004) Transnationalism in question', *American Journal of Sociology*, 109 (5):1177–95.

Wallendorf, M. (2001) 'Literally literacy', *Journal of Consumer Research*, 27 (4): 505–512.

Wallendorf, M. and Arnould, E.J. (1991) 'We gather together': Consumption rituals of Thanksgiving Day, *Journal of Consumer Research*, 18 (June): 13–32.

Wallendorf, M. and Reilly, M.D. (1983) 'Ethnic migration, assimilation, and consumption', *Journal of Consumer Research*, 10 (December): 292–302.

Waller, D.S. and Fam, K.S. (2000) 'Cultural values and advertising in Malaysia: Views from the industry', *Asia Pacific Journal of Marketing and Logistics*, 12 (1): 3–16.

Walton-Roberts, M. (2004) 'Returning, remitting, reshaping: Non-resident Indians and the transformation of society and space in Punjab, India', in Jackson, P., Crang, P. and Dwyer, C. (eds) *Transnational Spaces*, London: Routledge, pp. 78–103.

Wang, H. (2000) 'Rethinking the global and the national', *Theory, Culture and Society*, 17 (4): 93–117.

Warde, A. (1995) *Consumption, Food and Taste: Cultural Antinomies and Commodity Culture*, London: Sage.

Warden, C.A., Lai, M. and Wu, W. (2002) 'How worldwide is marketing communication on the world wide web', *Journal of Advertising Research*, September–October: 72–85.

Ware, V. and Back, L. (2002) *Out of Whiteness: Color, Politics, and Culture*, Chicago: University of Chicago Press.

Waters, M.C. (2002) 'The social construction of race and ethnicity', in Denton, N.A. and Tolnay, S.E. (eds) *American Diversity: A Demographic Challenge*, New York: State University of New York Press.

Webster, C. (1992) 'The effects of Hispanic subcultural identification on information search behaviour', *Journal of Advertising Research*, 32: 54–65.

Webster, C. (1994) 'Effects of Hispanic ethnic identification on marital roles in the purchase decision process', *Journal of Consumer Research* 21 (September): 319–49.

Webster, C. (1996) 'Hispanic and Anglo interviewer and respondent ethnicity and gender: The impact on survey response quality', *Journal of Marketing Research*, 33 (1): 62–72.

Weismantel, M. (2001) *Cholas, Pishtacos: Stories of Race and Sex in the Andes*, Chicago, IL: University of Chicago Press.

Welch, C. and Wilkinson, I. (2004) 'The political embedding of international business networks', *International Marketing Review*, 21 (2): 216–231.

Wells, L.G. (1994) 'Western concepts, Russian perspectives: Meanings of advertising in the former Soviet Union', *Journal of Advertising*, XXIII (1): 83–93.

Werbner, R. (2002) 'Introduction: Challenging minorities, difference and tribal citizenship in Botswana', *Journal of Southern African Studies*, 28 (4): 671–684.

Westwood, S. (2002) '"Diamond time": Constructing time, constructing markets in the diamond trade', *Time and Society*, 11 (1): 25–38.

Wetherell, M. and Potter, J. (1992) *Mapping the Language of Racism: Discourse and the Legitimation of Exploitation*, New York: University of Columbia Press.

Wheeler, D.L. (2006) *The Internet in the Middle East*, New York: State University of New York Press.

Whittler, T.E. (1989) 'Viewer's processing of source and message cues in ad stimuli', *Psychology and Marketing*, 6 (Winter): 287–309.

Whittler, T.E. (1991) 'The effects of actor's race in commercial advertising: Review and extension', *Journal of Advertising*, 20: 54–60.

Whitty, M.T. and Carr, A.N. (2003) 'Cyberspace as potential space: Considering the web as a playground to cyber-flirt', *Human Relations*, 56 (7): 869–891.

Wilkie, W.L. (2005) 'Needed: A larger sense of marketing and scholarship', *Journal of Marketing*, 69 (4): 8–10.

Wilkins, R. and Gareis, E. (2006) 'Emotion expression and the locution "I love you": A cross-cultural study', *International Journal of Intercultural Relations*, 30 (1): 51–75.

Wilkinson, I. and Cheng, C. (1999) 'Multicultural marketing in Australia: Synergy in diversity', *Journal of International Marketing*, 7 (3):106–124.

Willett, C. (1998) *Theorizing Multiculturalism: A Guide to the Current Debate*, Oxford: Blackwells.

Williams, P. and Vlassis, D. (2005) *Combating Transnational Crime: Concepts, Activities and Responses*, London: Frank Cass.

Williams, R. (1983) *Keywords: A Vocabulary of Culture and Society*, London: Fontana Paperbacks.

Williams, R. (1983) *The Year 2000*, New York: Pantheon.

Williams, R. (1993) *Culture and Society*, London: Hogarth Press.

Williams, T.K. (1997) 'Race-ing and being raced: The critical interrogation of "passing"', *Amerasia Journal*, 23 (1): 61–65.

Williams-Leon, T. and Nakashima, C.L. (eds) (2001) *The Sum of Our Parts: Mixed Heritage Asian Americans*, Philadelphia: Temple University Press.

Williamson, D. (2002) 'Forward from a critique of Hofstede's model of national culture', *Human Relations*, 55 (11): 1373–1395.

Willis, J. (2003) 'New generation drinking: The uncertain boundaries of criminal enterprise in modern Kenya', *African Affairs*, 102: 241–260.

Wills, J.R. and Ryan, J.K. (1977) 'An analysis of headquarters executive involvement in international advertising', *European Journal of Marketing*, 11 (8): 577–584.

Wilmsen, C. (2007) 'Maintaining the environmental–racial order in northern New Mexico', *Environment and Planning D: Society and Space*, 25 (2): 236–257.

Wilson, A. (1999) 'The empire of direct sales and the making of Thai entrepreneurs', *Critique of Anthropology*, 19 (4): 401–422.

Wilson, M. (2003) 'Chips, bits, and the law: An economic geography of Internet gambling', *Environment and Planning A*, 35: 1245–1260.

Wilson, W.J. (1973) *Power, Racism and Privilege: Race Relations in Theoretical and Sociohistorical Perspectives*, New York: Macmillan.

Wing, A.K. (2004) *Global Critical Race Feminism: An Integrated Reader*, New York: New York University Press.

Winick, C. (1961) 'Anthropology's contributions to marketing', *Journal of Marketing*, 25 (5): 53–60.

Witkowski, T.H. (1989) 'Colonial consumers in revolt: Buyer values and behavior during the Nonimportation Movement, 1764–1776', *Journal of Consumer Research*, 16 (September): 216–226.

Wolf, E.R. (1994) 'Perilous ideas: Race, culture, and people', *Current Anthropology*, 35 (1): 1–12.

Wong-MingJi, D. and Mir, A. (1997) 'How international is international management?', in Prasad, P., Mills, A., Elmes, M. and Prasad A. (ed.) *Managing the Organizational Management Melting Pot: Dilemmas of Workplace Diversity*, Thousand Oaks, CA: Sage, pp. 340–366.

Wood, L.J. and Grosvenor, S. (1997) 'Chocolate in China the Cadbury experience', *Australian Geographer*, 28: 173–84.

Woodlock, D. (2005) 'Vitual pushers: Antidepressant internet marketing and women', *Women's Studies International Forum*, 28: 304–314.

Woolgar, S. (2004) 'Reflexive internet? The British experience of new electronic technologies', in Castells, M. (ed.) *The Network Society: A Cross Cultural Perspective*, Cheltenham: Edward Elgar, pp. 125–144.

Worcester, R. and Dawkins, J. (2006) 'Surveying ethical and environmental issues', in Harrison, R., Newholm, T. and Shaw, D. (eds) *The Ethical Consumer*, London: Sage, pp. 189–203.

World Bank (2000) Poverty in an age of globalization, available online at http://www.worldbank.org/html/extdr/pb/globalization/povertyglobalization.pdf.

Yancy, G. (2004) *What Whiteness Looks Like*, London: Routledge.

Yang, K.C.C. (2007) 'A comparative study of internet regulatory policies in the Greater China Region: Emerging regulation models and issues in China, Hong Kong SAR and Taiwan', *Telematics and Informatics*, 24 (1): 30–40.

Yang, M., Roskos-Ewoldsen, D.R., Dinu, L. and Arpan, L.M. (2006) 'The effectiveness of "in game" advertising', *Journal of Advertising*, 35 (4): 143–152.

Yano, Y. (2001) 'World Englishes in 2000 and beyond', *World Englishes*, 20 (2): 308–321.

Yeoh, B.S.A. (2004) 'Cosmopolitanism and its excursions in Singapore', *Urban Studies*, 41 (12): 2431–2445.

Yeoh, B.S.A. (2005) 'The global cultural city? Spatial imagineering and politics in the (multi) cultural marketplaces of South-east Asia', *Urban Studies*, 42 (5/6): 945–958.

Young, W. (2004) *Sold Out: The True Costs of Supermarket Shopping*, London: Fusion Press.

Young, C., Diep, M. and Drabble, S. (2006) 'Living with difference? The "cosmopolitan city" and urban reimaging in Manchester, UK', *Urban Studies*, 43 (10): 1687–1714.

Young, M.M. and Wallendorf, M. (1989) 'Ashes to ashes, dust to dust: Conceptualizing consumer disposition of possessions', Proceedings Educators Conference, American Marketing Association, pp. 32–37.

Zabid, A.R.M. (1989) 'The influence of socio-cultural factors on perceived unethical practices', *Malaysian Management Review*, 24 (3): 47–53.

Zabkar, V. and Brencic, M.M. (2004) 'Values, trust and commitment in business-to-business relationships: A comparison of the two former Yuoslav markets', *Journal of International Marketing Research*, 21 (2): 202–215.

Zafar, R. (1999) 'The signifying dish: Autobiography and history in two black women's cookbooks', *Feminist Studies*, 25 (2): 449–469.

Zaheer, S. and Manrakhan, S. (2001) 'Concentration and dispersion in global industries: Remote electronic access and the location of economic activities', *Journal of International Business Studies*, 32 (4): 667–686.

Zaltman, G. (2000) 'Consumer researchers: Take a hike!', *Journal of Consumer Research*, 26 (March): 423–428.

Zeleza, P.T. (2002) 'The politics of historical and social science research in Africa', *Journal of Southern African Studies*, 28 (1): 9–23.

Zhou, N. and Belk, R.W. (2004) 'Chinese consumer readings of global and local advertising appeals', *Journal of Advertising*, 33 (3): 63–76.

Zinkhan, G.M. (1994) 'International advertising: A research agenda', *Journal of Advertising*, XXIII (1): 11–13.

Zinkhan, G.M., Roth, M.S. and Saxton, M.J. (1992) 'Knowledge development and scientific status in consumer-behavior research: A social exchange perspective', *Journal of Consumer Research*, 19 (2): 282–291.

Zmud, J. (1992) 'Ethnicity and the consumption relationship', *Advances in Consumer Research*, (19): 443–449.

Zou, S. (2005) 'Contributions to international advertising research: An assessment of the literature between 1990–2002', *Journal of Advertising*, 34 (1): 99–110.

Zurawicki, L. and Braidot, N. (2005) 'Consumers during crisis: Responses from the middle class in Argentina', *Journal of Business Research*, 58: 1100–1109.

Index